# RELIGION IN POLITICS:

## A WORLD GUIDE

Edited by

STUART MEWS

## ST. JAMES INTERNATIONAL REFERENCE

Contributors: Shirin Akiner, Louis Allen, D.A. Brading, Ian Breward, V.C. Chrypinski, Christopher Clapham, Marius Deeb, Mary-Jane Deeb, Marion Farouk-Sluglett, Paul Furlong, Tom Garvin, George Gelber, Paul Gifford, James H. Grayson, Göran Gustaffson, Sergei Hackel, David Hanley, Jeff Haynes, Allen D. Hertzke, Alan Hunter, Mark Juergensmeyer, Lionel Kochan, Fred H. Lawson, Dorothea McEwan, Kenneth Medhurst, Lawrence Moore, Peter Moore, Paul Morris, J.S. Nielsen, James O'Connell, Ron O'Grady, Farzana Shaikh, Norman J. Shanks, Peter Sluglett, R.B. Smith, John O. Voll, Fred R. von der Mehden, Michael Walsh, Gavin White, Virgil Wiebe, H.S. Wilson

ST. JAMES PRESS
CHICAGO AND LONDON

RELIGION IN POLITICS: A WORLD GUIDE

Published by Longman Group UK Limited, Westgate House,
The High, Harlow, Essex, CM20 1YR, United Kingdom.
Telephone (0279) 442601
Telex 81491 Padlog
Facsimile (0279) 444501

Published in the USA and Canada by St James Press,
233 East Ontario Street, Chicago 60611, Illinois, USA

ISBN 0-582-05058-8 (Longman)

1-55862-051-6 (St James)

**British Library Cataloguing in Publication Data**
Religion in politics.
   1. Politics. Role of religion
   I. Mews, Stuart
   291.1′77

   ISBN 0-582-05058-8

Phototypeset by Quorn Selective Repro Ltd, Loughborough, Leics.
Printed and bound in Great Britain by Mackays of Chatham PLC, Kent

# RELIGION IN POLITICS:
## A WORLD GUIDE

**Other recent titles from St. James Press include the following:**

*Political Parties of the World*, edited by Alan J. Day (1988), ISBN 0–912289–94–5, $85.00

*Elections Since 1945: A Worldwide Reference Compendium*, general editor Ian Gorvin (1989), ISBN 1–55862–017–6, $150.00

*Trade Unions of the World, 1989–90* (1989), ISBN 1–55862–014–1, $85.00

*World Directory of Minorities*, compiled by the Minority Rights Group (1989), ISBN 1–55862–016-8, $85.00

*Political and Economic Encyclopaedia of the Pacific*, edited by Gerald Segal (1989), ISBN 1–55862–033–8, $85.00

# CONTENTS

# INTRODUCTION

Newspapers and television every day carry stories in which religion and politics are intertwined. Today it may be the challenge of Islamic hardliners in Iran to President Rafsanjani, yesterday in South Africa Archbishop Desmond Tutu appeared to be in danger of arrest, tomorrow in Tibet there may be further clashes between Chinese troops and Buddhist monks. Conflicts may be about religious issues as in India or involve religious personnel as in Burma where Buddhist monks have joined in the opposition to what is widely perceived to be an inhumane regime; in either case they represent a religious dimension in politics which has in the past often been played down or treated as an archaic survival.

Media attention could be the artificial fabrication of journalists wishing to present an incident economically by using the shorthand of widely accepted stereotypes. Edward Said has brilliantly shown how this has happened in the Western treatment of Islam.[1] Alternatively this coverage might be the belated recognition of phenomena which were present before but went unnoticed. The secularization of Western academic elites had led to the assumption that religion was a declining force in politics. "Neither preachers nor the religious laity matter", wrote C. Wright Mills of the USA in 1959; they could "be readily agreed with and safely ignored".[2] This book contains many examples of the perils for politicians in many parts of the world today of ignoring religious factors.

To assess adequately the complex interaction between religion and politics, both sides need to be considered. Numerical growth of religious bodies need not in itself give rise to tension. What seems to have happened in many parts of the world is that both the state and its religious bodies have enlarged their spheres of operation. Many states have chosen to legislate on a range of "deep-life" matters "such as definitions and *raisons d'être* of birth, death, old age, sexuality, and other dimensions of individual and collective meaning, suffering and reward".[3] Moreover there is a new recognition of human rights, concern about global inequalities, and about national identities. As Roland Robertson rightly observes, the state has taken up quasi-religious questions.

Outside the Western world, how can we know whether the signs of religious resurgence in the political sphere are anything more than the heightening of consciousness on the part of the detached observer? One recent academic assessment insists that African nationalism had been basically secular, but that the situation had begun to change in the 1970s. This development, it was suggested, was due to three causes: the Africanization of religious institutions, the situation created by the failure of economic expectations, and the influence of external factors such as the new fundamentalist self-confidence of religious preachers, both Christian and Islamic.[4]

It has been argued from the Western European evidence that the religious perspective does not operate in politics in isolation but, as might be expected, in conjunction with other social variables. Political questions are not decided exclusively in religious terms but by a process which allows for some input from religious as well as other sources.[5] In recent years, ethnic consciousness has emerged as one of the most potent pressures in the political system. Though religion often combines with, and reinforces ethnic consciousness,[6] it does not do so in all cases, as the sensitive studies of Nigeria and Sri Lanka clearly demonstrate.

The emergence of traditionalist or fundamentalist versions of the historic faiths has been much discussed in recent years. One explanation, which perhaps partially fits the Islamic case, highlights the crisis of identity experienced by those caught up in the great population migrations of the past 30 years which have placed them in alien environments, often exposing them to the traumas of city life for the first time. Even more likely to be ripe for religious traditionalism are those who have experienced the double emotional shock of the transition to urban life in a different and hostile culture (e.g. Bangladeshis in London).

In the twentieth century Islam has played a complex role in the political process. In a traditional Islamic kingdom like Saudi Arabia, religion has been a conservative force, but in the Islamic republic of Iran, it has been used to sanction a radical theocratic programme. In Libya, Islam has been interpreted by Colonel Qadhdhafi in reformist terms, and in Syria the Ba'ath party has followed the path of secularist socialism but tried to avoid alienating Muslims. Needless to say, the effect of the Iranian revolution has been to inspire and increase Islamic traditionalism and create new levels of tension between governments and radical religious groups, especially in Egypt, Pakistan, Bangladesh and Malaysia.[7]

One incident in which the political–religious conflicts of the Islamic world were crystallized was the uproar aroused by the publication in September 1988 of a novel, *The Satanic Verses* by Salman Rushdie.[8] In India, Rajiv Gandhi, with a general election imminent, lost no time in submitting to a Muslim MP's demand for a ban on the book, Governments in Muslim countries, especially those whose commitment to the idea of an Islamic state had been questioned, have found it expedient to condemn the book. Within a short time, it was banned by Saudi Arabia, Pakistan, Egypt, Sudan, Somalia, Qatar, Bangladesh, Malaysia and Indonesia. South Africa became the only white government to impose a ban. The stakes were raised in February 1989 when in Iran Ayatollah Khomeini issued his *fatwa* and condemned the author to death, a decision which undermined attempts to rebuild relations with the United Kingdom and other European states. The incident drew attention to the presence of substantial numbers of Muslims in European towns and cities, especially in France and the United Kingdom.

Christianity in its Protestant evangelical form has also been growing rapidly, especially in the USA, Central and South America, South Africa, and the Philippines. Pentecostalism has increased in Latin America from 12 million in 1968 to 55 million in 1988; by the mid-1990s, it has been estimated that Guatemala will become the first country in the region to have an evangelical majority. These major shifts in religious alignments have important political consequences. The new movements are fiercely anti-communist and have been accused of being agents of right-wing oppression. However, in the USA itself, "baptized in the spirit" Christians include some Catholics and many blacks whose cultural conservatism often merges with liberal views on many social questions.

In Latin America, despite the phenomenal growth of Pentecostalism, the major religious tradition is still Roman Catholicism, which used to be, and in some countries still is, a deeply conservative force. More progressive sentiments began to be heard from the Catholic church in Chile, and then from Brazil. It was the Brazilian hierarchy which dominated the historic Medellín conference of 1968 when the Latin American bishops accepted the need to work for radical social change. This set the scene for the emergence of Liberation Theology with its rejection of "developmentalism" and the promotion instead of the preferential option for the poor. The radicalization of the church has had important consequences for the politics of Latin America but has not found favour in the Vatican; a 1984 "instruction" issued with papal authority warned against that "politicization of existence, which . . . begins to sacralize politics and betrays the religion of the people".[9] Recent episcopal appointments in the region have strengthened those opposed to change. Disappointment with the political and theological caution of Vatican nominations has been expressed not only in Latin America but also in the German Federal Republic, Holland, Switzerland, Ireland, and the USA. In the 1980s, theologies of liberation seemed to be heading in directions which were logically opposed to the goals of the papacy. Pope John Paul II, having spent most of his life in opposition to the totalitarian Marxism of the government of Poland, had no intention of watching his Church provide the window-dressing for Communism in the Third World. From the outset of his reign in 1978, the Pope has spearheaded a Catholic human rights movements which he has explicitly linked to the democratic revolution in world politics. In Poiand, the Philippines, South Korea, southern Africa, El Salvador, Chile, Nicaragua, Paraguay and elsewhere, he has consistently condemned corrupt, dictatorial and authoritarian forms of government and called for their replacement by the politics of democracy and participation. In several states the Catholic Church has given institutional support to a change of regime, notably through its backing for Corazon Aquino in the Philippines, and the installation of a government led by a Catholic in Poland.

In other aspects of human life, the Pope's human rights campaign has extended to the rights of the unborn, which has led to political activity in the USA, the United Kingdom and elsewhere in opposition to abortion. This has brought the Church into conflict with the women's movement, which in many countries insists on a woman's right to control her own life and destiny. This current of thinking has led to demands for opening the Christian ministry to women, a development which has occurred in most Protestant churches in the USA and Europe, but is stoutly resisted by the Roman Catholic Church, Eastern Orthodoxy, and a minority of Anglicans.

In recent years there have been efforts by sociologists to explore the religious situation in post-industrial society by reference to globalization. In this view, global integration has led to the revitalization of religion, especially in transnational movements. Concern for justice, peace and the integrity of creation has been widespread throughout the world's religions, and has in many countries led to differences with governments. This book does not present global theses but provides an account of the religious-political situation in every country in the world. Many entries will be found to provide the empirical richness which will provoke further study and lead to the drawing of wide-ranging conclusions. No constraints were placed on contributors about the form in which they were asked to present their findings, but they were requested to take special account of developments since 1987. Considerable effort has been taken to secure contributions from an international team of scholars, who have been able to write with authority about the countries assigned to them.

**References**

[1]Edward W. Said, *Covering Islam* (London, Routledge & Kegan Paul 1981).

[2]C. Wright Mills, *The Causes of World War Three* (London, Secker and Warburg 1959) p.150.

[3]Roland Robertson and Joann Chirico, "Humanity, Globalization and Worldwide Religious Resurgence: A Theoretical Exploration", *Sociological Analysis* 46(1985) p.224.

[4]Naomi Chazan, Robert Mortimer, John Ravenhill and Donald Rothchild, *Politics and Society in Contemporary Africa* (Basingstoke, Macmillan 1988) p.93.

[5]Gordon Smith, *Politics in Western Europe* (5th ed. Gower 1989) p.20.

[6]David Brown, "Ethnic Revival: perspectives on state and society", *Third World Quarterly* 11 (1989) p.1; *Religion and National Identity*, ed. Stuart Mews (Oxford, Basil Blackwell 1982).

[7]*Islam in the Political Process*, ed. James P. Piscatori (Cambridge, Cambridge University Press in association with the Royal Institute of International Affairs, 1983).

[8]*The Rushdie File*, eds. Lisa Appignanesi and Sara Maitland (London, Fourth Estate 1989).

[9]*Instruction on Certain Aspects of the "Theology of Liberation"*, p.17.

*Stuart Mews*                                                    *November 1989*

Publishers' note: The abbreviations BCE (before Common Era) and CE (Common Era) used for dates in this book are the equivalent of BC and AD respectively.

# AFGHANISTAN

Afghanistan is a land-locked country whose strategic importance derives from its proximity to Central Asia, the Persian Gulf and the Indian sub-continent. Its total size is estimated to be around 637,397 sq km of which only 22 per cent is deemed to be arable land. The economy is primitive, depending heavily on livestock farming characteristic of nomadic societies, although more settled forms of agricultural farming were actively encouraged in the 1960s and '70s.

The last population census held in 1979 put Afghanistan's population at 15.5 million. More recent estimates suggest however that this could be anything between 14.7 million and 19.7 million. There are roughly 20 languages, the dominant one being Pushto, although Dari (a derivative of Persian) is accepted as the language of government and business. The majority of Afghans are Pashtuns who coexist with other minority ethnic groups of which the most important are the Tajik, the Baloch, the Brahui, the Turkoman, the Farsiwan, the Aimaq, the Siailbash, the Hazara, the Mughal, the Uzbek and the Nuristani.

Most Afghans are Sunni Muslims of the Hanafi school of jurisprudence. Of those who are Sunni, the majority belong to the Pashtuns, Tajiks, Aimaqs, Mughals, Uzbeks, Turkomans, Baloch, Brahui and Nuristani. There is also a sizeable Shia minority, comprising both Twelver and Ismaili Shias. Shias tend to predominate among the Turis (a line of ethnic Pashtuns), Farsiwans and Hazaras, although some are also present among Tajiks.

## Government and politics

Until 1973, Afghanistan was a monarchy whose independence in the nineteenth and early twentieth centuries was guaranteed alternatively by Britain and her great Russian rival. The 1950s and '60s witnessed closer relations between Afghanistan and the Soviet Union. Much of the dynamism characteristic of government policy in this period is attributed to Mohammad Daoud, Prime Minister from 1953 to '63. Daoud's reformist programme and his passionate commitment to "Pashtunistan", an independent Pathan homeland on the north-western frontiers of Pakistan, lost him the support of the political establishment and the royal family. His subsequent dismissal did not, however, herald political isolation. By July 1973, Daoud had mustered enough support among reform-oriented army officers, many of whom had links with the Parcham group of People's Democratic Party of Afghanistan (PDPA), to stage a bloodless coup that deposed King Zahir Shah.

Once in power, the new regime sought to distance itself from left-wing elements by purging the army and bureaucracy of Parchamites and by reducing the number of Soviet advisers. Liberal dissent was silenced, while Muslim fundamentalists came increasingly to be the object of repression. By the spring of 1977, opposing sections of the PDPA, namely Parcham headed by Babrak Karmal, and Khalq led by Hafizullah Amin and Nur Mohammad

Taraki, managed to reach a fragile agreement. This in turn enabled the PDPA
to concentrate on penetrating sections of the army which made possible the
coup which finally overthrew Daoud in April 1978.

## The Saur Revolution

The new PDPA-led government of the Democratic Republic of Afghanistan
was dominated by urban, Kabul-based, middle-class Marxist intellectuals.
Few among its members could lay claim to a provincial or rural base.
Pashtuns dominated the first cabinet, although Tajiks, Hazaras and Uzbeks
were also represented. The new government's attempts to reflect the social
and cultural make-up of Afghanistan were matched, particularly in its early
days, by a recognition of existing political realities. The new president,
Nur Mohammad Taraki, stressed that his government's policies would be
non-communist and tolerant of Islam.

The months following the Saur (April) Revolution revealed the absence of
any real consensus between rival factions in the new government. Hardliners
led by Hafizullah Amin clearly preferred a Soviet-style social revolution
based on a more secular social and economic system. Others, like the
moderates who included Babrak Karmal, stressed the need to retain Islamic
policies acceptable to the traditional leadership. Moderate opinion was,
however, steadily marginalized (Karmal himself was frequently dispatched
as ambassador abroad), and anti-communists increasingly hounded.

With the Khalq faction under Hafizullah Amin firmly in control, the
new government lost little time in forcing through a series of radical
measures. These were intended to effect changes in the rural economy
and the pattern of traditional social relationships, particularly between men
and women. A series of decrees issued between April and November 1978
introduced measures which aimed at a more equitable distribution of land in
the countryside and the abolition of usury and rural indebtedness. Changes
were also envisaged in the legal and social status of women. Limits were set
on the amount of bride-price and a minimum age established for marriage at
18 years for men and 16 years for women. More importantly, women were
to be encouraged to participate in an adult literacy programme which would
be secular in character and coeducational in practice.

The government's reforms alienated substantial sections of the traditional
ruling classes. Little, if any, attempt was made to incorporate the opinion of
the clergy, many of whom resented the potential threat to their standing as
a result of the abolition of the Islamic system of justice. By May 1978, there
were clear signs of growing political opposition to government. One significant
development was the consolidation of a National Rescue Front composed of
nine Islamic and anti-communist groups, under the leadership of Professor
Burhanuddin Rabbani, a Tajik from Badakhshan in the north-east who had
recently formed the Jamiat-i-Islami. By September 1978, political opposition
gave way to armed resistance. Guerrilla insurrections were reported in the
Nuristan region and Paktia and Ghazni provinces in the east, followed by
Herat and Farah provinces in the west.

## The Saur Revolution and the Islamic resistance

The period preceding the Soviet invasion of Afghanistan witnessed the consolidation of two distinct opposition groupings, both of which were part of a more broad-based Islamic resistance: the first consisted of conservatives, also known as the "moderates", who included dispossessed landlords, tribal chiefs critical of the government's intrusion into local affairs, and *mullahs* (religious preachers), fearful of the radical rhetoric espoused by Muslim fundamentalists; the second, of Muslim fundamentalists committed to a radical restructuring of Afghan society along explicitly Islamic lines. Although several attempts have been made to unify these groups into a single Islamic alliance, none have as yet met with any success. Together they represent seven different Islamic organizations, also known as the "Peshawar Seven", indicating their subsequent dependence on bases located in and around Peshawar in the North West Frontier Province of Pakistan.

The "moderates" are divided into three organizations characterized broadly by their links to prominent Sufi families and loyalty to the ex-king, Zahir Shah. These are as follows:

- Afghan National Liberation Front (Jabh-e-Nejat Milli Afghanistan), led by Sibghatullah Mojaddedi, a noted religious scholar;
- National Islamic Front of Afghanistan under Pir Sayed Ahmad Gilani, a spiritual leader with a large Pashtun following who combines a liberal outlook with pro-monarchist views;
- Islamic Revolutionary Movement (also known as the Harkat-e-Enqelab-e-Islami), led by Maulvi Muhammad Nabi Muhammadi, a traditional Islamic scholar known for his anti-Shia views.

There are four main "fundamentalist" organizations:

- Islamic Party, (Hizbe Islami), (Hekmatyar Group), led by Gulbadin Hekmatyar. This is the largest and most organized of the "fundamentalist" groups with close links to the Jamaat-i-Islami in Pakistan and to sections of the Pakistani intelligence agency handling Afghan affairs;
- Hizbe Islami (Khalis Group), led by Maulvi Muhammad Yunus Khalis who developed differences with Hekmatyar in 1979, but who shares with Hekmatyar the belief that only devout Muslims should rule Afghanistan. It has a wide following among Afghan refugees in Pakistan and receives substantial aid from the United States;
- Islamic Society of Afghanistan, (Jamiat-i-Islami Afghanistan), led by Professor Burhanuddin Rabbani, a Tajik, who has a large following among non-Pashtun nationalities, most notably the *mujahadin* of the Panjsher Valley associated with Ahmad Shah Masood, also a Tajik;
- Islamic Alliance for the Liberation of Afghanistan, (Ittehad-e-Islami), led by Abdur Rab Rasul Sayyaf, who is noted for his preference for a military solution to the Afghan problem.

One important factor which contributed substantially to the development of an Islamic resistance in Afghanistan was the Iranian revolution of 1979. The opposition of Afghanistan's sizeable Shia minority to the PDPA is expressed through the "Iran Eight". These are:

- Sazmane Nasr, the biggest Iran-based group led by Abdul Karim Khalili, who also heads the eight-party alliance;
- Harkat-i-Islami, an Iran-based group close to the present Iranian government and led by Ayatollah Mohsini;
- Pasdaran-i-Jihad, led collectively by a council of 10 members;
- Hezbollah, a militant Shia group operating inside Afghanistan and led by Qari Ahmad, also known as Qari Yakdasta;

- Nehzat, based in Afghanistan mainly in the Jogore area and under the command of a council of three members;
- Jabhe Muttahid, based in the Hazarajat area of Afghanistan under a collective leadership;
- Narave Islami, a small group based inside Afghanistan whose most prominent member is Zaidi Mohazzizi;
- Dawat-i-Ittehad-Islami, a small group operating in Ghazni Province;
- Shoora-i-Ittefaq, the largest and most organized Shia group, with broad-based support and headquarters in the Hazarajat Area of Afghanistan. One section was rumoured to have been under the command of the late Ayatollah Syed Ali Beheshti, a close associate of Ayatollah Khomeini.

## The Soviet invasion: containing the fundamentalists

Growing dissent within the PDPA, the ferocious pace of reform and the alienation of increasing numbers of landlords, peasants, ethnic tribesmen and *mullahs*, constituted the immediate context of the Soviet invasion in December 1979. There is evidence to suggest that the Soviet Union, concerned by developments in Afghanistan, had pressed the PDPA leadership under Amin to reconsider its political line. Amin's intransigence is one among many factors that led the Soviets to favour his replacement by the more moderate Babrak Karmal.

The Parcham phase of the Revolution, undertaken under Soviet auspices, stressed a more conciliatory policy towards Afghanistan's religious leadership. Under Karmal all Afghans were constitutionally entitled to practise and profess Islam, while Karmal himself stressed his personal devotion to Islam. Karmal's reforms, announced in June 1981, which suspended laws relating to debts and bride-price, were also evidence of a change in government policy. There were to be some rewards. In June 1985, it was reported that two Afghan spiritual leaders, namely Abdullah Agha and Asmatullah Muslim, each with a substantial following, had lent their support to Karmal.

Karmal's more moderate policies did not, however, affect the course of the Islamic resistance. Between 1985 and 1987 the *mujahadin*, operating chiefly from Pakistan, stepped up their campaign with sustained military assaults on government positions inside Afghanistan. Some, like Hikmatyar's Hizbe Islami, enjoyed substantial military and political support from American sources, notably the Central Intelligence Agency, and Pakistan's Inter Services Intelligence (ISI) which was directly responsible to General Zia-ul Haq.

The election of Dr Najibullah as President in November 1987 signified fresh attempts to resolve the political deadlock in Afghanistan. A new constitution stressed the identity of Afghanistan as an "Islamic nation" and endorsed the right to private property. Najibullah also proposed a programme of national reconciliation aimed at initiating discussions with "moderate" *mujahadin* groups. These overtures, however, met with little response partly because of divisions within the *mujahadin* concerning the role of ex-king Zahir Shah in a future Afghan government. A stalemate also dominated the military front where, during 1987 and 1988, Soviet and Afghan forces held on to major cities while the *mujahadin* achieved numerous local victories.

The signing of the Geneva Accords in April 1988 and the subsequent withdrawal of Soviet troops from Afghanistan has done little to obtain a political solution. Neither Pakistan nor the United States (signatories of the Accords) were willing to recognize the Najibullah government, while the *mujahadin* have steadfastly refused to participate in any negotiations with the government in Kabul. Even if *mujahadin* groups are ideologically united over the question of an Islamic State, politically they remain deeply divided. The formation of an interim government based principally in Pakistan has done little either to resolve differences between "moderates" and "fundamentalists", or to persuade the Shia *mujahadin* to join the government. Militarily, the *mujahadin* are far from establishing control over Kabul, or indeed over major cities like Jalalabad. In the meanwhile, dreams of an Islamic Afghanistan continue to elude the three million refugees now resident in Pakistan.

Farzana Shaikh

# ALBANIA

Until the communist takeover in 1944, 70 per cent of Albanians (about 800,000) professed Islam: Sunni Muslims in the north and a smaller group of Shia Bektashi in the south, while the Orthodox (about 220,000) and Catholics (about 120,000) formed much lesser religious organizations. Although in neighbouring countries religion played a very important role in the development of local ethnic consciousness, Islam was not a significant factor in establishing the national Albanian identity, and religious diversity was an obstacle in the process of its formation.

These reasons encouraged ideologically-motivated communists to "abolish religion" in 1967. To assure full submission to their order, the rulers resorted to harassment and repression. The Muslims, whose leadership was mercilessly purged in 1945, offered little open resistance. Orthodox and especially Catholic oppugnation was stronger but it was also broken after dreadful persecution.

The 1976 constitution formalized the end of religious organizations and of public religious activities. But religion was not dead and enforced atheism was very superficial, particularly in regions settled by Catholics and Bektashis.

Thus animosity against religion continued. In 1985, an old Jesuit priest, Fr Pjeter Meshkella, was arrested again for saying a Christmas Mass in a private home. It was his third imprisonment for pastoral activities. The first time, he spent 25 years in jail (1946-71). Re-arrested again in 1973, he was condemned to nine years. His third life sentence ended with his death in a labour camp in July 1988.

In 1987, the Albanian Union of Working Youth dispatched 70 teams to intensify an atheist campaign throughout the country, especially in the Catholic north. An attempt by Dutch tourists, in 1988, to distribute the Bible among the workers of a textile mill near Berat resulted in the confiscation and burning of books.

Recently, however, there appeared signs of a subtle change. Old people were not punished for praying in the privacy of their own homes; the atheist museum in Shkodra, a showpiece of the regime's propaganda, was closed: a permanent exhibition of iconography was opened in an Orthodox church in Berat. Most significantly, the only living bishop, Mikol Troshani, Apostolic Administrator of the Archdiocese of Durres and diocese of Lezh, was at 73 years old freed from prison where he had spent the last 20 years.

It is possible that the re-entrance of Albania on the European political scene may also bring Europeanization of the official attitude towards civil rights and political freedom.

V. C. Chrypinski

# ALGERIA

In Algeria Islam has long been associated with politics. During more than 130 years of French colonial rule Islam served as a source of national identity against the "mission civilisatrice" that sought to supplant and eventually eradicate all vestiges of the indigenous culture. It was the Islamic reformist movement of Sheikh 'Abd al-Hamid Ben Badis, founded in 1931, that set the foundations of the nationalist struggle with its slogan "Islam is my religion, Arabic my language, Algeria my fatherland".

In 1956 Ben Badis' Association of Reformist Ulamas joined forces with the Front de Libération Nationale (the FLN) in the war of independence against the French. In the process it became subordinate to the Front and was incorporated into its organization.

When the FLN emerged triumphant from the war, organized Islam was seen by the new leaders as part of the state structure. From the outset it became a means to mobilize support for the new state and to reinforce the national identity which had been forged during the nationalist struggle.

Although Islam became the religion of the state in the new Algerian Constitution, the *shari'a*, or Islamic law, was not made an integral part of the legal system of the state, nor were Muslim jurists allowed to play an independent role in legislative matters on the national level. Instead a Minister of Religious Affairs was appointed by the Algerian leaders to head a bureaucratic organization that had the final authority to appoint or dismiss clergymen, review Friday sermons, administer religious endowments, control religious publications, and set up Islamic institutions of higher learning.

In 1964, the first autonomous Islamic movement to emerge in independent Algeria, *Al-Qiyam* (the values) was a precursor of the Islamic fundamentalists of the 1980s. It called for a more visible role for Muslim practices in society, and opposed western cultural manifestations in clothing and entertainment in Algeria. One of its leaders, Muhammad Khider, was a founding member of the FLN, who had broken away from the party and set up the nucleus of an opposition to Ben Bella and later to Boumediene. The movement was eventually suppressed by the Boumediene regime, and Khider was assassinated in 1967.

Islamic revivalism in Algeria began to emerge in the mid-1970s as a consequence, in part, of state policies advocating a Cultural Revolution.[1] Opposition to the nationalization of private property and in particular of agricultural land, was expressed in Islamic terms. The Arabization of the educational curriculum adversely affected an underclass of rural migrants to Algeria's large urban centres who could not find employment, partly because of their limited linguistic skills, and began to swell the ranks of the Islamic movements.[2] Finally, the shift of the government towards the left, in the mid-1970s, and its association with the Socialist Vanguard Party, an Algerian Communist group, was perceived as a threat to Islam and mounting criticism of atheistic ideologies took place.[3]

By the end of the 1970s an autonomous Islamic movement *Ahl al-Da'wa*, the People of the Call, began to voice the dissatisfaction of many Algerians with state policies and with the direction they were taking the country. But it was only after the death of Boumediene in 1978, and the emergence of an Islamic Republic in Iran the following year, that the movement became organized and active.

Ideologically, the Algerian Muslim fundamentalists are among the most radical in North Africa. Unlike most of their Tunisian or Egyptian counterparts they advocate a complete restructuring of society "in an attempt to realize the City of God on Earth".[4] They have pushed for the application of Islamic law, *shari'a*, to replace the civil code of law of Algeria. They have also pushed for reforms based on Islamic principles such as a stricter dress code for women, more religious broadcasts on radio and television, and the banning of consumption of alcohol in public places.

The Algerian Islamists did not confine themselves to haranguing their followers, or to writing pamphlets but moved to action in the early 1980s. They took over mosques which had been under government control for two decades, and established independent places of worship of their own, even ousting officially appointed *imams*, or clergymen, and replacing them with members of their own movement. When government security forces attempted to stop the takeover (in Laghouat, in 1981, for instance) bloody clashes erupted and resulted in a number of casualties. They also attacked public places suspected of selling alcoholic beverages to their customers, and harassed women in Western clothes. University campuses witnessed pitched battles between Muslim fundamentalists and left-wing students culminating in the death of a student in November 1982 on the Ben Aknoun campus of the University of Algiers.

This event led the government of Chadhli Ben Jadid, whose policy towards *Al-Da'wa's* activities had hitherto been rather tolerant, to clamp down on them. During the rest of the 1980s the Algerian state began a systematic campaign to undermine the movement, by arresting its leaders, conducting police raids on the homes of suspected members, and branding them in the mass media as "criminals" and "agitators".

In 1984 one of those leaders, Sheikh 'Abd al-Latif Sultani died at the age of 82, while under house-arrest. Tens of thousands demonstrated emotionally at his funeral and it became clear to the authorities that Islamic fundamentalists were much more numerous and had a much greater appeal than had at first been thought. They could also be found among varied strata of urban society and did not merely belong to one organization.

The government's response was to attempt to steal the thunder of the fundamentalists by founding numerous Islamic institutes, schools and teaching centers, training a greater number of *imams*, and cloaking itself in Muslim garb by using Islamic idioms in official speeches. A number of Muslim fundamentalists were also set free from jail as a gesture of reconciliation. In the spring of 1985, another 135 Muslim fundamentalists were released, while a number of others who had been arrested the previous year received very light sentences.

Apparently the olive branch was not effective in reconciling the fundamentalists with their government. In the summer of 1985, Mustafa Bouyali, an independence war veteran and Muslim fundamentalist, robbed a factory of its payroll and a few days later attacked police barracks in Souma, south of Algiers, taking the arms and ammunition that were stocked there. He and his men then fled to the Atlas mountains, where security forces could not find them, and remained in hiding until January 1987 when he was finally caught and killed in a bloody conflict with an elite army force. On June 15, 1987, those who had fought with Bouyali as well as other Muslim fundamentalists, numbering more than 200, were brought to trial in Medea, south of Algiers. This time the courts did not show any clemency, and the defendants were given harsh sentences including the death penalty for four of their members.

In October 1988 riots broke out in the Bab al-Oued sector of Algiers over government austerity measures to cut state subsidies on some basic commodities. The riots spread quickly to the rest of the capital, and to Oran, Constantine, Annaba, Blida, Tiarret and Sinya and beyond to Tizi-Ouzou in the Berber Kabylie region. Demonstrators were protesting against the high unemployment, the shortage of basic consumer goods, and the unavailability of affordable housing in the cities. The armed forces who were brought in to quell the riots were unable to restore law and order for 10 days, at the end of which more than 200 people were reported dead and over 1,000 injured while an estimated 3,500 were arrested.

Although the riots were not initiated by the Muslim fundamentalists, they tried to exploit the disturbances to mobilize support for their views. Two days after the riots broke out several thousand young Muslim fundamentalists demonstrated in the Belcourt District of Algiers, while the army attempted to keep them away from demonstrations in other sectors of the city. On October 14, they staged another peaceful demonstration and submitted a 12-point proposal for reform to the government, asking it to lift the state of emergency which had been imposed on the country at the outbreak of the clashes. A young religious leader from the Bab al-Oued sector of Algiers, 'Ali Bin al-Haj, led a march mobilizing the local residents of the district and apparently clashing with soldiers, leading to a number of deaths. Finally, an Islamic group calling itself the Movement for Algerian Renewal issued a communique assuming responsibility for the riots and calling on the government to meet the demands of the rioters.

When the riots were over President Chadhli Ben Jadid met with Muslim fundamentalist leaders including Sheikh Sahnoun, Sheikh 'Ali Bin al-Haj, and Sheikh Mahfouz Nahnah. The religious leaders condemned acts of violence and sabotage, and submitted to him a number of proposals for economic and social reforms including a demand that Islam constitute the basis of all such reforms.

It is not yet clear what compromises the Algerian government had to make with the Islamists, but negotiations took place during that meeting and may have included some *quid pro quo* for the maintenance of law and order in the country. This became evident in March 1989 when the first Algerian Islamic political party, The Islamic Salvation Front was proclaimed in Kouba, a suburb of Algiers, with official government approval. It has a consultative council or *shura* made up of 14 members, some of whom are very important Islamic leaders in Algeria. They include: Sheikh 'Abd ·al-Baqi, Sheikh Bin 'Azzuz and Sheikh Al-Mukran, as well as Sheikh 'Ali Bin al-Haj, the leader of the Bab al-Oued demonstrations in Algiers who had met with the Algerian President in the aftermath of the riots.

The government-controlled Ministry of Religious Affairs, however, warned the Islamic Salvation Front that it would not allow it to set up offices or party headquarters in mosques or to use such religious institutions for any other purpose than for the practice of religious functions. No political or non-political activity would be tolerated, and the ministry threatened that it would use every legal means to prevent such activities.

### References

[1] For an excellent discussion of the impact of Boumediene's policy on the Islamic fundamentalist movement in Algeria, see Hugh Roberts, "Radical Islamism and the Dilemma of Algerian Nationalism: the Embattled Arians of Algiers", in *Third World Quarterly*, Vol. 10, No. 2, April 1988, pp. 567–575.
[2] *Ibid.*, pp. 566–567.
[3] *Ibid.*, p. 569.
[4] John P. Entelis, *Algeria: The Revolution Institutionalized* (Boulder, Colorado, Westview Press, 1986) p. 85.

Mary-Jane Deeb

# ANDORRA

Foreign residents account for some two-thirds of the tiny population of this principality, the indigenous inhabitants being almost wholly Roman Catholic. Since 1278 the bishop of Urgel in Spain has been co-prince with the King (now President) of France. France supports some French-language schools, while those in the Spanish-speaking areas have hitherto been supported by the Church.

Michael Walsh

# ANGOLA

The former Portuguese colony of Angola has considerable natural resources, oil and iron ore, as well as coffee growing areas which once made it the world's fourth largest coffee producer. Unfortunately for its people, Angola was ill-prepared for independence. Catholic-controlled schools taught only basic skills and did little to nurture an elite or train for leadership. Consequently the country has experienced a serious skills shortage and been riven by guerrilla warfare. Dissatisfaction in the colony led to armed struggle in 1961, and though the army used great brutality in attempting to maintain control, the Portuguese withdrew after the death of Salazar in 1974. Since then the armed conflict has continued, only now it is between the Marxist-Leninist MPLA, who form the government, backed by 50,000 Cuban soldiers with equipment supplied by the USSR, and their chief opponent, UNITA, led by Dr Jonas Savimbi, backed by South Africa and the USA.

The largest religious body is the Roman Catholic church which began its mission in 1491, and today claims the allegiance of over 60 per cent of the population. Its strength lies amongst the largest tribe, the Ovimbunda of the central region. Always loyal to Lisbon, the Catholic hierarchy in Angola as late as April 1974 was condemning armed insurrection and expressing support for the colonial regime. Two months later, it was forced by events to backpedal and denounce the atrocities of the previous regime.

About 18 per cent of the population belong to Protestant denominations and sects, but their growth was hindered by government restrictions. Protestants were prominent in the revolutionary movement and five Methodist ministers were put in prison soon after the armed struggle began. In 1976 the new constitution stated that Angola was a secular state with freedom of conscience and religious liberty, but the government has become increasingly hostile to the churches. In 1977, the president of MPLA, Agostinho Neto, the son of a Methodist minister, said, "No party member can be a church member, and no church member can be a member of the party". The following year, the Catholic radio station in the capital, Luanda, was taken over by the government and used to carry atheist propaganda. All religious holidays including Christmas, have been abolished.

The UNITA rebels had agreed to a cease-fire in June 1989, but it collapsed two months later.

Stuart Mews

# ANTIGUA AND BARBUDA

Antigua and Barbuda (population 80,000 mid-1984 estimate) became independent in 1981. Anglicanism is the primary denomination, but other Christian groupings are represented. The Antigua Labour Party (ALP), long under the control of Vere Bird Sr, won its fourth straight election in March 1989, weathering allegations of corruption earlier in the eighties and the coalition of opposition parties into the United National Democratic Party in 1986.

Virgil Wiebe

# ARGENTINA

Argentina's modern history has been characterized by political instability and economic decline. A central issue has been the military's repeatedly unsuccessful efforts to create viable political institutions whilst simultaneously seeking to marginalize the mass urban labour movement created by President Juan Perón (1946–55 and 1973–74). The repressive military dictatorship of 1976–83 failed to solve basic economic problems or to eliminate dissent and it was finally discredited by defeat in the Falklands War. The initial beneficiary of the resulting return to democratic politics was the Radical Party led by Raul Alfonsin, but his government's credibility was undermined by problems in handling the military and especially by economic difficulties. Consequently, in 1989, a *Peronista*, Carlos Menem, came to power charged with confronting a huge national crisis of confidence.

Over 90 per cent of the nation's 31,029,694 inhabitants are Roman Catholics. Their Church's senior leaders remain preponderantly conservative and opposed to the minority within the hierarchy who advocate "a preferential option for the poor", liberation theology and base communities. Initially leading Churchmen were attracted by Peron's authoritarian nationalism but were subsequently alienated by his demagogic anti-clericalism which tended to reinforce alliances with conservative military and economic interests. With notable exceptions they remained silent during the repression of 1976–83. By contrast Alfonsin's government was attacked for introducing divorce (1987) and for educational reforms threatening to ecclesiastical interests. In recent election campaigns support has been voiced for ultra-conservative positions.

Kenneth Medhurst

# AUSTRALIA

There are six states and two territories in this federally ruled nation. All states except Queensland have two houses. At present their governments are equally divided between Labor and conservative parties in the lower houses, with conservative majorities in the upper houses. The federal government is Labor, but it does not have control in the Senate, where Democrats hold the balance. The population of almost 17 million is preponderantly Australian born and of Anglo-Celtic origin, with the political and religious traditions that flow from that heritage. Migration since 1945 has brought substantial European settlement, but has not significantly changed political or religious patterns. There is an influential Jewish lobby and significant Muslim and Buddhist minorities, but there is as yet no sign that they have changed the century-old secular relationship between politics and religion.

## Religious patterns

An overwhelming majority of Australians give census allegiance to some form of Christianity, with the 1986 Census indicating percentages as follows: Roman Catholic 26.1, Anglican 23.9, Uniting 7.6, Presbyterian 3.6, Orthodox 2.7, Baptist 1.3, Lutheran 1.3. There is no established Church, but there are a number of privileges given to Churches through tax exemption. There are still limitations on Sunday trading, major Christian festivals are public holidays and there is a great deal of government financial assistance to the Churches for education, health and welfare. There are differences in the religious demography of each state and territory which have affected the important but informal links between government and leaders of the churches. No Church has its headquarters in the federal capital, Canberra.

The relation between politics and religion can be characterized as a combination of partnership and separation. The latter is due to the historic importance of sectarian rivalries and the influence of secularism on Australian elites. This, however, has been modified by the growth of ecumenism since the 1960s, with important common initiatives by religious leaders, such as their Bicentennial statement in January, 1988 — *Towards reconciliation in Australian society*.

## Constitutional issues

The Preamble to the Federal Constitution of 1901 noted that the people of the states "humbly relying on the blessing of Almighty God, have agreed to unite in one indissoluble Federal Commonwealth under the Crown . . .". Section 116 laid down that "the Commonwealth shall not make any law for establishing any religion, or for imposing any religious observance, or for prohibiting the free exercise of any religion, and no religious test shall be required as a qualification for any office or public trust under the Commonwealth". That did not abolish the reserve power of the states to legislate on religious matters, but they have not used that power very often. In June 1901, the two houses of the federal parliament agreed to follow the example of state parliaments and open their proceedings with an agreed prayer.

The importance of these historic boundaries was underlined in the debate preceding the referendum on constitutional amendments in September 1988. One amendment which purported to establish freedom of religion was decisively defeated, with the opposition of Roman Catholic and Anglican bishops undoubtedly swaying some voters, who feared that the amendment might lead to legal challenge to the Commonwealth's and states' subsidies to Church schools, hospitals and welfare services. Another issue raised in these debates was the legal status of UN conventions ratified by the federal government where they bear on religion. This has not yet been clarified.

## Religion in politics

Australian political parties have not had explicit links with churches. Even The Call to Australia Party, which has three seats in the New South Wales Upper House, has no formal links with any Church, despite being led by a Uniting Church minister, the Rev. Fred Nile and having a conservative Christian agenda. Earlier attempts to establish Protestant and Roman Catholic parties failed. No Church leader has been able to deliver a recognizable block vote, but the Roman Catholic vote is treated warily by politicians. It played a substantial part in the dramatic 1954 split in the Labor Party which, through the formation of the Democratic Labor Party, kept it out of power until 1972. Mr. B. A. Santamaria, an important figure in the split and in the victory over Communist Party union leaders, still exercises an important influence on Roman Catholic opinion, especially in Victoria. Earlier sectarian rivalries and class issues, which tended to ensure that Roman Catholics mostly voted Labor and Protestants mostly voted for the conservative parties, have been seriously weakened by ecumenism and Catholic upward mobility. But until very recently, the leadership of the Liberal, National and Democrat parties has been predominantly Protestant. An exception is the Liberal Premier of New South Wales, since 1988, Mr. Nick Greiner, who is a Roman Catholic of Hungarian origin.

The only state premier who made large claims to represent Christian values was Sir Johannes Bjelke-Petersen, an active Lutheran who frequently denounced Labor atheists in Canberra and in the states. Sir Joh was quick to denounce any Christian view that differed from his own. In 1986 he told the visiting Archbishop of Canterbury to go home for daring to criticize anti-union legislation. The Fitzgerald Inquiry which published its findings in July 1989 showed that this allegedly Christian facade was a front for pervasive corruption. A more responsible use of Christian insight to illumine political life can be seen in the Rev. Dr. J. D. McCaughey, Governor of Victoria and a former President of the Uniting Church. His wide-ranging interests and wise judgement have made him one of Australia's most influential leaders.

## Patterns of partnership

Direct and provocative announcements about political issues by Church leaders have diminished over the last two decades. The 1988 retirement of the Anglican Dean of Sydney, Lance Shilton, a major voice for the Festival of Light and its traditional moral stance, has removed the last conservative spokesman of national stature outside the ranks of bishops. The minor Churches make little or no input into the formation of social policy and discussion of national change. The major Churches have tended increasingly to work through parliamentary inquiries and commissions. Submission of carefully researched evidence has undoubtedly informed legislation on in-vitro fertilization and experimentation with embryos in Victoria, where medical research in these areas is of world importance. In addition, Churches and other religious groups have representatives on the ethical committees appointed by state governments to monitor such research — an interesting example of partnership, where expertise in moral theology and social ethics has much to contribute to matters of life and death. Reports on housing, prostitution, liquor licensing reform, video pornography, youth homelessness and prison reform all reflect religious interest in wise solutions to major social problems. This trend has undoubtedly been encouraged by the Labor government's conviction that social change by education and legislation is vital. The Churches are willingly heard if they can present reasoned positions on such issues.

## Indigenous religion

That is not the case on Aboriginal land rights. For Aboriginal people land is not a commodity. It is the basis of their spirituality, a fact ignored or derided by many otherwise sensitive Christians, who are in positions of political and economic power. Graziers and miners now give slight recognition to Aboriginal sacred sites, but often Aboriginals' religious attitude to land is actively opposed, despite the unanimity of all major religious leaders and Church bodies in supporting and pleading for federal Aboriginal land rights legislation. Even the attempt to open the first session of the Commonwealth Parliament in its new building on August 23, 1988, with a declaration that Aboriginal people were the prior occupants of Australia was rejected by the Liberal and National parties. That was a dramatic illustration of the gap between religious and political perceptions on a very divisive issue.

Secular, Australia may be. Many members of its elites see little value in religion or actively repudiate it. Yet there is still a substantial level of commitment to Christianity and other world faiths, even if Christianity is no longer the assumed basis for national values. Politicians can find Church priorities difficult to fathom and be infuriated when religious leaders refuse to leave politics to politicians. There is much evidence that, for the foreseeable future, religious convictions will influence political perceptions and realities, even though the process is more subtle than in countries with a historic majority faith. The Roman Catholic Bishops' enquiry into the distribution of wealth, begun in 1988, indicates that even arcane matters of finance and economics are not immune from Christian scrutiny and comment.

Presence without power was underlined at the Queen's opening of the new Parliament House in May 1988. Initially, no religious ceremony was planned by the Hawke Government, but finally pressure from the Churches resulted in an inter-faith religious service being included. Even more interesting was the unofficial gathering of Christians to pray for the nation May 7–8, 1988. Up to 50,000 were present, far more than at the official celebrations.

Ian Breward

# AUSTRIA

For a second time in the history of the second Republic the Socialist Party and the conservative People's Party entered into a coalition in January 1987 stressing partnership over confrontation in politics. Because of a combination of state industries performing chronically badly and an overgenerous social security system the economy was crisis-ridden and remains in critically poor shape. Scandals over the modernization of the municipal hospital in Vienna, arms production and illegal arms shipments contravening Austria's pledges of neutrality, the squandering of huge sums of money at major construction works alarmed not only the Austrian taxpayers but also the international community.

A deepseated uneasiness about a government that could not come to grips with the economy coupled with an ambivalence towards the state President Kurt Waldheim who seemed to polarize rather than draw the people together, spread. Waldheim is in many ways the politician whose virtues and vices make him representative of his people. The former UN General Secretary had been nominated by the People's Party for election for President. (The party with the highest votes in parliamentary elections traditionally came second in presidential elections.) With a nomination like his, a long overdue and necessary process of coming to terms with the past was initiated; of acknowledging many Austrians' willing participation in the war as Hitler's allies and of discussing and re-evaluating Austria's role in 1938 and since; all things which the older generation had previously had difficulties in facing.

After his win at the election his past came under scrutiny, especially the role he played as an officer of the German *Wehrmacht* in World War II stationed in the Balkans. On April 28, 1987, the US government took back the decision by the US Justice Department to put Waldheim's name on the "watch-list" of undesirable people in case he planned to travel to the US. The President started court proceedings against the president of the Jewish World Congress for libel, that Waldheim had been part of the Nazi murder machinery. At the same time the President charged an international commission of historians to investigate his past impartially and pledged himself to work actively to root out emerging anti-semitism and reappearing fascism.

The commission of historians reported on Feb. 8, 1988 that Waldheim could not be said to be implicated in Nazi atrocities, deportation of Jews and war crimes, at most in violations of human rights. Despite national and international protests at Waldheim's presidency and calls for his resignation, especially in view of the commemoration of the annexation of Austria, the *Anschluß* in March 1938, Waldheim declared in March 1988 that it was a basic principle of democracy that election results could not be changed after the election and as a consequence did not resign. In a TV speech he refuted the notion of collective guilt for Austria.

This struck a chord in a population, the majority of which profess Roman Catholicism. Anti-semitism was endemic in Austria for centuries and discussions about the fate of Jews and Austria's collaboration with Hitler's Germany in the extermination of Jews was a topic hotly contested. In a nation of some seven million people where 84.3 per cent are Roman

Catholic, 5.6 per cent Protestant, 3 per cent other Christian denominations, 1 per cent Islamic, 0.1 per cent Jewish and 6 per cent without religious denomination, the attitude of the main Church carried enormous weight with the believers and the politicians. Traditionally the People's Party was termed the "clerical" party, while the Socialist Party was the anti-clerical party and at the same time the party mostly concerned with stamping out any form of anti-semitism or a re-emergence of fascism. It was precisely this stance which made the former Cardinal Archbishop of Vienna, Franz König, acceptable to the Socialist party because he could not be termed a conservative Churchman.

Despite the fact that the Jewish presence has plumetted to an all-time low with some 7,000 Jews, anti-semitic sentiments are still heard. They form part of a pattern of wider xenophobia which is directed equally against the immigrant workers, mostly from Yugoslavia and Turkey, who are Muslims.

There is a dichotomy between an adherence to traditional humanitarian or gospel tenets of co-operation on the international stage as practised by the second Republic and the intransigence towards the neighbour who might be different or have a different political or ideological outlook on the national or internal stage, the bitter inheritance of the centuries old anti-semitism, the Civil War of 1934, the *Anschluß* of 1938 and the exigencies of the post-war reconstruction of the Austrian economy. International co-operation and practical assistance find expression in Austria's work inside international fora and the many international conferences and UN agencies located in Austria, notably the Conference of Security and Co-operation in Europe (the Helsinki Agreement), and Austria's exemplary record in the provision of asylum for political prisoners. This sharply contrasts with its treatment of minorities (notably when it comes to questions of educational provisions) and immigrant workers and the partisan way party politics are conducted on a day-to-day basis.

Religious practice is declining among the once traditional social groups of worshippers. The peasantry has largely disappeared in a modern highly industrialized country, the salaried middle classes increasingly leave the Church mainly upon entering the labour market. The reason given is that the individual member is assessed to pay Church taxes on the basis of his or her income and receives an instruction to this effect, based on a law introduced by Hitler and never repealed. Thus instructions to pay Church taxes are automatically sent out to every baptized member whether he or she is a practising Catholic or not. Since practising Catholics are only some 15 per cent of the membership a huge change in the pastoral situation has to come about if the Church is not to lose the income of those 85 per cent not practising but (still) paying nominal members.

Controversial appointments by Rome to Austrian sees have done nothing to improve the climate between those alienated from the Church and the Church authorities. After the resignation of Cardinal Franz König in 1985 because of age, dubbed the "red" cardinal because of his enlightened and compassionate views on birth control and divorce and remarriage, the bishop conference was gradually reshuffled and packed with conservative appointees. Hans Groer who succeeded as Archbishop of Vienna in 1987 and Kurt Krenn as auxiliary bishop are both viewed by the Austrians as Roman appointments, appealing with their neo-conservatism in pastoral work only to the right-wing conservative circles, including the neo-Nazis. At his induction into St. Stephan's Cathedral in Vienna, the police had to intervene to protect Kurt Krenn from angry protesters who tried to prevent the new bishop from entering the cathedral. It was noted that Archbishop Karl Berg of Salzburg, president of the Austrian Bishops' Conference, together with other members of the conference, were absent. Austrian Protestants feel particularly uncomfortable with these appointments as the ecumenical climate favoured under their predecessors has cooled off. Protests increased with the appointment of the head of the Austrian section of Opus Dei, the sect-like Catholic traditionalist group, Klaus Küng as bishop of Feldkirch and the conservative militant anti-communist Georg Eder as archbishop of Salzburg.

At the same time the second papal visit to Austria by Pope John Paul II from 23 to 27 June 1988 hard on the heels of these appointments and the commemorations of the 50th anniversary of the *Anschluß*, was a test whether or not the Austrian faithful accepted papal decisions and statements by their political leaders. Significantly some of the events drew more people from neighbouring states than from Austria itself.

Kurt Krenn, the former Professor of Theology in Ratisbon, sent a reply to the signatories of the Cologne Declaration of German, Dutch, Swiss and Austrian theologians in February 1989 refuting their complaints and concerns. He could not share their criticism of the Pope.

Ex-empress Zita Hapsburg-Lorraine who died on March 14, 1989 in Switzerland was buried in Vienna with all the traditional pomp the official Roman Catholic Church could muster, mourned by a small minority of monarchists, notably members of the aristocracy and traditionalist Catholics.

For the present it appears that the social change which has taken place has, because of the Church's failure to recover from old crises, been met by some Church authorities and centre-right parties moving more to the political right. It remains to be seen whether they have recovered lost ground by these means or marginalized themselves.

Dorothea McEwan

# THE BAHAMAS

The Bahamas is home to some 235,000 people (1986 est.). The major religious groupings are the Baptists, the Anglicans, and the Roman Catholics, each with between 22 and 30 per cent of the population as adherents. Other groups active include the Methodists, Adventists, Lutherans, Assembly of God, Church of God, Greek Orthodox, the Salvation Army, and the Assembly of the Brethren. The Bahamian Council of Churches includes the broad spectrum of Christian churches on the islands. A small Jewish community is present.

The Progressive Labour Party commands a majority over the opposition Free National Movement, but has been embroiled in controversy over the use of the Bahamas as a transit point for drug trafficking and money laundering. Considerable pressure has been brought to bear on the Bahamian government by the US government for greater drug interdiction.

Virgil Wiebe

# BAHRAIN

Bahrain's heterogeneous population is ruled by the pre-eminent sheikhs of the Khalifah clan, in conjunction with prominent members of the indigenous commercial elite, who occupy many of the senior positions in the central administration. The Al Khalifah are followers of the orthodox Sunni branch of Islam and adhere to the Maliki school of Islamic jurisprudence, which favours relatively strict interpretations of the Koran and the traditions of the Prophet (Hadith), but which also tolerates some flexibility in applying the law for the benefit of the community as a whole. The commercial oligarchy is divided into Sunnis following the *Shafi'i* school, most of whom immigrated to Bahrain from the southern coast of Iran, and Twelver Shias with close ties to the main Shia centers in Iran and southern Iraq. There are also small but significant pockets of Sunnis who adhere to the more literalist Hanbali school of interpretation and Shias who accept the tenets of the more ecstatic Akhbari school, which places primary emphasis on the received traditions of the Koran and the twelve original *Imams* as the source of doctrine and legal practice. It is estimated that Shias make up almost 70 per cent of the general population, a substantially higher proportion than that reported for the 1941 census, the last that registered religious affiliation.

Discontent among the country's Shia inhabitants became more pronounced in the wake of the 1979 revolution in Iran. Reformist organizations such as the Sunni Society for Social Reform and the Shia Party of the Call to Islam lost ground throughout the 1980s to activist groups like the Sunni Islamic Action Organization and the Shia Islamic Front for the Liberation of Bahrain. In mid-December 1981, the government announced that it had broken up a network of saboteurs affiliated with the last of these groups; these activists were handed lengthy prison sentences by a tribunal presided over by a senior sheikh of the Khalifah clan the following March. Sporadic arrests of members of militant Islamist cells have occurred since that time, but the evident efficiency of the state security forces in rounding up dissidents and the relative magnanimity of the authorities in dealing with those arrested have largely stifled the political activities of the country's Islamist movement.

Fred H. Lawson

# BANGLADESH

Over 80 per cent of the population of Bangladesh are Sunni Muslims.
Although Islam is recognized as the official religion of Bangladesh,
successive governments have tended to pursue a policy of secularism
and religious tolerance. This is accounted for in part by the fact that
over 13,000,000 Bangladeshis are Hindus, while just over half a million
subscribe to Buddhism. In the late 1970s, the government's policy of religious
co-operation was seriously undermined when military troops were used to
forcibly re-settle the predominantly Buddhist population of the Chittagong
Hill Tracts.

Like most other Muslim countries, the role of Islam in Bangladesh has
recently assumed greater importance. Because of its cultural and linguistic
affinities with Hindu West Bengal, Bangladesh's Islamic identity has needed
constantly to be re-affirmed. Although many Bangladeshis perceive little
or no conflict between their Islamic heritage and their Bengali culture,
religious parties continue to press for a more rigid adherence to Islamic
law and practice. More recently the government of General Ershad has
chosen to respond to fundamentalist demands by endorsing the idea of an
Islamic State. Mounting political opposition to Ershad, some of which stems
from religious parties, suggests that Ershad's enthusiasm for an Islamic State
may well amount to no more than a ploy to muster popular support. Like
other Muslim countries, Bangladesh was also affected by the controversy
surrounding the publication of *The Satanic Verses*. The book was officially
banned; protest marches were organized and the author, Salman Rushdie,
roundly condemned by Bangladesh at the Islamic Conference Organization
in March 1989.

Farzana Shaikh

# BARBADOS

Reflecting the uninterrupted colonial presence of the British from 1624
until full independence in 1966, the predominant Christian faith in a
predominantly Christian nation is the Anglican one, which commands well
over half the population of 253,000 (1985 est.). Numerically it is followed
by Roman Catholics (Barbados and neighbouring St. Vincent comprise the
diocese), the Methodists and Moravians and rapidly growing Evangelical and
Pentecostal and other Nonconformist Churches and sects. Small groups of
Hindus, Muslims and Jews are also present.

Three parties find representation in the 350-year old parliamentary system:
the ruling Democratic Labour Party (DLP), the opposition New Democratic
Party (NDP), a recent split-off from the DLP, and the once-ruling Barbados

Labour Party (BLP). Most notable has been the political consensus between the public and private sectors with changes of government resulting in change of emphasis rather than substance. The unexpected death of long time leader of the DLP Errol Barrow in June 1987 removed a key opponent to US policy in the eastern Caribbean but caused no serious problems of transition.

The Caribbean Council of Churches is headquartered in Barbados and under the leadership of Methodist minister Allan Kirton has taken an active role in the region, for instance sending observers to the November 1987 elections in Haiti and voicing criticism of US influence in the region. Dame Nita Barrow serves as ambassador to the UN while also serving as a president of the World Council of Churches.

Notable growth has occurred in wealthier evangelical Churches such as the People's Cathedral and Abundant Life Assembly, reflecting spiritual revival as well as attraction to "successful" Churches. In January 1988 local opposition was voiced by Anglicans, Catholics and some evangelicals to the then upcoming visit of Jimmy Swaggart.

Virgil Wiebe

# BELGIUM

Belgium must still be counted an overwhelmingly Catholic country. A decade ago over 90 per cent were baptised and over 80 per cent married in church.

After independence in 1830 Catholics collaborated with liberals who represented the secularist and democratic thrust of 1789, along with the emergent socialists. The two traditions split over the question of schools, Catholics resisting attempts at secularization and obtaining parity of funding — an arrangement reaffirmed in the 1950s after another lengthy dispute.

The lack of conflict on this issue compared with other states says much about the nature of Belgian politics, where compromise has been the rule. Christian Democracy was slow to organize politically, only really emerging in its present form as the Social Christian party in 1945. Previously there had existed a loose federation of *stande* (socio-professional groups). The new party organized as a mass party and soon became an indispensable member of the coalition governments inevitable in a multi-cultural state which uses proportional representation. The Christian Democrats did much to build the welfare state and to anchor Belgium firmly within the European communities and NATO.

Since the sixties the party has in effect split into two (like the socialists and liberals), with the CVP (*Christelijke Volkspartij*) in Flemish-speaking areas and the PSC (*Parti social chrétien*) in Wallonia. In the last two decades the divide between Walloons and Flemings has increased, with nationalist parties making headway in each camp. At stake is not religion (there are probably more non-Catholics among Walloons, but liberalism and socialism both flourish in Flanders) but resources and status: Flemings are now richer and more powerful after years of subordination to French-speakers, and the latter fear decline. The moves towards a more federal type of arrangement in recent years owe much to the Christian Democrats who have used their tradition of compromise to preserve a Belgian state. So often a divider, religion might in this most polarized of countries for once have played the role of a healer.

David Hanley

# BELIZE

Faced with a multi-ethnic, multilingual and plural society, the former British colony of Belize faces a religious/political mix of some complexity, with a historically strong Catholic Church (currently 63 per cent of the population are Catholic) and established Anglican presence. Dynamic cultural and political interaction occurs between the following groups, many members of which are multilingual: In 1980, 40 per cent of the population were Creole, 33 per cent *mestizo*/"Spanish", 8 per cent Garifuna, 7 per cent Maya, 4 per cent white, 3 per cent Kekchi, 2 per cent East Indians, and small groups of Arabs and Chinese. A massive influx of refugees from the rest of Central America has since led to a process of "hispanization", with estimates that up to 10 per cent of Belize's estimated 170,000 people are refugees, most of them *mestizo*. The previously open door refugee policy has been taxed severely, leading to greater governmental restrictions and considerable tensions. Clear response from the religious community to the crisis has not yet emerged.

Roman Catholicism crosses ethnic lines and is growing in the Creole, Mayan, and Garifuna communities. In 1980, the Anglicans numbered about 12 per cent (down from over 20 per cent in the 1940s), followed by the Methodists and the rapidly growing Pentecostals and Adventists. The Mennonites, who migrated to Belize in the late 1950s, maintain relatively closed and "apolitical" communities. Two parties dominate Belizean politics. The People's United Party (PUP) led the country to independence in 1981 and has long been influenced by middle class Catholics garnering considerable labour support. Since 1984 the neo-conservative United Democratic Party (UDP) has dominated the political landscape. Elections are to be held by the end of 1989.

In late 1986 and early 1987, an internal dispute between Jamaican born Anglican Bishop Keith McMillan and Canon Eric Williams (a presumed supporter of the UDP) led to an involvement of a government minister on the side of Williams and intervention on the side of McMillan by Anglican bishops in the West Indies. McMillan charged the authorities with failing to protect freedom of worship while supporters of Williams protested his transfer from the Cathedral in Belize City to the parish of Belmopan. Nationalist sentiment against a "foreign" bishop may have been the origin of the dispute rather than theological differences.

Virgil Wiebe

# BENIN

In a population of over four million, just under a quarter are Christian, located mainly in the south, and some 15 per cent are Muslim. Over 60 per cent adhere to the traditional religions which have displayed great strength and resilience; the Yoruba god, Ogun, the god of iron and war, has, for example, become the god of the highways. (It is significant that religions from this area survived slavery and industrialization in the New World and are today celebrated in the Caribbean and Brazil.)

After independence from France in 1960 there were several coups. In 1972 Major Mathieu (now Ahmed) Kérékou came to power proclaiming a Marxist-Leninist state. The sole legal party is the Parti de la Révolution Populaire du Bénin. The economy enjoyed a boom in the 1970s by taking advantage of the Nigerian oil bonanza, chiefly through smuggling. The slump in oil prices has forced Kérékou to pursue a much more pragmatic policy as he has manoeuvred between Côte d'Ivoire and Nigeria, France and Libya in search of political and financial assistance. Local wits dub the official philosophy "Marxism-Beninism". Kérékou is threatened by the dissatisfaction of younger officers, many of them educated in eastern Europe, who resent his trimming and their own lack of promotion prospects, due to the constraints of the budget. Kérékou has in fact survived several attempted coups. His spiritual and security adviser is a wealthy Malian businessman and marabout, Mamadou Cissé, known as "Djine", "the devil".

H. S. Wilson

# BHUTAN

In the Himalayan kingdom of Bhutan, Buddhism is the state religion. 75 per cent of the 1.3 million inhabitants are Mahayana Buddhists whose ancestors came from Tibet and Burma as early as the eighth century CE; most of the other 25 per cent are Hindus of more recent Nepalese origins.

The history of Bhutan is intimately tied to its Buddhist monastic organizations. The Drukpa sect became dominant in the seventeenth century, and under Ngawang Namgyal, a Tibetan lama, several feuding religious factions were consolidated and a theocratic system of government was created. It had two leaders: one in charge of religious organizations, the other in charge of civil matters. This dual pattern continues today, although since 1907 the power of the civil authority has been taken over by a hereditary kingship.

The parity between political and religious institutions in Bhutan is symbolized by the roughly equal status given to the governmental leader, the king, and the Buddhist spiritual leader, the *je khempo*, the only person beside the king allowed to wear the saffron scarf. A central organization of Buddhist monks nominates the *je khempo*, who must be approved by the king. The monks hold a variety of governmental positions at all levels. Two of the 11 members of the Royal Advisory Council (*Lodoi Tsokde*) are representatives of the monastic hierarchy. The government, in turn, maintains the major Buddhist temples and shrines.

The present monarch, Jigme Singye Wangchuck, has ruled Bhutan since 1972. There are no political parties and no organized religious opposition to the government.

Mark Juergensmeyer

# BOLIVIA

Bolivia is Latin America's poorest country. Twenty-five per cent of its 6,611,351 inhabitants are unemployed. Over 60 per cent of the employed are in the informal economy. The formal economy is largely dependent on agriculture and a now-declining mining sector. Politics has been characterized by instability and military intervention though, since 1982, there has been constitutional government. President Paz Estenssoro, elected in 1985, attacked foreign debt and inflation with neo-liberal policies that have intensified poverty and heightened social tensions.

The population is preponderantly Roman Catholic (87 per cent) though approximately 75 per cent of clergy and the majority of bishops are foreigners. The episcopate is one of Latin America's most progressive with a strong commitment to structural change, "a preferential option for the poor" and base communities. Their impact is limited by the prevalence of traditional individualistic or popular "folk" expressions of Catholicism. In the 1980s they have moved from seeking to act as mediators in political disputes towards advocacy of the cause of miners, peasants and other impoverished groups. For example, they have pressed the claims of land reform and opposed plans to privatize the mines. Their questioning of official policies found particular expression during Pope John Paul's visit (May 1988).

Kenneth Medhurst

# BOTSWANA

Overshadowed by its powerful neighbour South Africa, the republic of Botswana has had a continuous struggle to maintain its political and economic independence. Over 100 years ago this threat led the rulers of the Tswana to ask for British help. In 1885 the protectorate of Bechuanaland was set up, its first British resident being a Congregational minister from the London Missionary Society. Consequently Congregationism became under King Khama I (1872–1930) almost the state religion. When independence was granted in 1966, the constitution provided for religious liberty, though local chiefs still exercise great influence over their peoples' religious activities.

Seretse Khama, the first president, was chief of the Ngwato. On his death in 1980, he was succeeded by Quett Masire, chief of the Kwena. At independence, the existing civil service was left undisturbed; expatriates still hold nearly a quarter of senior posts. With its colonial style civil service, a House of Chiefs in Parliament and a democratically elected government, Botswana appears to have successfully forged a partnership between traditional and bureaucratic elites which has been legitimized by popular election.

The Christian Council of Botswana set up in 1966 has both Protestants and Catholics as full members. In recent years the number of African indigenous sects has grown. Despite official support for Christianity, 60 per cent remain traditionalist. The Bushmen of the Kalahari desert have been particularly resistant to Christian preaching.

Stuart Mews

# BRAZIL

The Brazilian Catholic Church is of special significance. Its 358-strong episcopate is the world's largest and it is responsible for the spiritual leadership of the world's biggest concentration of Roman Catholics. (The nation's population is over 135 million people of whom the great majority remain officially Roman Catholic.) It consequently exercises a special influence upon the Church elsewhere in Latin America and, given that region's great strategic importance for the universal Church, it is bound to receive special attention from the Vatican.

Its international significance began to become particularly clear during the 1960s. Progressive elements within the Brazilian episcopate then emerged as pace-makers within both the national and the wider Latin American Church. Their influence was especially marked at the Second Conference of Latin American bishops held in Medellin (in 1968) — a conference which constituted a watershed in Latin American Church history. It was they, in particular, who then persuaded the region's episcopal leaders to command the Church to work for a radical transformation of inherited socio-economic and political structures. Equally, they helped to create that ecclesiastical climate that subsequently facilitated the emergence of liberation theology, the spread of ecclesiastical base communities and the development of a "popular Church" depending substantially on lay leadership.

The roots of such development can be traced back to the period immediately prior to the Brazilian military takeover of March 1964, when portions of the Church became caught up in the radicalization process then generated as a consequence of competition within the governing populist coalition bequeathed by former President Getulio Vargas (1930–45 and 1950–54). Most notably, Archbishop Helda Camara of Recife led a movement to provide the National Bishops' Conference (CNBB) with a bureaucracy that would stimulate radical pastoral and political initiatives. A mass literacy campaign came under this heading. In the immediate aftermath of the military coup such activities were suspended but they provided the Church with important precedents when it subsequently emerged as a major source of opposition to authoritarian rule. That regime's doctrine of "national security" and its overriding concern for economic growth entailed such abuses of human rights and such systematic impoverishment of majority lower-strata groups that large portions of the Church's leadership provisionally closed ranks behind outspoken radical colleagues. Progressive Catholics were thus again able to set the Brazilian national Church's agenda. At the episcopal level the policies of the regime were subjected to strong criticism. At the local level pastoral programmes were mounted in defence of the urban and rural poor and of threatened indigenous populations. Also, spreading "ecclesiastical base communities" (over 60,000 in number) offered the poor novel forms of participation in Church life and a means of promoting their own solidarity. Not least, they helped to produce leaders for mass movements, protected by the Church, capable of mobilizing opposition to the military government. Unofficial trade unions and the new "Labour Party" were in this category. It was a process of popular mobilization that ultimately helped to undermine the credibility and viability of the military dictatorship.

The return to civilian rule, in 1985, led to some official ecclesiastical disengagement from the political arena. The resumption of conventional political activity meant that political groups had much less incentive to seek out the Church's patronage or protection. Equally, Church leaders perceived a need to avoid embroilment in partisan politics and to concentrate upon more conventional pastoral activities. For example, they were reluctant to become involved in a campaign to move the election of the national President away from Congress to the electorate.

Nevertheless, the Church has, to some degree, been drawn back into public controversy. In practice the economic and social policies of the new civilian regime, headed by President Sarney, have shown such continuity with those of the military dictatorship that Catholic spokesmen, still committed to a "preferential option for the poor", have been constrained to resume a critical running commentary upon the government. At the same time they have remained the subject of pressure from Vatican authorities, and their local allies, concerned to curb the Brazilian Church's autonomy and so to foster a conservative counter offensive.

This counter offensive had its roots in the 1970s and took the form of a campaign, spearheaded by Colombian Church leaders, to curb the post-Medellin influence of liberation theology. At the following regional bishop's conference held in Puebla, Mexico (in 1979) the "neo-conservatives" only partially succeeded in placing their stamp upon the official conclusions. Progressive forces remained strong enough to secure a series of compromises between their positions and those advocating a wholesale return to conventional understandings of evangelism and pastoral practice. Competing tendencies consequently remained free to vie for pre-eminence and, because of its relative size, attached particular importance to the Brazilian Church's future direction.

## The post-military period

Church–State conflict was evident in a CNBB statement of January 1988 which attacked the government for corruption and a failure adequately to address continuing economic and social problems. A further statement of May 1988, making policy recommendations, also, implicitly, attacked official priorities.

The relative moderation of Sarney's response hints at the significance attached, at the highest level, to avoiding head-on collisions with the Church. On the other hand the sharpness of the controversies surrounding the activities of particular Church agencies indicates the extent of opposition from specific entrenched interests. This has been especially evident in the matter of agrarian reform and of protecting indigenous peoples.

The Church addresses the problems of rural dwellers through its Pastoral Land Commission (CPT), established in 1979 to attend to the interests of poor peasants and landless labourers. It continues to monitor agrarian issues, to offer support to poor rural communities and to press the claims of agrarian reform upon political and land-owning interests.

The CPT's own studies have indicated the extent to which policies pursued under the military promoted a greater concentration of Brazilian land ownership and a relative impoverishment of rural society's lower strata. Against this background Sarney's administration, in 1985, promoted an apparently significant land reform measure. In practice, however, the legislation was less far-reaching than Church and other radical bodies desired. Moreover, land-owning interests organized under the auspices of "the Democratic Ruralist Union" (UDR — founded in 1985) have apparently slowed up the legislation's implementation and, according to the CPT, have been responsible for much grass-roots intimidation. In 1987, for example, the Commission alleges that the UDR was behind the killing of 153 rural workers. Clergy asserting the claims of the landless have also been the objects of violent attacks or, as in the case of the theologian Leonardo Boff, of detention (in March 1988) by public authorities. Equally, radical Churchmen have been subjected to campaigns of attack in such conservative newspapers as *O Estado* of Sao Paulo. The latter distinguishes between politicized clergy, subject to inappropriate Marxist influences, and those concerned with the salvation of souls and evidently appropriate forms of spirituality or evangelism. Such attacks are an indicator of the tensions in much of Brazil's countryside and of the extent to which the Church's more radical sectors have emerged as one of the more effective voices speaking on behalf of the rural poor.

The Church's Indigenous Missionary Council (CIMI) has similarly emerged as the defender of indigenous populations threatened by the activities of large companies, private prospectors or the state. Clergy and others operating under CIMI auspices have been the subject of press attack and, in 1988, collided with the government's National Office of Indian Affairs (FUNAI). In particular there have been conflicts over official attempts to divide Indians into "acculturated" and "non-acculturated" categories on the understanding that the former would effectively be compelled to abandon traditional life-styles in order to open up forest and other Indian lands to business interests. On this, as on the agrarian front, fierce running battles are likely to persist.

In 1988 particular international attention was drawn to the destruction of Amazonian forests and the subsequent plight of rubber tappers. The assassination of the rubber tappers' leader, Chico Mendes, especially highlighted the issue. Mendes' roots in a local Catholic community further points to the part played by portions of the Church, in alliance with other groups, in challenging the beneficiaries of established social and economic policies.

The position of negroes in Brazilian society was another divisive issue to engage the Church's attention in 1988. In May the country celebrated the 100th anniversary of the abolition of slavery and in response the National Ecumenical Commission to combat racism drew attention to the Church's past responsibility for the legitimization of slavery. It also made use of the Church's annual Lenten programme to promote an educational campaign on the subject of racism. Not least the campaign formed part of a longer-term effort to come to terms with and theologically to affirm religious practices with mixed African and Christian roots.

The unwillingness of the Cardinal Archbishop of Rio fully to co-operate in this exercise and the contrary efforts of others in his archdiocese hint at some of the divisions engendered in the Church by the need to respond to cultural, socio-economic or political changes. In this instance there is a division over the significance to be attached to popular or folk religion. Those primarily concerned with the Church's visible unity and the reassertion of hierarchical controls tend to advocate uniform and substantially clericalized pastoral practices inimical to radical liturgical experimentation. Those primarily concerned to mobilize the laity and deeply to root the Church at society's base are much more likely to attribute a positive pastoral value to non-orthodox popular liturgical practices.

Such differing conceptions of ecclesiastical authority and pastoral practice underlie more generalized controversies. The contesting groups in question may ultimately be boiled down to three. Firstly, there are those "progressives" who clearly espouse liberation theology, a "preferential option for the poor", a commitment to structural change and to those decentralized understandings of the Church associated with base communities. Secondly, there are "moderates" who may be generally sympathetic to "the preferential option for the poor" and the autonomy of the Brazilian National Church but who may be generally less inclined than the "progressives" to encourage the spread of a popular grass-roots Church. Thirdly, there are "conservatives" who wish strongly to reassert the claims of traditional hierarchies, pastoral practices and evangelical strategies. They wish to withdraw the Church from avowedly political commitments of a radical character and are disposed to promote a strengthening of the Vatican's control over the local Catholic community.

Developments during 1988 suggest the continuation of a deliberate Vatican attempt to strengthen the numerical strength and influence of the "conservatives". This strategy manifested itself at an earlier stage (1984) in Cardinal Ratzinger's negative comments upon liberation theology and in the summons to Rome of the Franciscan theologian of liberation, Leonardo Boff. More recent events indicate longer-term plans for eroding the influence of liberation theology and for outflanking those Church leaders who have been willing to offer it their support.

One important signal of Vatican intentions was the 1988 appointment to the College of Cardinals of Archbishop Lucas Moreira Neves of Salvador, in the state of Bahia. Neves had himself long served in the Vatican as Vice President of the Congregation of Bishops and Secretary of the College of Cardinals. His elevation to that College, following upon his move back to Brazil, was clearly intended to boost the prestige and influence of a leader formed more by the Vatican bureaucracy than by the local Brazilian Church.

Similar priorities have underlain recent papal appointments to vacant Brazilian archbishoprics. Nine such appointments, by John Paul II, have involved the replacement of "progressives" by "conservatives". Consequently it is now estimated that of Brazil's 36 archbishops no more than 12 are "progressives", only eight are "moderates" and the other 16 are "conservatives". Similarly it is a "conservative", like Cardinal Eugenio Sales of Rio, who is more likely than "progressive" colleagues to be appointed to influential Vatican commissions.

A deliberate attempt to re-fashion the episcopate has been most evident in the economically backward north-eastern region of the country. Within that area the last three years have seen the replacement of six "progressives" by "conservative" successors, the most notable case being the replacement of Helda Camara by José Cardoso Sobrinho. In this latter case, moreover, episcopal powers of appointment were used to remove senior diocesan officials associated with earlier radical priorities.

Alternative steps have been taken to curb the influence of those major "progressives" who have already been appointed. These steps are of at least three kinds. Firstly, as in the case of Bishop Pedro Casaldalgia, who has been outspoken in his support of such causes as the Nicaraguan Sandinista regime, pressure may be applied by the local *Papal Nuncio* to elicit silence. (In Casaldalgia's case even threats of physical violence from conservative political interests have failed to produce this result.) Secondly, as in the case of the radical Auxiliary Bishop of Sao Paulo, Luciano Mendes, there may be a move away from an existing base which ostensibly constitutes promotion but which, in reality, may threaten a diminution of influence. Mendes was known for his radical pastoral work amongst the slum dwellers of Sao Paulo and as the first Auxiliary Bishop ever to be elected President of a National Episcopal Conference. His move to a bishopric in the state of Minas Gerais clearly constituted a formal promotion but also had the effect of removing him from his established base in a major ecclesiastical and political centre. Thirdly, as also in the case of Sao Paulo, there may even be attempts radically to re-draw ecclesiastical boundaries. Thus, in 1988, the Vatican proposed to divide this key archdiocese (the most populous in the Catholic world) into four. The practical result of this move, if implemented, would be to leave the existing Archbishop, Evaristo Arns, to preside over an essentially middle-class and upper middle-class area whilst removing from his jurisdiction those heavily-populated working-class and shanty town neighbourhoods which operated as the centre of his archdiocese's innovative and radical pastoral activities. (During the last years of military rule Church-supported labour and political movements concentrated in Sao Paulo played an especially important role in mobilizing the opposition which helped to undermine the incumbent regime's credibility.) Clearly enough the aim is to deprive the Brazilian hierarchy's most senior radical of his base and to diffuse the impact of his diocese upon the national Church.

Strong ecclesiastical resistance to the proposal, reinforced by protests from politicians, labour leaders and intellectuals, indicates the strength of the position carved out by the Brazilian Church's "progressive" elements. The latter (accounting for about 100 bishops) can count on the backing of many of the "moderates" who constitute the majority of the nation's bishops and so, despite recent developments, are able to question or challenge the Vatican and its local conservative allies. For example, the CNBB was able, in 1988, to launch an essentially new nation-wide periodical designed to counter the influence of Vatican-sponsored and business-supported evangelization campaigns. Progressives and some moderates are opposed to what they perceive as the ostensibly apolitical but effectively conservative and individualistic thrust of the campaigns. In the medium term, at least, they retain the numbers, confidence and institutional resources to sustain the radical cause and to preserve a substantial degree of autonomy for the Brazilian Church. Much will ultimately depend upon the extent to which radical innovators have succeeded in institutionalizing their initiatives at the base level. It seems unlikely, however, that the changes of recent years can be wholly reversed.

Kenneth Medhurst

# BRUNEI

Brunei (*Negara Brunei Darussalam*) is officially a Muslim state, although there is a sizeable non-Muslim minority. The Sultan actively attempts to advance Islam through public pronouncements, control over "un-Islamic" behaviour and media, fostering Islamic studies in the schools and publicly symbolizing religious identity. Internationally, Brunei has participated frequently in Islamic affairs, is a member of the Islamic Conference Organization, strongly criticizes Israel, and supports the Palestinian cause.

There is also an effort to curb both Islamic "extremism" and other religious activities deemed dangerous to Islam. Thus, in recent years *dakwah* groups, the Jehovah's Witnesses, B'nai Br'ith, the Marharishi Movement and several secular organizations charged with having links to freemasonry and Zionism have been banned.

Fred R. von der Mehden

# BULGARIA

After taking over the country in 1944, the communists initiated an intensive secularization of Bulgarian society. But to achieve this goal, they had to subdue the Orthodox Church (total number of believers 6.8 million, i.e. about 85 per cent of the population), which commanded the loyalty of the great majority of the people. Their efforts met only feeble resistance from the Church leaders who were historically conditioned to obey infidel and despotic masters. They felt that submission to secular authority did not compromise their faith and allowed them not only to protect their flock but also to serve national interests. The restoration of the patriarchate in 1953 was a symbol of such hopes.

The 1949 Law of Confessions established a strict system of controls over all denominations, but the Orthodox bishops were able, despite pressures, to defend canonical purity of the Church. They were much less successful in protecting its integrity and in avoiding the excesses of servility.

The most visible sign of the bishops' obsequious behaviour was shown in the insistent promotion of false propaganda that the Church was developing in freedom and peace. Another was the shameful denial and denouncement, in 1989, of Fr. Hristofor Sabaev's "Committee for Religious Rights, the Freedom of Conscience, and Spiritual Values".

More complex was the prelates' posture on issues involving national interests since in these cases governmental directives were in line with their own convictions. Thus they enthusiastically supported the regime's claims to Macedonia against Yugoslavia and fortified them with religious justifications. It appears that the devotion to Bulgarian nationalism was treated by them as a moral vindication of their servile conduct.

Other religious groups (1.2 million Muslims; 70,000 Catholics; 20,000 Protestants) were exposed to political repression similar to that used against the Orthodox Church. Instead, however, of bringing them into total submission, the regime dealt with them differently. Muslims were forced either to assimilate and abandon their faith or to emigrate; Catholics and Protestants were destined for extinction. (Unexpectedly, the Uniates were not liquidated). Despite persecutions, especially intensive during the 1948–52 period, both denominations survived. Their existence, however, is very precarious, since the regime is still rigidly adhering to its policy of attempting to atrophy the religious life of the people by depriving them of their leaders (e.g. in 1987, Pastor Pavel Ignatov of the unregistered Pentecostal congregation in Sofia was sentenced to internal exile), banning religious education of children, and by eliminating, discouraging or adapting religious rituals to their own secular goals.

V. C. Chrypinski

# BURKINA FASO

Burkina Faso was known as Upper Volta before 1984. Once one of France's West African colonies, it was for some years administered as part of the Ivory Coast. Since independence in 1960, there have been several military coups, the latest in 1983 by radical officers led by Captain Thomas Sankara. The largest ethnic group is the three million-strong Mossi, amongst whom French Catholic missionaries have found support. Islam can claim the allegiance of about 35 per cent of the population but its strength lies chiefly among the Fulani, Mandingo and northern groups. The Sahel famine prompted evangelical missionaries to set up relief work.

Stuart Mews

# BURMA (MYANMA)

Religion has been a focal point in Burmese politics throughout the twentieth century. During the pre-independence decades Buddhism provided one of the rallying points for Burmese nationalists against the British colonial regime and Buddhist religious and lay leaders were spokesmen for the nationalist cause. There were also tensions between the dominant Buddhist population and Muslim and Christian minorities. Alleged insults to Buddha in a book written by a Muslim led to bloody riots in the 1930s and Christian-led hill tribes expressed little sympathy for the nationalist movement, preferring the retention of British protection. Christian–Buddhist tensions increased during World War II, when hill tribes aided the Allies and the nationalists initially co-operated with the Japanese.

The post-independence years prior to the military takeover in 1962 saw two major religious issues arise: efforts to emphasize Buddhism led by Prime Minister U Nu, and ethnic-religious conflict involving the hill tribes. U Nu, often referred to as the monk-politician, actively fostered Buddhism. He sought to employ Buddhism to support his development programmes, was at the forefront in an effort to reform the Buddhist clergy (*sangha*), spent heavily on religious activities, implemented policies to aid Buddhist education, was responsible for the implementation of a constitutional amendment establishing a Buddhist state, and led a nation-wide campaign to build thousands of sand pagodas. In the 1960 parliamentary elections his party's polling boxes were Buddhist yellow with a picture of U Nu on them. This emphasis on religion was looked upon with suspicion by non-Buddhists and viewed as an obstacle to modernization and national unity by the armed forces. It was one of the factors leading to the military coup of 1962.

This was also a period of insurgent activities based upon ethnic, ideological and religious divisions. The religious factor was most apparent among the Karens whose Christian leadership sought autonomy or independence, but was also present within sections of other hill tribes. However, for the bulk of the insurgents disagreements were of an ethnic or ideological character.

Until the past two years, the military-dominated government of the post-1962 period found two of its most formidable adversaries were the stubborn rural insurgents and the Buddhist monks. Having eliminated the political and economic bases of power of the previous regime, the military was still faced with opposition from elements of the *sangha*. After the initial rejection by many monks of government efforts to register and otherwise control the *sangha*, the authorities moved to severely limit the influence of the Buddhist clergy in public life. The *sangha* was put under the power of a government-directed committee, the Sangha Mahanikaya, and attempts were made to weed out dissident younger monks. The military government also granted the *sangha* special privileges and carried out symbolic acts, such as building a new pagoda, in order to co-opt the Buddhist monks. As a result of these policies, the *sangha* remained relatively docile until the recent popular resistance to military rule.

During 1988 there were mass demonstrations in urban centres against the often ineffective and corrupt military-led regime. The opposition was ultimately put down by force, resulting in the killing of hundreds of civilians. Disturbances continued during 1989, but without the previous extensive violent reaction by the government and many opponents went into exile or joined the rural insurgents. The students have been at the forefront of this conflict with the regime, joined by workers and other elements of urban Burma. Members of the Buddhist clergy also actively participated in the opposition. During the height of the demonstrations against the military in 1988, elements of the *sangha* were involved in giving anti-government speeches, marching with students and others, providing sanctuary to students against the authorities, giving food and intelligence to the demonstrators, and acting as shields to the students in order to protect them against military and police attempts to fire at them. There were pictures of young monks holding rifles and in Mandalay members of the *sangha* were reportedly handling the day-to-day activities of local government. Allegedly monks were therefore the targets of military threats and repression. There were also official allegations that individuals had dressed as monks in order to incite the population. During the demonstrations Muslim and Christian organizations also participated in opposing government policies and rural insurgent groups offered support. However, religious issues as such were not at the core of the recent popular movement against the military regime.

Fred R. von der Mehden

# BURUNDI

Situated on the east side of Lake Tanganyika with few natural resources, Burundi is possibly the poorest country in the world. Until 1962, it was under Belgian trusteeship. The population is 60 per cent Roman Catholic and is increasing by 2.4 per cent every year. A mass movement into the Catholic Church began in 1930 but there is a great shortage of priests. Some parishes have had to be placed under lay catechists. The Church has followed the state in giving its most eminent positions to the Tutsi, the politically dominant group who comprise only 15 per cent of the population. The Hutu who number 84 per cent were slaughtered in their thousands in 1972 when they rose in revolt. Amongst those killed were 18 Catholic priests and over 2,000 catechists and teachers. In 1972 missionary religious superiors challenged the Catholic bishops to take a "firm and unambiguous position" on the repression. Several critical European missionaries were expelled. With many widows and orphans, the scars of the 1972 bloodbath remain.

Stuart Mews

# CAMBODIA

Cambodia, until recently known as Kampuchea, lying between Vietnam and Thailand, covers an area of about 180,000 sq km and has an indigenous population of around eight million. Its recent history has been bloody and troubled. In 1975 the Maoist Khmer Rouge took power and imposed radical social changes, adopting brutal measures to enforce collectivization. In 1979 the Vietnamese army invaded and established the People's Republic of Kampuchea. Many thousands of soldiers and almost one million immigrants from Vietnam now live in the country. Anti-Vietnamese factions are conducting guerrilla warfare and have formed a "Government of Democratic Kampuchea" in exile which is recognized by the United Nations. It is possible that with warmer relations between China and the USSR the Vietnamese will agree to withdraw in favour of a provisional national government, perhaps under Prince Sihanouk, but the political situation is highly complex and volatile.

Before 1975 the state religion of Cambodia was Theravada Buddhism, which was permeated with elements of popular belief in spirits and demons. There were some 20 thousand Buddhist priests and two thousand monasteries including the renowned temples of Angkor Wat. Under the Khmer Rouge, religious activities were banned and monks persecuted. The PRK government has been more liberal, allowing the Patriotic Kampuchean Buddhist Association to represent the interests of Buddhist monks. Religious life at popular level has somewhat revived but Buddhism is no longer a state religion and there are fewer monks and temples.

Alan Hunter

# CAMEROON

Cameroon displays a fine balance of religious allegiance: approximately 21 per cent Catholic, 18 per cent Protestant, 22 per cent Muslim and 39 per cent followers of traditional religions make up its 10 million population. Ahmadou Ahidjo, a Muslim and northerner, guided the country with a strong hand during the first decades of independence, forcefully dealing with left-wing opposition. In 1984 he resigned from the presidency handing over power to Paul Biya, a southerner and Christian. (Some months later though Ahidjo was implicated in an unsuccessful attempt to overthrow Biya.) The only legal party is the RDPC, the Democratic Assembly of the People of Cameroon. President Biya has relied heavily on support of people from his own area of the centre south. As the politics of presidential decision-making, appointments and demotions, have increasingly centred around manoeuvring factions within his own Beti ethnic group, Biya's relations with the RDPC as a whole have deteriorated. More and more he has withdrawn behind an Israeli security shield led by the leader of the Entebbe raid.

H. S. Wilson

# CANADA

Politics and religion have always clashed in Canada, though usually by mistake. The French regime was Catholic; the British regime which followed tried to be Anglican. But in Nova Scotia this was thwarted by Congregationalists from New England, and the Quebec Act of 1774 conceded rights to Roman Catholics lest rebellious Americans should do the same thing. In the nineteenth century Anglicans were established in Ontario and, with some Scottish Presbyterians, had lands set aside for their support, but opposition, mainly from Methodists, soon brought about religious equality in law if not in social status.

As a two-party system developed it was inevitably a two-religion system for some generations, and in some areas it still is. Usually Protestants have favoured Conservatives, and Catholics have favoured Liberals, but in some sections this pattern is reversed. French-speaking Quebec favoured Conservatives and regarded Liberals as irreligious until the last years of the nineteenth century when Conservatives were seen as Empire-minded Anglo-Saxons and Liberals as protectors of the French tongue and the Catholic religion, and Quebec has been generally Liberal ever since. The present Conservative federal government is almost the first to enjoy widespread support in Quebec; for once it is the Liberals who are now thought to be weak on local rights. But these alignments are no longer primarily religious.

Newfoundland, which only united with mainland Canada in 1949, always enjoyed a sectarian political life, with the Catholics in a minority — though it was one which was itself divided between what was called the "Bishop's Party" and the "O'Sheas' Party". The architects of the 1949 union formed a provincial government which was, like the federal government of the day, Liberal, and the opponents of that union became Conservatives and were overwhelmingly Catholic. When Diefenbaker's populist Conservative regime swept Canada in 1957 the Newfoundland Conservatives shared in power at the federal level and Catholics ceased to oppose confederation. In due course even provincial power fell to them, but denominational and party loyalties are still intermixed.

On the prairies, the depression years saw the birth of two contrary Protestant parties, both replacing farmers' unions. In Alberta a radio-evangelist, William Aberhart, led Social Credit to power in 1935 on a programme of monetary reflation (never achieved) and old-fashioned virtues, while in neighbouring Saskatchewan it was not until 1944 that the CCF, an agrarian party of social gospel origins, took power under Tommy Douglas, a Baptist minister utterly unlike Aberhart. Later the CCF (now the New Democratic Party) held power in British Columbia and in Manitoba, while Social Credit also took power in British Columbia. Neither party controls a provincial government today, but the New Democrats have held their share of seats in the federal house, while Social Credit has declined. The Quebec wing of Social Credit was particularly strident and spoke for the neglected rural areas and a "poujadiste" Catholicism, but was ignored by most Catholics. And it must be added that British Columbia has a polarized political–ideological nature; to call it Southern California north is perhaps an exaggeration, but political movements there have the flavour of religious movements without being actually religious.

As elsewhere in the world, the late nineteenth century saw the state demanding full control of education and the Church resisting; in most provinces Catholic "separate schools" have had only marginal public funding. In Ontario attempts to increase this funding have led to complaints from quite respectable Protestant leaders, and there is obviously more suspicion here than anyone would like to admit. In Quebec there are separate French-speaking Catholic, English-speaking Catholic, and English-speaking Protestant school systems, and bitterness is aroused not by religion but by government restrictions on whose children may be educated in English. Manitoba was given a constitution allowing for bilingualism and Catholic schools on the Quebec model, but French rights were whittled down as English-speaking settlers swamped others. It is only recently that the French minority has asserted its constitutional rights, though the result has been the frantic translation of thousands of laws rather than the redressing of practical injustices.

All religious communities in Canada are outspoken on matters of social responsibility. Governments, both federal and provincial, are responsive to them. In recent years the main issue has been free trade with the United States, which became effective at the start of 1989. All major religious bodies expressed concern at this, not in opposition to tariffs being abolished, but over the apparent requirement that Canada should not subsidize workers with social programmes which are far more advanced in Canada than in the United States. As a United Church document noted, more exposure to market forces would "leave the weakest and poorest more vulnerable". On the same issue, it was noted that 3.7 million Canadians live below the poverty line; an outstanding Anglican study of 1978 held that in Canada the problem of poverty could be solved with relative ease, and it was thus a scandal that it had not been solved. There have also been representations in the last two years about hasty legislation against those who help refugees, against the reintroduction of capital punishment, and in 1989 the Catholic bishops have spoken against budgetary cuts which hurt the poor and, specifically, cut university places for native Indian and Eskimo students. In 1987 a major Church concern was the intention to re-equip the armed forces, and this led to Roman Catholic preference for "living by the Gospel vision and of having that vision transform the political order", while the United Church appeared to argue for neutrality in world affairs. Plans to build a fleet of nuclear submarines to maintain Canada's Arctic sovereignty were regarded as exporting the cold war to new areas, since there was no real evidence that Soviet or even American submarines were using Canadian waters. Yet on this subject the Churches were less convincing than they were on the scandal of homeless families living in the streets, and if the armed forces were not re-equipped it was for purely financial reasons and not due to Church pressure. On the other hand, a Conservative government favouring free trade was elected despite Church reservations. It is possible that the electors did not share those reservations, but it is also possible that they felt the final draft of the treaty allowed sufficient Canadian individuality in social policy.

Yet churchgoers are not usually as unanimous on social concerns as the Churches might suggest. If Roman Catholics are adamant on divorce and abortion, surveys would indicate that their members do not differ greatly from the generality of citizens on the subject of divorce, while on abortion there is stronger feeling but some division. Nonetheless, the issue of abortion is one on which millions in Canada, not all of them Catholics, hold strong convictions which cannot be ignored by any democratic government. But Roman Catholics are generally cautious in their detachment from politics. It is only in the last 30 years that the Church has ceased to be the major political force in Quebec, and if the moral authority and the actual strength of Roman Catholicism in that province were previously overrated, both are now underrated. But it is thought, rightly or wrongly, that too much involvement in the machinery of what is now seen to have been corrupt government has been partly responsible for the decline of the Church.

As for Protestants, the United Church of Canada, the major Protestant body, has a long tradition of support for liberal causes and the downtrodden. But when their General Council of 1988 decided that homosexuals were eligible to be considered for the ministry by local conferences, presbyteries, and congregations, there was a tremendous uproar, even though this decision made little practical difference. As for the Anglicans, when it became known that their Primate had led a session of the Lambeth Conference in 1988 and had chosen to do so in French, this led to an embarrassing reaction from some Churchmen who made it clear that their religion was closely tied to English language and heritage and any use of French was a betrayal. These two issues are not strictly political, but they show that when churches take public stands for tolerance they sometimes find their members less than willing to follow.

Religious persecution is unusual in Canada, but since World War II two groups have suffered. The Dhoukobors are a religious community who came from the Ukraine at the start of this century and settled, mostly quite peacefully, in western Canada. But one branch in British Columbia took to dynamiting railway bridges and the tombstones of their enemies, as well as mass disrobings in front of public buildings. Their rejection of secular education eventually goaded the provincial government into placing their children in a special boarding school. The Dhoukhobors were profoundly shocked at this, but photographs of parents and children communicating through a chain-link fence shocked a public previously exasperated by the sect and its excesses. The children returned to their parents who sent them to school with certain safeguards. The Jehovah's Witnesses were banned during the war and attracted a lingering suspicion for the next 20 years. In Quebec they were particularly successful in converting lapsed or lapsing Catholics, and the provincial government subjected them to legal and illegal harassment. A few Churchmen were prominent in their defence, and they themselves used the legal system to such good advantage that when their rights were finally respected they made the ironic claim that their activity had provided the state, which they regarded as evil, with the legal machinery to protect the rights of all.

Gavin White

# CAPE VERDE

Cape Verde, which is over 98 per cent Roman Catholic, became independent of Portugal in 1975. With a population of only 350,000 (although 600,000 Cape Verdeans live abroad) union with Guinea-Bissau seemed logical and was originally favoured by the vast majority of Cape Verdeans. But the troubled politics of Guinea-Bissau and the development of more friendly relations with Portugal than are enjoyed by any other of its ex-colonies, along with Cape Verde's overwhelmingly Catholic culture, combined to reverse this. The constitution of February 12, 1981 removed all references to future union with Guinea-Bissau and under President Aristides Maria Pereira the Partido Africano da Independência de Cabo Verde is the only legal party. The Roman Catholic suffragan see of Cape Verde is attached to the metropolitan see of Lisbon.

H. S. Wilson

# CENTRAL AFRICAN REPUBLIC

This former French territory became independent in 1960. It suffered under the cruel and capricious regime of the Emperor Bokassa who was deposed in 1979. It has a population of just over 2.75 million but statistics of religious adherence are unreliable. Some estimate religious traditionalists as approximating 60 per cent of the population, with 35 per cent Christian (20 per cent Roman Catholic and 15 per cent Protestant) and five per cent Muslim.

President André Koligba took over in September 1981 when he was head of the army. The sole legal party is the Rassemblement Démocratique Centrafricain. The government is heavily dependent on French support.

H. S. Wilson

# CHAD

Chad gained independence from France in 1960 under the leadership of François Tombalbaye who ruled the country through an army and bureaucracy based on his own Sara ethnic group from the south. With a population of around 5.5 million, Chad divides into 45 per cent Muslims, living mainly in the north, six per cent Christians and the rest followers of traditional religion. Both Christians and traditionalists are grouped mainly in the south. Widespread dissatisfaction with Tombalbaye's regime led him to call on France for permanent military support. In 1975 his political base had become so narrow that a group of Sara junior officers overthrew and killed him. In the Muslim north, meanwhile, Frolinat, the National Liberation Front, was formed in 1966. Two leading figures emerged in a decade of warfare: Goukoni Oueddeye, the aristocratic leader of the northern fighters, and Hissène Habré who had served briefly as an administrator after university education in France. In 1978 the National Liberation Front defeated the southern-dominated government of President Félix Malloum. At once, however, the northern movement broke up into contending factions. Goukoni was the leading figure in the capital, Ndjaména, from 1978 to 1981. In 1980 he called on Libya for military assistance to hold on to power. Habré left the country but soon put together an effective army in the Sudan from which he entered Chad and took Ndjaména. Goukoni fled but was soon back with an army supported by Libya. Habré has shown himself an adroit politician and effective military leader whose forces severely mauled the Libyans. His main problem has been that in broadening the base of his support he has disaffected some of his formidable early supporters.

H. S. Wilson

# CHILE

Until the military coup of September 1973, which overthrew the popularly-elected Marxist coalition government of President Salvador Allende, Chile possessed one of Latin America's most durable and apparently deep-rooted democracies. Prior to the military-based regime created in the coup's wake, under the leadership of General Augustino Pinochet, the country's experiments with dictatorial rule had been infrequent and brief. The prevailing tradition was of constitutional government based upon a relatively smooth-working multi-party system that sprang out of a society containing a substantial middle class and, by Latin American standards, a relatively strong organized labour movement of partially Marxist inspiration. The system ultimately collapsed under the combined weight of political polarization, deep-seated economic problems and external pressures — difficulties which led to harsh political repression and to free market, monetary policies obviously intended to place the interests of capital and economic growth before those of labour and social welfare. Nevertheless, continuing opposition and the electoral defeat of Pinochet in the plebiscite of October 1988 (initially designed to prolong his personal rule by another decade) testify to the persistence and strong reassertion of previous traditions.

This general background helps to explain why, until the 1960s, the Chilean Catholic Church was in the vanguard of the Latin American Christian community's first major moves toward changes of theological, pastoral and political perspective. In particular the emergence of a Marxist left, as well as of a relatively strong Pentecostalist movement, provided an early indicator of the extent to which the Church had lost touch with the country's newly urbanized lower strata. Equally, the Church, from the 1920s onwards, was provided with unusually strong incentives to reconsider its previous reliance upon alliances with upper-class interests associated with the traditional Conservative Party. Minorities of European trained clergy were consequently able to mobilize support for more socially progressive understandings of Catholicism that came to emphasize pastoral work amongst the urban poor and reform programmes aimed at the promotion of greater economic and social justice.

In the 1950s this reformist and socially progressive form of Catholicism found expression in the creation of a "Christian Democratic Party". This was not organically linked to the Catholic hierarchy and was officially non-confessional in character (Protestants and non-believers were free to join). It was, however, heavily influenced by Catholic social teaching and represented an attempt, on the part of some lay Catholic leaders, to come to terms with the realities of a pluralistic society. The aim was to mobilize multi-class support for a pattern of economic development and a programme of social welfare that would substantially benefit the lower strata of both urban and rural society. It was also intended to provide a progressive middle way between the competing claims of Marxism and right-wing authoritarianism.

In 1964 the party leader, Eduardo Frei, was elected President with a degree of popular and Congressional support that seemed to bode well. It momentarily seemed as if Chilean Christian democracy offered the rest of Latin America a model of evolutionary but significant change. In practice, however, political and economic constraints combined to undermine the reforming thrust of Frei's administration. Adverse economic circumstances reduced the necessary freedom of manoeuvre. Equally, divisions emerged within the party's electoral constituency and membership between radicals concerned to accelerate change, conservatives primarily concerned to neutralize the Marxist left and moderates seeking, with increasing difficulty, to pursue a consensual approach. The ultimate result was that of polarization which first produced Allende's narrow electoral victory over a conservative adversary and then led to the establishment of military rule.

Such difficulties partially underlay the discrediting of reformism which occurred, outside of Chile, in the late 1960s, amongst many progressive Latin American Catholics. The role of pace-maker, which had belonged to leading groups within the Chilean Church, passed to radical elements in the Brazilian hierarchy. In Chile itself the new more radical currents of opinion produced divided responses which were further confused by the need to come to terms with Allende's administration and its mounting economic and political difficulties. Left-wing Christian Democratic elements actively supported Allende's radical reform programme and they had clerical allies amongst a radical group, "Christians for Socialism", which openly confronted episcopal leaders in an attempt to push them in an unambiguously pro-Socialist direction. The episcopate, however, remained concerned for the Church's visible unity and sought to reassert hierarchical controls over those, in their own ranks, perceived as a threat to established ecclesiastical authority or as an unduly partisan source of division. Equally, ambivalence or uncertainty surrounded their official dealings with the state. Initially there was a cautious yet respectful attitude to the Marxist government but increasingly ecclesiastical opinion tended to move in the direction of that minority of senior Church leaders who, from the outset, were wholly opposed. This was partly a matter of responding to an apparent breakdown of political and economic order. It was also a question of reacting to threatened attacks upon Church interests in such institutionally vital areas as education. Eventually, most senior clergy were disposed to give at least qualified approval to the government's overthrow. Military intervention was perceived as a temporarily necessary means of saving the country from a descent into chaos.

During the period of the ensuing dictatorship, however, the Church emerged as a significant source of opposition and as virtually the only major national institution capable of offering some sustained resistance. Faced with the brutal repression of all conventional political activity, the systematic abuse of human rights, the arbitrary arrest and torture of political opponents, and the pursuit of economic policies that systematically impoverished most of Chilean society's already poor lower strata, the great majority of Church leaders moved toward more obviously critical positions. Particularly once it became clear that the dictatorship was more than a transient expedient they lent the institution's weight to the support of those being made to suffer by official policy. This was partly a question of responding to pressure from the international Catholic community. It was also a question of responding to pressure from clergy and others working close to the victims of governmental activity. Finally, it was a matter of Church leaders themselves reinterpreting the Church's mission in the light of unfolding circumstances. Confronted by a repressive regime, unwilling to surrender power, the Chilean hierarchy, undergirded by the findings of Vatican II and the Medellin Conference of Latin American bishops, gave renewed expression to their national Church's socially critical traditions.

The Church–State conflict of the Pinochet period has been sustained on different fronts and at differing levels of the national ecclesiastical system. Firstly, there has been an ideological struggle over the regime's legitimacy. From the outset the regime's supporters, including Pinochet himself, have shown an awareness of the potential legitimating capacities of organized religion and the desirability of obtaining a religious sanction for the exercise of political power. Thus official propaganda has consistently stressed the regime's mission to save Chile from atheistic Marxism and to align the country with "the Christian West". Equally, its Doctrine of National Security asserts the need of a strong state in order to eradicate the enemies of Western civilization and to provide necessary levels of social discipline or cohesion. In a more explicitly religious vein, Pinochet has claimed a divine mandate to act on Chile's behalf and divine protection against his enemies. The failure of a 1987 assassination attempt was openly attributed to providential protection. Similarly, the regime's propaganda apparatus sought to derive political benefit from the 1987 visit to Chile of Pope John Paul II. Though the Pope used the visit to criticize the regime's human rights record, and to assert the claims of social justice, official propagandists sought to present images of Pinochet appearing alongside the Pope in order to convey the idea of papal approval for the status quo. By contrast most official national Church leaders have, to varying degrees, identified themselves with calls for a return to democracy and with criticisms of the regime's human rights record which amount to a denial of all claims to legitimacy.

At the back of such disputes lie differing images or representations of God. Official propaganda finds little room for the figure of Jesus but focuses, instead, on a magisterial Triune God who favours the militaristic virtues of order, discipline and hierarchy. It is very much an unreformed pre-Vatican II and anti-ecumenical version of the Catholic faith. Church spokesmen, by contrast, have stressed a concern for justice and reconciliation springing much more directly out of New Testament-based understandings.

Such differences help to explain why Pinochet's regime has permitted a major erosion of the Catholic Church's erstwhile religious monopoly within the armed forces. It is estimated that approximately 15 per cent of army officers now identify with anti-Catholic, anti-Marxist and anti-ecumenical forms of Evangelical and, particularly, Pentecostal Protestantism. There are seven Protestant Churches, grouped in "the Confraternity of Chilean Christian Churches", who have actively opposed the dictatorship, but the latter's supporters clearly perceive an affinity between themselves and some of the more militantly Protestant groups.

Conflicts of an ideological or symbolic kind have been accompanied by more substantive conflicts. Thus the Roman Catholic Church, in parallel with the Lutheran and other Church bodies, has been actively involved in aiding the victims of oppression. This has partly been a question of providing material assistance to the unemployed and to other victims of the state's social policies. It has also been a matter of offering advice, support and protection to the victims of human rights abuses. Most obviously the Church's "Vicariate of Solidarity" has made legal and welfare services available to those under official threat. Governmental intimidation of agencies and individuals engaged in such activities constitutes a measure of the importance of such work in encouraging the regime's opponents and in subjecting its claims to rule to a measure of critical public scrutiny.

Church activities, at the senior level, have been underpinned by work done through parochial networks and urban base communities. It is work that has drawn parish clergy, nuns and local leaders into "the front line" of opposition to the dictatorship. The occasional expulsion of foreign priests, engaged in these forms of struggle, indicates the sometimes exposed nature of such grass-roots activity.

The same activity (particularly in the case of base communities) can also be a source of internal Church controversy. In the present circumstances radical Church activists can generally count upon senior ecclesiastical protection but in the longer term, and when the pressure of an authoritarian state has been removed, latent tensions seem likely to become more obviously manifest. Even now more conservative Church leaders are anxious to assert firm clerical control over decentralized lay-led groups which, from their vantage point, threaten to destroy unity and to subvert authority. In the longer run they are likely to have their hand strengthened by a

Vatican appointments strategy designed to tilt the Chilean hierarchy in a more obviously conservative direction and by at least tacit support from moderates who, in the post-Pinochet period, may be disposed to retreat to less obviously politicized positions. The net result is likely to be struggle between minorities of local activists, committed to the continuing pursuit of radical strategies, and those inclined to return to more conventional pastoral priorities. Present evidence suggests that, in such a struggle, the former are now too deeply entrenched to be eradicated but without the institutional resources needed dramatically to extend their influence.

The extent to which the Church is united in its opposition to Pinochet's regime may be gauged by the fact that only three of Chile's 33 bishops are known as government supporters whilst 17 are avowed opponents. Moreover, the episcopate's public stands suggest that, at critical points, the outright opponents can count on the support of many of the less obviously committed. The national episcopal conference's continuing inclination to elect anti-regime officials points in this direction.

The episcopate's critical attitude to the referendum of October 1988 further confirms the extent of Church opposition. Only a minority of bishops explicitly recommended rejection of Pinochet's candidature but there was general support for statements highly critical of government attempts to outlaw left-wing parties and otherwise to restrict debate. There was also support for statements issued after Pinochet's electoral defeat (which found echoes in the Protestant community) urging the government to negotiate with opposition parties, including the still-active Christian Democrats. For its part the government identified the Church, political terrorists and foreign pressure as the chief sources of its discomfiture. Clearly, Church leaders are likely to play a significant role in the process of moving slowly away from dictatorial rule.

Kenneth Medhurst

# CHINA

The People's Republic of China, founded on October 1 1949 by the Chinese Communist Party, covers almost 10 million sq km and has a population of 1.1 billion (1989). Geographically and culturally there are significant differences between the maritime east of the country and the north/western interior. East China, particularly the central plains, is mainly low-lying, intensively cultivated and densely inhabited by the Chinese-speaking Han people who comprise about 95 per cent of China's total population. Western China is dominated by high mountain ranges, plateaux and deserts. It is far less heavily populated and is home to various national minorities of non-Han people who inhabit sensitive areas bordering with the USSR, India and Vietnam. The population of China is still 80 per cent rural, partly as a result of policies to prevent mass migration from country to city. In the

1980s agriculture and then industry became regulated by market forces rather than central control. Production increased dramatically but there are signs of increasing social tensions caused by corruption, inflation and unemployment. Over-population, pollution and land exhaustion will be serious problems in the immediate future.

## Political system

Demarcation between the Chinese Communist Party (CCP) and the governmental apparatus is ill-defined, state and party having a symbiotic relationship which would be impossible in a pluralist democracy. The Communist Party, the largest in the world, is hierarchically organized on Leninist principles. The Standing Committee of the Politburo forms an inner cabinet which determines strategic policies and fundamental long-term issues. In theory the Standing Committee is answerable to the full Politburo, the Central Committee and ultimately the Party Congress. The CCP organization extends right through the country and has branches in factories, villages and most institutions. Its officials are responsible for relaying Party and government decisions to the population, and provide feedback from local level to the higher authorities.

The State Council oversees the work of the ministries and governmental departments, implementing the policies of the Party leadership but holding little independent policy-making function. The State Council is formally elected and supervised by the National People's Congress which is supposed to meet every five years. A handful of small political parties are represented at the Congress but have minimal influence. Elections play little part in the Chinese political process and national media are firmly controlled by central government. The daily business of government is conducted by the secretariat of the CCP together with senior figures from the State Council.

Chinese political life has experienced periodic oscillations as different factions in the CCP gained ascendancy. The cultural revolution brought to power the "leftist" tendency, led by Mao Zedong and the Gang of Four, which aimed at centralization, egalitarianism and strict party control. The "rightists", represented in the 1970s and '80s by Deng Xiaoping, advocate economic reforms, efficiency, modernization and limited political liberalization. In the 1980s China was in a relatively liberal phase, although "leftists" were still influential and held powerful positions in state and party. It is too early to evaluate the effects of the student protests in Beijing and other cities in spring 1989. Demands for more democracy and an end to corruption received massive support but the movement appeared to be thoroughly crushed by the army and security forces in June 1989.

## Religions in traditional China

The Chinese people have a rich and varied religious heritage, ranging from popular cults and folklore to sophisticated philosophies. "Folk religion" is a generic term for the diverse beliefs and practices which were widespread at the popular level before 1949.

*Ancestor worship* was most common in South China where it played a central role in kinship, lineage and clan systems. Ancestors were thought to bring prosperity provided that descendants protected their graves and performed appropriate ceremonies.

*Local deities* in each region made up a varied pantheon from which the believer was free to choose. Gods included the spirits of local heroes, versions of Taoist or Buddhist deities, and local or animistic spirits. Particular gods were sometimes propitiated by members of particular professions, e.g. sailors or firework manufacturers.

*Religious specialists* were widespread, including monks, shamans, diviners, mediums, ritual leaders, astrologers and healers.

Great emphasis was laid on practicality. Ancestors, gods and specialists were all expected to provide results and answer requests. If they failed to do so, the supplicant was perfectly entitled to switch allegiance to others. Temples were often dedicated to several different gods, and there was little concept of mutual exclusivity. The entire system was decentralized, unsupervised and subject to local conditions. Formal religions were more the concern of the educated elite, although elements did filter down to the common people: Buddhism achieved a mass following at certain periods, and Taoism influenced popular cults. The imperial government maintained strict state control over institutional religions, and heterodox sectarian groups, which sometimes organized major popular rebellions, were often outlawed and suppressed by force.

*Buddhism* was introduced into China in the early centuries of the common era. It was at first mostly confined to foreign residents, but under the Eastern Chin (fifth century) began to spread among native Chinese. The following centuries saw a rapid expansion of Buddhism which reached its peak in the Tang dynasty (seventh to ninth centuries). The most popular sects were the Pure Land and the Chan, the latter being well known in the west via its Japanese derivative Zen. Buddhist philosophy, iconography and monasticism made a profound impact on Chinese culture which is still discernible.

*Taoism* is a term applied to the philosophy expounded by Lao Zi and Zhuang Zi, who asserted the existence of an unseen, inexpressible absolute (Tao) pervading the universe. Their works, dating from about the third century BCE, discuss how a person might become a sage by following the Tao, abandoning worldly desires and acting spontaneously. Taoism later evolved an esoteric system of religious beliefs centred around the achievement of immortality. This quest was pursued by a variety of occult means including alchemy, rituals, exercises akin to yoga and chanting of scriptures. Taoism was regarded by many of the elite as an alternative to the conventional state philosophy of Confucianism.

*Confucianism* could be considered a philosophy rather than a religion, but in either case is essential in any consideration of the Chinese world-view. Originally the teachings of Confucius (c.550–480 BCE) focussed on humanistic ethics and moral conduct. He dismissed speculation about the supernatural and insisted on the need for personal responsibility in the context of formal relationships between men and women, parents and children, rulers and subjects. In later centuries Confucianism was adopted as the state orthodoxy and came to dominate official thinking, culture and education. Its political expression was the veneration of the emperor as supreme ruler by virtue of a heavenly mandate and the creation of an elaborate ritual around him. The imperial system was totally discredited and overthrown in the twentieth century but as the dominant ideology of the scholar–official class Confucianism exerted enormous influence on the Chinese consciousness.

*Islam* was taken to China in the eighth century by Arab and Persian merchants. By the sixteenth century, at least in China proper, many Muslims were integrated into Chinese society, but in the nineteenth century, under the influence of the Naqshbandi Sufi Order, there were fierce Muslim revolts in outlying provinces. Apart from c.20 million signified and integrated Chinese Muslims, there are today important minorities in Xinjiang, Ningxia, Gansu and Yunnan, totalling perhaps 15 millions.

*Christianity* spread through the treaty ports of southeast China and into the hinterland owing to missionary efforts in the nineteenth century. Mission schools, hospitals and even universities were founded and many thousands of Chinese adopted Christianity. These converts were often regarded with suspicion by their compatriots and occasionally attacked, most notoriously during the Boxer uprising of 1900–01. All missionaries were obliged to leave China in the early 1950s and Christians came under increasing state control.

## Religion and politics in contemporary China

The CCP has traditionally been hostile to religion, regarding it in conventional Marxist terms as opium for the masses and feudal superstition. This attitude perhaps had some justification in a tradition-bound society where religious dogmas were often reactionary in the fields of medicine, women's rights, social equality and other areas. The policy adopted since 1949 has been to allow a limited degree of freedom of worship and belief, which was guaranteed by the Constitution of 1954, but to maintain strict supervision and control over religious organizations. Policies are determined by the United Front Work Department (a CCP organ) and implemented by the Religious Affairs Bureau, a body under the State Council. Religious movements are officially represented by national associations, such as the Buddhist Association of China, The China Taoist Association and the Islamic Association of China, all of which were founded in the 1950s. Protestants and Catholics also have their own official national associations.

In theory, since 1954 religious believers have been free to practise their religion in private and to maintain temples, churches and monasteries. In fact the CCP became increasingly harsh towards religious movements during the 1950s and '60s. After 1955 the Christian churches were attacked as crypto-imperialist forces and obliged to sever links with foreign bodies. All religions came under increasing attacks which culminated in the Cultural Revolution, particularly in 1966–67. In September 1966 the Red Guards conducted a fierce campaign against temples, churches, religious art and literature, believers and religious specialists. Almost all religious buildings were forcibly closed and immeasurable destruction done to China's religious heritage. The devastation was particularly severe in Tibet.

As part of the stabilisation and reconciliation undertaken after the Cultural Revolution, policies on religions were considerably relaxed. Religious freedom was specifically guaranteed in the new constitution of 1982. Native Chinese religions are generally allowed to proceed without state interference, except in occasional cases of fraudulence or other disreputable practices. The determining factor in this new orientation is probably the government's wish, in line with "United Front" theory, to minimize social conflict and to adopt a stance of co-operation rather than confrontation. Christianity and Islam, with their substantial international connections, are more closely monitored than native religions, and Islam in Xinjiang remains a sensitive issue since the province, which borders on the USSR, has seen violent protests against Chinese rule. However, foreign connections also provide a measure of protection since religious toleration creates a far better impression internationally than repression. It is interesting to compare the current approach with the recent warming of relations between government and Church in the USSR.

Religion continues to play a significant part in Chinese life. Many people, particularly peasants, are deeply affected by folk beliefs which influence ceremonies, customs and attitudes. Some Chinese intellectuals and artists are influenced by traditional Taoist/Confucian ways of thought. Buddhist monasteries are flourishing and continue to attract devotees, mostly from families with a Buddhist background, but also occasionally among overseas Chinese and intellectuals. Christianity made a strong revival in the 1980s, Protestant churches alone now having over 20 million adherents according to some estimates. There is a new mood of searching among a population to some extent disillusioned with traditional Chinese values and with communist policies, and it seems that religions and philosophies will fulfil an important social function in the coming years. Religious organizations were not involved in the 1989 student protest, but their recent popularity is perhaps another indication of growing opposition to state ideology.

However, it should also be noted that the CCP is essentially critical of religion and its long-term aim is that the masses turn away from it. Religion is strictly excluded from schools, and there are periodic campaigns against excessive liberalism in the cultural field. Religious groups such as pro-Vatican Catholics or evangelical Protestants who refuse to accept state policies are still liable to arrest and imprisonment. Religion is tolerated, but within limits.

## Recent events

*Tibet*: Autumn 1987 and spring 1989 saw demonstrations against Chinese rule suppressed by security forces. resulting in an estimated 100 dead. Tibetans demanded national independence and the return of the Dalai Lama.

*Shanghai*: January 1988 — Gong Pinmei, former Roman Catholic Bishop of Shanghai, rehabilitated. Signs of rapprochement between China and the Vatican.

*Xinjiang*: Summer 1988 — protests by Muslims against Chinese occupation and racism.

*Guangdong and Fujian*: 1988–89 — reports of stricter controls over Christian activities, including compulsory registration of meeting points.

*Hebei*: April 1989 — two Catholics reported dead and hundreds wounded after police attacked a (pro-Vatican) Catholic community in Youtong, Hebei province.

*May 1989*: Public protests in Beijing and elsewhere by thousands of Muslims against a book allegedly blaspheming Islam. The book was withdrawn and authors criticized.

*May/June 1989*: Student movement in Beijing and other cities suppressed by army; imposition of martial law.

Alan Hunter

## Tibet

Virtually all inhabitants of the Himalayan nation of Tibet, which is currently controlled by the People's Republic of China, are Buddhists of the distinctively Tibetan Vajrayana variety. Religion and politics have been intimately linked throughout Tibet's history, and the Dalai Lama has been the highest officer of both religious and secular administrative organizations.

In 1959, when the Chinese government severely repressed an uprising in support of Buddhist rule, the Dalai Lama and a large number of his followers fled to India and established a government in exile at McLeod Ganj near the Indian mountain resort of Dharamsala. It is the headquarters of a large monastic community and provides leadership for the 120,000 Tibetan refugees located throughout India.

On September 24 1987, the first of a new series of violent encounters erupted in Lhasa, Tibet's capital. Monks protesting against the Chinese authorities were interrogated, and when rumours spread that they were to be executed large crowds protested in front of police stations, burning police vehicles. At least 12 Tibetans including several monks were killed when police fired on the crowd. Several encounters occurred in 1988, including an uprising of Buddhist monks following a prayer festival on March 5; in the ensuing repression by Chinese authorities, 24 monks were killed.

In March 1989, an even more violent encounter left as many as 75 dead and scores wounded. It occurred on the twentieth anniversary of the 1959 uprising. Thousands of Tibetans poured into the streets for three days of protests led by young monks and nuns, centring on the Jokhang Temple, the most holy of Tibetan Buddhist temples. The protests escalated to rioting against Chinese and Chinese-owned businesses, and the Beijing government sent an estimated 2,000 troops to quell the riots.

The Dalai Lama, in a conciliatory gesture, announced that he deplored the violence from both sides and assured the Chinese government that he had no ambition of returning to political power in Tibet. Earlier he had proposed a five-point basis for peace talks with the Beijing government which involved the withdrawal of Chinese troops, an end to Chinese settlements in Tibet, a restoration of human rights, the restoration of Tibetan ecology and culture (including the removal of nuclear waste dumps in the area), and the creation of a new political status for the country.

Mark Juergensmeyer

# COLOMBIA

Since the 1960s Colombia has experienced major social changes which have eroded the power base both of the nation's traditional ruling elite and of the traditionally influential Roman Catholic Church. Underlying political changes have been revealed in the inability of successive presidents from the predominant Liberal and Conservative Parties to resolve the problems of left-wing guerrilla-inspired violence; the counter-violence of established interests; and of massive drug-related crime.

The Catholic Church, in principle, commands the loyalty of 95 per cent of the nation's 27,867,326 inhabitants. It initially depended on an alliance with the Conservative Party and still counts on the institutional support provided by a Concordat (first signed in 1887) between the Vatican and the Colombian State. Partisan violence in the 1950s persuaded it to move toward a position of neutrality in the traditional Conservative versus Liberal competition. In practice, however, the institution's freedom of manoeuvre was not greatly increased. By backing the Liberal Conservative power-sharing arrangement ("National Front") of 1958–74 it remained effectively associated with established and partially discredited elites. Equally, its popular base has been eroded by processes of secularization. The consequent weakening of its influence has been revealed by the failure of attempts to promote dialogue between the State, guerrillas and other contending groups. It has also been the subject of attempts by the Liberal President Barco (1986–90) to renegotiate the Concordat. The institution's longer-term viability seems to depend on a fundamental reassessment of traditional elite-orientated strategies.

Kenneth Medhurst

# THE COMOROS

The Comoro archipelago in the Indian ocean has a population of 378,000, who are predominantly Sunni Muslims. Three of the four largest islands declared themselves unilaterally independent from France in 1975, though one island, Mayotte, voted to remain a French overseas department. The first president, Ahmed Abdallah, was overthrown by a left-wing coup within two months of taking office. The economic policy of the new regime soon proved disastrous and a counter-coup supported by right-wing religious groups restored Abdallah. There are 780 mosques and Islamic law is followed on marriage and divorce.

Stuart Mews

# CONGO

The country became independent from France in 1960 with a large, rapidly growing urban sector. Knowledge of the French language, moreover, though instruction had begun late, was almost universal. Congo has a population of almost 2.25 million, over 50 per cent of whom are Roman Catholic, 25 per cent Protestant, 20 per cent followers of traditional religion and three per cent Muslim. The first President, Fr. Fulbert Youlou was, for Africa, a uniquely ambitious and successful political priest. He was deposed by a populist revolution spearheaded by the trade unions in 1963. In January 1970 a Marxist-Leninist state was introduced. The state was henceforth officially atheist with Christmas Day, for example, to be known as Children's Day. Since 1969 the Parti Congolais du Travail has been the only legal party. Colonel Denis Nguesso has been president since 1979. He has seen his role as reconciler rather than follower of an ideological hard line, balancing the influence of regions, ethnic groups and right and left within the country. He has played a similar role both within the UDEAC, the Customs Union of Central African States, and as host to talks on the future of Namibia and Angola in 1988. The Roman Catholic Church, which publishes the only independent newspaper, *La Semaine*, has been able to accommodate this pragmatic brand of socialism.

H. S. Wilson

# COSTA RICA

Seeing themselves as the Swiss of Central America, the Costa Ricans pride themselves on a stable social democratic system lasting 40 years, built in part on Catholic social doctrine. This stability is threatened by turmoil in its neighbours Nicaragua and Panama and persistent economic crisis (social crisis being averted largely due to a well-developed social security system, strong labour movement, and massive inflows of largely US foreign aid). The political landscape has been dominated by the *Partido de Liberación Nacional* (PLN), a social democratic party, but the centre-right *Coalición Unidad* (in power from 1978–82) may coalesce into a more permanent party during the 1990 election campaign.

Once at the vanguard of progressive Catholic social action in the region, the Catholic Church in recent years has been marked by a conservative stance allied with the existing political system, using its influence to defuse potential civil unrest during the deepening economic and social crisis facing the nation. While it garners about 90 per cent of the country's 2.5 million people (mid-'85 est.), historic Protestant Churches such as the Central American Mission and the Presbyterians exercise considerable societal influence. Growth of the pentecostal groups over the past decade has come at the expense of the Catholic Church and traditional Protestant Churches, offering answers to insecurity, anxiety, and economic difficulties, particularly for *campesinos* and urban poor. A Pentecostal church exists for every 3,000 in the capital in comparison to one for 13,000 10 years ago. On the banana-growing Caribbean coast the ratio rose from one church for 22,000 people to one for every 600, according to a study commissioned for the Catholic archdiocese of San José.

In early 1988, Archbishop Roman Arrieta of San José refused to mediate a dispute between high school students who had occupied the cathedral and the government over the imposition of mandatory school uniforms. The occupation was objected to by Arrieta, as he has done with previous occupations by miners and farmers. In March the Catholic Bishops' Conference issued a pastoral letter deploring the high cost of living, the foreign debt, corruption, sterilization, pornography, alcoholism, and drug trafficking but did not mention IMF-imposed austerity plans. In May 1988, the Catholic Bishops' Conference released a document reaffirming labour rights the same day as a new government draft of the labour code. It affirmed the right to strike, equal pay for equal work, protection for *campesinos*, and wage adjustments for rises in the cost of living.

Virgil Wiebe

# CÔTE D'IVOIRE

Côte d'Ivoire became an autonomous state in 1958, an independent one in 1960. Forty-five per cent of its inhabitants follow tribal religions, 30 per cent are Christians, and 24 per cent are Muslim. The Muslims are primarily in the north west. Because of the Catholic schools in colonial times, there is a high percentage of Catholics prominent in government and business. The Catholics are predominantly in the south — Abidjan is reckoned to be 50 per cent Catholic. Although the constitution respects all religious beliefs, Felix Houphouët-Boigny (president since independence) has repeatedly urged people to turn from animism or traditional religions to one of the three major religions. Israeli Prime Minister Shamir visited Côte d'Ivoire on June 19–20, 1987 as part of a tour of four African countries which had established diplomatic relations with Israel. Diplomatic relations with Israel were restored in February 1986, having been broken off after the Arab–Israeli war of 1973. Shamir later called Côte d'Ivoire "Israel's best friend in Africa". In response, in mid-1987 the Council of the Arab League decreed that those League members with diplomatic links with Côte d'Ivoire should sever them. Houphouët-Boigny has in recent years attempted to transform his birth-place, the village of Yamoussoukro, into an African Versailles. The latest project is the basilica of Our Lady of Peace, a church comparable to St Peter's in Rome. It is due for completion in September 1989, and Houphouët-Boigny, a Catholic, has offered the basilica to the Pope as a gift. There had been doubt that the Pope would associate himself with such extravagance, but on July 18, after three months of silence, the Papal Nuncio announced its acceptance.

Paul Gifford

# CUBA

While the Catholic Church claimed as adherents 40 per cent of Cuba's 10 million people in 1984, only 1 per cent are practising Catholics, with a roughly equal number of practising Cuban Protestants. But religious renewal and rapprochement with the state are well under way on the largest Caribbean island. This may be one way of thinking to coincide with Castro's current return to the "spiritual" side of socialism and the economic "rectification" put in place in 1986 by Fidel Castro which has rejected market-based reforms and Soviet notions of *perestroika* and *glasnost*. One indicator of spiritual revival has been the tripling of Catholic baptism since 1979 to over 20,000 a year in 1986, many of those for young people. Yoruba, the Afro-Caribbean rite, has also experienced revival.

The Cuban Catholic Church has until recently been a weak institution unable and/or unwilling to shelter independent political movements or promote human rights but since the mid-1980s has been providing good offices, along with a number of US bishops, to facilitate the freeing and migration of several hundred political prisoners and their families to the US and to call for greater respect for individual rights and freedoms. For its part, the communist party and the state has revitalized its religious affairs office and promoted a greater openness to dialogue with Protestants and Catholics and allowed in greater numbers of foreign religious workers for visits and work. Most notable was the April 1988 visit of New York Cardinal John O'Connor who celebrated mass and met Castro. In May 1989 the Vatican accepted an invitation for Pope John Paul II to visit Cuba in the near future. Several Protestant and Catholic conferences with foreign participation have been held recently in Cuba to consider theology and religious practice in a socialist society. Plans in 1989 included Catholic broadcasts on state radio, expansion of religious printing and the opening of mobile libraries with French and German Church support.

In spite of such progress, a visit in September 1988 by a UN observer team which met with religious leaders revealed human rights abuses including restrictions on the right to worship (especially against smaller groups like the Jehovah's Witnesses and the Adventists) and free association. After prolonged harassment, Ricardo Bofill, the leading human rights activist in Cuba and tacitly supported by the Catholic hierarchy, left the country for exile the same month.

Virgil Wiebe

# CYPRUS

An Ottoman possession from 1571 to 1878, Cyprus became a British colony in 1925 and an independent republic in 1960. The island's political problems spring from the conflicting interests of its mixed population of Sunni Muslim Turks (one-fifth) and Orthodox Christian Greeks (four-fifths). Divided by religion and language, but above all by Greek Cypriot agitation for *Enosis*, union with Greece, the two communities have never formed an integrated people.

The Church of Cyprus, autocephalous within Eastern Orthodoxy since the fifth century, is quite distinct from, though having close ties with, the Orthodox Church of Greece. Its Archbishop is traditionally also Ethnarch, national as well as spiritual leader. Its political activism is a legacy of the Byzantine church–state alliance and of the Ottoman *millet* system, whereby the Church administered the civil as well as the ecclesiastical affairs of its own community. Ecclesiastically nourished, the *Enosis* ideal was rooted in the same Hellenic Christian nationalism that helped create Greece itself.

First president of Cyprus (1960–1977) was Archbishop Makarios, who abandoned earlier support of *Enosis* in favour of a united, independent Cyprus. In 1973 an episcopal bid to depose him for refusing to relinquish secular office was condemned by a pan-Orthodox synod that left him stronger than ever. In 1974 a pro-*Enosis* coup against Makarios engineered by the dictatorship in Athens prompted Turkey's invasion of northern Cyprus. Coup and dictatorship crumbled together.

The island's *de facto* partition progressively hardened. In 1983 the North illegally declared itself the independent "Turkish Republic of Northern Cyprus". The South continues as the Republic of Cyprus.

Peter Moore

# CZECHOSLOVAKIA

Due to historical circumstances, in Czech lands Catholicism and Protestantism competed for the allegiance of the population, and in the struggle weakened their popular acceptance. In Slovakia, on the other hand, the Catholic Church retained the fidelity of the predominantly peasant masses of Slovaks, while the Ukrainian minority remained faithful to the Uniate Church. In both cases, the Church became a major force in the striving for national independence of both ethnic groups. While the Catholics formed the leading religious group (about two-thirds of the total population), the rest of the Czechoslovak citizenry was affiliated mostly with a variety of Protestant denominations, such as the Czechoslovak Hussite Church, the Slovak Protestant Church of the Augsburg Confession, the Evangelical Church of Czech Brethren, and others. In January 1989, the government authorised the formation of the Czech Apostolic Church, a Pentecostal denomination with about 2,000 members. A relatively small group of about 150,000 believers belonged to the Czechoslovak Orthodox Church. Thus, at present there exist in Czechoslovakia 19 legally recognized denominations.

After the 1948 *coup*, which gave them complete control of the government, the Communists oriented their religious policy along the pattern that fundamentally followed the example set by their Soviet mentors. Thus, they accorded favoured treatment to smaller religious organizations, especially to the Hussite and Evangelical Churches, and concentrated on attacking the Catholic Church. Especially strong repressions were applied toward the Uniate Church in Slovakia (about 320,000 strong), considered by the regime to be the hotbed of Ukrainian separatism. After unsuccessful attempts to force it into the Orthodox Church, the authorities declared its dissolution.

There were many methods used by the Communists against the Church, including brute force, administrative chicanery, creation of splinter groups, and a very extensive system of controls over all Church activities. Although they were not able to achieve their most cherished goal and create a schismatic "Czech Catholic Church", they succeeded in severely curtailing religious life.

The state's supervision was — and still is — exercised by the Office for Religious Affairs which regulates all Church functions, including episcopal appointments, pastoral letters, construction and repair of churches, as well as clerical salaries, admissions to theological studies and licensing of priests. As might be expected, the control was highly discriminatory, especially in regard to the recruitment to the priesthood, whose membership was dramatically curtailed. The situation was made even more difficult by the dissolution of Catholic orders. Last but not least, the Office, part of the Ministry of Culture, was carefully monitoring religious instruction, which for purely pragmatic reasons was allowed in grades two to eight of primary schools.

During the 1968 "Prague Spring," the Communist Party took a more liberal attitude toward the Church. Among several new measures, the Uniate Church regained its legal status.

The post-Spring "normalization" brought back the former anti-Church policy to the fore. In August 1971, a new dissident organization *Pacem in Terris*, was formed. Its first congress, held in 1975, was attended by about 400 members. It was clearly an instrument to infiltrate the clergy and to undermine the Church's unity. This role was easily recognized by the Vatican, and the association was condemned by John Paul II in 1982. After this firm action many members left the organization.

Special repressions were again applied by the regime in Slovakia. The reasons were twofold: the close relationship between Catholicism and Slovak nationalism, and the impact of the Polish events, i.e. the election of Cardinal Wojtyla to the throne of St Peter and the birth of "Solidarity".

But the coercion proved counterproductive and instead of forcing Catholics into submission, it made them more assertive. The solemn celebration of the 1,100th anniversary of the death of St Methodius, the Christian apostle to the Moravian pagans, observed at Velehrad in July 1985, was attended by hundreds of thousands and became a visible manifestation of the new spirit. Significantly, youth formed a big part of the faithful. This phenomenon repeated itself on numerous other occasions. For instance, among about 230,000 pilgrims to the shrine of the Virgin Mary at Levoca, in July 1987, close to 70 per cent were young people of both sexes.

This was not all, however. The massive participation in religious demonstrations gave rise to a sense of Catholic strength and provided an incentive for political demands. In 1987, a group of Catholics from Moravia started collecting signatures on a formal request to the government for religious freedom. By May 1988, the petition was signed by about half a million people, including some Protestants, Jews and even non-believers. Among Catholic endorsements one was from the Primate, Cardinal Frantisek Tomasek of Prague, who not only signed the appeal but also called on Catholics to support it as their moral duty.

Somewhat earlier, Cardinal Tomasek sent a letter to the Minister of Culture requesting a basic revision of the existing Church–state relationship. Among others, he demanded the complete separation of these two entities, establishment of Catholic youth organizations, restoration of the suppressed religious orders, permission to build new churches, and no state obstructions in filling 10 (out of 13) vacant episcopal sees. The officials refused and indicated their determination to continue in the same fashion their supervisory activities.

The year of 1988 witnessed a continuous advance of religious life. On March 6, after attending a mass at the St Vitus cathedral in Hradcany, thousands of Catholics from all over the country walked to the Primate's residence (next door to the official mansion of President Gustav Husak) and openly proclaimed their allegiance to the Church, demanded religious freedom, and expressed respect for the aged prelate. On March 25, a similar manifestation took place in Bratislava where 2,000 Czechs and Slovaks, defying official prohibition and police brutality, demonstrated against religious persecution. The protest as well as the savage behaviour of the authorities received wide publicity in Western mass media and strong remonstrations from the Pope and several democratic governments.

A significant element in the religious revival of young people in increasing the awareness of their responsibility and the willingness to make sacrifices for the Church, formed the initiative of the Great Novenna in preparations for the 1000th anniversary of the death of St Adalbert. The plan, undoubtedly inspired by the analogous Polish millennial celebrations of Christianity (1957–1966), was proposed by a mixed group of lay and clerical activists, and gained wide popular acceptance.

In May 1988, the Primate wrote another letter to Premier Strougal in which he condemned the repressions against the signers of the petition and against the peaceful demonstrators in Bratislava. He termed the regime's religious policy as "crisis-ridden" and requested — "on behalf of Latin and Greek Catholics" — a change in the state's attitude, and non-interference in the internal affairs of the Church and in the private lives of believers. At the same time, he declared that "we do not want to follow the path of confrontation; we want a dialogue".

The Primate's plea was urgent for there was a score of pressing problems, among them a severe shortage of bishops, for no new hierarchs were appointed since 1973. (The diocese of Kosice, for instance, was without a bishop for 25 years.) Negotiations with the Vatican, resumed after a four-year interval, were stalled because the government insisted on the elevation to the archbishopric of

Olomouc Father Frantisek Vymetal, the leader of the pro-regime association *Pacem in Terris*. The Holy See, fully supported by the Czechoslovak Church, was unwilling to give in to the government's demands. Ultimately, the regime agreed, toward the end of April, to the appointment of two auxiliary bishops for Prague (Rev. Jan Lebeda and Rev. Antonin Liska), and a bishop to function as Apostolic Administrator for the Trnava archdiocese (Rev. Jan Sokol). None of them was a member of *Pacem in Terris*.

Two Prague auxiliaries were consecrated on June 11 at a solemn service in St Vitus cathedral. It was conducted by Cardinal Tomasek in the presence of Cardinal Macharski of Cracow, the special Vatican envoy Archbishop Francesco Colasuonno (who delivered the papal message in Czech), very many priests and thousands of the faithful. The next day Bishop Sokol was consecrated in Trnava and expressed hope that the event marked the beginning of a new era. Over 20,000 Catholics present rejoiced in the prospect.

Significant at the Prague ceremony was the presence of two Czech bishops who were elevated without governmental approval: Kajetan Matousek and Karel Otcenasek. The latter, speaking at the beginning of the mass, greeted Cardinal Tomasek in the name of all priests and lay Catholics, and declared that: "Our Church has only one voice; it is yours, Your Eminence."

As might be expected, the religious revival, associated with growing militancy, was not welcomed by the communist authorities. Their apprehension was increased when the members of the Charter 77 human rights movement manifested their support for the struggle for religious freedom. The regime's worries were expressed in a variety of ways. Thus, the press accused religious activists that their goal was political and that they aimed toward destabilization of the existing socio-economic system. The term "political clericalism" was constantly invoked in print, radio and TV, and branded as a tool of the anti-communist emigres. It was imputed that they would like to turn Catholics into "the largest anti-socialist opposition" and use the Church as a main instrument of undermining the building of socialism in Czechoslovakia. The Pope was not spared either. He was charged with attempting to transform the Catholic Church into a superpower and of using "secret churches" in socialist countries to promote this grandiose plan of the Vatican's new *Ostpolitik*. Numerous officials publicly deplored "illegal pressures" instigated from abroad, and warned that they might destroy constructive approaches to the solution of confessional problems. Fortunately — they proclaimed — Czechoslovakia has enough loyal and conscientious priests.

Moreover, there were still cases of harassment for religious activities. The most notorious was the case of Ivan Polansky, a Catholic layman from Slovakia, who was sentenced to four years' imprisonment for "subversion against the Republic". His crime consisted of duplicating some *samizdat* publications, mostly of a religious nature, in particular items on strained Church–state relations. Another case was that of Augustin Navratil, committed to a mental asylum for authorizing a petition for religious freedom. Several lay Catholics were charged with "incitement" or a "breach of public order", after they took part in the Bratislava peaceful vigil.

Stanislav Devaty, a Catholic and former Charter 77 spokesman, was singled out for criminal prosecution after an unofficial May Day manifestation and was held in prison, where he went on a hunger strike. His sufferings prompted several hundred people to organize a committee for his defence and send a letter to Premier Ladislav Adamec. It expressed outrage with Devaty's treatment and complete solidarity with his actions. The protest was signed, among others, by civil rights activists Jiri Wolf, just released from 1983 incarceration, Peter Pospichal, Dana Nemcova, and by a Protestant pastor, Jan Dus. A Catholic teacher, Vera Zak, was dismissed from her job for her religious beliefs. Dissatisfied, she took her case to court, but lost. Fr Vaclav Maly was detained for 48 hours, his house was searched, and a number of items were confiscated, including a statue of the Virgin Mary. Afterwards, he was accused of "spreading alarmist propaganda" about the possibility of another protest suicide.

Despite persistent misinformation, prohibitions and repressions, the dissident movement continued unabated, and Catholics as well as other Christians played an increasingly important role in it. In October 1988 the "Association of Believing Catholic Laymen" was formed and issued a declaration calling for religious freedom. It was signed by Augustin Navratil, Radomir Maly, and Frantisek Zalesky. On January 16, 1989, a memorial service was held in St. John's church in Brno on the twentieth anniversary of Jan Palach's self-immolation. Afterwards, many participants marched peacefully to the Freedom Square, where for hours they prayed in silence at the Marian column. The next and the following days similar demonstrations took place at the Wenceslas Square in Prague. This time, unlike police behaviour in Brno, security organs used brutal force against non-violent demonstrators, several of whom — among others Dana Nemcova and her son, David Nemec — were arrested.

In Slovakia, Catholics requested permission to hold three days of prayers to mark St Joseph's Day (March 19). The authorities, however, were insisting on one day of services only, but relented when priests and lay Catholics warned that the refusal might trigger young people's manifestation, similar to the last year's demonstration in Bratislava.

A Mass, celebrated before Easter in Kosice by Cardinal Jozef Tomko, Prefect of Congregation for the Evangelization of Peoples in Rome, visiting his sick mother, was attended by over 15,000 faithful. The funeral of the Cardinal's mother in Uddavske, eastern Slovakia, gathered over 150 priests, many nuns, and over 20,000 people from all over the province.

Seventy-eight priests from the Kosice diocese sent a letter to its administrator, Rev. Onderko, demanding dissolution of the *Pacem in Terris*. They called the association "the rock of evil, which is destroying the unity among the faithful and among priests". Members of the pro-regime organization were accused of "being favoured by the state", and for occupying "almost all key positions" in the curia, often in violation of canon laws. (According to Cardinal Tomasek only about 15 per cent of priests in Bohemia and Moravia, and about 5 per cent in Slovakia belonged to the splinter group. They were mostly older men who naively expected that the membership would give them greater freedom in pastoral activities.)

Cardinal Tomasek did not fail to manifest his posture. On January 20, he dispatched a memorandum to Premier Adamec in which, citing the Czechoslovak access to the Helsinki agreement, he urged the implementation of governmental pledges regarding civil rights and religious freedom. He also protested against brutal police methods during the tranquil Prague demonstrations. The Premier's reply, published in *Rude Pravo* on January 28, assured the Primate of the government's intentions to carry out the Helsinki treaty but expressed strong reservations against "attempts to create relations with the socialist state by means of ultimatum". He also insisted that the police actions were reasonable, and the information the Cardinal quoted was biased. After receiving the reply, the Cardinal wrote another letter to the Premier. This time, he dealt exclusively with the Prague demonstration, and stressed that — contrary to official accusations — the rallies in memory of Jan Palach were not incited by foreign instigators but manifested the genuine and popular desire for full freedom.

In Church affairs, the Primate called a meeting of 20 superiors of Catholic orders, required that they come dressed in monk's habits, and urged them to demand the same in churches from their subordinates. He also preached that the life of the Church was unthinkable without male and female religious communities. Subsequently, the abbots asked him for the acceleration of efforts for the re-establishment of religious orders in Czechoslovakia.

More joyful was the occasion when, on February 18, the Primate personally ordained in Prague 14 graduates of the Litomerice seminary (one of the two still in operation; the other exists in Bratislava). On the same day in Brno, the Prague auxiliary Bishop Lebeda conferred priestly ranks on five students of the diocese of Brno, and Bishop Liska, the second Prague auxiliary, consecrated as deacons 16 students of the archdiocese. These occurrences, however, were not enough to meet a great shortage of priests. The problem existed mainly due to the negative attitude of the State Secretariat for Church Affairs (formerly known as the Office for Religious Affairs). This executor of the government's religious policy habitually prohibited admission of candidates for theological studies who were accused, or suspected, of links with the dissident movement.

Another hopeful development took place in relations between Prague and the Vatican. In January, Vladimir Janku, head of the Secretariat for Church Affairs, paid an unofficial visit to Rome and held talks with Archbishop Colasuonno. While no communique was issued afterwards, it may be reasonably assumed that the main topic of conversation dealt with the issue of vacant episcopal sees. The same problem was discussed when an official Vatican delegation visited Prague in April. The question became even more pressing since meanwhile one more bishop died, and all of the living were over 60. Characteristically, the Czechoslovak episcopate was, on the government's request, excluded from participation. The results of negotiations were not announced and no new bishops were appointed. There were speculations, however, that there existed a possibility that three or even four dioceses might soon regain their pastors.

Although recent developments in Czechoslovakia seemed to indicate some improvement in the Church's situation, there still existed many problems to be solved. One of these was the restriction on religious publishing. A good indication of the need for more and freer publications was the quantity and quality of Catholic *samizdat*, which were issued more or less regularly and were distributed throughout the country in disregard of official repressions.

V. C. Chrypinski

# DENMARK

Like the other Scandinavian countries, Denmark has a state Church, the Danish Folk Church. 93 per cent (1984) belong to this church and about 2 per cent of the citizens belong to other Churches and denominations. The Catholic Church and Islam have grown through immigration and are the religious creeds with the largest number of adherents next to the Lutheran.

The Danish Folk Church is more tightly bound to the state, the government and the central bureaucracy than its Scandinavian counterparts and it has almost no central organization of its own. The traditional political parties (Social Democrats, Conservatives, Liberals) have a unanimously positive view of the State Church system as it has developed up to now. Some new parties such as the (non-communist) Socialist People's Party and the populistic Progress Party, which have both been successful in the latest elections, are critical of the present system.

In 1970 Denmark acquired a Christian People's Party; Conservative Christian groups, especially within the pietistic Inner Mission Movement, were critical of new abortion and family laws and formed a party of their own. This party fared best in the election in 1975 when it won 5 per cent of the votes; in the latest election (1987) the percentage was two. The Christian People's Party has for some years been one of four members of a conservative coalition government and its leader has held the position as Environment Minister; this gives some indication that the priorities of the party are not only those traditional issues centring around the family and Christian education.

The Danish Folk Church seldom takes a position on political issues. When individual members of the clergy have used the pulpit to express opinions on issues that are regarded as belonging to the political sphere, such as the peace issue, they have often been strongly criticized by different political authorities.

Göran Gustafsson

# DJIBOUTI

Virtually the entire indigenous population of Djibouti is Sunni Muslim, as are most of the members of the sizeable Arab commercial community. Religion thus provides a means of bridging differences between the country's two roughly equal ethnic groups, the Afar and the Issa Somali. It has also enabled Djibouti to obtain economic aid from neighbouring Arab states (notably Saudi Arabia), and to gain membership of the Arab League. Since Djibouti also depends on French aid and military protection, resentment at the French presence sometimes takes on a religious colouring, but this is better regarded as a legacy of colonialism than as a genuinely religious issue.

Christopher Clapham

# DOMINICA

Dominica's predominantly Roman Catholic population of 74,000 (1981 census) reflects French colonial influence, though significant Methodist enclaves exist and in recent years fundamentalist and Pentecostal sects from the US and neighbouring islands have made inroads. Their arrival has stimulated greater direct involvement of other clergy in the daily lives of parishioners.

The conservative Democratic Freedom Party, led by Prime Minister Eugenia, has been in power since 1980, survived two coup attempts and an election, and drawn much public support from national and local Catholic clergy. The opposition Labour Party of Dominica has been damaged by in-fighting and the imprisonment of former leader Patrick John for attempting to overthrow the government.

Virgil Wiebe

# DOMINICAN REPUBLIC

As well as 90 per cent of its approximately 6.5 million people being Roman Catholic, the Dominican Republic is also home to Baptists, Evangelicals, Seventh Day Adventists and Jews. While no longer totally unified, the Roman Catholic Church continues to play an influential role in the political life of the country. The forthcoming 500th anniversary of Christopher Columbus' arrival in 1492 will certainly occasion intense debates over that legacy and the nature of Church in society, including specific issues such as land reform and peasant land occupations, the role of the clergy in Christian base communities, protection of Haitian migrant workers, and response to the acute economic crisis.

Elections in May 1990 will pit the opposition Partido Revolucionario Dominicano (PRD), which has split into factions in spite of efforts by the Catholic hierarchy to keep it together, against the ruling Partido Reformista Social Cristiano (PRSC) of President Joaquin Balaguer. The more radical Partido de la Liberación Dominicana (PLD) of former President Juan Bosch has been staging a comeback by softening its image and courting the Catholic Church while the other two parties are faced with disarray.

Austerity measures and price increases sparked off nation wide demonstrations and strikes in June, July and November, 1987 and February and March, 1988. Rank and file Catholics were often involved in their organization. The government met the strikes with force and, following mediation by the Church hierarchy between business, labour and the government in mid-1988, with an easing of prices. Representatives of popular organizations were left out of the talks.

In late 1987, Archbishop Nicolás Jesús López Rodríguez returned an unsolicited gift from former PRD president Salvador Jorge Blanco (1982–86), who later went on trial in early 1989 on charges of corruption (elements of the Church hierarchy have had long connections with the PRD). The Archbishop has also been critical of the Balaguer government's handling of the economic crisis and its acceptance of former Duvalierists from Haiti and Basque separatists from Spain as political exiles.

Virgil Wiebe

# ECUADOR

Ecuador is a small country with an estimated (1986) population of 9,647,107. Its economic development continues to underline the vulnerability of small, relatively backward countries to changes in international economic circumstances. The discovery of petroleum in 1972 facilitated modernization, and moves away from dependence on agricultural products but the oil boom's termination (1986) left behind increased economic inequalities and, in some regions, archaic agrarian structures. National political life has been characterized by instability and, particularly since 1963, recurrent military intervention.

The Roman Catholic Church officially claims the loyalty of 90 per cent of the population. A prophetic episcopal statement, "Opciones Pastorales", issued in 1979, indicated that, in general, its bishops fully accepted the conclusions of the Medellin (1968) and Puebla (1979) Latin American Bishops' Conferences. However, an ageing clergy, particularly concentrated in Quito and especially involved in conventional sacramental life or in Catholic schools, has tended to impede the emergence of a dynamic socially committed Church. Similarly, the bishops were slow to criticize the abuses of power especially associated with the right-wing, neo-liberal government of President Febres Cordero (1984–88). Radical activists were also dismayed by the appointment (1988) to the Archbishopric of Guayaquil of a very conservative *Opus Dei* sympathizer. On the other hand the base community movement continues to develop and has resulted in some dynamic areas of (particularly) rural activity. Similarly, important episcopally-encouraged work continues to be done in defence of threatened Indian communities. A successful episcopal intervention in the 1988 presidential election campaign, which persuaded candidates to moderate their demagogic manipulation of religious language, indicates some still significant capacity to influence the quality of public debate.

Kenneth Medhurst

# EGYPT

The relationship between Islam and politics in Egypt, which had been inter-twined and inseparable, began to change with the rise of a "modern" Egypt under the rule of Muhammad 'Ali (1805–1849). The forces of modernization which the Ottoman leader unleashed by creating a modern army (building factories to arm, clothe and feed this army), sending the educational missions to Europe and introducing cash crops such as cotton, together with the influx of Levantines and Europeans as merchants and entrepreneurs, began a process of modernization which continued unabated until the mid-twentieth century. Gradually during this period the ideology of Egyptian nationalism, which consciously separated Islam and politics, became the dominant ideology. This was symbolized by Mustafa al-Nahhas (1879–1965), the leader of the Wafd Party (which was, prior to the 1952 Revolution, the epitome of Egyptian Nationalism *par excellence*), who prayed and fasted as a pious Muslim, but regarded any attempt to utilize Islam in politics as smacking of charlatanism. Thus al-Nahhas had separated the private domain of Islam from the public domain of politics.

As Egyptian Nationalism had emphasized the need to liberate Egypt from indirect British colonial rule and to Egyptianize the economy, which was dominated by local foreign minorities, it unleashed xenophobic sentiments which remained subordinated to secular nationalism within the Wafd Party itself, but found full expression in the Society of Muslim Brothers, (*Jam'iyat al-Ikhwan al-Muslimin*), and in the Young Egypt Society (*Jam'iyat Misr al-Fatat*). (The Society of Muslim Brothers was founded in 1928 by Hasan al-Banna, who was educated in Dar al-'Ulum with no knowledge of foreign languages, and the Young Egypt Society was founded in 1933 by Ahmad Husain, who was a lawyer by profession and whose ideology, as expounded in his major early work "My Faith" (*Imani*), was an amalgam of militant nationalism, Islam and fascism.)

Although secular Egyptian nationalism continued to be the dominant ideology on the eve of the 1952 Revolution, it began to be seriously challenged by the rising tide of Islamic ideology, and particularly that of the Muslim Brothers. It was indicative of the times that the vast majority of the 100 Free Officers (with no Coptic representation to speak of) who actually executed the *coup d'etat* of July 23, 1952 were at one time or another either members of, or strong sympathizers with, the Muslim Brothers. The list included Jamal

'Abd al-Nasir (Nasser), Anwar al-Sadat, 'Abd al-Hakim 'Amir, Kamal al-Din Husain, 'Abd al-Latif Baghdadi and Khalid Muhyi al-Din. It was not surprising that the Muslim Brothers had claimed that through the Free Officers and with civilian support they had actually "made" the 1952 Revolution. Similarly Ahmad Husain, whose Young Egypt Society became the Socialist Party by 1949, had also claimed with some plausibility that his ideology had inspired the Free Officers Movement led by Nasser. The latter's adoption of Pan-Arab Nationalism was in the Egyptian context a reaction to the secular nationalism of the Wafd, and was definitely rooted in the ascendancy of the Islamic ideology as enunciated by both the Muslim Brothers and the Young Egypt Society (Socialist Party) of Ahmad Husain. In the 1950s, the struggle between the Egyptian Muslim Brothers and Nasser was basically over power and not of an ideological nature. The unsuccessful attempt at Nasser's life in October 1954 led to the incarceration of the leaders and members of the Muslim Brothers until 1958, but when the Egyptian Communists parted company with Nasser in 1959, the Egyptian Muslim Brothers were released, and enjoyed a certain degree of tolerance. Ideologically the Egyptian Muslim Brothers had little to complain about Nasser then. Mosques were built at an increasing pace, the educational system was largely Arabized, the Egyptian economy had become gradually Egyptianized, and the ideology of Pan-Arab Nationalism, with a strong Islamic colouring, was propagated from the Voice of the Arabs broadcasting station in Cairo with its thundering *Allah Akbar* (God is Great) anthem.

Nasser and the Egyptian Muslim Brothers were at loggerheads again when Nasser began his nationalizations in the early 1960s, which affected both local foreign and Egyptian financiers, industrialists and merchants. As the Egyptian Communists were released from prison in 1964, and eventually dissolved their party and joined the newly formed Arab Socialist Union as individuals, the Muslim Brothers, who were strongly against Nasser's adoption of "scientific socialism" which they regarded as incompatible with Islam, were imprisoned in droves after being implicated in an attempt to overthrow the Nasserite regime in 1965.

The leading figure among the Muslim Brothers at that time, Sayid Qutb, who was eventually executed in 1966, had inspired not only the mainstream of the movement, but also some of its offshoots which resorted to violence in the 1970s and the 1980s. Qutb's influence among the Muslim Brothers exceeded that of their founder Hasan al-Banna, especially among the militants such as the *Takfir wal-Hijra* and *al-Jihad* organizations.

When Sadat took over power after Nasser's demise, he released the imprisoned Muslim Brothers whom he had tried to utilize in counterbalancing his Leftist (Nasserite and Communist) critics. Nevertheless Sadat was hardly immune from the militants who attempted to undermine his regime by resorting to violence. Incidents such as that undertaken by the so-called Military Technical College organization which targeted the Cairo Military Technical College in April 1974, or by the *Takfir wal-Hijra* organization which kidnapped the eventually executed the former Minister of Waqfs Sheikh al-Dhahabi in July 1977, and the most dramatic incident of all, namely, the assassination of Sadat himself by the *al-Jihad* organization in October 1981, were stark reminders of the presence of militants among the Muslim fundamentalists.

The mainstream moderate Muslim Brothers have been gradually drawn into the political system since Mubarak took over power. Under the leadership of al-Talmasani, the Muslim Brothers formed an alliance with the New Wafd Party and participated in the parliamentary elections of May 1984, and ended up with eight members of the People's Assembly (parliament). The Wafdist–Muslim Brothers alliance did not survive the demise of al-Talmasani in 1986. The rapport which had existed between the leader of the New Wafd Party, Fu'ad Saraj al-Din, and the leader of the Muslim Brothers, al-Talmasani, was pivotal in building and keeping the alliance between the two political organizations. After al-Talmasani's death, the leaders of the Muslim Brothers, Muhammad Hamid Abu al-Nasr, Mustafa Mashhur, and Muhammad Ma'mun al-Hudaybi sought a different alliance which they could dominate. They allied the Muslim Brothers with the Socialist Labour Party led by Ibrahim Shukri who formed it (with Sadat's blessings) in 1978, and who was a former member of the 1950 Chamber of Deputies (the lower house of parliament) representing Ahmad Husain's Socialist Party (Young Egypt Society). Furthermore the Muslim Brothers "took over" the Liberals' Party (*Hizb al-Ahrar*), a tiny conservative party which advocates free enterprise and which is led by Mustafa Kamil Murad, who began to sport a beard, while the Sheikh Salah Abu Isma'il, a prominent Muslim activist, became the vice-president of the party (he resigned from the party in February 1988); while Al-Hamza Da'bas, the editor of *Al-Nur* weekly, and Sheikh Yusuf al-Badri, another prominent Muslim activist, became *Wakils* of the Party. Under the banner of the Alliance (*Tahaluf*), the Muslim Brothers, the Socialist Labour Party and the Liberals' Party campaigned and formed joint electoral lists in the parliamentary elections of April 1987.

The Muslim Brothers led this alliance and to a large extent put forward their own ideological platform as that of the Alliance as a whole. In an open letter, dated February 1987, and addressed to President Mubarak, the leader of the Muslim Brothers, Abu al-Nasr, outlined the way the mainstream Muslim Brothers view the problems of Egypt. First there is the strong Egyptian identity of the Muslim Brothers, for Abu al-Nasr takes pride in the ancient Egyptian civilization which goes back seven thousand years. During this time-span he finds elements of continuity with more recent history; so just as ancient Egyptians believed in religion and followed its sacred rituals, Egyptians in modern times have become "the guardians of the Islamic Nation (*Ummah*) and the Islamic Caliphate". Second, Abu al-Nasr maintains that the problems of Egypt are basically ethical in nature. As long as the masses of the people as well as those who rule them lack this element of ethical conduct then whatever the government policies are, they will not make significant progress. Third, as religion is essential in remedying the plight of Egyptians at present it follows that Islamic values should permeate all aspects of Egyptian society, whether the educational system, the mass media, or the various government agencies. Fourth, the various Islamic organizations should be allowed to operate freely without any restrictions. The declared state of emergency since 1981 has affected the economic crisis because it has discouraged both the foreign and domestic investor.

The mainstream Muslim Brothers led by 'Umar al-Talmasani had tended to support Sadat with some reservations until the latter's round up of practically all opposition leaders in September 1981. Nasser's tyranny and Sadat's last days of intolerance of all political opposition had "converted" the Muslim Brothers into advocates of democracy, the rule of law, and the need for safeguarding public liberties. Nevertheless there is still a basic tension in the ideology as well as in the policies pursued by the Muslim Brothers between championing political and economic liberalism on the one hand, and the demand for the spread of Islamic values and norms in the entire Egyptian society on the other hand (including social, legal, economic and political aspects).

The actual electoral programme of the Alliance (*Tahaluf*) had the appealing headline "Islam is the solution" (*Al-Islam Huwa al-Hal*), thus stealing the thunder from all other opposition parties. Nevertheless, the electoral programme lacked specific elements or guidelines on how to implement it. For instance the first item on the platform states that the starting point for resolving Egypt's economic and social problems is faith in God. The abolition of the state of emergency and the guaranteeing of public freedom, including free elections, are among the few specific demands which are clearly spelled out. The monolithic dimension in the ideology of the Muslim Brothers, which has been the target of criticism by secularists such as Faraj Fuda, comes out in the call for making all forms of artistic expression as the means "to strengthen genuine religious values".

The elections of April 1987 gave a strong boost to the Muslim Brothers as they were able to get 38 seats out of the 56 seats which the Alliance had won, putting them slightly ahead of the New Wafd Party which won 36 seats of its own. Among those elected were Ibrahim Shukri, the leader of the Socialist Labour Party, Ma'mun al-Hudaybi a leader of the Muslim Brothers, the son of Ahmad Husain, Majdi Ahmad Husain, and the son of Hasan al-Banna, Ahmad Sayf al-Islam Hasan al-Banna. In terms of the total number of seats in People's Assembly (448), the opposition parties are still less than 20 per cent of the total. But the parliamentary elections of 1984 and 1987 were *not* free elections. The last time Egypt had a free parliamentary election was under the monarchy in 1950.

The Muslim Brothers have adapted to parliamentary politics, and therefore they have been incorporated into the political system. The idea of making them participate politically was to weaken the appeal of the Muslim militants, but it has not been successful so far. Some of the leaders of the Muslim Brothers (e.g. Sheikh Salah Abu Isma'il) are directly or indirectly linked to the Islamic Groups (*Al-Jama'at al-Islamiya*) which have flourished in Cairo, Alexandria, and the various provincial cities, especially among university students and youth groups in general. Some of these Islamic Groups have been to some degree linked to militant organizations which are engaged in violence; the best known is the *al-Jihad* Organization.

The incidents which took place in the aftermath of the parliamentary elections of April 1987 are most revealing. A splinter group of the *al-Jihad* Organization, called "Those Redeemed From Hell", attempted in May–June 1987 to assassinate a former Minister of the Interior, Hasan Abu Basha, and a leading journalist Makram Muhammad Ahmad, and, in November 1987, 33 members of that organization were indicted. The Egyptian authorities also discovered, in July 1987, another organization called the "Islamic Vanguard", linked to Iran, and arrested 85 members. Despite the Muslim Brothers' participation in the political system, the Islamic Groups have continued to gain in strength and clashes between them and the police took place in al-Minya and Asyut in September 1987. The situation worsened in al-Minya in October 1987 when the local YMCA was stormed by Muslim militants, which led to the arrest of a few hundred of them. Clashes took place between Muslim militants and the security forces in Bani Suwayf in February 1988, and consequently 14 militants were arrested. In March 1988, one person was killed near Asyut as police dispersed a crowd of protesting Muslim militants. Leaflets were distributed "calling for *jihad* against the authorities" in Cairo, and 85 Muslim militants were arrested consequently at the Ikhlas Mosque in Imbaba.

The *Al-Jihad* Organization was the target of the Egyptian authorities when its members staged a demonstration in the Ayn Shams quarter of Cairo, in August 1988, demanding the imposition of Islamic *Shari'a*, which led to the arrest of 92 members. *Al-Jihad* members also clashed with members of the Muslim Brothers in Asyut in July 1988, revealing a difference in outlook between the mainstream Muslim Brothers and the more militant organizations. In December 1988 100 people were injured as clashes erupted between rival Islamic Groups.

The fear of the militant Islamic Groups prompted the Egyptian Minister of the Interior to ban in September 1988 meetings and gatherings at universities and inside mosques for a period of one year. Measures were taken in anticipation of demonstrations by students at al-Azhar and Ayn Shams Universities, and at mosques all over the major provincial cities including al-Minya and al-Uqsur. After one officer, a policeman, and three Muslim fundamentalists were killed in clashes with Muslim militants in the Shubra and Ayn Shams quarters of Cairo in December 1988, hundreds of Muslim militants, including five leaders of the *al-Jihad* Organization, were arrested by the end of that year, and the authorities discovered a new group called the "Reformation of the Jihad Organization". In April 1989 serious clashes took place between members of the *al-Jihad* Organization and the Egyptian police in al-Fayyum in which a police officer was critically wounded, and consequently tens of members of the *al-Jihad* Organizations were arrested including the Organization leader, 'Umar 'Abd al-Rahman, who was accused of "exploiting religion to propagate ideas with the intention of creating sedition".

The *Al-Jihad* Organization and its splinter groups constitute a qualitatively different ideological school of thought from that of the mainstream Muslim Brothers, despite their common origins. According to Muhammad 'Abd al-Salam Faraj, who had written the Abscent Obligation (*al-Farida al-Gha'iba*): "The rulers of Muslims today are in a state of apostasy from Islam . . . they are Muslim in name only even though they may pray and fast and claim to be Muslims". The first thing to do to achieve the Rule of God, according to the author of the Abscent Obligation, is to get rid of the enemy within, that is, the rulers of Muslims. Thus fighting or *Jihad* against the present regimes to overthrow them becomes the foremost obligation (*farida*) of all Muslims.

Marius Deeb

# EL SALVADOR

The civil war between the FMLN (Farabundo Martí Front for National Liberation) and the government is the major issue in El Salvador and the context for all other activities. The war started in earnest in 1981 when the guerrillas retreated to the mountainous northern part of the country after mounting an abortive "general offensive", which was intended to spark off an uprising in imitation of the insurrection which had brought the Sandinistas to power in Nicaragua in July 1979. Since 1981, 65,000 Salvadoreans, the great majority of them civilians, have been killed by death squads and the armed forces. The FMLN too has been responsible for some hundreds of civilian deaths over the same period.

The civil war in El Salvador was preceded by a decade in which reforms had been blocked, elections nullified by fraud and intimidation, demonstrators massacred and peasant and union leaders detained, tortured and killed by the army and the economic elite in order to preserve their monopoly of power. For many — not only active supporters of the FMLN — the blocking of all avenues to peaceful change by the right legitimized the armed struggle. The grafting of elections in the 1980s on to a regime locked in a civil war did little to change how the protagonists on both sides of the conflict saw the fundamental issues.

The Salvadorean churches — not only the Catholic Church — live in the shadow of Monseñor Oscar Romero who was Archbishop of San Salvador from February 1977 to March 1980. His inauguration coincided with the fraudulent election which installed the Minister of Defence as president. This government unleashed the death squads and launched a campaign of repression against the unions and the anti-government coalitions known as "popular" organizations. Nine priests were killed by security forces or death squads before Romero himself was killed by a death squad on March 24, 1980.

Romero was regarded as a conservative and therefore a safe choice to succeed Archbishop Chávez y González, who had allowed priests within the archdioceses to work with peasants and urban workers seeking greater economic and social justice. One week after Romero was installed as archbishop on March 5, 1977, however, his close friend, Fr. Rutilio Grande SJ, was shot and killed. The killing of Grande shocked Romero. In the months that followed Romero received direct reports of abuses and atrocities from the members of the "base communities" in the Church, many of whom had taken the lead in the defence of human rights. Romero set up a legal aid office to document these abuses and denounced them publicly from his pulpit every Sunday. Romero did not personally form the base communities. Other priests and religious, who were themselves a minority among the clergy, had been working with the poor since the early 1970s, putting into practice the guidelines which emerged from the Latin American Bishops' Conference held in Medellín, Colombia in 1968. This conference used the phrase "institutionalized violence" to describe economic injustice and called on the Church to "defend the rights of the poor and oppressed according to the Gospel commandment . . .". In a country where the official

Church had been a conventional support of the *status quo*, the open taking of sides by an archbishop amounted to a revolution.

Today the Catholic Church in El Salvador is the only independent institution with a presence throughout the country. Monseñor Rivera Damas, who was made archbishop in 1983, maintains this independence with difficulty in the archdiocese of San Salvador. *Tutela Legal*, the human rights office of the archdiocese, investigates, documents and denounces human rights violations by both government and FMLN forces. The Social Secretariat of the archdiocese distributes aid for development and welfare purposes to war victims and is responsible for the running of the refuge for displaced people at Calle Real on the outskirts of the city. The Social Secretariat is also a member of *Diaconía*, an ecumenical organization in which the Emmanuel Baptist, Episcopalian and Lutheran Churches also participate, which is also involved in development and welfare work with displaced people, returning refugees and other victims of government repression. The other dioceses do not support similar programmes and the work of the archdioceses of San Salvador does not have the approval of the Bishops' Conference.

Archbishop Rivera has also permitted a few priests to work in the areas controlled by the FMLN in Chalatenango which, until the creation of the new diocese of Chalatenango in 1988, formed part of the archdiocese of San Salvador.

The Society of Jesus is a significant presence in the Church in El Salvador. It runs the Universidad Centroamericana "José Simeón Cañas", known as the "UCA", to which traditionally the elite families of El Salvador have sent their children for education. The university is the base for Jon Sobrino SJ, one of the best-known liberation theologians in Latin America. The rector is Ignacio Ellacuria SJ, who has been a consistent and outspoken advocate of dialogue between the FMLN and the government. Other religious men and women, working with the authorization, but not under the direct supervision of, local bishops also work with the base community movement of the cities and the rural areas.

The twin aims of Monseñor Rivera Damas since he was made archbishop have been the "humanization" of the war and dialogue between the FMLN and government forces. By "humanization" of the war, he means that the government — and indeed the FMLN — should show a minimum of respect for the lives and property of non-combatants. In practical terms, Rivera Damas has helped to negotiate prisoner exchanges and has gained tacit acceptance for wounded FMLN combatants to be evacuated to the church-run refugee camp at Calle Real on the outskirts of San Salvador. In practice this refugee camp, which the security forces are forbidden to enter, is used by people who would feel at risk from the security forces anywhere in the country.

Rivera Damas has also been the principal official intermediary between the FMLN and the government for the meetings between the guerrilla leaders and their political allies on the one hand and President Duarte and the army chiefs on the other. The two sides first met face-to-face in late 1984 and then there was a gap of three years before they met again in October 1987. In 1985, however, Rivera was involved in an intensive negotiation for the liberation of Duarte's daughter who had been kidnapped by the FMLN. Her release started the practice of prisoner exchanges which has been continued sporadically ever since.

Rivera Damas has been criticized by army leaders and the right for being too soft towards the guerrillas. At the same time Christian groups on the left have complained that Rivera is not outspoken enough in his denunciations of the right and human rights abuses by the security forces. They often hearken back to the declarations of Archbishop Romero. One of the associations of relatives of the disappeared bears the title Madres y Familiares de los Desaparecidos "Oscar Arnulfo Romero". Rivera was close to President Duarte and, like many in the Church, susceptible to the claim made by Christian Democrats that they offered a middle way between the extremes of right and left.

In August 1987 the five Central American presidents signed a peace agreement (known as Esquipulas II or the Guatemala Accord) which, though technically binding on all of them, was, in reality, more directed to bringing the contra war in Nicaragua to and end. In El Salvador, it brought about another round of negotiations with the FMLN and the release of 450 political prisoners but it did not change the dynamics of the civil war. Indeed, after the announcement of the agreement the war intensified and the number of death squad killings increased. The negotiations between the FMLN and the government were broken off after one meeting by the FMLN in protest against the killing by a death squad of Herbert Anaya, the head of the independent Salvadorean Commission for Human Rights. The major achievement of Esquipulas II in El Salvador is that it made dialogue respectable, allowing politicians in alliance with the FMLN, Guillermo Ungo of the *Movimiento Nacional Revolucionario* (a Social Democrat party) and Rubén Zamora of the *Movimiento Popular Social Cristiano*, to return in early 1988 to El Salvador, after seven years of exile, to rebuild their parties.

After these initial gains, however, the war continued very much as before, with the right gaining ascendancy among the military and in the political arena as the political collapse of the Christian Democrats became evident, coinciding with the announcement that Duarte was suffering from terminal cancer. In June 1988 Archbishop Rivera attempted to revive the dialogue by inviting "all the social forces most representative of national life" to a national debate in order to "identify the fundamental points of agreement which might help the government, the armed forces and the political parties, on the one hand, and the FMLN–FDR on the other, to put an end to the conflict by means of dialogue". Rivera was supported by an extremely short and lukewarm declaration of the Bishops' Conference which made clear that it was the archbishop's initiative. The real support came from the UCA which provided the accommodation and the organization of the event. A total of 102 different organizations were invited. They ranged from some of the most right-wing business groups, such as the Cattle Raisers Association (AGES), through all the professional associations, universities — of which there are now a score as a result of new laws encouraging the setting up of private universities — the Lutheran, Episcopalian and Emmanuel Baptist Churches to unions and humanitarian and human rights organizations. The right, in general, refused to attend, with the exception of the Party of National Conciliation, which had been the party of government up to 1979. The right clearly thought that the national debate favoured the FMLN: the letter of refusal sent by the Chamber of Commerce and Industry of El Salvador said: "It is the terrorists upon whom the Church should concentrate greater effort. The bishop should speak forcefully with those who kill and destroy and should seek to persuade them to incorporate themselves into society, alongside those who work, invest, live by their own exertions and do not take justice into their own hands." *Estudios Centroamericanos*, the review of the UCA, accused the business sector of taking the same attitude which it had taken in 1970, when it had boycotted the first Congress of Agrarian Reform organized by the legislative assembly.

Archbishop Rivera's national debate had no lasting effect on the structure of politics in El Salvador but it did enable groups normally deprived of a voice to express themselves. The refusal to attend of the great majority of the right-wing groups made it a more one-sided affair than was intended by Rivera. The groups which did participate set up a "Permanent Committee of the National Debate" to carry the initiative forward. On November 15, 1988, 40 organizations, including *Tutela Legal del Arzobispado* and the UCA, organized a "march for peace", and called on Archbishop Rivera and his auxiliary bishop, Monseñor Gregorio Rosas, to lead it. In his homily on November 13, Rivera not only said that the bishops would not participate but forbade parishes and official church movements to do so. The march, in which 25–30,000 people participated, included a religious service which was conducted by representatives of the Lutheran, Baptist and Episcopalian Churches. Rivera's open withdrawal of support was criticized by grass-roots organizations within the Catholic Church because it reinforced the claim of the right that the national debate was a front for the FMLN and its sympathizers.

The expected victory of the ARENA candidate, Alfredo Cristiani, in the presidential elections of March 19, 1989, has ended the political ascendancy of the Christian Democrats. The election took place as planned after an offer by the FMLN to take part in elections if they were postponed until September. The FMLN threatened both to disrupt the elections and to step up the war if its proposal was not accepted. With a majority in the National Assembly won in elections in March 1988, the right enjoys formal political control of El Salvador for the first time since 1979. The most important political debates will now take place within ARENA and, as before, between the civilian government, the US government and the armed forces.

The effect on opposition forces and the Churches of the election was immediate. Repression has been stepped up; disappearances and death squad killings are on the increase; and humanitarian and Church-linked organizations are being harassed. After a bomb exploded harmlessly on April 14 outside his house, the vice-president-elect, Francisco Merino, with no evidence at all, accused eight people, including a Catholic priest, of having planted the bomb. ARENA also publicly attacked the parish priest of Sonsonate and Fr Segundo Montes SJ, who heads the UCA's human rights institute, accusing him of collaborating with subversion and terrorism.

On the morning of April 19 the Attorney General, Dr Roberto Garcia Alvarado, was assassinated. Although the FMLN did not claim responsibility for the killing and there are equally plausible explanations which place the blame on the right or Christian Democrat groups, the media and ARENA immediately accused the FMLN. Hours later, on the same day, security forces stormed the offices of CRIPDES (Christian Committee for the Displaced), detaining 75 people, including 30 children. Six members of the CRIPDES leadership were sent to prison.

In the following week, the UCA was accused by an army colonel of being the centre of operations where the assassination of the Attorney General was planned. On April 28, the UCA was bombed. Charges exploded at three sites in the campus. This was a clear reminder of the early 1980s when the UCA was bombed 13 times and the Jesuits were told by death squads to leave the country or face the consequences.

The growing polarization of politics in El Salvador is also increasing tension within the Salvadorean Church. On February 5, 1989, the bishop of Zacatecoluca, Monseñor Romeo Tovar, who is now also the President of the Bishops' Conference, organized a "march for peace" — attended by some 200 people — in which he denounced the FMLN as responsible for the violence in El Salvador. The march was applauded by the right-wing press, such as the *Diario de Hoy*, which ran the headline "The archbishopric [of San Salvador] plays the game of the FMLN terrorists".

ARENA has produced a book called "The Popular Church was born in El Salvador", written by Fr Fredy Delgado, a well-known conservative cleric, in which several Church leaders are accused of preferring Marxist theory to the Bible.

In April also the army press office, COPREFA, launched new attacks on *Tutela Legal*, suggesting that it was part of a broad-based effort to "lobotomize" the US Congress in order to bring about a cut-off in US aid and stating that it would soon be "saturating Congress and the North American people with criticism and false human rights violations by the Salvadorean army."

This campaign against groups within the Church is a pre-emptive bid by the strong faction within the armed forces and ARENA which wishes to wage a total war on the FMLN without, as they see it, being hamstrung by human rights policies. *Tutela Legal*, which also documents violations committed by the FMLN, is seen internationally as independent and gives the Archbishopric of San Salvador a unique authority when commenting on the human rights situation. Humanitarian organizations connected with the church are deeply concerned about the escalating threats and violence against their own personnel and the people with whom they work. They are afraid that these attacks are intended to brand all who work for the victims of the war as "Marxists" and to intimidate Archbishop Rivera into withdrawing his protection from them. So far, this strategy has not worked and Rivera has energetically defended both *Tutela Legal* and the humanitarian organizations.

This account has concentrated on the Catholic Church in El Salvador. Approximately 28 per cent of the Salvadorean population is Protestant, however, with a majority belonging to the Baptist churches. The attitude of the Protestants has, in general, been to turn their backs on the conflict. The exceptions are the Lutheran and Emmanuel Baptist Churches which have a long record of working to support the victims of war. The Emmanuel Baptist Church in particular has taken strong stands on the need to struggle for justice. Both Churches continue to suffer because of this commitment to social justice. María Cristina Gómez, a member of the Emmanuel Baptist Church, is the most recent victim. María Cristina, a 40-year old teacher, an activist in ANDES, the teachers' union and the women's movement, was kidnapped outside her school on April 5 by a group of men in a Cherokee Chief station wagon with darkened windows — the usual mode of transport of the right-wing death squads. María's Cristina's body was found 45 minutes later. She had been tortured and was shot as she was tossed out of the vehicle.

The Lutheran bishop, Medardo Gómez, has received death threats for taking seriously the "option for the poor." On December 26, 1988, his church was completely destroyed by a bomb.

There is no end in sight to the civil war in El Salvador. The main protagonists, the military and the ARENA government, on one side and the FMLN on the other, are each preparing to seize the initiative by taking the war to the enemy. There is no indication of a change in policy on the part of the United States government whose military and economic aid, running at approximately $500 million a year, prevents the armed forces and the government from collapsing. Being a civil war, the Salvadorean conflict is above all a war for the "hearts and minds" of the Salvadorean people. The Catholic Church and, to some extent, the Protestant Churches, will continue to play an important role in succouring the victims of the conflict and more importantly in this very religious country, in interpreting it both to ordinary Salvadoreans and to Churches, aid agencies and governments in the world at large.

George Gelber

# EQUATORIAL GUINEA

Colonel Teodoro Obiang Nguema Mbasogo became President of this former Spanish colony in August 1979 having ousted his lunatic predecessor President Macias. Most inhabitants are Roman Catholic and the Church suffered under Macias' terror when over a quarter of the population fled the country. Spanish bishops and nuns were expelled and all Christian names abolished. Most Christian churches were closed in 1975 and in June 1978 the Roman Catholic Church was banned. President Obiang began a policy of reconciliation by ordering the opening of all churches immediately after the coup.

H. S. Wilson

# ETHIOPIA

The relationship between religion, ethnicity and politics in Ethiopia (the People's Democratic Republic of Ethiopia) is important but complex. Historically, Ethiopia's national identity was closely associated with the monophysite Orthodox peoples of the northern plateau region, where Christianity was first established in the fifth century. The peoples of the surrounding lowlands were largely Muslim (to the north and east) or animist (to the west and south), and though these were incorporated into Ethiopia, mostly in the later nineteenth century, high political office was dominated by Christians. There are also small Catholic and Lutheran Churches, and a remarkable indigenous Jewish community, the Falasha, many of whom emigrated to Israel in 1985. After the 1974 revolution, the constitutional status of the Orthodox Church was abolished, and Christianity and Islam were accorded formal equality under an atheist Marxist-Leninist regime. Despite some repression, especially of the convert Churches, in the early years of the revolution, the regime has been anxious not to alienate organized religion, which retains an overwhelming hold on popular belief. The commission established in 1986 to draft a new socialist constitution included the Orthodox and Catholic archbishops, and the leaders of the Muslim and Lutheran communities; a prohibition on polygamy in the original draft was removed in deference to Muslim feelings. Despite revolution and secularization, Muslims are still heavily under-represented in government; only five of the 200 Workers' Party of Ethiopia central committee members, for instance, have Muslim names. Much of the resistance to central government correspondingly comes from Muslim peoples, including the Somalis in the south east, and movements claiming to represent the Afar of the Red Sea plain and the southern Oromo. In Eritrea, however, a Muslim-dominated resistance movement, the Eritrean Liberation Front, has been ousted by its secular Marxist rival, the Eritrean People's Liberation Front, much of whose leadership comes from the Eritrean Christian community; some Arab states have nonetheless supported Eritrean separatism on a pan-Islamic basis. Another major regional opposition movement, the Tigray People's Liberation Front, is drawn almost entirely from Orthodox peoples. Though religion remains an important source of social and political identity in Ethiopia, conflict between the central government and its numerous regional opponents by no means corresponds to the simple Muslim-Christian division as which it is often portrayed.

Christopher Clapham

# FIJI

Until their independence in 1970, the Fiji islands were governed by Britain. The tropical climate was ideal for growing sugar cane and the industry was developed by the British who used indentured Tamil labourers from South India to tend the crops. Between 1879 and 1916, so many Indians arrived that they threatened to outnumber the indigenous Melanesian people of Fiji. The Indians gradually came to control much of the commerce and the professions in Fiji, causing simmering resentment among the conservative Melanesians of the islands.

Matters came to a head in 1987, when the election of Timoci Bavandra as Prime Minister was perceived by some to be a threat to the power of the Melanesian chiefs. In May 1987 Colonel Rabuka, a high army officer, led a coup which overthrew the elected government and placed the country under military rule. Subsequently there have been several attempts to normalize the situation but it is still unresolved. The Hindu and Muslim communities represent the Indian half of the population and have been strongly opposed to the military takeover. Many have sought asylum overseas, especially in Australia and New Zealand.

Melanesian Fijians number 300,000, 98 per cent Christian and almost all Methodist. All the current coup leaders and chiefs are Methodist and their actions have split the Church. Rabuka preaches a fundamentalist piety which considers it a criminal act to work on Sunday. The constitution of the Church has been suspended while opponents fight for control of the Church and try to determine how to resolve the political conflicts in their country.

Ron O'Grady

# FINLAND

Finland has two Churches with the status of state Church. The Evangelical–Lutheran Church of Finland has (1987) 89 per cent of the population as its members. The Orthodox Church comprises only one per cent of the citizens. There have been strong revivalist movements in Finland but the great majority of those who profess conversion have stayed within the Evangelical–Lutheran Church although they sometimes supplement official services with religious meetings of their own. All other Churches and denominations are weaker than in other Nordic countries.

The Church of Finland has a strong position against the state and the political system and its formal standing as a state Church is indisputable. It fulfils more civil religious functions than other Nordic state Churches. All political groups, except the communists, accept and support the present situation. The conservative National Coalition Party has done so for a long time, the Social Democrats accepted it during the war years and have supported it since the Church got a democratic constitution in 1970. The political parties contest elections for the parish councils and through these elections they can gain an indirect influence on the elections for the Synod. It is a sign of the strength of the position of the Synod (and the Church) that it can both take initiatives of its own and let the government know what it sees as being wrong in society, and ask for political remedies. In 1970 Finland got a religious party, the Finnish Christian Union. It was founded as a protest against the rejection of basic Christian values which was seen to have found expression in the rising divorce rate and drug addiction. This protest party got enough votes for parliamentary representation and was most successful in 1975 when nearly 4 per cent of the electorate supported it; in 1987 the Finnish Christian Union won 2.6 per cent of the votes. The party has had only insignificant political influence.

Göran Gustafsson

# FRANCE

The 1789 revolution with its confiscation of the Church's lands and demotion of its role in public life ushered in two centuries of conflict which are slowly ending. The Concordat which Napoleon signed with Rome created a truce whereby in return for recognizing Catholicism as the official religion and subsidizing it, the state obtained considerable leverage over the hierarchy. But Catholics (hierarchy or laity) were never reconciled to the idea of republican democracy. In the struggles between this and authoritarianism which plagued France until recent times they were usually in support of the latter. Church and state were officially separated in 1905, following noisy Catholic support for anti-democratic factions during the Dreyfus case. By then Catholics and secularists (*laics*) had become accustomed to fearing and suspecting each other, often in highly caricatural fashion. It took the experience of occupation and resistance after 1940 for Catholics to come round to acceptance of the republic and for republicans to accept that they had a legitimate role to play. In 1945 a fully fledged Christian Democrat party, the MRP (*Mouvement Républicain Populaire*), appeared; it and its successors have been central to French politics ever since. But recent events suggest that the old wounds are not entirely healed, even if the "clerical question" can never assume the saliency it once did.

The most recent issues have concerned schools, the role of the clergy and the Christian Democrat movement itself. Many believed that the Debré laws of 1959 had solved the schools dispute. They effectively gave grants to non-state (i.e. 90 per cent Catholic) schools in return for the latter's conforming to certain standards; no attempt was made to suppress the Catholic nature of the school. Such a compromise was never to the taste of the left, especially the

Socialist Party (PS), many of whose activists are teachers and members of the teachers' union FEN (*Fédération de l'Education Nationale*), the last redoubt of traditional *laicité*. When Mitterrand won the presidency in 1981 he was saddled with a commitment to "nationalize" the private schools. After two years of delicate negotiations by education minister Alain Savary a deal was concocted with the hierarchy which would have brought the private schools into the state system (and considerably improved pay and conditions for teachers), while respecting their character; the only sticking point (and arguably that was bargainable) was the status of the teachers (should they be employed by the state or not?). Under pressure from the PS MPs Prime Minister Mauroy insisted on this point and so scuppered the whole negotiations. Backed by the opposition parties and Catholic associations, a million-strong petition and demonstration were organized, forcing Mitterrand into a humiliating withdrawal of the bill. There are two lessons from this. One is that part of the left still remains attached to an anti-clericalism that now commands little echo in the country. The other is that opposition to the bill was motivated less by religious sentiment (80 per cent of the French will admit to the description "Catholic" but probably less than 10 per cent actually practise their religion) than by parental fears about the performance of state schools and the desire to keep an alternative available.

Some analysts believe that the hierarchy has been encouraged by this success to assume a higher profile. For years after Vatican II the clergy generally had moved leftwards, often speaking out on issues such as human rights, poverty, the third world and racism. Latterly there have been attacks on contraception (the pharmaceutical giant Rhône–Uclaf had to withdraw a contraceptive pill largely as a result of Church pressure) and on certain cultural manifestations. A Paris cinema was bombed by extremist supporters of the integrist Cardinal Lefevre (recently excommunicated) for showing Scorsese's film about Christ; this incident followed strong criticism by the hierarchy (though this is not to suggest that there is any connection between the two events or indeed that Lefevre supporters are more than a minute fringe of Catholics). But such incidents, together with opposition to contraceptive advertisements on television and calls for religious instruction in state schools, have made some wonder if part of the hierarchy is not overstepping the mark at the risk of reviving old demons.

There has been movement of late within the Christian Democrat family. During the Fourth Republic (1946–58), the MRP was a pivotal party. At one stage it was in fact the largest, with a panoply of associations (farmers, youth, workers, women) close to it and a sympathetic relationship to the major Catholic trade union. It played a major role in reconstructing the economy, creating a welfare state and taking France into the Atlantic Alliance and the European Community. Unfortunately the Republic's failure to decolonize and its demise tended to be blamed on the MRP; it shrunk rapidly, losing some of its vote to Gaullism, which shrewdly combined populism with deference to traditional Catholic values. As religious practice declined (cf. the "deconfessionalization" of the major Catholic trade union in 1964) it would incur further losses on its left, particularly to the new PS in the 1970s which had modernized its discourse sufficiently to attract Catholics, practising and non-practising, across the sectarian divide. The remains of the MRP struggled on under Jean Lecanuet, the party assuming its present name of CDS (*Centre des Démocrates Sociaux*) in 1976. But the growing bipolarization of the electoral system (where at the second ballot voters are effectively forced to choose between left and right) cut down the space available to the centre, where Christian Democracy has always positioned itself. Lecanuet accepted the logic of this by taking the CDS into alliance with Valéry Giscard d'Estaing during his presidency (1974–81), in the hope of being the reforming catalyst of the coalition. Results were disappointing not least because the CDS was distinctly cool towards some of Giscard's attempts at modernization (notably laws facilitating divorce and abortion). But party activists showed growing impatience with the social and economic conservatism of the right and the disinterest of some of its parts in European integration. Demands increased for the CDS to show more autonomy from the mainstream right, and this feeling lay behind the movement's support for Raymond Barre in the presidential campaign of 1988. Barre's defeat left the CDS in more of a mood to listen to the offer of *ouverture* from the victorious President, Mitterrand. Yet it remained very unclear as to what sort of collaboration between his own socialists and the centre Mitterrand was proposing. The CDS set up its own parliamentary group as a first timorous gesture of autonomy. One major difficulty remained: the electoral system which pinions the centre to the right when it comes to support at the second ballot. The European elections of 1989, being run on a PR basis however, presented an opportunity for the centrists to test their strength; accordingly they ran their own list headed by Simone Weil (who is Jewish herself and whose presence must be seen as an attempt to give the list an appeal going beyond Catholics). The poor 8 per cent which the list won suggests perhaps that the hour for an autonomous Christian Democrat force in the centre of French politics has come and gone, and that the future of the CDS lies somewhere in a revamped right. This would be an unfortunate end to the Christian Democrat tradition (though its exponents have stopped using this term long ago) and a strange paradox that the eldest daughter of the Church could not sustain viable politics of this type, compared with virtually all its neighbours.

Other religions have played political roles also. France has always had a Jewish community with a distinguished record in many spheres. Traditionally Jews voted for republican and later left-wing candidates, seen as the best guarantee of minority rights. Latterly this is probably less true, and there is probably very little now by way of specifically Jewish voting behaviour. Protestants were also long considered to be in the vanguard of progressive politics in France; many of the founding fathers of modern republicanism were of this persuasion and the Prime Minister Michel Rocard and the late Minister of the Interior Gaston Defferre are fairly typical. Protestants are concentrated in a few areas in France (the Cévennes, Alsace, parts of the West) but again it is not possible to speak of a protestant vote *per se*.

Of greater numerical importance now is Islam, which is France's second religion. This is mostly due to the waves of immigration, especially from the Maghreb, in recent decades. Most Muslims are of orthodox persuasion and fundamentalism appears to have made as yet relatively little impact even in the very Muslim areas which are now evident in many towns (though recent terrorist attacks by fundamentalists have been exploited by those opposed to Muslim immigration — see below). The politics of Islam have two dimensions, active and passive. That is to say many Muslims have immigrant status and therefore cannot vote, unlike the situation in the UK, for example. The second generation (*les beurs*) who do have French nationality and rights are probably tending increasingly towards a secularist view, especially those who show signs of political activity. In other words there is no real Islamic constituency for anyone to mobilize. But despite itself Islam has become a major political stake, insofar as the rise of the hard right in the shape of Le Pen's *Front National* undoubtedly owes a great deal to its exploitation of the fears of French people, who have to come to terms with a new culture and way of life which is firmly based on a religion of which they know little.

Thus if the old clerical/secular antagonism may well be on the way out (although the passions it releases are such that a resurgence can never be totally ruled out), it may be that it is being replaced with a different kind of politico/religious conflict whose potential for damage is even greater.

David Hanley

# FRENCH OVERSEAS DEPARTMENTS/TERRITORIES

## French Guiana

French Guiana is France's largest overseas department. Its estimated population (1986) is 84,177. Separatist organizations exist but the bulk of the population support greater autonomy within a continuing association with France. Economic development is retarded by the impenetrability of the forests covering 90 per cent of the department's territory and the poor navigability of rivers. Recently it has been assisted by the creation of a French space station and of EC links.

The Roman Catholic Church, based on the single diocese of Cayenne, claims 63,000 adherents (about 75 per cent of the population). (The Anglican Church and four Protestant sects are also represented.) The main social problems the Church confronts arise from racial tensions engendered by immigration, the presence of a European population, enlarged by the space station's creation. Significant support for France's right-wing "Front National" indicates the scale of the problem.

Kenneth Medhurst

## French Polynesia

French nuclear ambitions received a setback in 1962 when Algeria became independent. Until that time, the northern Sahara had been a convenient place to test nuclear weapons. French testing then moved to the island of Mururoa in remote French Polynesia, a move which was resisted by most of the South Pacific countries. Christians make up 93 per cent of the population in the 120 islands of French Polynesia, with the majority belonging to the Evangelical Protestant Church. Church leaders have tried to publicize the negative effects of the continued nuclear testing but without much success. The main island, Tahiti, is a major tourist destination and the Church has had a strong influence in curbing the growth of legalized prostitution and the development of casinos.

Ron O'Grady

## New Caledonia

Violent clashes in New Caledonia since 1986 have highlighted the difficulty for France of maintaining a hold over its largest Pacific colony. Annexed by France in 1853, the islands became a prime source of nickel and chrome for French industry. In 1984, in response to growing unrest, the French National Assembly offered a degree of internal autonomy to New Caledonia and opened the door to eventual independence. French settlers in New Caledonia wanted to retain French ties and opposed the move vigorously.

Most of the country's 200,000 people are Christian. The Protestant Evangelical Church membership is almost entirely Kanak, the indigenous Melanesian people, and it has been a strong voice for independence. The Catholic Church comprises predominantly white French settlers with just a scattering of Kanak members and priests. It has generally been opposed to independence. The leader of the liberation movement (FLNKS), Jean-Marie Tjibaou, a former Jesuit priest, played a key role in moderating between the two opposing factions. His assassination in May 1989 was a setback to progressive forces.

Ron O'Grady

# GABON

Gabon, celebrated as the most successful missionary field in francophone Africa, "the bastion of the cross", gained independence from France in 1960. Eighty-four per cent of its 0.25 million inhabitants are now held to be Christian (65 per cent Roman Catholic) and most of the rest follow traditional religion with about 10,000 Muslims. The first President Leon M'ba died in 1967 and was succeeded by his Vice-President, Albert-Bernard (now Omar) Bongo. The sole legal party is the Parti Démocratique Gabonais. Political stability has been helped by a relatively high per capita GNP based on oil (US$4,250 in 1983). By the mid-1980s Gabon was suffering from the oil slump but the discovery of a vast new onshore oil field in 1988 has renewed optimism. Like some other West African rulers, President Bongo has his personal Malian marabout, M'Baba Cissoku, to act as general adviser, matrimonial go-between and political fixer.

H. S. Wilson

# GAMBIA

Gambia became independent in 1965, and has been a republic since 1970. Its population of 500,000 is 85 per cent Muslim, 3 per cent Christian and 11 per cent adherents of traditional religion. Sir Dawda Kaibara Jawara (a Muslim) was Prime Minister between 1965 and 1970, and has been President since 1970. He was re-elected for a further five year term on March 11, 1987, when his party again won an overwhelming majority. On June 23, 1988, three men were convicted for taking part in a "Libyan plot" to overthrow the government, a plot allegedly uncovered at the end of January 1988.

Paul Gifford

# GERMAN DEMOCRATIC REPUBLIC

The major religious organization in the German Democratic Republic (GDR — East Germany) was the Evangelical Church, which in 1946 claimed 15 million believers out of the total population of 17 million. Over the years, however, the number of Protestants was steadily declining and, according to recent estimates, the figure fell to 7.7 million. The distant second was the Catholic Church whose size since 1948 also decreased from 1.75 million to about 1.05 million members. In addition to these two Churches, there existed a number of other religious groups, including the new Apostolic Church (about 100,000), Methodists (about 28,000), Baptists (23,000), Adventists (11,000), Mormons (4,500), Mennonites, Quakers, Old Catholics, Russian Orthodox, and Jews (less than 1,000). All of them were recognized by the state, which, however, refused to register the Jehovah's Witnesses.

The Evangelical Church, which until 1969 was a member of the all-German Evangelical Church, operated as the Federation of Evangelical Churches (BEK) in the GDR. It consisted of eight regional organizations, each having its own structure with elected synods and bishops. The whole body operated through a "Conference of Church Directorates" with its chosen chairman, currently Bishop Werner Leich.

The Catholic Church in the GDR was, since 1975, also detached from the canonical organization of West Germany. It comprised six territories under the jurisdiction of either diocesan bishops (two) or apostolic administrators. The appointment of either did not require official governmental sanctions. The hierarchs formed the Berlin Bishops' Conference, presided over by an elected chairman. Until recently, the position was occupied by Cardinal Joachim Meisner of Berlin who, in 1989, was designated to head the archdiocese of Cologne in West Germany.

Since the formal creation of the GDR in 1949, the communist leadership was rather amicably inclined toward religious organizations. In time, however, its relationship, especially with the Evangelical Church, became incrementally worse. The main reason for the deterioration was the Church's outspoken opposition to the government's militaristic policies, and the support given by clergymen to the unofficial peace movement. Not least important was the Church's efforts to preserve the concept of one Germany.

In the strained situation, the regime resorted to a variety of "carrot and stick" methods but for pragmatic reasons — not the smallest of these being the hard currency assistance from West Germany — the Church was never exposed to the harsh treatment experienced by Christians in other communist-ruled states of Eastern Europe. Consequently, the BEK was able to maintain its organizational independence and conduct reasonably free religious activities.

A partial rapprochement between the two sides was achieved in 1978 when the leaders of both entities realized the need for establishing a *modus vivendi* for mutual benefits. As might be expected, the agreement did not deal with philosophical questions but attempted to establish a conciliatory relationship. The state intended to turn the Church into a partner in "the construction of a developed socialist society", while the Church was primarily concerned with protecting its interests and the rights of Christians.

The theoretical foundation for the Church's friendly gesture rested on the concept of "the church in socialism", which was elaborated at the Eisenach Synod in 1971. It was a result of a passionate debate among the Lutheran clergymen after a Politburo member, Paul Verner, suggested that the Church should abandon its "critical distance" from the state. But due to its vague nature, the design was controversial and caused many tensions and disagreements within the Church. Walking the line "between opportunism and opposition" was especially taxing on the Church leaders, though most of them were of exceptionally high calibre.

In any case, the Church did not refrain from exercising its critical function toward the government on issues of societal importance. Already in 1978, the Conference of Church Directorates declared its determined opposition both to the government plan of inserting compulsory military training into school programmes and to the growing animosity towards the West. The resulting strain in mutual relations was aggravated when, in 1980, the Church — as its reaction to the East–West controversy on atomic weapons in Europe — initiated country-wide peace "decades", which laid foundations for the unofficial peace movement. The idea attracted many East Germans, especially the young, and in consequence not a few of them began looking to the Church for political guidance.

The regime, while not prohibiting peace meetings, intensified its campaign for strong deterrent under the slogan: "Peace Must be Defended — Peace Must be Armed." But the effects of these efforts were meagre, and throughout 1981 and 1982 the disapproval of the state's policy continued. In January 1982, the so-called "Berlin Appeal" was issued by 35 activists, among them an outspoken critic of the regime, Pastor Rainer Eppelmann. The plea called for the withdrawal of all alien soldiers from Germany, the establishment of a nuclear-free zone, and the substitution of military duty by the "social peace service". It also urged public debate on the issue of peace. At about the same time, Bishop Werner Krusche advocated the disengagement of both Germanies from their military coalitions, and the annual Lutheran synod called on the government to disarm unilaterally. When, despite all the protestations, the government proclaimed a new law on military conscription and the Church's proposals for "social peace service" were not in the text, Bishop Krusche, acting as the head of the BEK, published a critical open letter that was read in all Evangelical churches of the GDR.

The authorities' reaction consisted of the usual mixture of repressions and inducements. Pastor Rochau of Magdeburg was sentenced to three years imprisonment, and about 20 peace activists were deported. On the other hand, the state joined the Church in the celebrations of the quincentenary of Martin Luther's birth, and for the first time a religious service was shown on television. In 1984, the government opened the borders for legal departures to West Germany in the hope that the offer would also attract many Christian activists. The expectations proved correct and several of them, including a number of clergymen, left the country. The relaxation did not last long and the government abruptly changed its liberal course, replacing it with harsh exit rules and new laws on the "disruption of socialist communal life".

The governmental measures and, even more, the deployment of NATO and Soviet missiles in Europe led to some disarray in the peace movement. But Gorbachev's "New Thinking" and changes taking place in Eastern Europe gave the people, especially the young, more ground for expressing popular dissatisfaction. Not unexpectedly, the Church became again the forum for dissident activities as peace, ecology and human rights groups sought the Church's guidance and protection. Characteristically, many young activists also demonstrated their interest in spiritual matters and organized hundreds of small groups associated with the Church. One of them, formed in 1987 and named "Church from Below", called on Church leaders to assume representation of the grass-root movement vis-a-vis the government.

The Church's leadership, though at times uneasy with the more radical pressures, readily responded to the people's calls and strongly supported more pressing demands. The issue of emigration was one of them, and synod after synod criticized the regime for the ban on travel to the West (e.g. the Berlin–Brandenburg of March 31–April 4, 1989). The rigging of results of May 1989 local elections prompted condemnations and mass protests. In Leipzig, for example, over 1,000 people took part in a demonstration denouncing the conduct of the poll.

Not unexpectedly, the new development brought the Church into conflict with the state, which — as usual — resorted to crackdowns on dissidents. In November 1987, the security forces raided a church in East Berlin that was suspected of providing shelter for a dissident group, and the censorship of Church publications was sharpened. A silent protest march through East

Berlin, in 1988, was dispersed by police and about 80 participants were detained. Over 100 protesters were arrested after taking part in the Leipzig manifestation against the manipulation of electoral procedures. Characteristically, the regime constantly attempted to create the impression that the current tension in Church–state relations is but a "passing turbulence" and that anti-dissident acts do not indicate any change in the official policy toward the Church.

The relations between the state and the Catholic Church followed a less dramatic course, which does not mean that the episcopate renounced its social responsibilities. On the contrary, the Church took a strong stand on the issue of abortion and *Jugendweihe*, and it joined the criticism of the militarization of the society. In 1983, the bishops issued a pastoral letter condemning the arms race and supporting the "construction-soldier" concept. In 1985, Cardinal Meisner called attention to the evils of a divided Germany. In 1987, the Dresden Congress (80,000 attendants) was devoted to discussions of politically sensitive issues and afterwards Cardinal Meisner urged the relaxation of travel restrictions. In 1988, the bishops initiated a collection for the rebuilding of a Berlin synagogue burned down by the Nazis 50 years before.

It is very likely that the growing activism of young Catholics, organizing themselves within the Church in autonomous groups (e.g. the Halle Action Circle) as well as a more open attitude toward ecumenism may contribute to an even stronger stand on political issues. In this way, the position of all Churches, especially the major ones, may become closer, and in consequence more effective in performing their tasks, which also include the building of a better society.

A good illustration of such an action was recently provided by an ecumenical conference in Dresden. Almost 150 delegates from 19 Christian Churches debated for four days (April 26–30, 1989) political and social issues and passed resolutions demanding "more democracy; more openness". For the first time, representatives of the Catholic Church had a hand in the proceedings not as observers, but as full participants.

V. C. Chrypinski

# GERMANY, FEDERAL REPUBLIC OF

In 1987 61.1 million people lived in the Federal German Republic of whom nearly 57 million were Germans, the rest mainly immigrant workers from southern and south-east Europe. The two major denominations are Roman Catholicism with 26.2 million people or 42.9 per cent of the population and the Evangelical Church with 25.4 million people or 41.6 per cent of the population, in all 84.5 per cent in 1987 in contrast to 91.6 per cent in 1970. At the same time the birth rate has dropped by half between 1965 and 1988.

The remaining 10 million people constituting 15 per cent of the population are members of fairly large Muslim communities and small Protestant, Orthodox and Jewish communities and atheists. Many immigrant workers, mainly from Turkey and Yugoslavia, drawn to Germany by the post-war construction boom, are Muslims and are only slowly asserting themselves as a political group.

In the Evangelical Church the number of pastors has increased by 27 per cent since 1964, the percentage of women among them was 1.9 per cent in 1964, while it was 10.5 per cent in 1986. On the whole the two large Church communities display a great deal of consensus on fundamental questions regarding the world economic order, nuclear energy, ecology and peace among nations. While Catholics tend more to stress the merits of a moral life for the individual, the Protestants tend to stress the societal context as the framework for a moral life. In 1988 Dieter Oberndörfer, Professor of Political Science, argued in his book on understanding the state in the present time that it was time to leave the "We Germans or We French" mentality behind, the belief that one's own nation is the chosen nation, in order to overcome the narrow nation state understanding of state. This is of key importance in the discussion about the re-unification of the two German states as begun by Willy Brandt, the former Prime Minister who resigned as head of the Social Democratic Party on June 14, 1987. These talks with the German Democratic Republic led to an improvement in the relationship of the two German states. In consequence in 1987 some 86,000 Germans and in 1988 some 200,000 Germans from Eastern Europe were repatriated to the German Federal Republic. On August 31, 1988 the Federal government set aside a special budget facilitating the housing and integration needs of German repatriates. On April 22, 1988 Minister Wilms answered the repeated accusation of Gottfried Forck, Bishop of the Evangelical Church in Berlin–Brandenburg, that the number of Germans wishing to settle in the Federal Republic was limited, by stressing that the Federal Republic did not operate a quota system.

The conservative Christian Democrats are in a politically strong position after the Social Democrats lost in regional elections to the Greens. The rise of the Green Party, mainly disaffected left-wing Socialists but also ecology-concerned Germans who traditionally voted for other parties, can be explained by their hostility towards NATO, their demands for the removal of American missiles from German territory (US intermediate range Pershing II rockets started being withdrawn from Germany from September 1, 1988) and generally by their demands for "alternative" lifestyles. However they were strongly criticized by Cardinal Joseph Höffner of Cologne who urged Catholics not to vote for them because of their views on NATO and abortion. The president of the Central Committee of the Catholic Church in Germany, Professor Hans Maier, Bavarian minister for culture, said in an interview in 1987 that the Church was not there simply to acknowledge trends in society and follow them, but to present arguments and views and imbue society with its values.

Politicians of all parties protested against the measure of the government in Bavaria which decreed on February 25, 1987 that all people suspected of AIDS had to undergo HIV tests. An all-party AIDS commission was set up to prepare political decisions by parliament in the fight against AIDS. In July 1988 the Evangelical Church issued a statement that society as a whole was called to create a climate of openness, togetherness and compassion in the face of the epidemic. It was noted that the Catholic Church had not yet issued a similar statement although questions of nationwide concern had usually been discussed jointly.

An event of historic importance was the state visit of the President of Israel, Chaim Herzog, to the Federal Republic from April 6–10, 1987, the first time an Israeli head of state visited post-war Germany, closely followed by Pope John Paul II who visited the Federal Republic for a second time in his pontificate (April 30 to May 4). The visit was controversial from the outset, because the Pope preaching against abortion (legislation for which differs between the various German provinces and is strictest in Bavaria) and euthanasia and calling for solidarity with migrants and the unemployed, omitted to touch on an issue very sensitive for Germans, that of the experiences of victims and perpetrators of Nazism. The Jewish community felt particularly incensed when the Pope beatified Edith Stein, a Jewess who became a Carmelite nun, but was despite her changed faith deported and perished in Auschwitz. A year later, in May 1988, the Pope told a delegation of Christian Democrat supporters that Europe's richest country had to be aware of the poor beyond its own frontiers despite the fact that the Catholic Church in Germany finances a number of missionary and developmental projects through "Misereor", "Adveniat" and "Caritas" among others in many overseas countries.

When Cardinal Höffner resigned in August and died on October 16, 1987, he was succeeded as president of the German Bishops' Conference by Karl Lehmann, the Archbishop of Mainz, a man noted for his commitment to dialogue. At 51, he was the youngest bishop to be elected to the presidency of the conference. A few weeks later the Vatican appointed from a list of three conservative candidates as successor to bishop Höffner the Archbishop of Berlin, Cardinal Joachim Meisner, who had gained a reputation as an authoritarian and conservative, in opposition to the wishes of the Chapter of the Cathedral in Cologne. The Chapter and the Vatican were unable to agree on a candidate. The archdiocese is one of the richest in the world and critics fear what might happen if these funds came under the control of a Vatican appointee. Church taxes in Germany based on a law of the Weimar Republic are paid by all baptized members of the churches deducted at source together with income tax.

The 22nd Congress of the German Evangelical Church took place in Frankfurt-am-Main from June 17–21, 1987; the next congress will be in Berlin in 1990. On May 26, 1988 the Confederation of the Evangelical Church in the German Democratic Republic and the Evangelical Church in the German Federal Republic published a "joint declaration" at the occasion of the 50th anniversary of the pogroms against German Jews on November 9, 1938, the so-called Night of Broken Glass (*Kristallnacht*).

In August 1988 the Sixth Assembly of the World Council of Churches met in Hanover to celebrate the foundation of the Council 40 years ago. Ever since the twin poles of its work had been faith and doctrine and social action to overcome centuries of distrust among Christians and to affirm "that we are one people".

On January 27, 1989, 163 theologians from Germany, Austria, Switzerland and the Netherlands made public the "Cologne Declaration", a statement of disquiet about the way the Vatican was filling episcopal sees without respecting the wishes of the local churches, was withholding from qualified theologians the permission to teach the Catholic faith and was attempting to enforce its views as competent in matters of doctrine and jurisdiction. In a very short time theologians from other countries, Spain, Belgium etc., endorsed this declaration, thus challenging the Vatican which had taken the line that the Cologne Declaration was a purely local matter.

Dorothea McEwan

# GHANA

The Gold Coast, independent in 1957, was renamed Ghana by the country's first president, Kwame Nkrumah. The first Europeans to visit were the Portuguese in 1471, followed by the Dutch and the British, with the latter establishing their rule by the end of the nineteenth century. Trade was the principal motivation for European interest — especially slaves and gold; the possibility of converting pagans to Christianity a strong secondary one. The Portuguese brought with them Catholic priests, but following the former's expulsion in the mid-seventeenth century by the Dutch, Protestant missions began to establish themselves. The first British missionary society to concern itself with the Gold Coast, the Church of England Society for the Propagation of the Gospel, established a mission in 1752. However, apart from supervising a school for African boys, the chaplains made little attempt to convert the people of the Gold Coast. The first active missions to the Gold Coast, arriving in the early nineteenth century, were the Basel Missionary Society, the Bremen Society and the Wesleyan Missionary Society which worked in the south of the colony among the Fante, the Ga and the Ewes.

Europeans, in their penetration and conquest of West Africa, encountered Islam which had arrived in the sub-region by 1600. Brought by Arab and Berber traders, Islam was adopted by African merchants with whom they traded to the extent of becoming important in the north of the Gold Coast. There developed a north-south religious divide, with southern nations, such as the Fante, the Ewe and the Ga becoming Christian converts, and those of the north becoming Islamicized. Unlike some other parts of West Africa, however, there was no overt Christian–Islam friction. It was rather the case that the north of the Gold Coast was neglected by the Europeans, not only in a religious sense but also in both economic and political terms. To this day, the north of the country is significantly underdeveloped in relation to the south, while retaining allegiance to Islam. According to the last census which produced relevant data, that of 1960, some 43 per cent of Ghanaians professed to be Christians, 12 per cent Muslims and the remainder — some 45 per cent — adherents of traditional religious beliefs. This clearly indicates that the impact of the two great monotheistic religions was significant, but did not remove all adherence to earlier religious beliefs.

Until British rule was established, Christian missions made little progress, with the number of active converts to Christianity small compared to the total population. Nevertheless, the influence of the early Protestant missionaries was of importance. They were aware that teaching a love of Christ was insufficient on its own, realizing that Africans were in need of material as well as spiritual assistance. It was, therefore, in the missionaries' interest to improve the material knowledge and skills of the Africans — such as reading, writing and health education — for in this way the latter would develop into more useful members of Christian society. As a result, in the southern areas of the Gold Coast where European influence was strongest, a class of educated Africans began to emerge. By the end of the nineteenth century this group became dissatisfied with merely serving Europeans and began to organize political societies to defend African rights and to work for the government of the Gold Coast by African Gold Coasters.

During the 1940s Kwame Nkrumah emerged as the most significant figure in Gold Coast politics before leading the country to independence in 1957. Nkrumah, himself possessed of strong Christian beliefs, led a government made up southern Ghanaians with northerners excluded. In 1954, a number of northern chiefs founded the Northern People's Party, a regional rather than religious party designed to defend the interests of northerners against the wealthy and more populous south. It foundered however, on rivalries between chiefs. Protest groups did flourish briefly amongst Ghana's northern Muslims in the mid-1950s, owing to feelings of disgruntlement, but there were neither strong leaders nor a well-developed feeling of Islamic identity. Following independence such religious-based political groups disappeared.

Nkrumah was overthrown in a military coup in 1966. In 1981 a self-described "revolutionary" government led by Flight-Lieutenant Jerry Rawlings came to power. The conservative leaders of the major Christian Churches displayed their dislike of the government by a series of pastoral letters, sermons and letters to newspapers which earned them the distrust of the government. The Catholic newspaper, *The Standard*, was banned in 1986 because of its continuing opposition to government policies. Many Ghanaians, however, saw *The Standard's* campaign as one which tried to protect the position of the Catholic hierarchy, rather than out of any other motivation. Such a feeling may have been a factor in the increasing number of spiritualist and other religious groupings which have surfaced in Ghana in recent times. Another reason may well be that in a continuing situation of economic underachievement, the new Churches are seen as a means of comfort and salvation which the Christian Churches have failed to deliver. In January 1989 the government banned Mormons and Jehovah's Witnesses whose activists it claimed to be subversive. In February, the Commission on National Culture ordered all religious groups to register within three months. The Interior Ministry has reminded them that political meetings may not be held on church premises.

Jeff Haynes

# GREECE

The Hellenic Republic is a secular state whose constitution recognizes the Orthodox Church of Greece as the national religion of the Greek people: 97 per cent of the population are members. Greece is the sole surviving officially Orthodox Christian country.

Although its prestige and influence have waned in recent years, the Church remains closely (sometimes narrowly) identified in popular sentiment and official ideology with the historical struggles and social values of the Greek people. During the four centuries of Turkish rule the Church was the protected institution through which the Ottomans governed their Greek subjects, but also the force that nourished Greek culture and nationalist aspirations, providing symbolic leadership in the War of Independence (1821–29) and in the subsequent formation of the modern Greek nation.

From 1833 the Church of Greece became autocephalous within the Eastern Orthodox communion, its primate the Archbishop of Athens. Previously it had come under the jurisdiction of the Ecumenical Patriarchate of Constantinople (Istanbul), whose ecclesiastical pre-eminence it continues to acknowledge, whose spiritual jurisdiction is still followed on Mount Athos, Crete and the Dodecanese islands, and whose hard-pressed situation in Istanbul constitutes a perpetual irritant in Greece's troubled relations with Turkey.

The complexity of Church–state relations derives from ancient Byzantine traditions re-focussed by the experience of modern Hellenic nationalism. Theoretically the Church is apolitical. Yet it seeks to influence government policy and legislation, while expecting state intervention in its own affairs. Significantly, Education and Religious Affairs form a single government ministry. The right-wing military dictatorship (1967–74), which proclaimed a return to Greek Christian values starting with a reform of the Church itself, split the ecclesiastical hierarchy politically. Church–state relations were stabilized under the New Democracy government of Karamanlis (1974–81), but became strained under the socialist PASOK government of Papandreou (1981–89), which sought looser ties between Church and State. The Church failed to prevent civil marriage becoming a legal alternative to church marriage (1982), but forced a substantial compromise (1988) on proposals to nationalize church property (even threatening to place itself under the jurisdiction of Constantinople, and thereby its property under Turkish control).

Peter Moore

# GRENADA

Of Grenada's 100,000 plus population, approximately 60 per cent are Roman Catholic, 20 per cent Anglican, with a number of other denominations represented. Main political parties following the US invasion in 1983 include the ruling New National Party (NNP) (currently riven by internal power struggles), the New Democratic Congress (a 1987 break-away from the NNP), and Grenada United Labour Party (Gulp) led by former strongman, President and UFO expert Sir Eric Gairy. Elections must be held by March 1990.

Following the collapse of the Maurice Bishop regime, there was a marked increase in the number of conservative evangelical missionaries arriving in the island, such as "Youth With A Mission", a conservative organization sponsoring short-term missions by students. During the August 1987 carnival, incidents occurred in the northern town of Sateurs (a centre of missionary activity), in which missionaries attempted to counter the celebrations by entering processions and singing gospel songs. In September 1987 ten Mormon missionaries were expelled from Grenada under accusations by the government of racism and working without waiting for work authorisations. The head of the Caribbean Council of Churches, Allan Kirton, offered lukewarm opposition to the action while at the same time "trusting the wisdom of the government of Grenada".

Virgil Wiebe

# GUATEMALA

Guatemala, in which over half its eight million inhabitants are of Maya Indian descent (speaking over 20 different dialects), has been beset by social, economic and political divisions for decades. The predominant religion is Catholicism, which in Indian areas is undergirded by indigenous belief systems. But a burgeoning evangelical community (35 per cent of the population in over 300 denominations and sects, some present since the late nineteenth century) challenges Catholic predominance and has led to considerable differentiation not only within its own ranks but those of the Catholic Church as well. By the mid-1990s Guatemala will become the first Latin America country to have a professing evangelical majority.

In a country racked by continuing civil war with a strong racial element, the new sects provide not only a safe haven but also a semi-autonomous base in which some elements of indigenous language can be preserved. Their appeal is considerable to a growing middle class as well. Many of the new sects have brought with them a crusading anti-communist, millennialist, and health and wealth theology which dovetails well with the military's counter-insurgency efforts. Both radical and reformist forms of Catholicism are viewed by the military as subversive and are subject to harassment. Some exiled religious workers have formed tacit alliances with the guerrilla movement. While repression has diminished since the return to full formal civilian rule in January of 1986, recent escalation of disappearances confirms that opposition to social change is strong. The summer of 1988 saw a war of words between the right wing leader of the *Movimiento de Liberación Nacional* (MLN), long linked with death squads, and the Catholic Archbishop Próspero Penados. Earlier that year an Indian priest was threatened by the military after he spoke out against the military on the radio and held mass for widows. In September 1988, an assassination attempt was carried out against the reformist Catholic priest Andrés Girón, leader of a land reform movement and potential presidential candidate for the 1990 elections.

The Catholic hierarchy's more prominent social profile in recent years reflects emergence from the terror of the early 1980s and a reassertion of its role as societal arbiter. Bishop Rodolfo Quezado Toruño has been the chairman of the National Reconciliation Committee (NRC) since its formation as part of the Central American Peace Plan signed by the region's Presidents in August of 1987. The bishops have also taken a leading role in offering good offices between the government, the independent trade union movement (UASP), the business community (CACIF), and the guerrilla movement (URNG). The issuance of pastoral letters, particularly about the land tenure system and the growth of the evangelical Churches, has kept the hierarchy at the midst of controversy. The Catholic community is far from unified, with a resurgent traditionalist element leading to greater *Opus Dei* involvement and also a vibrant charismatic movement led by the flamboyant Salvador Gómez providing strong challenges both to indigenous practice and the evangelicals.

Should 1990 elections successfully take place (which is uncertain given that there have been at least three coup attempts in the past three years), the transfer of at least formal power from one civilian government to another would be the first in nearly half a century. A leading opposition neo-conservative politician and evangelical, Jorge Serrano Elías, serves on the NRC and has used his exposure to boost his chances for the presidency (he ran third in the elections of late 1985). The controversial neo-pentecostal President of 1982–83, General Efraín Ríos Montt, accused by human rights organizations of sanctioning brutal counter-insurgency tactics resulting in the deaths of thousands of rural dwellers, is also making a bid for the presidency (he reportedly supported the most recent *coup* attempt of May 1989).

The late 1988 formation and ongoing participation in the National Dialogue by the Permanent Assembly of Christian Groups marked a new effort in co-operative efforts between Catholics and Evangelicals. The Assembly has stressed the need for respect for human rights, examination of the land issue, and refugee rights to return to Guatemala.

Virgil Wiebe

# GUINEA

Guinea became an independent republic in 1958, and under President Sékou Touré pursued a policy of fierce independence. The country of five million inhabitants is predominantly Muslim (65 per cent), with a large section of traditional religionists (30 per cent) and very few Christians (1 per cent). In 1961 all denominational schools were nationalized. At the same time the French Catholic Archbishop of Conakry was deported. In 1964 two Christian ministers served in the government for a short time. In May 1967 all foreign missionaries were given a month to leave the country. After an attempted invasion with Portuguese backing in 1970, hundreds were arrested, among them the Catholic Archbishop Tchidimbo, a Guinean, who though known as a committed anti-colonialist, was sentenced to life imprisonment on January 24, 1971 for "collaboration with the enemy". Touré became more accommodating later, and the Archbishop was released in 1978. After Touré's death in 1984, Lansana Conté came to power in a coup of April 3, 1984. He has opened the country, allowed Christian missionaries back, and attempted to implement IMF recommendations. On October 18, 1988 a National Islamic League was created to replace the Ministry of Religious Affairs. El Hadj Amadou Tidiane Traore, formerly a Secretary of State in the Ministry of Education, was appointed first Secretary General with the rank of Cabinet Minister.

Paul Gifford

# GUINEA-BISSAU

Although the colony of Portuguese Guinea existed for almost 100 years, Lisbon was never in total control. The long fight for independence began with the massacre of dockers and ended with a bankrupt state. The new government proclaimed itself to be socialist and looked for assistance to the USSR and China. Traditional African beliefs are held by 58 per cent, while another 33 per cent are Muslims and 8 per cent Roman Catholic. Christianity is strongest among the Balanta, but Islam is growing as it spreads to the coast.

Stuart Mews

# GUYANA

Guyana acquired independence from Britain in 1966. Its modern politics have been overshadowed by racial tensions between the descendants of former black slaves and of East Indian indentured labourers imported in the nineteenth century. The conflict found expression in the rivalry of the two politically dominant figures of modern times — Cheddi Jagan (East Indian) and James Burnham (black). In 1950 the two formed the People's Progressive Party (PPP) but by 1957 Burnham had formed his own People's National Congress (PNC). As independence approached the avowedly Marxist PPP was the largest single party but Jagan was outmanoeuvred by Burnham who ultimately consolidated a monopolistic grip on power which enabled him to pursue his brand of socialism. Economic difficulties exacerbated underlying racial tensions which were met by repression and electoral fraud. Burnham's death (1985) entailed "the roll-back of co-operative socialism" but did not change the underlying ethnic and political realities.

Most major Christian denominations are represented amongst the 790,000 inhabitants. Anglicans and Catholics are especially numerous. There are similarly large Hindu and Islamic populations. Particularly in the 1980s Christian Churches and human rights groups have been drawn into conflict with the government over abuses of power. The "Jonestown massacre" of 1978 (when 900 members of the People's Temple cult committed suicide) revealed how cults were officially encouraged as counterweights to orthodox, politically critical religious bodies.

Kenneth Medhurst

# HAITI

Haiti is the poorest country in the western hemisphere. In 1985 public expenditure amounted to 1 per cent of GDP or $3.70 per capita; public expenditure on health in the same year was estimated at 0.9 per cent of GDP or $3.44 per capita. For each secondary school teacher there were 189 members of the security forces, while for every secondary school there were 35 prisons. The country's infant mortality rate was 124 per thousand (in the United States the figure is 13 per thousand and in Cuba 14 per thousand).[1] Since 1985 social and economic indicators have deteriorated even further. Corruption and brutality are still the norm. Each year thousands of Haitians try to leave, selling all their possessions and risking their lives in leaky boats in an attempt to reach the shores of Florida. This desperate poverty and the hopes kindled by the successful movement to oust the Duvaliers underly the tensions within the church.

Before François "Papa Doc" Duvalier came to power in 1957 the Haitian Catholic hierarchy was dominated by French bishops. Duvalier appealed in his election campaign to the black majority of the Haitian population, pitting them against the lighter-skinned mulatto elite. Once elected, Duvalier moved quickly to remove any potential challenge to his rule. He expelled the French bishops in 1961 and succeeded in negotiating an agreement with the Vatican in 1966 under which he could present his own candidates for the Haitian sees. While 10 of the country's 11 bishops were foreign in 1957, all but one were Haitian by the time of Francois Duvalier's death in 1971. Restrained by an obligatory oath of allegiance to the government, the bishops were largely silent throughout the worst excesses of Duvalier's 14-year rule. Seven of Haiti's 10 Catholic bishops today were appointed under the agreement which was terminated at the time of the visit of Pope John Paul II in 1983. Six of those seven were appointed under Jean-Claude "Baby Doc" Duvalier while one, Frantz Wolff Ligondé, the present Archbishop of Port-au-Prince, was appointed under Papa Doc. By marginalizing foreign priests, however, Duvalier's measures created the conditions for the emergence within the Haitian clergy of a self-confident and nationalist group with a strong personal commitment to social justice.

Catholicism is the official religion of Haiti, co-existing uneasily with the practice of voodoo which reaches into almost every area of life, especially among the poor. The outright hostility of the anti-superstition campaigns of the 1940s has been replaced by grudging acceptance of voodoo which was officially recognized as a religion by the 1987 constitution. François Duvalier clothed his repressive rule with the mystique of voodoo and some voodoo priests or "houngans" were undoubtedly informers. For this reason they became targets of spontaneous revenge attacks after the downfall of Jean-Claude.

Around 20 per cent of Haitians are Protestants. The Methodist Church is the longest-established Protestant Church in Haiti with a distinguished tradition in education and social welfare. Recent decades have also witnessed a proliferation of fundamentalist Protestant Churches, commonly referred to as "sects", many of which are US-based and funded. There are at least 50 such active in Haiti. While some provide health and other services in the countryside, their proselytizing activities are generally seen as promoting US interests.

By the late 1970s Church-linked groups were growing up throughout the country to help peasants organize to improve their conditions and promote small-scale development projects. Their education programmes helped to produce a new generation of peasant leaders and critics of the Duvalier dictatorship. Radio Soleil, the Catholic radio station, also became a principal channel for criticism of the government in the 1980s. The visit of Pope John Paul II to Haiti in 1983 provided support for those in the Church who were demanding change. His message that "things must change so that the poor can regain hope" gave the bishops a new confidence in denouncing the government's human rights violations and the conditions of extreme poverty under which the majority of the population lived.

Following Jean-Claude Duvalier's departure, Haiti was ruled by a provisional government, known as the Conseil National du Gouvernement (CNG) headed by General Henri Namphy, who had been a loyal supporter of Duvalier. The bishops made clear their support for social justice and democracy. New tensions appeared, however, as Church-linked groups, known collectively as the "Ti L'Egliz" (Little Church) and the priests and religious linked to them became prominent in the growing opposition to the provisional government. In the months of unrest preceding the elections in November 1987 attempts were made on the lives of several priests. Among the priests attacked was Père Jean-Bertrand Aristide who was at the centre of growing controversy with the country's bishops. An outspoken critic of the provisional government who commanded widespread popular support, he was removed from his shanty-town parish in the capital in August 1987 but reinstated after thousands of his parishioners crowded the capital's cathedral in his support.

In September 1987 the bishops' conference issued a warning to Church-linked groups and the radical clergy as they increasingly became the targets of violence at the hands of landlords whose armed gangs, including former Tontons Macoutes, could muster scores of men. In the same month as many as 500 peasants belonging to the *Tèt Ansamm* (Heads Together) movement, founded by the respected Catholic priest, Père Jean-Marie Vincent, were massacred at the instigation of local landowners at Jean Rabel in the remote north-west of the country. "The expression 'Popular Church' ", they said, "is not acceptable as it inevitably introduces the class struggle, acceptance of violence and a certain political radicalization into the Church". The term "Popular Church" was hardly used in Haiti and its use by the bishops sounds like an echo of the concerns of the Vatican in Central America.

Tension in the church was exacerbated by the demand of grass-roots activists that "déchoukage", literally uprooting, of Duvalierists from positions of privilege should apply also within the Church. This demand was aimed particularly at priests who were well known for their Duvalierist sympathies and included Archbishop Ligondé who, the activists suggested, should take a year off in Rome to reflect. The bishops' criticism of politically active priests might have met with a less hostile response if they had also acted against right-wing activists within the church.

The tension between the grass-roots church and the hierarchy has increased since the abortive elections of November 1987. The bishops denounced the elections of January 17, 1988 as fraudulent, saying that ". . . fundamental moral values had been violated, during the electoral process and on election day, values relating to truth, liberty, justice and respect for human rights". The inauguration ceremony of Leslie Manigat, the victorious candidate, was boycotted by the Catholic hierarchy. In February, however, Manigat called on the Church to assume its role as a "pacifier of spirits" and reminded it that its mission was "fundamentally spiritual."

From this date onwards the bishops seemed to be retreating from their commitment to social change. On April 30, 1988, without warning, they shut down Mission Alpha, their own literacy programme based on the "conscientization" methodology of Paulo Freire. The only fault of Mission Alpha, it seems, was that it was successful in raising awareness, provoking accusations within the church that it was infiltrated by "communists". In early 1989 they announced that the Church would resume its literacy programme following a purely technical methodology, that is, without conscientization. It is doubtful whether it will have any impact since the success of Mission Alpha as a literacy programme was the result of its use of Paulo Freire's methods.

In June 1988 General Namphy deposed Leslie Manigat who had placed him under arrest in an attempt to gain greater control over the army. This coup gave heart to all those who had benefited from the brutality and corruption of the Duvaliers and was the signal for renewed attacks on peasant organizations in the rural areas. On September 11, the church of St Jean Bosco in central Port-au-Prince was attacked by a gang of Tontons Macoutes as Père Aristide was saying mass. At least 12 people were hacked to death in this attack and many more were wounded. The church was burnt to the ground. Père Aristide himself managed to escape and went into hiding. The savagery of the attack and the outcry against it provoked the downfall of General Namphy and his replacement by another army commander, Colonel Prosper Avril. The Catholic bishops responded with one of their strongest declarations identifying for the first time "macoutism" as the true enemy of democracy. At the same time the Salesian superior publicly denied the widespread rumour that Aristide was about to be sent abroad. It seemed that the events of September 11 had brought about a rapprochement between the bishops and the more radical sectors of the Church for whom Père Aristide was the unofficial spokesman.

The hopes raised by this declaration were dashed. On December 8 the Superior General of the Salesians in Rome overrode the conciliatory advice of the Haitian superior, issuing a detailed denunciation of Aristide as a political agitator and expelling him from the order. This measure has been interpreted by supporters of the Ti L'Egliz as a colonial edict called for by the Nuncio and the Haitian bishops. This conflict is symbolic of the more general divisions within the Haitian Church. There are many more priests who support the general stand taken by Aristide and who have reacted with dismay to the actions of the hierarchy and the Nuncio. Aristide himself remains in Haiti and is working in the refuge for street children which he founded.

Early in 1989 the bishops accepted the resignation of Père Hugo Triest, a Belgian priest, who had been director of Radio Soleil since 1984. Despite repeated requests from Père Triest and the staff they made no provision for an orderly handover. New appointments and dismissals since March indicate a brusque move to the right. Three key staff members have been dismissed, including the respected programme manager, who had worked for Radio Soleil for 11 years. He has now been replaced by Hervé Bros, the son of Jean Claude Duvalier's Treasury minister. The new director, Fr Arnoux Chery, is reported to be a "protégé" of Archbishop Ligondé and Georges Martin, one of the new council members, is notorious for his attacks on liberation theology in the Petit Samedi Soir, the Duvalierist weekly.

On June 7 the bishops issued a pastoral letter calling for reconciliation between Haitians, urging employers to treat their workers fairly and politicians to work for the common good. They end by saying that "this is the moment to forget our old quarrels, to put our differences on one side and work together to carry out this common project". This letter has been criticized as an evasion of all the major problems of Haiti. The growing polarization of Haitian society and the frustration of the hopes raised by the successful movement against Jean-Claude Duvalier will undoubtedly continue to be felt within the Catholic church. The Ti L'Egliz, and the priests and religious who work with it, will not simply fade away in response to the bishops' call for reconciliation.

**Note**

[1] James Ferguson, *Papa Doc, Baby Doc: Haiti and the Duvaliers*, Basil Blackwell, Oxford, 1987.

George Gelber

# HONDURAS

Honduras, its 4.5 million people the second poorest per capita in the western hemisphere, faces internally- and externally-induced crises. The presence of the Nicaraguan *Contra* rebels and massive US assistance dependent on political quiescence combined with the presence of thousands of refugees from neighbouring conflicts and economic crises make political stability difficult. The summit of Central American Presidents held in Tela in August 1989 calling for the removal of the *Contras* by the year's end may relieve some of the pressure. Logistical assistance for the *Contras* has in part come from US fundamentalist agencies such as the Christian Broadcasting Network. According to a 1987 report, Protestants make up 12 per cent of the population (46 per cent fundamentalist, 40 per cent pentecostal, and 2 per cent historic) with a missionary tendency to impose US based theology indifferent to the country's poverty.

Compared to the Catholic Church in the rest of Central America, the Honduran hierarchy with the exception of several bishops has until recently taken a less political role. In late 1987 a Catholic bishop accused the armed forces of promoting Protestant sects to counter Catholic social activism, a charge dismissed by the high command with a reminder of the constitution's prohibition of clerical political involvement. Prior to his fall from grace, Jimmy Swaggart held a crusade attracting tens of thousands in Honduras in January of 1988. The former defence chief and US ally accused of masterminding death squad activity from 1982 to 1984 (when he was forced into exile), Gustavo Alvárez Martínez, returned to Honduras in April 1988 after converting to a Pentecostal Church. His assassination in early 1989 was claimed by the Chinchonero guerrilla movement, which claimed his recent conversion was an attempt to pass himself off as "a meek repentant Christian". The assassination has led to a resurgence of the shadowy Alianza de Acción Anticomunista.

Harassment of pastoral workers, including the deportation of foreign Protestant and Catholic personnel and death threats by members of the armed forces, has been directed particularly at those working with peasant co-operatives, refugees, and those accused of carrying "subversive materials". The Catholic Bishop's Conference created a legal aid office in early 1988 to assist clergy and lay workers harassed by the government. Church–state conflict has also occurred over the handling of drought relief efforts in southern Honduras.

Virgil Wiebe

# HUNGARY

Religion, whether Catholic (about 6,000 believers), or Protestant (about 2.5 million), formed a formidable impediment to communist plans of transforming the Magyar nation into a "progressive socialist society". But the united front of Christians, forged and led by strong-willed Cardinal Jozsef Mindszenty, was exposed to persistent persecution, and gradually succumbed to domination by the state. The following years were filled with suffering and sacrifices. But in the 1960s, the Kadar regime adopted, undoubtedly for pragmatic reasons, a more conciliatory approach.

Relations between the state and the Catholic Church were governed by the so-called "alliance", which provided for a progressive increase in the Church's activities conditioned on public support given to governmental policies. The course of political loyalty, practised by the episcopate presided over by the late Cardinal Laszlo Lekai and, since 1987, by his successor Cardinal Laszlo Paskai, was expected to facilitate the re-evangelization of Hungary and satisfaction of the most urgent needs of the Church, such as the critical shortage of bishops and priests. Indeed some of the expectations were realized. Among others, the regime gave permission for the employment of laymen in pastoral functions and for the opening of an order of sisters. In 1987, an agreement between the regime and the Vatican was concluded on the appointment of new bishops, and in 1988 an invitation, agreed with the government, was extended to the Pope to visit Hungary in 1991. In June 1989, the Hungarian government announced its intention to re-establish diplomatic relations with the Holy See. But the posture of the episcopate met with publicly expressed criticism. The greatest controversy arose around Fr Gyorgy Bulanyi and his followers from small communities known as *Bush* who refused to bear arms.

A very characteristic strife on the issue of submissiveness to the state erupted, in 1984, within the Lutheran Church whose leader, Bishop Zoltan Kaldy, promoted the concept of *diakonia*, in essence unconditional support for the regime. The view was opposed by Pastor Zoltan Doka, who was joined, in 1986, by a Lutheran Reform Group calling for political pluralism.

The Church leaders, obviously emboldened by changes taking place abroad in the 1980s, also took a more aggressive stance and demanded more freedom for confessional organizations. Under growin ' pressure, the government relented and made a number of concessions, including permission to conduct religious services in hospitals, to restitute religious orders, and, in May 1989, to resume activities of the Christian National Democratic Party. To top it all, the regime announced its intention to close the State Church Office, the main instrument of control over religious organizations. Somewhat later, the regime decided to do away with preventive censorship.

V. C. Chrypinski

# ICELAND

The Icelandic population is homogeneous Lutheran and the majority of the 7 per cent who are not members of the Church of Iceland, which has the status of a state Church, are members of free Lutheran congregations. The Catholic Church is the second largest religious organization.

Iceland differs from the other Nordic countries in not having a (small) Christian political party. Traditionally, both the Progressive Party, which has had its stronghold among the farmers, and the Conservative Independence Party have been in favour of religion and the Church. Support from the Social Democrats has been more passive but neither this party nor the party to the left of it, the People's Alliance, have for a long time questioned the State Church system.

The Synod and the bishop have protested against permissive abortion legislation. The protests had no results but this religious interference into what is seen as a political issue was criticized by radical groups. On other issues, such as peace and disarmament, the statements of the Church leadership have been more in line with the positions of the political left; but the Independence Party complained that the Church was too engaged in political actions.

Göran Gustafsson

# INDIA

The interaction of religion and politics is a persistent feature of life for the some 800 million inhabitants of India, 83 per cent of whom are Hindu, 11 per cent Muslim, and 2.6 per cent Christian; slightly over 1 per cent is Sikh, and there are also small communities of Jains, Parsis, and Buddhists.

In traditional India there was no clear distinction between the spheres of religion and politics. One indication of this is the fact that the words "India" and "Hindu" are etymologically linked. Both terms were coined by outsiders to refer to the land and the people along the Indus river. Therefore, although today one can speak of "Hindus" as one among several religious communities in India, Hindu culture traditionally embraced all people and aspects of life in the Indian subcontinent. In classical Hindu social theory, each role in society, including kingship, had its own *dharma* (moral responsibility), and the prime duty of the king, as enunciated by the fourth century BCE Hindu political theorist Kautilya in the *Arthashastra*, was to maintain power and uphold the *dharma* of the social whole. The religious importance of kingship is indicated by the fact that gods are portrayed as playing regal roles in the great Hindu epics, the *Ramayana* and *Mahabharata*, which became written down in their present literary forms around the first century BCE.

During most of India's history, however, there has not been a single centralized monarchy. Instead there have been hundreds of small princedoms and a pattern of local governance involving representative committees, or *panchayats* ("councils of five"). The vacuum of leadership at the centre made it possible for Muslim rulers from Central Asia and Persia to establish great imperial powers, including the Mughal dynasties that ruled during the sixteenth to nineteenth centuries. The Mughals and their British successors formed alliances with local kings and left traditional Hinduism largely untouched.

The leaders of Hinduism's devotional reform movement — the *sants* and *gurus* who led the *bhakti* movements of the fifteenth to seventeenth centuries — tended to avoid politics, but since they belittled the spiritual value of any form of ritual or social status, they are sometimes touted today as prophets of social as well as spiritual reform. Hindu movements originating in the nineteenth century, such as the Brahmo Samaj and the Arya Samaj, were also reform-minded. They promoted mass education, rights for women, and the improvement of conditions for Untouchables.

In the twentieth century religion and politics have continued to interact. Although officially secular, India's independence movement preached nationalist loyalties in terms that carried echoes of the Hindu notion of dharmic obligation, and its espousal of devotion to mother India incorporated some of the characteristics of worship of a Hindu goddess. Mohandas Gandhi brought Hindu ethical values to the nationalist movement when he applied the principles of *satyagraha* ("the force of truth") and *ahimsa* ("nonviolence") to political conflict.

Mohammad Ali Jinnah and his Muslim League, suspicious of what they felt was the Hinduization of the nationalist movement, broke with Gandhi and demanded that the British create a separate nation for Muslims. When the British withdrew from India in 1947 they carved Pakistan out of portions of Bengal in the east and sections of Punjab, Sindh, and other areas in the west. Jinnah was named Pakistan's first Governor-General. Not all Muslims in the remainder of India moved to the areas designated as Pakistan, but eight million people moved from one side of the borders to the other, and as many as a million lost their lives in the communal rioting that occurred in the transition. Gandhi strongly protested the partition of the country and the communal hatred it unleashed. Militant Hindus felt that he had capitulated to the Muslims, and it was a member of a radical Hindu organization, the Rashtriya Swayamsevak Sangh (RSS), who assassinated Gandhi in 1948.

After independence many of these tensions remained. Although the government was officially secular, the doctrine of the separation of religion and politics was often interpreted as meaning that the state should treat all religions equally. As a result, the government protected and maintained some religious institutions, allowed religious colleges to be a part of secular universities, and permitted aspects of traditional Islamic law that pertain to marriage, divorce and inheritance to be applicable to members of Muslim communities. Christians and other minority religious communities were given legal sanctions similar to those given the Muslims. Despite its attempt to be impartial, there were accusations that the government leaned toward the sentiments of the Hindu majority. In 1987–89 the government television network, Doordarshan, sponsored a serialized presentation of the *Ramayana*, followed in 1988–89 by the *Mahabharata*, claiming them to be traditional stories and not religious myths. They have been the most watched programmes in India's history, and many devout Hindus performed rituals of worship before their television sets when they saw the gods flicker across the screen. Some political parties, such as the Jan Sangh, have openly pandered to the interests of conservative Hindus, but only recently have political organizations directly catering to Hindus been widely supported.

## Hindu revivalism

Recent years have seen a remarkable rise in Hindu activism. The RSS is back, even bigger than before, the new Hindu political movements, such as the Vishwa Hindu Parishad (the "All Hindu Conference") or VHP, are on the rise. Many of these were spurred on by reports of mass conversions of lower caste Hindus to Islam at Meenakshipuram in south India in 1981. The secular government became a target for the conservative Hindu's wrath, since the state's policy of religious neutrality was read as favouring Muslims, Sikhs, Christians and other religious minorities.

Conservative Hindus were particularly incensed over the government's protection of mosques that had been built over Hindu sacred sites during the Mughal period. In 1984 the VHP called for a reassertion of Hindu control over a dozen such sites, including especially the Babri Mosque built by the emperor Babar on the location of the major temple in Ayodhya, the home and capital of the God-king, Ram. An image of Ram had magically manifested itself in the mosque, and some Hindus insisted on worshipping there. Riots broke out between Muslims and Hindus as to which group should be allowed to worship at the site, and the government barred them both. In 1986, after the VHP's efforts to liberate Ram from what they called his "Muslim jail", a judge again opened the site. Violent encounters between Muslims and Hindus soon ensued, with the VHP calling for the mosque to be destroyed and a new temple to be built in its place. A report of the Archeological Survey of India published in January 1989 concluding that there is very little likelihood that Ram was born on the site has done little to deter the VHP's efforts.

The leadership of the VHP was taken over in 1985 by a new all-India organization, the Dharma Sansad. Based in Karnataka in south India, it consists of 900 representatives of a variety of Hindu sects and orders of *sadhus* who have vowed to fight for Hindu purification and the propagation of Hindu nationalism. By 1986 the VHP had 3,500 branches throughout India and over a million dedicated workers. It targeted politicians whom it felt were unfaithful to the Hindu cause, and lobbied for pro-Hindu legislation. Another movement, the Shiv Sena, has been active in Maharashtra, Gujarat and Punjab in attempting to purify the government of what it regards as pro-Muslim and pro-Sikh policies. The Shiv Sena now controls major temples in Punjab's central cities.

A significant political incident occurred in Rajasthan following the *sati* (suicide of a widow on her husband's funeral pyre) of 18-year old Roop Kanwar on September 4, 1987. The Indian government, which has followed the British practice of outlawing *sati*, attempted to suppress the *cunari* rite that would have consecrated her suicide two weeks after the event, and a new organization, the Sati Dharma Raksak Samiti ("Committee for Defending the Righteousness of Sati") was created in Jaipur to defend the custom of *sati* and the *cunari* rite. Some 70,000 sympathizers marched in protest against the government, and on December 15, 1987 the Indian parliament passed a bill imposing death or life imprisonment for anyone abetting an act of *sati*, and up to seven years' imprisonment for anyone "glorifying" the act. Nontheless the debate continued, and the Sankaracarya of Puri, a conservative Hindu leader, courted arrest by speaking out on April 2, 1988 in defence of the practice. He also berated the government for allowing women to study the scriptures and for requiring Hindu temples to admit Untouchables into their precincts.

## Muslim communalism

What is sometimes called Muslim "communalism" is often a reaction to prejudicial acts against the Muslim minority. In July 1986, for example, rioting between Muslims and Hindus in Ahmedabad, which resulted in at least 50 deaths and further violence throughout the state of Gujarat, began when a small crowd of Muslims responded to Hindu taunts by stoning a Hindu religious procession. A communal clash in Meerut on May 18–26, 1987, which led to over 100 deaths, was part of an ongoing reaction to the attempts of the Hindu VHP to take over the Babri Mosque in Ayodhya. Muslims throughout India formed an All-India Babri Masjid Conference in December 1986, to protect the sanctity of the mosque at Ayodhya and 150 other mosques throughout India that are listed by the Indian government as historic monuments. In January 1987 the Conference's leader, Syed Shahabuddin, called for a boycott of India's Republic Day celebrations. Disagreements among the committee's leadership, however, led to the establishment of a splinter movement in December 1988.

Another political issue that has exercised Muslims in recent years is the Indian Supreme Court's 1986 decision in the Shah Bano case. At issue was the fairness of the Muslim laws regarding compensation for a divorced wife. A Muslim woman in Indore, Shah Bano, argued that she should receive compensation equal to what a Hindu woman would receive under such circumstances, not the meagre settlement that is allowed under Muslim law. The Court agreed, and the Chief Justice added fuel to the fire by stating that the time had come for a unified legal code for all religious communities in India. The outcry from Muslims in response was considerable, and in Bombay a procession of 100,000 people denounced the Court's verdict. At first Rajiv Gandhi's government defended the Court, but then with mounting Muslim resistance it reversed itself, proposing a new piece of legislation known as the Muslim Women Bill, which would nullify the effect of the Supreme Court's decision by exempting Muslims from the provisions of Section 125 of the Criminal Procedure Code, which prescribed the way in which husbands were to support their divorced wives. The new bill attempted to be egalitarian, however, by allowing Muslim women to appeal to the Muslim *waqf*, the charitable fund, for compensation equal to what Hindu women in such circumstances would receive. The bill was attacked by Hindus, secularists, and feminists, but on May 6, 1986 it became law.

Muslims in the state of Kashmir have also been involved in politics for a religious cause, but the situation in Kashmir is unique. It is the only state in India in which Muslims are in the majority, so the issue is not the protection of a minority's rights, but the degree to which the state can assert its Islamic identity without becoming estranged from the rest of the Indian nation. One point of tension in recent years has been the continuing power exerted in Kashmir by a small group of Brahmins, and in February 1986 there were demonstrations and outbreaks of violence against them. There was also rising opposition in 1987, led by a new group, the Muslim United Front, and other Muslim fundamentalists, against the government of Farooq Abdullah. They felt it was not sufficiently supportive of the interests of orthodox Islam. In 1988 some elements of the opposition took a more strident turn, becoming a paramilitary operation: the Kashmir Liberation Front. Allegedly supported by Pakistan, the Front called for secession from India. It organized demonstrations and responded to police attempts to suppress it by throwing bombs and shooting automatic weapons, incurring a considerable amount of bloodshed on both sides. In May 1989, the separatists began calling themselves *mujahadin* ("holy warriors"), and characterized their conflict with the government as a holy war.

One other issue that has caught the attention of Indian Muslims in recent years is the publication of *The Satanic Verses* by Salman Rushdie. Even though it was banned in India, violent demonstrations against the book in March 1989 left 20 dead. Most Muslims favoured a ban on the book, but disagreed over the Ayatollah Khomeini's decree calling for Rushdie's death.

## Sikh separatism

The rise of Sikh separatism in the 1980s was in part a response to what many Sikhs saw as the increasing Hinduization of Indian politics. It was also an assertion of the military power and political independence that Sikhs have enjoyed throughout much of their 500-year history. Whereas most Sikhs supported the assertions of Sikh pride and identity, few endorsed the violent extremes of the movement which were perpetrated by a small, intensely-committed group of young Sikh men.

The early years of Sikhism were quite peaceful, and the teachings of the first Sikh spiritual master, the sixteenth century *bhakti* saint and poet, Guru Nanak, were introspective and devotional. The movement that survived him became increasingly militant, however, partly in response to the political dominance of the Moghuls and partly as a result of the infusion of tribal Jats into the Sikh community at the end of the sixteenth century. They contributed their own martial customs to the growth of the tradition. The tenth and final teacher in the historic lineage of Sikh masters, Guru Gobind Singh, presided over an army of considerable size, and martyrdom was the supreme honour bestowed on those who gave their lives to the cause. The symbols he is said to have imposed upon his followers in 1699, and which are still observed by the faithful, included such emblems of militancy as a sword and a bracelet-like shield worn at the wrist. The most frequently displayed symbol of Sikhism today is a double-edged blade, surrounded by a circle that surmounts a pair of scabbards.

The eighteenth century was an era of small kingdoms in the Punjab; each had its own army. Early in the nineteenth century the land and the armies were consolidated by Maharaja Ranjit Singh, whose expansive kingdom lasted until the middle of the century. The late nineteenth century was a period of decline for Sikh cultural and political influence until 1873, when a reform movement, the Singh Sabha, began reviving the tradition and imposing standards of faith and practice. The Sabha was especially exercised about what it regarded as the display of Hinduism in the Golden Temple and other Sikh shrines and *gurdwaras* (religious meeting places). In 1920 groups of Sikhs began agitating for reforms in the management of *gurdwaras*, calling for an ouster of Udasis (a semi-Hindu sect that revered Guru Nanak to the exclusion of the other nine founding gurus of Sikhism) and others who had been in control of the shrines.

In 1925 the British government capitulated to these demands and established a political body, the Shiromani Gurdwara Parbandhak Committee ("Central Gurdwara Management Committee"), consisting of elected representatives of Sikh *gurdwaras* (which can here be translated as "congregations"), to control and maintain all Sikh holy-places. The congregations, in turn, were to be managed by locally elected bodies. The SGPC became an arena for Sikh politics. One group of partisans in the Gurdwara reform movement, the *Akali Dal* ("The Group of Immortals") later became a political party, and after independence they successfully contested elections for legislative seats, alternating with the Congress Party in forming Punjab's ruling governments.

The partition of India and the creation of Pakistan raised in the minds of many Sikhs the expectation that they should also have political autonomy. At first, however, they did not even have control of their own state in India, since the Sikhs constituted less than half of Punjab's electoral population. In the 1960s a new political movement called for redrawing the state boundaries of the Punjab so that only Punjabi-speakers would be included. Since India's States Reorganization Act in 1953 specified that state boundaries should follow linguistic boundaries, this was a reasonable suggestion; and since the majority of people willing to identify themselves as primarily Punjabi speakers were Sikh, this would ensure a Sikh-majority state. The charismatic leader at that time was Sant Fateh Singh, who went on a well-publicized fast and threatened to immolate himself on the roof of the Golden Temple's *Akal Takht* unless the government made concessions that would lead to the establishment of a Sikh-majority state. In 1966, the Indian government, captained by Prime Minister Indira Gandhi, conceded, and the old Punjab state was carved into three to produce Haryana and Himachal Pradesh, states with Hindu majorities, and a new Punjab, where the majority was Sikh.

The violent movement that developed in the 1980s had some ties with these earlier movements for Sikh autonomy and political power, but it was in many ways more fanatical, more religious. The origins of the movement may be traced to a clash in 1978 between the *Nirankari* movement, a semi-Sikh sect, and a group of Sikh religious extremists led by Jernail Singh Bhindranwale, the young leader of the *Damdani Taksal*, a religious school and retreat centre once headed by the great Sikh martyr, Baba Deep Singh. Bhindranwale, who was being promoted as a Sikh leader by the Prime Minister's son, Sanjay Gandhi, in order to undercut the Sikhs' support for the *Akali Dal*, found the *Nirankaris'* worship of a living guru to be presumptuous and offensive. In the escalating violence lives were lost on both sides, and on April 24, 1980 the *Nirankari* guru was assassinated. A new organization, the *Dal Khalsa*, associated with Bhindranwale and supported by Sanjay Gandhi and other Congress party leaders (such as Zail Singh), contended with the *Akali Dal* for control of the SGPC. On September 9, 1981, Lala Jagat Narain, the publisher of a chain of Hindu newspapers in Punjab was shot dead, and Bhindranwale was implicated. In response to his arrest and the destruction of his personal papers, Bhindranwale turned against the government. Bands of his young supporters began indiscriminately killing Hindus, and on September 29 a group of Sikhs hijacked an Indian Airlines plane in Pakistan. The violence had begun.

In his sermons Bhindranwale often spoke of the Sikhs' separate identity, using as his term for religious community the word *gaum*, which carries the overtones of nationhood. He did not unambiguously support the notion of a separate Sikh nation, Khalistan, which had been advocated by Jagjit Singh Chauhan among Sikhs living in England and Canada, but Bhindranwale did emphasize the Sikh concept of *miri-piri*, the notion that spiritual and temporal power are linked. He projected the image of a cosmic war between good and evil that was being waged in the present day, and demanded that Sikh political and military support be marshalled on the side of righteousness.

In 1982 the *Akali Dal* replaced the Congress Party as Bhindranwale's protector. The *Akalis*, led by a religious teacher, Sant Harchand Singh Longowal, felt that they needed to regain the support of the religious conservatives in the state, and since Bhindranwale had begun to mistrust the Congress Party, they thought he could be wooed to their side. The *Akalis* used the militancy of Bhindranwale and his followers as leverage in their own demands to the government, although they were unsuccessful in their negotiations.

The violent attacks of Bhindranwale's supporters against Hindus and police were met with repression from the government, and this encouraged more acts of violence. Thus the violence spiralled upward, and by 1983 scores of innocent people and an equal number of police and Sikh activists — now called "terrorists" by the press — were killed monthly. On October 6, 1983 Mrs Gandhi suspended the Punjab government and ran it directly from Delhi. Bhindranwale had set up something of an alternative government of his own, ruling from the protected quarters of the Sikhs' most sacred shrine, the Golden Temple, in Amritsar. The *Akali* leader, Langowal, was also staying in the Golden Temple, but in separate quarters, since he and Bhindranwale had had a disagreement which led to a series of killings in both camps.

The situation came to a head on June 5, 1984, when Mrs Gandhi sent troops into the Golden Temple in what was code-named "Operation Bluestar". In a messy military operation that took two days to complete, as many as 2,000 or more people were killed, including a number of innocent worshippers. Bhindranwale was killed, and Langowal was taken into custody. In retaliation, two of her Sikh bodyguards assassinated Mrs Gandhi on October 31, 1984, and on the following day over 2,000 Sikhs were massacred in Delhi and elsewhere by angry Hindu mobs. Rajiv Gandhi, who became Prime Minister after his mother's death, entered into an agreement with Langowal in July 1985 to bring the violence to an end, but Langowal himself was assassinated, presumably by members of Bhindranwale's camp, later that year.

The Rajiv–Langowal accord has never been completely implemented, nor has the violence in the Punjab abated. The followers of Bhindranwale have become more strident, increasingly aiming at the Longowal faction of *Akalis*, led by Punjab's Chief Minister, Surjit Singh Barnala, and other moderate Sikhs. On February 15, 1986, the Golden Temple was again occupied by militants, but this time they were extracted by the Indian security forces in what was called "Operation Black Thunder" without the tragic results of "Operation Bluestar". Sporadic acts of violence continued, however: many of the 350 killings in 1986 were random acts of violence. 1,400 suspected terrorists were arrested. On August 10, 1986, General A. S. Vaidya, who had commanded "Operation Bluestar", was gunned down in a revenge attack.

Although the leader of the *Akali Dal* faction most supportive of the militants, Parkash Singh Badal, and the leader of the SGPC, Gurcharan Singh Tohra, were in jail, they still commanded a great deal of power in Sikh politics, and in February 1987 they attempted to join forces with the militants by appointing several religious leaders who were sympathetic to the extremists' cause. These religious leaders were members of the council of five who have traditionally made decisions regarding religious matters in Sikhism. They include the *jathedar* ("leader") of the *Akal Takht*, the organizational office of Sikhism, and the *granthi* ("worship leader"), of the Golden Temple. These are often misleadingly referred to in the press as the "five priests" of Sikhism; this is a misnomer, because Sikhism is largely a lay community with no authoritative clergy.

The newly appointed council of five declared its support of Khalistan, and proclaimed Chief Minister Barnala to be excommunicated. On August 8, the least radical of the five religious leaders, Jathedar Darshan Singh Ragi, took a "leave of absence" from his position, and Jasbir Singh Rode, nephew of the martyred Bhindranwale, became the *jathedar* of the *Akal Takht*. Radical organizations such as the Khalistan Commando Force, the Khalistan Liberation Force and extremist factions of the All-India Sikh Students Federation had direct control of the official Sikh leadership. Violent assaults in the villages increased, and in the month of January 1988 alone, 129 people were killed by extremists.

The Golden Temple again became a hideout for militants seeking protection from the police. The *granthis* of the temple were charged with harbouring criminals and were jailed, but despite that action — or because of it — there were more violent incidents in the villages than before. By April 1988 more than 10 persons were being killed daily in terrorist encounters, a number three times that of the previous year. The government freed some of the worship leaders in an effort to diffuse the violence, and on May 18 in the second "Operation Black Thunder" the Indian security force again entered the Golden Temple and routed the militants. On May 28, 1988, the Indian parliament enacted a law prohibiting religious shrines from being used for political and military purposes. While it applied to all religious institutions throughout the country, it had immediate applicability to the Sikh situation.

On May 30, 1988, the SGPC broke with the militants and dismissed the Golden Temple *granthis*, claiming that they had neglected their duties and allowed "bad elements" to occupy the temple precincts. Paradoxically, the government regarded this dismissal of the *granthis* as a setback, since it found it convenient to deal with the militants through the *granthis*, and wished to discredit the SGPC by identifying it with the radicals. The militants responded to the dismissal of the worship leaders with even greater violence: bombs exploded in several cities early in July, killing 73. Darshan Singh Ragi again became the *jathedar*, and he and other moderate worship leaders allowed for conciliation between factions of the *Akali Dal*; later in 1988 Chief Minister Barnala was allowed to undergo acts of penance, including cleaning the shoes of Sikh worshippers, in order to reverse his excommunication from the faith.

The situation in 1989 was considerably brighter than in the previous year. The numbers of violent incidents in the Punjab decreased — owing in part to the increasing efficiency of police surveillance. An indication of the changing mood was the relative absence of demonstrations in response to the hanging of Satwant Singh and Kehar Singh, convicted assassins of Indira Gandhi, on January 6, 1989. In April 1989, even though Badal, the leader of one faction of the *Akali Dal*, and Tohra, head of the SGPC, were still in jail, representatives of their parties met with the moderate *Akali* leader, Barnala, and with militants who had formed their own faction of the Akali Dal, to initiate discussions about the possibility of forming a united party.

## Religious protests of Untouchables

The fact that Beant Singh, one of the Sikhs who assassinated Indira Gandhi, was an Untouchable is an indication of the attempts of some members of India's lowest castes to be accepted by the majority communities. In this century there have been a number of movements that have attempted to assert the rights and dignity of Untouchables, and since the notion of caste is essentially a religious one (because the hierarchy of caste groups is based on the ritual polarity between purity and pollution) many of these movements are religious as well. At the turn of the century the Arya Samaj attempted to bring Untouchables back into the Hindu fold through the practice of *shuddhi*, "purification". Gandhi also attempted to dignify the role of Untouchables by calling them *Harijan*, "people of God".

Thousands of Untouchables left the Hindu fold by converting to Christianity in mass movements that swept through North India from 1880 to 1920. Others turned to Islam. Dr Bheem Rao Ambedkar, leader of Untouchables and father of India's constitution, turned to Buddhism in 1956 and brought many of his followers with him. Beginning in the 1920s a number of new movements, such as *Adi Hindu* in Uttar Pradesh and *Adi Dharm* in Punjab, asserted themselves as religions of Untouchables, and became a significant force in local elections. Since independence several of these movements have revived, and in 1988 the *Bahujan Samaj* ("Party of the Minority") organized 300,000 Untouchable labourers in Uttar Pradesh for the purpose of making political demands and religious reforms. The leader, Kanshi Ram, a member of the Ambedkar Buddhist movement, has called for the end of India's acceptance of what he calls "Brahminism".

## Christian conversions

Since many Christians in North India are from lower castes, the political aspirations of Christians are often in league with those of other Untouchables. In south India, where there has been a thriving Indian Christian community since the second century of the Christian era, the cause of Christians is often joined with Muslims' in asserting the rights of religious minorities in Hindu India. In 1986, Christians in Goa led the fight to make the indigenous language, Konkani, the official language of the region. A persistent issue among Christians is the right to proselytize, an issue that is politically sensitive in the far north-east province of Arunachal Pradesh. A "Freedom of Religion Act" in 1978 outlawed conversions of tribals to Christianity (or any other religion) but by 1988 a third of the region had become Christian, largely through the efforts of missions operating across the province's border in the neighbouring state of Assam.

## Political power of new religious movements

The growing power of new religious movements in India may create new political tensions in the future, especially when they are seen as threatening old orthodoxies. One new movement, the *Nirankaris*, has played a significant role in exacerbating Sikh xenophobia in Punjab. Other movements that have grown rapidly in the 1980s and that together have attracted millions of adherents, such as the *Swaminarayan* movement in Gujarat, the *Radhasoami* movement in Uttar Pradesh and Punjab, *Satya Sai Baba* in South India, and the *Brahmakumaris* in Rajasthan, have also produced tremors of fear among the religious orthodoxies of their regions. Since throughout history significant religious changes have had a political impact in India, many observers of India's religious and social milieu expect that these new movements will have a formative effect as well.

Mark Juergensmeyer

# INDONESIA

Indonesia has the largest Muslim population of any country in the world composing 87 per cent of its 165 million people. During the colonial period, Islam was frequently employed as a unifying symbol against Dutch rule and the first mass nationalist party, Sarekat Islam, was Muslim-based. In this period most Christians (now approximately 9 per cent of the population) were more sympathetic to the colonial authorities, although a minority were pro-nationalist.

After the Dutch left in 1949 there was a decade of local insurgency based upon ethnic and religious factors. In West Java, South Sulawesi and other parts of the country a radical Muslim movement, *Darul Islam*, fought in a long conflict intended to establish a Muslim state. Meanwhile, in places like Ambon and Sulawesi Christian insurgents unsuccessfully fought the Indonesian armed forces in order to achieve autonomy or independence from the authorities in Java. By the 1960s these activities had generally been eradicated. However, in 1965–66, following an abortive coup attempt in which the Communist Party was implicated, Muslim organizations co-operated with the military in a campaign to destroy the communist movement, resulting in the deaths of several hundred thousand Indonesians.

The major religio-political tensions of the past decade have centred on differences between the Suharto government, which came into power in the late 1960s, and elements of the Muslim community. At the electoral level the most active opposition to the government had come from the Islamic PPP (Partai Persatuan Pembangunan), but in the 1980s its most important member, the NU (Nahdatul Ulama) withdrew from politics to concentrate upon religion and education. This, plus strong efforts by the Suharto government to eliminate

Islam from politics led to a decline in public support for the PPP to only 16 per cent in the 1987 national parliamentary elections.

Muslim opposition to government policies has revolved around a variety of issues from marriage laws to perceived efforts by the Suharto regime to weaken religious instruction in the schools. Many Muslims have characterized the government in Jakarta as too secular or dominated by non-Muslim ideals. However, the issue that dominated the 1980s was the government effort to require all social and political organizations to adopt the Pancasila (Five Principles). The crux of the dispute was the fifth principle, belief in God. This principle was not defined in Islamic terms and included Buddhist, Christian and other religions, which many Muslims viewed as at best agnostic. Ultimately this was accepted by all the mainline Muslim and Christian organizations, but was a major factor in increased religious tensions during the decade.

Since Suharto came into power, violent religiously-based activities have been minimal but not absent. There have been incidents of bombings, arson, a plane hijacking and alleged efforts to overthrow the regime by Muslim radicals seeking to establish an Islamic state and opposed to what they see as a secular order. Charges have also been made that foreign powers, supposedly Libya and Iran, have been involved in some of these activities. While this violence has generally not received widespread support from the Muslim community, there have been cases where forceful crackdowns on alleged "extremists" have been criticized by some Muslim and foreign spokesmen. These include cases such as deaths and arrests during the Tanjung Priok riots in 1984, related to government policies perceived as efforts to control Muslim organizations, and the bloody attack in 1989 by the military against a village in Southern Sumatra that was initially described as involving Muslim extremists and then characterized as largely a local land dispute. The government has been very active in efforts to contain possible anti-government religious opponents and long prison sentences have been given to Muslims accused of subversive actions including speeches, anti-government cassettes and tracts, and public demonstrations.

Fred R. von der Mehden

# IRAN

## Background

The Islamic Republic of Iran has one of the fastest growing populations in Asia. Some estimates suggest this could be as high as 3.6 per cent a year. The last Census, held in 1987, put Iran's population at a little over 47,000,000, but more recent figures suggest that it exceeds 53,000,000.

The country's economy and source of wealth owed much to its substantial oil reserves which were most intensively exploited in the late 1960s and '70s. The years since the Iranian revolution have witnessed a rapid decline in the country's economic performance. The strains of a vicious war between Iraq and Iran and political instability resulting from ongoing power struggles have compounded the problems of economic regeneration. Of an estimated work-force of 13 million in 1989 (which does not include women and children under 15), more than four million are officially designated as unemployed. Although oil revenues are up, inflation — officially 22 per cent but thought to be nearer 50 per cent — is at an all time high.

The dominant language spoken by just over half the population of Iran is Farsi, or Persian as it is known outside Iran. Related to the body of Indo-European languages, Farsi is also the language of government and business. The Turkic languages, Kurdish and Arabic are also important.

Persians constitute the largest ethnic group (about 65 per cent), followed by Kurds, Azerbaijanis, Lurs, Baktiaris, Qashqais, Baluchis and Arabs.

Shia Islam is the official religion. The majority of Iranians, approximately 90 per cent, are adherents of the Ithna Ashari (Twelver) brand of Shiism which subscribes to the Ja'fari school of jurisprudence. Several thousand Ismaili Shias who owe allegiance to the Aga Khan, are concentrated in the northern mountainous region bordering the Caspian Sea. There is also a small Sunni minority whose members are concentrated mainly among Kurds, Baluchi, Turkomans and Arabs.

Other religious minorities include Jews, Zoroastrians and Christians, all of whom are officially recognized and entitled to practise and profess their religion, but none of whom may hold political office. There is some concern that the toleration traditionally accorded to these established minority religions may now be under threat. There are reports of the maltreatment of Jewish Iranians, and in November 1986 the Jewish member in the Majlis, Mr Manusheh Niqruz, was arrested on charges of alleged corruption and immorality.

A notable omission in the category of legally-recognized religions are the Bahais whose beliefs are officially proscribed and who have been the subject of intense persecution under both the Pahlavis and the present regime. The Bahais represent a schismatic break from Shiism in the nineteenth century when one Bahaullah declared himself to be the long-awaited messiah. Although Bahais claim to be Muslims, their beliefs which question the finality of the Prophet Muhammad and regard the Koran as an allegorical rather than a revealed text, are deemed to be profoundly heretical by Shias and Sunnis alike. Anti-Bahai campaigns in the last century, and as recently as the 1950s, have provided the basis for some unusual alliances between clergy and State in Iran.

The early years of the Islamic Republic witnessed a concerted effort to repress the Bahais on both religious and political grounds. (Many are alleged to have links with Israel.) Official support for extreme measures, which included the final and complete eradication of the 300,000 strong community, were known to have the backing of the foreign minister, Aliakber Veliayati. In December 1981 and January 1982, 18 Bahais were executed for refusing either to opt for one of the established minority religions, or to convert to Islam. Since 1979, a total of 100 Bahais are known to have been executed although the figure is likely to be higher. Pressure from international human rights groups in the early 1980s persuaded the Iranians to shelve temporarily some extreme measures which included denying food ration coupons to Bahais who refused conversion. Fresh evidence emerged in 1987 which suggested that Bahais continue to be harassed and persecuted.

## The roots of the Islamic revolution

The antecedents of the Iranian Revolution of 1979 lie partly in a long tradition of political activism among the Iranian clergy, and partly in the social and economic polarization initiated by the reforms of Reza Khan Pahlavi. The Tobacco Revolt of 1892 which led thousands of Iranians to refrain from smoking as a result of a religious ruling issued by Iran's leading clerics, and the Constitutional Revolution of 1905–1909 which ensured that no laws repugnant to Islam were passed by an elected Assembly, are just two of the more notable instances of the political influence wielded by the Iranian clergy.

The secularization of Iranian politics and society initiated by Reza Khan and continued by his son, Muhammad Reza, also contributed substantially to the tensions which were finally to explode in the Revolution of 1979. The Pahlavis who were deeply impressed by Ataturk's Turkish experiment sought, by reform, to emulate the Turkish model. Reza Khan's reform of Iranian law led to the substitution of the *Shari'a* (Islamic law) by a secular legal code based on the French *Code Civil*. His educational reforms which were designed to create a westernized bureaucracy, also reduced the scope of Islamic influence by undermining institutions of traditional Muslim education like *maktabs* (mosque schools) and *madrassas* (seminaries). The modernization of Iranian society was reflected in changes in the position of women who were legally required to abandon the veil, and in a series of land reforms which sought to modify proprietary relations between landlords and peasants.

## The Islamic opposition

The accession of Reza Shah in 1953 witnessed a greater commitment to the programme of westernization and secularization. However, the Shah's "White Revolution" was sustained not by popular consent, but by an increasingly repressive state apparatus whose worst features were embodied in the dreaded and ruthless secret police (SAVAK). The opposition to the Shah's economic and social reforms came especially from the class of *bazaar* merchants, urban poor, and peasants, who had benefited little from the "White Revolution". Their opposition was most effectively articulated by the clergy, many of whom were already deeply disturbed by the relegation of Islamic law; the government's assault on centres of religious training; its programme for the enfranchisement of women and the end of official protection for religious endowments (*waqfs*).

One of the earliest organizations to reflect what was later to become an "Islamic Opposition" was the fundamentalist *Fedayeen-i-Islam* (Devotees of Islam). Established shortly after the end of World War II, the Fedayeen were organized along the lines of the semi-conspiratorial Egyptian *Ikhwar al-Muslimin* (Muslim Brotherhood). The *Fedayeen* were led by the young and barely-educated Mulla Nawab Safavi, and enjoyed the support of prominent *ulama* (religious leaders), including Ayatollah Kashani. The *Fedayeen's* involvement in the assassination of prominent Iranians in the 1950s and '60s led to the purge and subsequent execution of many of its leading members. The aims and methods of the organization, however, continued to inspire the policies of some members of the present regime like Sadegh Khalkhali, commonly known as "hanging judge", who once claimed to be a long-time member of the *Fedayeen*.

Opposition to the Shah and his reforms in the early 1950s came also from the *Mujahadin-i-Islam* (Defenders of Islam) led by Ayatollah Abul Qasim Kashani who enjoyed strong support in the Iranian Majlis and among sections of the clergy, the lower middle classes, peasants and *bazaar* merchants. Kashani's group did not, however, survive the purges that followed the coup against Prime Minister Mossadegh and his coalition of nationalist forces.

In addition to these better known organizations, there were also others which operated secretly, namely the *Nihzat-i Muqavamat-i Milli* (National Resistance Movement) led by Ayatollah Taleghani, and the *Ruhaniyat-i Mobarez* (Combatant Clergy) headed by Ayatollah Beheshti. Both were committed to the institution of an Islamic order and were fiercely anti-monarchist. The "Islamic Opposition" also manifested itself in informal groups associated with leading intellectuals, most notably the sociologist, Ali Shariati, who attracted large numbers of the Iranian intelligentsia, and religious scholars like Ayatollahs Motahhari and Khomeini.

By the summer of 1963, popular discontent enabled the radical *ulama* led by Ayatollah Khomeini to seize the initiative. This was made possible partly as a result of the political vacuum that followed the purge of liberal and nationalist groups which had coalesced around Prime Minister Mossadegh in the 1950s, and partly as a result of the death of the senior cleric, Ayatollah Muhammad Husain Burujirdi, who had led the conservative wing of the *ulama*. Khomeini's active involvement in the protest movement against the Shah's reforms was followed shortly by his imprisonment and exile in November 1964.

From his exile in Iraq and later (in 1978) in France, Khomeini laid the network of an Islamic movement that was to prove as effective outside as inside Iran. In the meanwhile, the Shah's policy of repression at home forced the religious opposition into quietism. The exile of Ayatollah Khomeini, the incarceration of large numbers of the radical clergy and the penetration of the clergy by the secret police, substantially reduced the scope for dissent and public protest. Strict censorship also meant that the dissemination of religio-political literature such as had sustained the protest movements of the early 1960s was severely curtailed.

By the late 1960s and '70s, however, the political activism of the *ulama* was once more in evidence. Much of it arose as a response to what many clerics and laymen believed was the steady erosion of Iran's Islamic identity by an imperial tradition which invoked the pre-Islamic past. A strident American presence which entailed increased personnel, joint business ventures and multinational corporation activities, also suggested Iran's growing subservience to foreign interests.

By the early 1970s increased contacts between Islamic resistance groups in Iran and those in exile in Iraq led the government to impose new restrictions on the freedom of movement. These did little to contain the spate of anti-government demonstrations at university campuses in Tehran and elsewhere in the autumn of 1970. In 1971 protesters led by Ayatollah Montazeri criticized the government's suppression of workers and students and distributed wall posters which denounced the commemoration of 2,500 years of the Persian monarchy on the grounds that it revitalized Zoroastrianism while debilitating Islam.

It was at this time that an important new organization, the *Mujahadin-i-Khalq*, came into existence. Founded along the lines of the *Fedayin-i-Islam* of the 1940s and '50s, the *Mujahadin* resorted to a campaign of urban-based guerrilla tactics against the government. Inspired by the works of Marx and Lenin and deeply influenced by the Islamic *Weltanschauung* of Ali Shariati, the group sought in its programme to achieve a synthesis of Marxism and Islam. In 1977, the *Mujahadin* suffered serious setbacks at the hands of the Shah's secret police, but later re-emerged under the leadership of Massoud Rejavi (now in exile in Iraq). The tensions between the secular and clerical opposition which surfaced soon after the establishment of the Islamic Republic in February 1979 led many Mujahadin to become targets of persecution. By 1982, open war between the Mujahadin and the incumbent Ayatollahs and their allies led many Mujahadin to opt either for exile abroad or face death by execution in Iran.

## The collapse of the monarchy

The revolution of 1978–1979 was the culmination of a series of developments in Iranian society which affected all classes, although it was the particular response of the *ulama* that proved absolutely critical. The growing censorship and the imposition of an official imperial culture was fiercely denounced by secular-minded intellectuals and clergy alike. The enormous revenues generated by Iran's petroleum boom in the mid-1970s bred inflation, corruption and cynicism. Resentment was widespread, especially among members of the clergy and sections of the small-merchant classes in the *bazaars*. Added to this were the grievances of agriculturalists and peasants who suffered from the regime's chaotic agrarian policies, and of industrial labourers who complained about the government's failure to induce divestiture of shares in favour of workers.

The ability of Iran's religious leadership to withstand co-optation by the regime in the 1960s and '70s permitted its members and their Islamic ideology to command a degree of legitimacy in the ranks of the opposition that was generally unique. This was reflected in part by the number of "Islamically-oriented" organizations spawned by the professional middle classes between 1978–1979 which included the *Nazhat-i Azadi-i Iran* (The Liberation Movement), a coalition of lay moderate forces led by Mehdi Bazargan, who was charged with the task of forming the first Islamic government.

By early 1978, Khomeini's growing personal influence and the co-ordination of an effective opposition from his exile in Neuphlé-le-Château near Paris, made it a matter of time before the final collapse of the Shah's political system. The forced departure from Iran of Reza Shah and his family (January 16, 1979); the return of Ayatollah Khomeini to Iran (February 1, 1979); the resignation of the caretaker government of Prime Minister Shapour Bakhtiar (February 11, 1979) and the referendum in favour of the Islamic Republic (March 1979), signified the end of a long struggle to displace a regime that had grown increasingly out of touch with popular sentiment.

## The Islamic Republic

On February 5, 1979, Mehdi Bazargan was nominated by Ayatollah Khomeini to form the first government of the Islamic Republic. However, intense power struggles between "moderates", committed to a western-style democracy, and "revolutionaries", dedicated to the creation of a theocratic state, imposed severe strains on the new government. The growing polarization of Iranian politics was also manifested in the dispute between laymen and clerics over the proposed constitution which envisaged an Islamic Republic managed by a Shia theocracy. Opposition to the policies of the new regime were also expressed by Iran's ethnic minorities, most notably the Kurds who demanded full autonomy. In November 1979 Bazargan and his government were forced to resign.

The American hostage crisis (November 1979 – January 1981) marked a turning point in the politics of the new Republic. Its most significant outcome was the consolidation of radical Islamic groups opposed to the secular–liberal wings represented by President Abol Hasan Banisadr and the Foreign Minister, Sadegh Ghotbzadeh. The radicals were organized, for the most part, within the newly-established Islamic Republic Party (IRP), founded by Ayatollah Beheshti (1928–1981). While the Party had the strong backing of the religious leadership, it also included in its ranks individuals who were not from among the clergy. Although the IRP sought institutional legitimacy through the Majlis, it tended also to rely heavily on extra-parliamentary forces like the *Pasdaran* or Revolutionary Guards loyal to Khomeini, and the *Hizbollahai* or Followers of the Party of God, which consisted of the urban poor, the homeless and the unemployed. In June 1987 Khomeini disbanded the IRP on the grounds that it had become "an excuse for discord and factionalism".

The dominant position of the radicals in the early years of the revolution was reflected in the IRP's electoral success in July 1980 which gave it a comfortable majority in the Iranian Majlis. Also important in the consolidation of the radicals was the growing political influence of a triumvirate consisting of Ayatollah Beheshti, the Speaker of the Majlis, Ali Akber Rafsanjani and the Prime Minister, Mohammadali Rejai. The death of Ayatollah Beheshti in a bomb blast at IRP headquarters in June 1980, and later of Rejai in a similar explosion in August 1981, did little to contain the political momentum initiated by the group to neutralize the liberal presidency of Abol Hasan Bani Sadr.

By the early 1980s, however, there were clear signs of growing resistance to the radical policies and programmes of the Islamic Republic. Opposition came from religious groups, ethnic minorities and liberal dissidents. One of the government's most severe critics was the senior cleric and Grand Ayatollah, Shariatmadari, who enjoys a wide following among the Turkic Azerbaijanis of north-western Iran. Shariatmadari's ideological position, which emphasizes the separation of the clergy from political affairs, was an early source of his differences with Khomeini. His own involvement in politics began somewhat unwittingly in December 1979, when large numbers of his Azerbaijani followers responded to a call by the Muslim People's Republication Party (MPRP) to boycott the referendum on the Constitution. This led to violent clashes in the cities of Qom and Tabriz, and later in Tehran, where an estimated one million Azerbaijanis threatened to stage an uprising against the government. Offers of reconciliation by government ministers, and Shariatmadari's personal intervention, secured a temporary peace. The government, however, failed to keep its promise of greater representation for Azerbaijanis and resorted instead to a purge of the MPRP. The MPRP was disbanded, 54 of its leading members executed and Ayatollah Shariatmadari placed under house-arrest in Qom.

Other clerics who voiced their opposition to Khomeini's Islamic Republic have included the clergy of the holy city of Mashad, most notably Ayatollahs Qomi and Shirazi. As late as November 1987, Ayatollah Qomi issued a *fatwa* or ruling, denouncing the regime policies as "un-Islamic". Qomi was supported by the elderly nationalist Ayatollah Zanjani, a keen supporter of Dr Mossadegh's National Front. Dissident clerics continue to express their opposition to the government. In May 1988, senior religious leaders, among them Ayatollahs Mohammad Reza Golpayegani and Shahabbedin Marashi-Najf, added their names to an open letter from the Society of Qom Theological Teachers calling on Khomeini to end the "un-Islamic" excesses of the Revolution.

Tenacious opposition to the regime has also come from members of Iran's ethnic minorities, especially the Kurds. In 1979, clashes between Kurds and security forces in Central Kurdistan led to formal demands by the Kurdish Democratic Party (KDP) for greater Kurdish autonomy, and for the right of Kurdish Sunnis to aspire to high office (a right presently denied under the Constitution which reserves the posts of President and Prime Minister for Shias). Khomeini responded by invoking the need for Islamic unity. The movement for Kurdish autonomy was given a fresh impetus in December 1979 when government troops entered Kurdistan to restore government control. This, in turn, set in motion a protracted struggle by Kurds to obtain recognition of their right to administer their own affairs within the framework of an Islamic Republic.

The opposition of liberal politicians and secular intellectuals, many of whom had rallied around Bani Sadr and the *Mujahadin-i Khalq* led by Massoud Rejavi, suffered a serious setback following the exile of Bani Sadr and Rejavi in July 1981. Sympathizers and members of the *Mujahadin* have been ruthlessly purged inside Iran, hundreds have been executed and many thousands arrested, tortured and imprisoned without trial. Although the *Mujahadin* and their allies continue to mobilize support, and have even attempted to co-ordinate their activities closer to home (Rejavi has been operating from Iraq after leaving exile in France in June 1986), their safe return is far from assured, even after the death of Khomeini.

The years 1980–1988 were marked by a long and bloody war between Iran and Iraq. Iran's foreign policy in these years continued to be characterized by a broadly isolationist stance in relation especially to the United States, the European Community (with the exception perhaps of Germany), and the majority of Muslim states, many of whose leaders are deemed by the Iranians to be un-Islamic. Domestically, however, the growing political influence of a more moderate group of "pragmatists" led by the Speaker of the Majlis, Hojotoleslam Aliakbar Rafsanjani, suggested subtle shifts in policy. Although the arrest, torture and execution of political opponents of the regime continued unabated, (a report by the United Nations Commission of Human Rights in February 1987 alleged that over 7,000 people have been executed since the establishment of the Islamic Republic), there were some indications that greater priority would be given to the urgent task of reconstructing an economy ravaged by war and revolution. Trade negotiations were initiated with Australia and New Zealand and there were signs of a growing rapprochement with the Soviet Union.

On the international front, Iranian officials made it clear that their government would be prepared to play an active and more positive role towards securing the release of Western hostages held by Shia groups in the Lebanon. It is also understood that it was primarily the influence of the "pragmatists" that persuaded the Iranian government to accept a ceasefire and end hostilities with Iraq in the summer of 1988.

The steady political consolidation of the "pragmatists" suffered a severe blow between February and March 1989. The publication of *The Satanic Verses* by the British author Salman Rushdie, which provoked widespread and sometimes violent demonstrations in parts of the Muslim world, led the Ayatollah Khomeini to issue a death sentence against Rushdie in February. Britain's refusal to ban *The Satanic Verses* and her insistence that Iran withdraw the death threat against Rusdhie led to a complete break in diplomatic relations between Iran and Britain. This was followed by a break in relations between Iran and the rest of the European Community. Iran's position on the Rushdie affair led also to a strain in the country's relations with the Muslim world. In March 1989, a meeting of the Islamic Organization Conference in Riyadh refrained, in the face of intense lobbying from the Iranian delegation, from endorsing Khomeini's death sentence, and opted instead for a declaration which merely charged the author of *The Satanic Verses* with apostasy.

The religious and political fervour aroused by the controversy over *The Satanic Verses* enabled hardliners led by Prime Minister Hussein Moussavi and Ahmad Khomeini (the Ayatollah's only surviving son) to regain the initiative. Their cause was substantially bolstered by Ayatollah Khomeini who publicly reprimanded Rafsanjani and President Ali Khamenei for having adopted a more conciliatory posture on the issue of *The Satanic Verses*. Khomeini's support for the hardliners was also demonstrated by his growing differences with Ayatollah Montazeri, his designated successor, who publicly deplored Khomeini's death sentence on Rushdie. In late March 1989 Khomeini accepted Montazeri's resignation as successor.

The death of Ayatollah Khomeini on June 3, 1989 did not, as was expected, erupt in a fierce power struggle. Khomeini's last political testament, which provided for Ali Khamenei to assume the position as supreme leader, suggests that Khomeini may well have been inclined, ultimately, to back the more cautious policies advocated by the "pragmatists". The election of Aliakbar Rafsanjani as President in July 1989 was fairly assured, and there is every sign that the existing triumvirate of Rafsanjani-Khamenei-Velayati (the foreign minister) may well put Iranian politics back on a moderate course. There is, however, strong resistance to any dilution of Iran's radical Islamic politics. The greatest political challenge comes from the hardliners inside the government who include the Prime Minister Hussein Moussavi, the interior minister Ali Mohatashemi, and the deputy Speaker of the Majlis, Mahdavi Karrui. Their greatest political asset presently is the support of Ahmed Khomeini who, while without any political office, may yet be persuaded to capitalize on his position as the only direct link with the late Ayatollah Khomeini.

Farzana Shaikh

# IRAQ

As in most Middle Eastern countries, religious affiliation has exerted a profound if inconsistent and uneven influence upon political life in Iraq over the past few decades. The population is divided along both racial and religious lines; about 75 per cent are Arabs, 18 per cent Kurds and the remaining 7 per cent Assyrians, Turcomans, Armenians and Persians. Some 90 per cent of the population is Muslim, the remaining 10 per cent consisting of a variety of Christian sects and the Yazidi and Sabaean communities which are only found in Iraq. Most Kurds are Sunnis, while the Arab Muslims belong to the Sunni and Twelver Shii sects; the Shiis account for about half the population, while the Sunni Arabs, the traditional rulers both of Ottoman Iraq and of the modern state since its inception in 1920, account for something less than a quarter of Iraqis. It should also be mentioned that four of the principal shrines of Twelver Shiism, the state religion of Iran, Kadhimain, Samarra', Karbala' and Najaf (the latter two being particularly venerated) are located in Iraq.

The first ruler of modern Iraq, Faisal, son of Sharif Husain of Mecca, came from a family able to trace its descent to the Prophet Muhammad, and this, together with his reputation as a leader in the Arab revolt and the support afforded to him by the British mandatory authorities, meant that he was generally acceptable to those whose countryman he became. Since the Ottoman Empire had been a Sunni institution, the Ottoman administrators in Iraq (most of whom were "Arabized Turks" by the end of the nineteenth century) were all Sunnis. For similar reasons, what modern educational facilities the Ottoman government had provided had generally not been patronized by middle and upper class urban Shiis, who, in addition, for various cultural and quasi-religious reasons, tended to prefer commerce and the learned professions to careers in government or military service. An important result of this was that when the British set up the modern state in 1920, very few Shiis had the necessary qualifications for political or public office, which meant that the Sunni Arabs were proportionally very much over-represented in both government and the bureaucracy.

Under the mandate and monarchy (1920–32; 1932–58) there were occasional instances of sectarian-based disquiet on the part of the urban Shiis, but on the whole, largely because the government did not seek to interfere with the affairs of the Holy Cities, such manifestations could be kept in check. There were other more burning issues at the centre of the political arena, most notably the question of the extent of British control of Iraq and the absence of political and other freedoms within the country as a result of that control. Under the mandate a constitution had been imported, with a monarchy, a cabinet and a bicameral legislature; these arrangements continued when Iraq became "independent" in 1932, but the system was weighted heavily in favour of the *status quo* and could not adapt to the major social, political and economic changes taking place both within and outside the country in the 1940s and 1950s.

During the 1940s and 1950s, the educational system expanded greatly, migration to the cities on the part of the Shii population of the rural south accelerated, and oil income came to dominate government revenue. These and other factors combined to produce a new educated middle and lower middle class (whose most articulate representatives were to be found in the professions and in the armed forces), the beginnings of a small proletariat, and a large urban underclass — of both Sunnis and Shiis — ekeing out its existence on the periphery of society. As "politics" remained the preserve of a few urban and rural notables, political activity was concentrated in two major tendencies, the Communist Party, then the most influential and best organized of its contemporaries in the Arab world, and a less formal grouping of Arab nationalists of various persuasions, whose aspirations were greatly encouraged by Nasser's rise to power and his nationalization of the Suez Canal in 1956.

While it is undeniable that Nasser's successful defiance of Britain and France earned him heroic status in the eyes of Iraqis of almost all political persuasions, there was a certain sectarian divide between communists and nationalists. Since most of the Arab world is Sunni, Arab nationalism and Arab unity was generally less attractive to the Shiis, who tended to feel themselves to be more Iraqi than Arab. Again, the Shiis, many of whom had migrated to the cities to escape virtual serfdom on the large estates of southern Iraq, formed the bulk of the urban poor, and for this and other reasons large numbers of them were attracted to the egalitarian ideals of communism. Although by no means all communists, or even most communists, were Shiis, it is true that most nationalists were Sunnis rather than Shiis.

Here, however, another important consideration needs to be taken into account. A general feature of the political, economic and intellectual climate of the Arab world between, say, the late 1940s and the middle 1970s was an emphasis on such secular themes as development, progress and equality. In Iraq, particularly with the considerable political and social advances made after the 1958 Revolution, and subsequently with the explosion in oil prices in 1973, the material standard of living of the poorer sections of the population improved. In this general climate, the notion that government service was not a suitable career for Shiis soon went by the board, and in this and other ways the Shiis were quick to catch up with their Sunni compatriots. One consequence of this tendency for the Shiis was that the traditional religious professions lost much of their status and appeal, and the numbers of students in the seminaries gradually decreased.

This state of affairs began to cause considerable alarm in the ranks of the clerical hierarchy, and to combat what they regarded as the spread of communism, which was more accurately the spread of secularism, the *ulama* of Najaf founded an association in the late 1950s which became known as *al-Da'wa al-Islamiyya*, the Islamic Call, in 1968. One of its leading members, Ayatollah Muhammad Baqir al-Sadr, formulated a theory of the ideal Islamic state somewhat similar to that of Ayatollah Khomeini, who lived in Najaf in exile from Iran between 1964 and 1978. In general this view amounted to a denunciation of the various un-Islamic regimes ruling in the Muslim world and a call for their replacement, through revolution, by a social and political order based upon Islamic principles. In the late 1970s two developments combined to exert a more direct influence on the course of events; the government's desire to incorporate the Holy Cities more fully into the Iraqi polity, and the rise of Islamic radicalism in Iran, culminating in the Iranian Revolution and the Iran-Iraq war.

Previous Iraqi governments had avoided confrontation by generally not interfering either with the Shii hierarchy or with the affairs of the Holy Cities, but the Ba'th, who came to power in 1968, seemed determined to extend their control over all parts of the country. Having defeated the Kurds in 1975, they turned their attention to the Holy Cities; in 1977 a protest demonstration was brutally suppressed, and several *ulama* executed. Ba'thist ideology, though somewhat incoherent, is Arab nationalist in orientation, and although the Ba'th leaders of the 1970s and 1980s have almost all been Sunnis, Ba'thism is essentially secular; the events of the late 1970s were more a reflection of the leadership's dictatorial pretensions than of sectarianism.

By 1978, when it became clear that the days of the Iranian monarchy were numbered, members of al-Da'wa began to attack Iraqi police posts and Ba'th party offices, and made no secret of their support for the Iranian Revolution. In response, the Ba'th launched a fierce campaign against al-Da'wa, culminating in the arrest and execution of Ayatollah Baqir al-Sadr and his sister, Bint Huda, in April 1980. The campaign was successful in the sense that there appears to have been little overt sectarian opposition to the regime within Iraq since then.

The war between Iraq and Iran, which Iraq initiated in September 1980, had two main aims. The first of these was to overthrow the Islamic Republic and install a regime which would be more acceptable to Iraq and its western supporters, and the second was to prevent the export of Islamic revolution from Iran to Iraq. At the time of the ceasefire in 1988, only the latter objective had been accomplished, but the war was not the only factor involved here.

There is no doubt that the present Iraqi regime is one of the most savage and repressive of all contemporary Middle Eastern governments, and for this reason it is impossible to gauge the actual extent of popular radical Islamic opposition within the country today. However, a number of other factors need to be taken into consideration. In the first place, "Iraqi Shiis" are not a unified body; in particular, there is a profound social gulf between the "religious professionals" of the Holy Cities, and the mass of urban and rural poor. Again, in broad terms, and in comparison with their contemporaries in Iran, the overwhelming majority of Iraqi Shiis are not as profoundly religious; many of them wear their Shiism fairly lightly and feel that they are Iraqi Arabs first and Shiis second. While many, in common with their Sunni counterparts, might welcome the overthrow of the present dictatorship and the establishment of a more widely representative government, they would not be in favour of an Islamic state or the version of militant Shiism espoused by the Iranian regime. In short, the prospect of an Islamic regime coming to power in Iraq is almost as unappealing to the Iraqi Shiis as it is to the bulk of their non-Shii compatriots.

Nevertheless, Saddam Hussein is taking no chances. He had decided to give himself an Arabo-Islamic image and to underplay the more secular aspects of Ba'thism. A major programme of mosque building has been inaugurated, and the government has given large donations to the shrines in Karbala' and Najaf. Saddam Hussein has had his family "traced back" to the Prophet Muhammad, and has also refurbished the image of the Hashemite monarchy, overthrown in July 1958, to whom, presumably, he claims to be related. Such policies, it must be said, are most unlikely to have the desired effect.

Although the traditional sectarian divide — between Shiis and Sunnis — had begun to be of less social significance during the decades preceding and following the Revolution of 1958, the repressive nature of Ba'th rule and more particularly the war with Iran have combined to reassert its importance. The process of nation formation, however hesitant, which had begun after the Revolution, now appears blocked, and local, regional, kinship and other, including sectarian, forms of identification have reasserted themselves. In this negative sense religion and religious affiliation continue to exert an important influence on Iraqi political life.

Marion Farouk-Sluglett

Peter Sluglett

# IRELAND

Relations between the majority Catholic religion and the state in independent Ireland since 1922 have been both intimate and, generally, harmonious, for certain historical and structural reasons. Before independence, nationalist separatists and the Catholic Church were natural allies against the British State and the mainly Protestant minority who ruled Ireland at that time. The revolutionary movement which created the independent state was itself overwhelmingly composed of Catholics. The young men who agitated for Irish independence were not merely nominal or sociological Catholics, but were usually believers and even fervent practitioners of their religion; Irish society had never experienced the secularization of British society, nor had it undergone the dechristianization that had occurred in so many continental Catholic countries. The ideology of Irish nationalism was nominally non-sectarian, but had a very noticeable tendency to identify the "Irish People" as being mainly, or even exclusively, the Catholic people of Ireland.

Furthermore, the partition of Ireland which was imposed by the Westminster Parliament in 1920 made it even more likely that independent Ireland would develop a strongly confessional public culture. This was because partition essentially attempted to segregate as many Irish Protestants as possible from the Catholic majority on the island. The British allocated one-fifth of the island to Protestants, and permitted the revolutionaries who led the Catholics to take the rest of it. The new independent country, originally entitled the Irish Free State, is now known as the Republic of Ireland because of constitutional developments of various kinds.

In the new independent Irish state, religious pluralism was effectively unnecessary, as there were not many Protestants around to press for it; a small Protestant minority of about 6 per cent remained in the new state. Protestants were not persecuted, but were provided with separate educational and health-care facilities on the lines of pre-independence arrangements. This had the perhaps desired effect of ghettoizing them in a comfortable way.

The rest of the people were devoutly Catholic, and continued to look to their Church for social and cultural leadership as they had since the seventeenth century. Discrimination against Catholics, echoing the anti-Catholicism of British elite culture since the Reformation, was now extinct in most of Ireland, but the habits of resistance against discrimination lingered on after independence. In Northern Ireland, they survive to the present day.

Even before independence, the confessional character of Irish culture had been acknowledged by the political authorities. The British state had conceded control of the education of Catholics to the Catholic Church. Similar arrangements were made with the other religious communities on the island. Health care was also by-and-large controlled by the Churches. During the Anglo-Irish War the underground *Dail* government gave the Catholic hierarchy to understand that no Irish government would disturb the comfortable arrangements that had been worked out with the British.

Independence in 1922 brought truly competitive electoral democracy to Ireland for the first time. However, the electoral contests were now between two sets of Catholics, ex-revolutionaries who had fought a bitter little civil war in 1922–23. Among other things, this entailed each side attempting to prove itself as being somehow "more Catholic" than the other. Clerically-approved bans on divorce and contraception were introduced, and an increasingly rigorous censorship of books and films was instituted under governments of both parties during the 1923–37 period. The public rituals of state were willingly associated with those of the dominant Church. Dignitaries of both Church and state celebrated a Eucharistic Congress in 1932 that marked 1,500 years of Christianity in Ireland. Catholic triumphalism pervaded the political system between 1932 and the late 1950s. Church–state separation, although it existed, was weaker and more qualified than in, for example, the United States or the secularized republics and constitutional monarchies of post-1945 western Europe.

In 1937, the Prime Minister, Eamon de Valera, promulgated a new constitution. This new constitution was an entrenched law; unlike the rather curious British arrangement, it can only be altered by vote of the people, and parliament is subject to the constitution as interpreted by the supreme court; Irish law is "judge-made" to an extent unimaginable in Britain. The new constitution contained several articles which were heavily informed by Catholic social thought of the period. In particular, it imposed an unconditional ban on divorce. In several other articles, it gave rhetorical support to Catholic values: for example, it urged the state to ensure that women were not to be forced to work outside the home to the detriment of family life. Since 1937, Church–state relationships have often been mediated by the judges, as constitutional issues are quite commonly involved. In the first 20 years, judges tended to take up positions sympathetic to "Catholic" opinion and also were inclined to go along with the purposes of elected politicians, à l'anglaise. In recent decades, by way of contrast, there has been a noticeable tendency to interpret the constitution in a more secularist, and almost "American", spirit.

The most serious clash between Church and state did not, however, involve a constitutional issue. Rather, it involved the creation of a state-run health service analogous to the British National Health Service, which was being put together by a consortium of politicians, medical administrators and civil servants in the years after World War II. Catholic bishops, encouraged by doctors' organizations, expressed their distrust of proposed state intervention in health services designed for pregnant women. The Mother and Child scheme involved some rudimentary sex and hygiene education, and this feature particularly aroused the bishops' ire and paranoia. The minister involved, Dr Noel Browne, was forced out of office in 1951, thereafter to become a folk hero in Irish politics. It became easier to assert that the Catholic hierarchy, rather than the *Dail*, supplied the true government of the Irish Republic. Northern unionists seized gleefully on the issue. While it would be an exaggeration to describe the bishops as the country's rulers, there is no doubt that the Catholic Church, because of its immense popularity, was able to exercise a near-veto in certain areas of policy; health, education and family law being the most obvious. It is also true, however, that most areas of policy are not regarded as being any business of ecclesiastics, and interventions by the hierarchy in areas which the culture regards as outside their ambit have commonly been struck down. In particular, issues involving economic policy or nationalist ideology have been consistently regarded as being no business of priests.

The partial secularization of Irish society that has occurred in the last 30 years has changed the situation somewhat. In the early sixties, economic prosperity and the liberalization of the Vatican Council combined to weaken the authoritarianism of the Church and also to make the religious life less attractive to young people. Vocations to the priesthood and to the convent fell dramatically. The consequence of this has been the inevitable laicization of the school system and of the hospitals. The various censorship systems fell into disuse at the same time.

The growing crisis in neighbouring British-ruled Northern Ireland erupted into violence in the early 1970s. There was widespread revulsion in the Republic from the terror tactics of the Provisional IRA, and this has forced a gradual liquidation of the old alliance between a certain kind of fervent Catholicism and visionary insurrectionist nationalism; the IRA have an armed struggle, but the Church realized that it must never be understood to be a *Catholic* struggle. In part, the point is that it is a deeply unpopular struggle among Catholics. Following the Vatican Council, the historic hostility between the different Christian communities in Ireland became a matter of public embarrassment on both sides, and elaborate public disavowals of sectarianism have become *de rigeur* in recent decades.

Secularism benefited from these trends in Irish society: consumerism, education, the scandal of Provisionalism and a general cultural modernization made the old idols of the clan increasingly unattractive. A series of attempts to secularize Irish law followed. In 1972, an article in the constitution granting a "special position" in Irish society to the Catholic Church was abolished by popular referendum. Aspects of the law prohibiting the sale of contraceptives were found to be in breach of the constitution by the supreme court. The law had been evaded openly by more and more people since the fifties, and it was eventually modified and then abolished by the *Dail*. Laws on adoption, which had, for example, prohibited the adoption by Protestants of a child born to a Catholic mother, were changed. Schools runs on lay lines by lay people became more common, and the Church retreated generally on the educational front. The old alliance between Church and state looked increasingly irrelevant. Protestant, Jewish and agnostic groups, hitherto quiet in the face of an overwhelming Catholic majority, became increasingly vocal, and found many Catholics to be, perhaps unexpectedly, willing listeners.

In the 1980s, international events and local circumstances combined to encourage a backlash against these tendencies. Catholic anti-abortion groups in the United States and Britain assisted in the organization of a similar group in the Republic. In 1983, the Irish government was manoeuvred into holding a referendum on abortion, the proposal being to insert a prohibition on abortion into the constitution; abortion was already illegal, but it was feared that the judges might eventually find the law to be unconstitutional in certain "hard cases". The amendment was passed by a two-thirds majority, after a long and bitter campaign between ardent Catholics and equally ardent secularists. The more urbanized and younger voters did, however, vote in considerable numbers against the amendment, despite the fact that the Irish are virtually unanimously hostile to abortion. In 1986, the government attempted to abolish the constitution's prohibition on divorce. Its amendment was defeated in popular referendum in proportions identical to those of 1983. There appear to be limits to Irish traditionalism, however; some Catholics proposed that existing rules recognizing foreign divorces in Ireland be weakened or abolished. This has proved too much for Irish legislators, some of whom have evaded the divorce prohibition themselves by getting British or other foreign divorces, and has been resisted.

Relationships between the hierarchy and the state are now less easy than they once were, because of the challenges that have been mounted to a hitherto rather cosy consensus. On the other hand, the Church has displayed an impressive ability to abandon positions which it sees are becoming untenable, and to avoid making unnecessary enemies. The referendums of the 1980s, forced by a lay Catholic group in one instance and by a secularizing government in the other, made the Church display, albeit reluctantly, its formidable influence on Irish public opinion. By so doing, it has, paradoxically, weakened itself somewhat by antagonizing some opinion-makers and policy-makers. It has also encouraged open dissidence in its own ranks; the days of monolithic Irish Catholicism seem to be numbered. The phrase *à la carte* Catholicism has come into use to describe the growing tendency of Catholics to pick and choose which doctrines and rules of their religion they are going to accept, and which ones they are going to ignore. No Irish government has yet successfully challenged the Church on its own ground, but that is in part due to the Church avoiding such challenges by conceding ground in advance. Both sides have tried to avoid collision; the relationship between Church and state in the Republic of Ireland resembles not so much a wrestling match as an eighteenth-century dance, reflecting accurately the subtleties of Irish political culture.

Tom Garvin

# ISRAEL

## "Is Israel a Jewish state or a state of Jews?"

This question, asked in the *Newsweek* article reporting the results of the 1988 elections, appeared under the headline "Israel: A Jewish Fundamentalist State?" and highlighted the unexpected "crisis" in Israeli politics.[1] Commentators, inside and outside of Israel, religious and secular, wrote of an impending "war" between the religious and non-religious, as the four religious parties attempted to create a theocratic state by using their new-found strength (18 seats) to lever further religious concessions as the price for their support in a coalition government.[2]

Although a more sober analysis reveals that the religious parties had merely regained the 15 per cent of the vote that they held from 1949 until 1981, it cannot be denied that Israel is currently undergoing a most profound period of self-questioning as to her identity as a nation. This self-scrutiny takes many forms — from the meaning of "Jewish" in the phrase "the Jewish State", as formulated in Israel's Declaration of Independence (1948), to the adherence to the democratic values, which are also enshrined in the same Declaration, in the light of an anticipated future Arab majority.

## Challenges to Jewish identity and destiny

Traditionally, Jewish identity has been understood as an overlapping amalgam of religion and nation. The people of Israel are a nation created by their covenant with God. The interpretation of the covenant and its implications gives rise to the characteristic beliefs and practices of the Jewish people. Vital to this covenant is the promise of the land of Israel. Following their dispersions under the Babylonians and Romans, Jews have prayed daily for the end of their God-given exile and the return to the land of Israel. Theologically this return became associated with the related doctrines of the messiah and the "end of days". Except for small numbers and periodic pseudo-messianic movements, Jews have lived in exile, under Christianity and Islam, in separate communities, their lives defined by *halakhah* (the system of religious law), awaiting the divine redemption in the land. This doctrine is significant in that it largely maintained the national component of Jewish identity.

Since the end of the eighteenth century, the Jewish world has undergone a series of transformations. Following the American and French revolutions and the granting of full rights of citizenship to Jews, emancipation seemed assured in Western and Central Europe of the 1860s. Emancipation and citizenship presented a challenge to the traditional notions of religious–national identity. The national element was rejected or suppressed as many Jews came to see themselves as citizens of France or Germany, for example, and Jews only by virtue of their religion. Thus began a massive programme of cultural assimilation associated with the *haskalah* (enlightenment) movement, and leading to the redefinition of "Judaism" along modernist lines.

Assimilationists were also to be found in Russia, where the vast majority of Jews resided until the end of the nineteenth century. Influenced by the

German *haskalah*, a number of Jews advocated assimilation. However, the rise of nationalism in Russia was accompanied by persecution and pogroms, and what came to be perceived as the failure of Jewish assimilation. Many Jews left Russia and Eastern Europe, providing the shape and structure of the present Jewish communities of America and western Europe. Although Jewish identity in Russia, in the main, continued to be conceived along traditional lines, a growing number of Jews, inspired by European state-nationalism, emphasized the national component of Jewish identity. Some became Russian Jewish nationalists and called for the recognition of the Jewish nation as an integral part of the Russian "multi-national" state, while others advocated Zionist Jewish nationalism and the return to the land of Israel. Both Russian and Zionist Jewish nationalism had groups calling for a "synthesis" of Jewish nationalism and Socialism.

## Zionism and/or Judaism?

The Zionist movement began with "practical Zionism" — the establishment of small-scale agricultural settlements in Palestine — and crystallized into a political movement with the first Zionist Congress in 1897. Fundamental to Zionism was the recognition of the national identity of the Jews, the rejection of the exile and a belief in the impossibility of assimilation. This rejection of diaspora Jewish existence often entailed the rejection of traditional Jewish religious practice and the secularization of Jewish beliefs concerning "the ingathering of the exiles" and the "redemption of the land". Jews, rather than being a people created by divine action, were a national people like all other nations and had an identity based on shared historical experience, language and culture. While the Bible was central to these non-religious Zionists as a "historical" document, they were unclear concerning the centrality of religious elements in Jewish cultural history and the rejection of Orthodox practice and supernaturalism.

Our concern, here, is with the growing tensions between those holding the traditional Orthodox, supernatural (religious–national) understanding of Jewish identity and destiny and those bound to a natural, historical and national conception, as the implications of these fundamental differences were developed in their associations with the Zionist programme of national renewal.

Zionism was opposed by the majority of Jews until after 1945. Reform Judaism, with its insistence on the Jews as a religious community, rejected the Zionist claim of the Jews as a national entity. The Orthodox understood the general Zionist aim of re-establishing Jewish sovereignty in the land before the coming of the messiah, as the sin of "forcing the end", that is, of using human means to hasten the redemption. The "political Zionism" of Herzl's World Zionist Organization (WZO, 1897) was condemned as "idolatry", by the Orthodox, who felt it replaced reverence for God and His *torah* by secular nationalism and the "worship" of the land.

There were, however, Orthodox Jews who supported the Zionist efforts to establish a Jewish state. This support was for a programme for Jewish security and/or as a fulfilment of the divine command to "dwell in the land" and more generally as the "beginnings of the redemption", that is acceptance of using human effort to prepare for the messiah's coming. These religious Zionists formed the *Mizrahi* (*Merkaz Ruhani*, Spiritual Centre) party which joined the

WZO in 1902, calling for "the land of Israel for the people of Israel according to the *torah* of Israel", and seeking to influence the WZO along traditional Jewish lines. In 1912, a second Orthodox group, *Agudat Israel* (Association of Israel) was formed, advocating Orthodox Jewish settlement in the land, particularly from the late 1930s. They were non-Zionist, in that they neither supported nor saw any religious significance in the aim of establishing a Jewish state *per se*.

## The *status quo* agreement and the State of Israel

The settlements of the *yishuv* (modern pre-state settlement) began under Ottoman rule, where a considerable degree of religious freedom was ensured by the millet-system. Each recognized religious community (or millet) was granted the right to administer its own system of officially recognized courts responsible for matters of religious law. The millet-system continued to operate under the British Mandate (1923–1947) and the Jewish religious courts became part of the official legal system.

In 1947 an agreement was made between the Jewish Agency (JA), the governing body of the *yishuv*, and the religious parties (*Mizrahi* and *Agudat Israel*), outlining the position of existing Jewish religious norms that were to be incorporated into the public life of the forthcoming State of Israel — the Jewish Sabbath would be the official national day of rest, government establishments would observe the dietary laws (*kashrut*), the religious courts would continue to have jurisdiction over marriage and divorce, and the religious educational systems would be maintained.

For *Agudat Israel* and the *Mizrahi*, the agreement was understood as a further move in the establishment of a *torah*-state, while for Ben-Gurion, the chairman of the JA executive, it was to ensure the Jewish character of the state and to secure Orthodox support.

Although this arrangement (known as the "*status quo* agreement" — SQA) was only a broad statement of principles, it was tacitly understood to entail an assurance that the pre-1948 religious situation would continue after the establishment of the state. It provided, and continues to provide, the framework for the Jewish public life of the state and the basis of co-operation between religious and non-religious Jews. As a result of the SQA, *Mizrahi* and *Agudat Israel*, together with their workers' parties, were able to participate in the first government of Israel.

In the absence of a constitution, the SQA provides Israel with a model of religion–state relations. The constitution, as promised in the Declaration of Independence, has yet to appear. The real tensions between secular and religious conceptions of the "Jewish State", as manifest in the Declaration itself, led to a stalemate in the discussions over the constitution, with the religious parties insisting that Israel already had one in the *torah*.

The SQA is the basis for both the two separate Jewish state-funded and controlled school systems (a religious sector, effectively controlled by the *Mizrahi*, and a secular sector) and the independent state-funded *Agudat Israel* schools. Parents have the right to patronize the educational system of their choice and presently some 35 per cent choose religious schools for their children (29 per cent to the state religious and 7 per cent to the *Agudat Israel* schools). This sizeable element of the Jewish population ensures that a strong religious presence will continue in the state.

On the Jewish Sabbath and religious holidays, non-essential businesses and services, with the exception of those vital to national security, can operate only when special work-permits are secured. Under the SQA, the application of the Sabbath regulations were administered at the local level, with the result that different localities have different regulations. Since 1955, the religious parties have constantly called for a national Sabbath law to curb what they see as increasing violations of the SQA (greater numbers of sabbath work-permits, etc.) but this has been resisted by a succession of governments on the basis of the same agreement.

The millet-system, as inherited by the State of Israel, provided for a system of religious councils and courts, together with two chief rabbis, one *Sephardi* (Jews of Asian and African origin) and one *Askenazi* (Jews of Eastern European origin). The two chief rabbis, with their selected advisors, constitute the Chief Rabbinical Council, the supreme religious authority in Israel. There are also local chief rabbis in the major cities and towns, generally one *Sephardi* and one *Ashkenazi*, and each area has a rabbinical council responsible for the provision of religious services. There are also rabbinical courts with jurisdiction over the Jewish population in matters of marriage and divorce.

This exclusive authority over Jewish marriage and divorce in Israel was officially recognized by the passing of the Rabbinical Courts' Jurisdiction Law (1953). The frequent calls for civil marriage and divorce have been rejected on the basis of the SQA and this act, and thus marriage between Jews, religious and non-religious, and non-Jews is not possible in Israel.

The Ministry of Religious Affairs is responsible for the supervision and financing of the activities of the four recognized religious communities (Jews, Christians, Muslim and Druze). The Ministry is influential in the appointment of the two national chief rabbis, rabbinical court judges and other rabbinical officials.

## The Israeli political system

Israel is a parliamentary democracy whose official head of state is the President, elected by the supreme authority of state, the *knesset*. The *knesset* is a unicameral parliament whose 120 members are elected for a four-year term which can only be ended prematurely by the *knesset* itself. Citizens over 18 have the right to vote, and the country forms a single electoral constituency. Each political party produces a list of candidates — ranging from a single name to 120 names — in order of priority. Voting is for one, fixed order, party list. Each party gaining 1 per cent or more receives the number of seats proportional to its share of the poll for all such parties. When the 120 seats have been allocated to the party lists, the candidates are elected in terms of their place in the order on their party list. The President then consults with the leaders of all the political parties in the *knesset* and invites a *knesset* member, usually the leader of the largest party or bloc, to form a government. As no one party has ever gained a majority, all governments have been coalitions, formed to secure the necessary 61 *knesset* seats. The Prime Minister-elect then submits a list of cabinet members, together with a statement of the principles and policies of the government coalition, to the *knesset* for the required vote of confidence.

# Israel's political parties

The major party groupings — the "left", the "right", and the religious parties — are much more than political parties in the usual sense. The major ones run banks, publishing houses, newspapers, insurance schemes, agricultural settlements, housing projects, industrial and commercial enterprises, educational establishments, social and welfare services and youth movements. Twenty-seven party lists, including 11 new parties, contested the 1988 election, representing an enormous variety of political viewpoints. They ranged from the socialist-nationalists, the right-wing nationalists and an anti-rabbinical list, to the Zionist and non-Zionist religious parties, ethnic parties, communists, and a number of Arab lists.

# Parties of the "left"

In its earlier guises, the Labour Alignment (*Maarah*) effectively ran the *yishuv* from the 1930s, and was the dominant party in government from 1948 until 1977. This dominance was based on its control of the economy via the *Histadrut* (Confederation of Labour) and other major business enterprises and its work as the main body involved with the settlement of new immigrants. For the sake of convenience we will refer to the precursors of the Labour Alignment (*Mapai*, founded in 1929, and the Israel Labour Party, founded in 1968) as *Maarah*.

*Maarah* is committed to a welfare state; a state-managed mixed economy; full employment; and trade unionism. However, since the "revolution" of 1977, it has been beset with considerable problems, including scandals; the loss of its traditional *Sephardi* support; internal dissension; the collapse of its peace plans, following the withdrawal of King Hussein's claims to the West Bank in 1988; and a lack of direction in its policies. After the inconclusive elections of 1984, it was a major partner in a Government of National Unity. Following the 1988 elections, after campaigning on a platform for "negotiations in the context of an international conference" and "peace for territory", a Government of National Unity was once again formed, with the *Maarah* as one of the two main coalition partners.

From 1948 until 1977 *Maarah* formed a series of governments with the *Mizrahi* (later *Mafdal*) as its major coalition partner. During this time, it demonstrated its support for the SQA and co-operation with the religious. This relationship came to an end in 1977, when the *Mafdal* precipitated an election by withdrawing from the government, after the delivery of American fighter planes, late on a Friday night resulting in a desecration of the Sabbath by the government welcoming party.

*Mapam* (the United Workers' Party which won three seats in 1988) has been a coalition partner in most governments since 1949 and was part of *Maarah* from 1968 until 1984. Calling for a classless society, with the public ownership of all enterprises, *Mapam* has historically been to the left of *Maarah*, and has a tradition of anti-religious policies. Two other smaller "left-of-centre" parties gained seats in 1988 — the Citizens' Rights Movement (five seats) and the Centre-*Shinui* (Change) party (two seats). The former is a secular liberal party opposed to what it sees as the religious coercion of the religious parties based on the SQA.

## Parties of the "right"

The *Likud* (Unity) alliance is the main bloc of the "right". *Likud*, formed in 1973, is comprised of the Liberal Party, a number of smaller elements and its dominant group, the *Herut* party. Based on its Revisionist party origins, *Herut* is committed to a Jewish state based on the market economy in "Greater Israel", the entire land on both sides of the River Jordan as promised to Israel by God. After the 1967 war, this "Greater Israel" doctrine became *Herut's* political programme which officially encouraged new settlements in the territories.

*Likud*, after years as the major Israeli opposition party, changed the face of Israeli politics with its victory in 1977, by unifying the disparate elements of the Israeli "right" and gaining a significant percentage of the *Sephardi* support. *Likud* has since been a major element in government (1977–1984 as the dominant bloc in the government, and from 1984 until the present, as one of the two major elements in the two governments of National Unity).

The *Likud* (and earlier, the Revisionists and *Herut*), with their support for "authentic" Jewish values and rejection of "non-Jewish secular liberalism", have been sympathetic to religious values. When *Likud* came to power in 1977, its leader, Menahem Begin, became the first Prime Minister who was an Orthodox Jew, and his ruling coalition included the two major religious parties, and since then, religious issues have become much more of a national concern.

The parties of the "right" also include the "ultra-nationalists". There is considerable overlap between these parties and the "religious ultra-nationalists" (see below). Both have their origins in groups such as the Land of Israel Movement, which were committed to a rejection of territorial compromise with the Arabs and Jewish settlement in the "whole land of Israel", and were radicalized by the "concessions" of the Camp David Accords which split the "right" after 1978. Three such parties successfully contested the 1988 elections (one party, *Kach* (Thus) was banned as racist): *Tehiya* (Revival or Renaissance, an Orthodox party founded in 1979 in response to the Camp David Accords, won three seats); *Tzomet* (Crossroads, a non-religious breakaway from *Tehiya*, gained two seats); and the most "extreme", *Moledet* (Homeland, advocating the "peaceful transfer" of all or some of the Palestinian population, gained two seats). The "extreme" nature of these parties gave impetus to the creation of yet another National Unity Government (*Likud* and *Maarah*) and the exclusion of these extreme parties from that government.

## The religious parties

Historically there have been two major religious party groups and the eight religious lists contesting the last election can be traced to these two. Although approximately 20 per cent of the Jewish population is strictly religiously-observant, since independence the electoral support for the religious parties has remained (with the exception of the elections of 1981 and 1984) consistent at between 12 per cent to 15 per cent. A number of orthodox Jews, therefore, vote for the non-religious parties, and it is evident that the orthodox use their votes, as in the 1980s, to prevent the secularist *Maarah* from gaining a majority.

*Mafdal* (National Religious Party) was founded in 1956 by the merger of *Mizrahi* and its earlier offshoot, *Hapoel Hamizrahi* (*Mizrahi* Workers). *Mafdal* (earlier as *Mizrahi* and *Hapoel Hamizrahi*) has participated, as a coalition partner, in every Israeli government: until 1977 with the ruling *Maarah*; from 1977 until 1984 with *Likud*; and in the governments of National Unity. *Mafdal* has been a major factor in Israel's political stability since 1948.

Traditionally, under pressure from both its non-religious coalition partners (seeking to limit its proposed religious legislation) and from the more separatist orthodox parties, *Mafdal* has sought a pragmatic accommodation of the religious sector in Israel's mainly non-religious society, while maintaining its long-term aim of the establishment of a *torah*-state. It has defended the SQA against secular interests and worked for co-operation between the non-religious and religious in the building of the Jewish state, the establishment of which *Mafdal* considers to be of religious-messianic significance.

*Mafdal* followers have been ardent supporters of the state and have generally accepted their national service, unlike the non- Zionist orthodox, and this has often been combined with *yeshivah* (religious institute of higher education) study. *Mafdal* institutions, where there is an attempted synthesis between religious and "secular" values, include the state–religious schools, Bar Ilan University, and the religious *kibbutzim* (collectives) and *Moshavim* (co-operatives), with their practical synthesis of Zionist labour and Orthodox values.

*Mafdal's* strategy of co-operation with the ruling non-religious parties has ensured its almost continuous control of the Ministry of Religious Affairs. This has allowed *Mafdal* to wield great influence over the chief rabbinate and the religious courts and councils and to operate an extensive system of patronage.

After holding between 10 and 12 *knesset* seats from 1949 until 1977, *Mafdal's* electoral support has fallen dramatically to only five seats in the 1988 election (the six seats that were won in 1981 were reduced to four in 1984). A significant factor in this decline is the growing radicalism of its younger supporters, beginning with the party's Youth Faction (*Tzeirim*, founded in 1963) with its call for the "change and renewal" of both the internal structure and policies of the party in the attempt to broaden party interests beyond purely religious matters, to issues of foreign policy and the economy. After 1967 they were instrumental in bringing about the eventual collapse of the coalition with *Maarah*, over the Israeli claim to the occupied territories, which they understood to be based upon the "covenant of God". Many of the religious ultra-nationalist movements have their origins in *Mafdal's* radical elements. The party's move to the right, particularly in relation to policy on the future of the occupied territories, has generated a further split among the more moderate elements, a number of whom left *Mafdal* in 1988, to form *Meimad* (Dimension), a religious Zionist party committed to alliance with *Maarah*, and although the new party did not win any seats it is indicative of yet further internal dissension.

A second factor in *Mafdal's* loss of support is the ethnic factor. *Likud's* ascendancy drew heavily on the votes of the *Sephardim*, a proportion of whom had been *Mafdal* supporters. In 1981 a financial scandal concerning the *Mafdal Sephardi* Minister of Religious Affairs, led to him claiming that the lack of support from the *Ashkenazi* leadership of *Mafdal* was based on ethnic indifference. He left the party to found the first (and now no longer existing) ethnic (and religious) party, *Tami* (Movement for a Traditional Israel), splitting *Mafdal's* support among the *Sephardim*.

Although *Mafdal* has made great efforts to overcome its electoral decline, by, for example, the election of a *Sephardi* leader, Avner Shaki, and the establishment of a new institute *Eretz Hemda*, for advanced secular and Jewish learning in a traditional *yeshivah* setting, in order to create a new generation of leaders, it would seem that their rather diminished status might be permanent.

Until 1988 the second largest religious party was *Agudat Israel* (Association of Israel). This non-Zionist, anti-secular, ultra-Orthodox, rabbinic-led alliance was established in 1973, by the reaffiliation of its earlier breakaway group, *Poalei Agudat Israel* (*Agudat* Workers), with the *Agudat Israel* parent party, although the two parties can now be seen to have merged. *Agudat Israel*, founded in 1912, sought to develop an international mass movement of Orthodox Jews to counter the growth of Zionism. Since its beginnings in Palestine in the 1920s, *Agudat Israel* has attempted to affiliate itself to the various representative Zionist bodies, but has found itself isolated as each of them refused to comply with its condition that these bodies limit their activities to the economic and political spheres. From 1937, under the impact of Nazi persecution, the party both encouraged its members to immigrate to Palestine and began to co-operate with the secular and religious Zionist parties, leading to the SQA. Although *Agudat Israel* shares — with the *Mafdal* — the ultimate aim of the establishment in the land of a *torah*-state, unlike the other major religious party, it sees no messianic import in the establishment of a Jewish state, and objects to all but the most limited co-operation with the non-religious. Its supporters are strictly Orthodox Jews, living in separatist religious communities centred around their *yeshivot* (religious institutes of higher education), and they do not usually serve in the army.

*Agudat Israel* and *Poalei Agudat Israel* formed part of the government of Israel from 1949 until 1952, when both parties withdrew over the question of religious education. Since then, *Agudat Israel* has retreated from its earlier aim of a *torah*-state, and until most recently has narrowly focussed its attention on securing the right of the ultra-Orthodox to practise their religion, extending the SQA, and for the state financing of religious education and activities. *Agudat Israel* has been a member of the ruling coalition since joining the *Likud* government in 1977, and is part of the Government of National Unity (taking five seats in 1988). In many ways it has come to replace *Mafdal* as the main religious party in Israeli politics.

Although *Agudat Israel* has been the major force for religious change during its time in government for the last 12 years, it still has a rather unclear policy on full political involvement. *Agudat Israel* rejects the notion that "real" values can come from society and accepts only those based on its authoritative tradition of the interpretation of religious texts. The party both refuses to fully recognize the legitimacy of the government of the "secular" state and yet works within it. As directed by its ruling Council of Torah Sages, *Agudat Israel* will not accept collective cabinet responsibility nor government ministries, but it does chair major government committees and after joining the present government coalition in 1988 it accepted the position of Deputy Minister of Labour and Social Affairs. Although still most active concerning issues of religious concern (abortion, the restriction of archeological digs, the call for a national Sabbath law, a ban on female conscription and the legal issues of Jewish identity), it has shown recent signs of a recovery of its earlier programme for a *torah*-state. This is most clearly manifest in the party's *volte face*, with its new hardline on the occupied territories ("not an inch") in the 1988 elections, in large part due to the influence and support of Menahem Schneerson, the Rebbe (spiritual leader) of the Brooklyn-based Lubavitch Hasidic sect.

The most unexpected result of the 1988 election was the taking of six seats by the ultra-orthodox, *Shas* (*Sephardi Torah* Observance) Party, thus doubling its representation and making it the largest religious party in the *knesset*. This highlights both the strength of religious support among the *Sephardim* and also the significance of the ethnic factor, in that the party was founded in 1984 by former members of *Agudat Israel*, dissatisfied with the *Sephardi* representation in that party (the Council of *Torah* Sages conducts business in Yiddish, the majority of funding has been used for *Ashkenazi* institutions and separate ethnic party lists have been operating at the municipal level since 1983). Although sharing many positions with *Agudat Israel*, *Shas* has a much broader view of its potential constituency and is less hawkish concerning the occupied territories. During *Shas*' coalition partnership in the 1984–1988 Government of National Unity, the party leader, Rabbi Yitzhak Peretz, resigned in 1987 over the registration of an American Reform convert to Judaism as a Jew on her identity card. As a member of the current Government of National Unity (from 1988 to the present), *Shas* controls the important Interior and Absorption ministries.

Closely related to *Shas*, and comprised of the followers of one of its major spiritual leaders, Rabbi Shach, is a new Ashkenazi ultra-orthodox party, *Degel Torah* (*Torah* Flag). Created just before the last election (1988), it took two seats. *Degel Torah's* support may in part be explained by Menahem Schneerson's influence on the *Agudat Israel's* 1988 campaign resulting in a more strident position on the occupied territories, a position which is in marked contrast to the more moderate views of the Lubavitch Rebbe's great rabbinic rival, Rabbi Shach.

## Extra-parliamentary "parties"

There are a number of religious movements which are not organized as political parties and yet have major and direct influence on Israeli politics.

The largely *Ashkenazi, Edah Haredit* ((God) Fearful Community) is made up of a number of Hasidic and other East European ultra-orthodox communities. These groups are characterized by the strict observance of the *mitzvot*, rabbinic leadership, *yeshivah*-centered lives, separatist Yiddish-speaking communities, anti-Zionism and their almost total lack of accommodation of the modern State of Israel, which they hold to be a sinful pre-messianic presumption. The three ultra-orthodox parties (*Agudat Israel, Shas* and *Degel Torah*) represent the elements within the *haredi* communities that have reached some degree of such accommodation and are referred to by many commentators as the *haredi* parties.

The most vocal of these *haredi* groups is the *Neturei Karta* (Guardians of the City), who refuse to speak Hebrew — the holy tongue — as a vernacular; will not use Israeli currency; would prefer to live under Palestinian Arab rule, and "celebrate" Israel's Independence Day as a day of mourning. The

*Edah Haredi* accuse the *Agudat Israel* and other ultra-orthodox parties of compromise, and this application of moral pressure restricts the political activities of these parties much as the pressure from *Agudat Israel* limits the political freedom of *Mafdal*.

A second group are the strictly Orthodox settlers. The major settlement group is *Gush Emunim* (Bloc of the Faithful), founded in 1974 (although its origins date back to the *Gahalet* youth group in 1952). It is held to be "the major extra-parliamentary force within Israel", and its members, after supporting *Likud* in 1977, have since then voted for a variety of parties. They represent a faction developing out of *Mafdal* and number only around 2,000. No other group has raised the core issues of the meaning of the Jewish State and the relationship between Zionism and Judaism so forcefully.

*Gush Emunim* offers a theological "answer" to the tensions between traditional Orthodox Judaism and modern secular Zionism — "there is no Zionism without Judaism and no Judaism without Zionism". This "answer" is based on the teachings of the spiritual leader of the *Merkaz Harav Yeshivah*, Rabbi Avraham Yitzhak Kook, and his son and successor, Rabbi Zvi Yehuda Kook. The major figures in the *Gahalet* group were students at the *yeshivah* and it represents the link between this group and the *Gush Emunim*.

Rabbi A. Y. Kook, the first *Ashkenazi* chief rabbi of Palestine, taught that the apparently secular activities of the Zionist pioneers were, when correctly understood, to be seen as possessing the "hidden spark" of the sacred. In explicating his doctrine of the "sacralization of the secular", he had recourse to a number of analogies, such as the building of the Holy of Holies in the Jerusalem Temple (the Jewish "state") where the holiness was preceded by the activities of "secular" workmen. His "theological" efforts failed to unite the different factions of the *yishuv*. His son, Z. Y. Kook, understood the state to be of ultimate religious significance, and the ingathering of the exiles and the re-establishment of Jewish sovereignty in the land to be signs of the impending redemption. The *Gush Emunim* share their teachers' views of the sanctity of the "whole" land of Israel.

The *Gush Emunim* are generally tolerant of the secularists and understand the present state of Israel to be "the kingdom in the making", although they insist that God's law always takes precedence over the democratic process. They seek to unite the different elements of Jewish Israel by their practical activities, that is, the establishment of religious settlement-communities (illegal and legal) in the occupied territories ("divinely mandated Israel"), and see themselves as the true pioneer heirs to the labour–Zionist pioneers. Their settlement plans have been both supported and opposed by the two major political parties. However, *Gush Emunim* elements have been involved in "terrorist" activities against Arabs, and their supra-historical, "Biblical" appreciation of the current situation has led them to see a war between "the sons of Amelek" (the Arabs) and "the children of Israel" as a necessary stage in the coming of the redemption. They hold that Palestinians can have no rights over the land, and understand them in terms of the Biblical concept of "strangers in the land". The combination of their emotive call for a revival of *halutziut* (pioneering) values (personal hardship, lack of materialism, collective spirit, etc.), harkening back to the foundational days of the pre-state settlement, and their "solution", which stands in marked contrast to the dearth of alternatives, has a broad appeal to Israeli Jews and a considerable influence on the political policies of the major parties. Their influence and appeal has only been enhanced by the recent, wide-scale insecurity generated by the *intifada*.

## Testing the *status quo*

Three factors have allowed the religious parties to exert an influence far exceeding their numerical and electoral strength: (i) the system of proportional representation and the specific conditions, particularly from 1949 until 1984, favouring a series of coalitions in which the major party has been dependent upon the support of the religious parties in order to secure a majority; (ii) the "inheritance" of the millet-system from the British Mandate, later established in Israeli law as the SQA; and (iii) the lack of certainty on the part of the non-religious parties, as to the part that religious traditions and values are to play in the life of the Jewish State.

In Israel's short history, the most frequent cause of political crisis and the subsequent collapse of government coalitions has been the withdrawal of the religious parties over religious issues. In the past, both at national and local levels, the religious parties have used their coalition-power to secure the passing of religious legislation, such as the Pork Prohibition Law (1961). With each new government, the funds available for religious institutions has increased and there are now tens of thousands of full-time *yeshivah* students who are funded by the state. Under the auspices of the SQA, all state institutions observe the Sabbath and Jewish religious holidays, and in the army, each unit has a rabbi, portable synagogue and Orthodox officers, and officially observe religious feasts and fasts. The chief rabbinate and the religious courts have considerable power over individual lives and the religious parties have ensured their influence over education, religion and the legal system. Their monopoly on the issuing of the required *kashrut* (dietary law) licences has been used to insist on further Sabbath restrictions.

From 1949 until 1977, *Mafdal's* policy was to maintain the SQA and to push for piecemeal "extensions" of the same. Since 1977, with the inclusion of *Agudat Israel* in the government, a policy of securing such "extensions" has been pursued, although critics claim that *Agudat Israel* invokes the SQA only to preserve existing legislation and not when attempting to extend the same. The set of specific religious issues has remained remarkably constant during the last 41 years, and crises have been precipitated by either the non-religious or religious seeking to test the SQA.

The demands made by the religious parties as the price for support of *Likud* in forming a coalition government, following the 1988 election, gives an excellent indication of such issues. The religious parties called for an extension of the Sabbath and Jewish religious holiday legislation; further state funding for religious institutions, without further state control; further exemptions from military service for *yeshivah* students; and the application of religious law in the determination of Jewish identity, in particular, the recognition of only Orthodox conversions to Judaism. In addition, the demands from the ultra-Orthodox included (as in 1977 and 1984) limits on post-mortem examinations; easier exemption of religious women from military service; tightening of the policy on abortions and pornography; extension of religious facilities such as ritual bath-houses; and further laws limiting the production and sale of non-kosher food. These demands have not changed greatly during the life of the State.

The "Who is A Jew?" debate has been the major source of religious/non-religious tension since the creation of the State. This issue has led *Mafdal* to withdraw from a number of governments. Potentially, the debate has the gravest consequences, in that it could split the fragile unity of the Jewish population into a number of separate, non-marrying camps. According to the *halakhah*, one born of a Jewish mother or converted to Judaism is a Jew. The religious parties, invoking the SQA, insist that as this is a matter of person status, it falls within their sole jurisdiction. The Israeli Orthodox authorities refuse to recognize the validity of non-Orthodox, modern forms of Judaism — Reform and Conservative Judaism — and do not accept the authority of these rabbis. These movements constitute the majority of diaspora Jews, who vigorously oppose the "Orthodox monopoly" and what they see as the absurdity of the chief rabbinate of Israel, recognizing Islam and Christianity, but not other forms of Judaism. Although the Orthodox in the diaspora and in Israel recognize individual Reform and Conservative Jews as Jews, if they satisfy the *halakhic* definition, they do not accept that non-Jews converted by rabbis of these movements are Jews. Thus many thousands of mainly American Jews are not recognized as such in Israel. In addition, Conservative and Reform divorces are not acceptable to the Orthodox, so that tens of thousands of Jews are considered illegitimate and technically subject to the marriage and other restrictions of this category.

There are Israeli (secular) laws which apply specifically to Jews, such as the Law of Return (1950) and the Nationality Law (1952). These statutes grant every Jew the right to reside in Israel and be granted Israeli citizenship. In a series of crisis-precipitating court cases, the secular authorities have determined definitions of "Jew" at odds with the *halakhic* requirements, and have ruled that persons who do not satisfy the Orthodox stipulations be registered as "Jews". In an attempt to resolve the issue in 1970, it was agreed that the *halakhic* definition would stand, but there was no determination that conversion to Judaism need be *halakhic*, so that non-Orthodox converts would still be able to benefit from the Law of Return. The Orthodox want to add the words "according to the *halakhah*" to these laws, thus limiting acceptable conversions to those carried out by Orthodox authorities. A condition of the 1981 and 1984 coalition agreements between *Agudat Israel* and *Likud* was an agreement to launch bills that would give the Orthodox this control of citizenship. However, these bills were defeated on a number of occasions, including July 1987 and June 1988. Raised as a coalition demand again, following the 1988 election, it led to protests in Israel and America, where there was also the threat of the withdrawal of non-Orthodox funding for Israel. These actions, plus the potential damage of a permanent split between large sections of the diaspora and Israel, were a major factor in *Likud's* forming of a Government of National Unity rather than a coalition with the Orthodox parties. In July 1989, in response to the *Shas*-controlled Interior Ministry, the Israeli Supreme Court ruled that non-Orthodox converts can benefit from the Law of Return and are to be registered as Jews.

The "Who is a Jew?" issue has also been raised in connection with the immigration of groups of Jews into Israel. The chief rabbinate has objected to the Jewish status of the Bene Israel of Bombay (1961), the Karaites (1971) and most recently, the Falashas (Ethiopian Jews, 1984), and each time, after public pressure and *knesset* debates, has finally recognized the Jewish status of these groups.

Since 1977, *Agudat Israel* has secured a number of changes in the law: so that it is easier for Orthodox girls to gain exemption from conscription (increasing actual exemptions by 10 per cent, together with greater numbers of *yeshivah* exemptions); the funding for religious institutions has increased by more than 350 per cent; abortions may no longer be performed in private hospitals or on the grounds of "sociological considerations"; increased state-housing for the religious; and in 1982, after a "strike" by employees of the national airline, El Al, concerned about job and profit losses, succeeded in stopping all flights on the Sabbath. It was the fear of the further religious legislation outlined in the religious parties' 1988 coalition demands that brought thousands of Israelis onto the streets protesting at the possibilities of a "theocracy", forcing *Likud* into an agreement with *Maarah*. While the *Likud–Maarah* coalition includes the four religious parties, it does so within a much larger coalition, thus greatly limiting the force of their demands.

Since 1977 it is clear that the religious parties have tried to promote religious legislation that cannot be incorporated into the non-religious sectors' ideological vision of the Jewish state.

## Israel's non-Jewish population

Israel's Arab voters number nearly a third of a million (Druze (8 per cent), Christians (15 per cent), and Sunni Muslims (77 per cent)) and account for approximately 18 per cent of the electorate. Historically, Israeli Arabs have been active participants in the electoral process and although numerically their vote could yield 15 or more seats, the communities are divided. From 1948 until 1964 the dominant *Mapai* party ran an Arab section in its list and received the support of some 60 per cent of Arab voters with six or seven Arabs regularly being elected. Although there is still substantial Arab support for *Maarah*, it can no longer command that majority.

In 1988 the Arab Democratic List (Arab candidates only) gained one seat, the Democratic Front for Peace and Equality, led by *Rakah* (Israel Communist Party), gained four seats and the Progressive Peace List, the Arab-led non-Zionist communist party, gained one seat. These last two parties, although mainly supported by Arabs, included Arabs and Jews on their lists. All three of these parties support the return of territories captured in 1967, the establishment of a Palestinian State and negotiations with the PLO. In the last two elections (1984 and 1988) there has been a clear indication that the Arab vote is being cast for Arab parties. Although in recent years the Palestine Liberation Organization has advocated an Arab boycott of the Israeli elections, in 1988 the PLO called upon Arabs to vote and some 75 per cent of them did so.

In recent years, both inside Israel and in the captured territories, the Arab Christian community (some 90 per cent of Israeli Christians) has become more closely identified with the Palestinian struggle, and its leaders consciously designated as "*Palestinian* Christians".

The Muslim community has felt the influence of "Islamic fundamentalism" in both its Sunni and Shia forms, and the *intifada* (since December 1987) in the captured territories has received wide support from Israeli Muslims, particularly amongst the young. In 1980 the "Young Muslims" association, inspired and funded by Ayatollah Khomeini's Iranian revolution, was established in Israel. This group is opposed to Israel, Arab nationalist groups, and the

Communist Party, on religious grounds. The proclamation of a Palestinian State — "in the name of *Allah*, with its capital Holy Jerusalem, al–Quds a-sharif" — made by the PLO in Algiers in 1988, has had an effect on Arabs in Israel, and has been the impetus for greater political activism.

In September of 1988, in Gaza, a new Islamic "fundamentalist" group arose in opposition to the leaders of the *intifada* and the PLO. This group, known as *Hamas* (Movement for Islamic Resistance) has become a major force in Gaza and is supported by Muslims in the West Bank (Judea and Samaria) and in Israel. It is a Sunni organization, tracing its roots back to the Egyptian Muslim Brotherhood, which has long been active in Gaza, and the more recent Islam War Organization. The *Hamas Covenant* (1988) calls on all Palestinian Muslims to wage *jihad* (holy war) on Israel as the only solution to the Palestinian problem. It advocates the creation of an Islamic state in Palestine and commands opposition to the PLO until it accepts Islam. *Hamas*' aim of establishing an Islamic state is violently opposed by Palestinian Christians, both in Israel and in the territories.

Although the Arab community in Israel is fragmented into Christian and Muslim communities, each with its own factions, there is a discernible move among young Muslims of the West Bank and Gaza towards strident forms of Islam. These developments will compromise Israeli peace efforts and are beginning to have an effect on the Muslim community inside Israel.

## The limits of "pluralistic legitimation"

Although the tensions between the non-religious and religious seem to be growing, and appear to threaten to fracture the unity of the Jewish people in Israel, these tensions must be seen in the context of an equally serious threat — that of continued Israeli security in the "war" against the Arabs. The major issues in the last two elections have been related to foreign affairs and the future of the occupied territories. The 1984 election was staged in the shadow of the Lebanese War coupled with hyper-inflation, and the 1988 elections took place amidst the daily killings of the *intifada*. Whether the responses to these issues are religious or non-religious, the maintenance of Jewish unity is of supreme importance and tends to suppress the implications of ideological and religious differences.

A second factor responsible for the perpetual delay of the long prophesied *Kulturkämpf* is the structure of Israeli society. The number of staunch anti-religious secularists is comparatively small and the calls to make Israel a secular state receive little public support. On the other hand, the Orthodox and ultra-Orthodox sector is also a minority and, in spite of its growing stridency, remains at around 20 per cent of the Jewish population. Also, the continued level of the political power of the religious parties is already in doubt with the recent successful first reading of a bill proposing electoral change from 1992, by dividing the country into 10 constituencies, while still allowing for half the *knesset* seats to be filled by proportional representation. This leaves the vast majority of the Israeli Jewish population which fits into neither of these extreme camps. Although some 40 per cent of Israeli Jews see themselves as *hiloni* (secularists), they generally observe the major Jewish religious festivals and many attend synagogue, even if their reasons are more "cultural" than religious. A further 40 per cent can be classified as *masorati* (traditionalists), those that subscribe to Jewish religious values and maintain beliefs and practices, but in a less than total fashion. Both these groups would be considered "religious" in most Western countries.

While more than 90 per cent of Jewish Israelis believe that Israel should be a Jewish State, it is not clear what should constitute the Jewish nature of this Jewish state. The religious parties, however, have an answer and wield a power much greater than their numerical strength, by continuously raising the issues that lie at the heart of the whole Jewish revival in the land of Israel, the meaning of the return, the land, and of Jewish destiny. They ensure that the nation does not become complacent by keeping these issues near the top of the national agenda. While the tensions between Jewish politics and Jewish religious values go back to the conflicts between the prophets and kings of ancient Israel, the state represents a new departure for Jews. A theocracy or a secular state are equally untenable, and a mono-linear Jewish path into uncharted waters is checked by the religious parties.

The nature of Israeli society is rapidly changing and the gap that has existed since the beginnings of Zionism between the religious conception of the *torah*-state and a majority Jewish democratic secular society is unbridgeable — a gap maintained by the enshrined system of separate education and culture. But a healthy situation obtains whereby these two radically opposed sides coexist, not on the basis of a common core (beyond the vaguest notions of supreme importance of the land, people and its history), but by the inclusion in their versions of Israel of specific policies and programmes, by a process of what we might call "pluralistic legitimation". That is, that the "same" policies and principles were interpreted radically differently by the different groups so that each group could legitimize its own programme by the incorporation of policies as consistent with its own overall programme. For example: settlement is understood as part of "the ingathering of the exiles" by the non-religious, by *Mizrahi* and *Agudat Israel* as the fulfilment of a *mitzvah* (divine commandment) or as messianic; the incorporation of Jewish religious norms into Jewish life in Israel is understood by the secularists as pragmatic concessions to the Orthodox in the interests of Jewish unity, but for the religious as the next stage in their programme for the *torah*-state; and the religious authority for such religious incorporations is held as being from God, while the secularists see it as derived from the democratic process. There is a fine line between agreements, such as the SQA, which can be pluralistically legitimized, and the over-stepping of that line to those that cannot, as in the case of the constitution. However, the system of pluralistic legitimization is dynamic and is constantly tested by both the religious and non-religious, reflecting the changes in Israeli society, and new working limits are being established, allowing for co-operation and even pre-messianic progress.

### Notes

[1] Hebrew words are rendered into English in their frequently used forms, but this is not linguistically consistent, so e.g. *Yitzhak* but *Agudat Israel*. *Newsweek,* 14 November 1988.

[2] E.g. the Israeli journal, *Politica* 2, 1989, on the crisis in the relationship between Israel's religious and non-religious Jews.

Paul Morris

# ITALY

The overwhelming majority (98 per cent) of Italy's 57.2 million inhabitants are nominally Roman Catholic. The head of the Catholic Church in Italy is Pope John Paul II, Bishop of Rome since 1978. Politically, the country has had a coalition government throughout the post-war period, which has been almost continuously headed by the Christian Democratic Party (DC). The period since the beginning of 1987 has been one of considerable activity. This is in part the unavoidable consequence of the high profile which religion necessarily has in the routine of Italian politics, and in part the result of long-running difficulties between the Vatican and Italy over particular issues.

The most important event in the first category was the general election of June 1987. Parliament was dissolved early, after the government led by Bettino Craxi (PSI) had had great difficulty in getting its budget approved by Parliament; the problems were largely caused by so-called "snipers" among the DC backbenchers using the secret ballot to defeat policies officially supported by their own party. This was in protest at the continued reluctance of Craxi to stand down in favour of the DC.

The election campaign was widely regarded as one of remarkable dullness. It was however characterized by a clear effort on the part of the DC secretary, Ciriaco De Mita, to reassert his party's links with the Church, which in the previous election campaign (1983) he had distinctly played down. In 1987 this new warmth for Catholic voters showed itself particularly in his stance on salient religious issues such as education and abortion, but also in his willingness to support a more centrist policy on state spending. The change in the religious climate was also indicated by the relatively outspoken intervention of the National Bishops' Conference (CEI), which called on voters "to remain loyal to the Italian Catholic tradition".

The Socialists and Communists steadfastly refuse to be engaged in political debate on particular religious topics. The PSI managed with some success the difficult trick (hitherto a specialty of the DC) of claiming credit for a period of governmental stability while denying responsibility for major problems such as the very large and increasing public sector deficit. The dullness of the campaign and the relative salience of macro-economic issues could not conceal the combativeness of the activist Catholic wing of the DC and the increasing concern of traditional Catholics at the pace of secularization in public life, to which De Mita was in part responding. The most important element within this grouping is *Communione e Liberazione* (CL), an evangelical Catholic group first established in the 1960s, which after these elections claimed to be worth one million votes to the DC. If this is so, they could claim credit for about 7 per cent of the DC vote, and 15 deputies. These figures are certainly exaggerated, but CL should not be ignored. Probably no more than six DC deputies are directly reliant on CL, for CL is an exclusive group; it requires strict standards of religious and political discipline from its associates, which few deputies could or would meet. But a far larger number of DC deputies have to acknowledge the electoral influence of the CL network and would not wish to fall foul of it.

The electoral system (PR, with a party list vote and personal preference votes) encourages factional developments of this kind. Also, the development of CL as a Catholic ginger group within the DC indicates the extent to which the Christian Democrat party as a whole has lost its distinctly religious identity. The DC is shedding its traditional reliance on religious-based support and has become reluctant to associate itself wholeheartedly with Catholic social policy. The 1987 election marked a slowing down of this process, but it is unlikely that it can be halted or reversed. The election results rewarded the DC with a slight improvement on their 1983 vote. The big winners were the PSI, who increased their vote by 3 per cent, a massive increase by Italian standards, largely at the expense of the Communists, who lost nearly 4 per cent and recorded their worst result for over 20 years.

The other category of religious issues is those which spring up often at politically-sensitive times such as government crises or elections and which serve to embarrass one or other side for a limited period. The best known of these is the series of scandals associated with the collapse of the Banco Ambrosiano in 1982, involving the Vatican Bank (IOR), the senior Vatican financial manager Archbishop Paul Marcinkus, the secret freemason lodge P2 and a considerable number of middle-ranking politicians and bureaucrats. On February 26, 1987, the Milan public prosecutor issued warrants for the arrest of Marcinkus and two other IOR officials, although as residents of the Vatican the three claimed to be outside Italian jurisdiction. The move was clearly timed to embarrass the Christian Democrats in the middle of a government crisis. In fact the Socialist-led government resigned on March 3, 1987. Italy's highest ordinary court, the Court of Cassation, annulled the warrants after the elections, citing the Lateran Pacts of 1929 even though these had been superseded for most purposes by the new Concordat of 1984. The Vatican has persistently maintained that Marcinkus as well as being innocent of wrongdoing is not punishable in any case in Italian law. After a suitably lengthy interval, Marcinkus resigned his post as chairman of IOR in March 1989, and was appointed to the more formal duties of Governor of the Vatican city state. The Vatican however had already acknowledged its financial responsibility in the Banco Ambrosiano bankruptcy by agreeing to pay $250 million to the Bank of Italy in settlement of outstanding debts.

One of the issues left unresolved by the 1989 Concordat was religious education. In December 1985 Franca Falcucci, the DC Minister of Education at the time, agreed with the Vatican that religious education or its alternative should be a compulsory part of the school day. In view of the difficulty of providing appropriate and acceptable alternatives, this was regarded by those opposed to Religious Education (RE) as making the subject virtually compulsory. However, a government directive implementing this in September 1987 specified that it should be timetabled at the beginning or end of the day, which would have the effect of discouraging attendance and would diminish its status. The CEI protested, and in October 1987 a socialist-led compromise was agreed which affirmed that the teaching hour for RE was indeed compulsory, though RE itself and the alternative "atheist class" were both optional. The precise timetabling was to be left to local officials. This typically vague compromise excited the suspicions both of the radical lay groups and of the conservative Catholics. In March 1989 the Constitutional Court overturned an earlier ruling by the Council of State that RE and its alternative were compulsory. The CEI again complained, this time of grave risks, to the new Concordat. The episode, though almost certainly not the series, closed with a government motion in Parliament in May 1989 affirming its support for the Concordat and for the principle of equal status for religion in schools. This was supported by the DC and the PSI against the minor governing parties including the Liberals and Republicans.

In the same pre-crisis period of February 1987, Craxi also reached agreement with Italian Jewish representatives for the repeal of discriminatory laws dating from the fascist period. The agreement assured Italy's approximately 40,000 Jews of future legislation covering respect for the Jewish religion in military service, in public hospitals and in marriage law.

In May 1989 an intense and public controversy occurred most unusually within the Italian Catholic hierarchy itself. The Bishops of southern Italy, led by the newly-promoted Cardinal Archbishop of Naples Michele Giordano, supported a report calling for ecclesiastical sanctions against the Mafia and other organized criminals. The resolution had the support in general terms of the Pope, and was accompanied by a statement from Giordano acknowledging the past silence of the Church on the issue. At the same time, the influential Jesuit commentator Fr Bartolomeo Sorge proposed an "anti-Mafia pastorate" of all 18 dioceses in Sicily. These initiatives aroused the objections of the Cardinal Archbishop of Palermo Salvatore Pappalardo. Pappalardo has a strong record of speaking out against the Mafia even at times when the cause was less popular, but in an interview in the leading Catholic daily *Avvenire* he referred to the Mafiosi as "criminal Christians" who had been baptised and confirmed in the Church and who needed not sanctions but the Church's ministry.

Finally, on July 23, 1989, Italy's 48th government crisis since the war was resolved. The crisis was caused by the resignation of the Prime Minister Ciriaco De Mita in May 1989. The new government was led by a 70-year-old DC politician whose record spans the entire post-war period. Giulio Andreotti was Under-Secretary to the Cabinet in the first DC-led post-war government, and since 1945 has occupied all the major offices of state. A former activist in Catholic Action and friend of the late Pope Paul VI, Andreotti has close links with the Italian hierarchy and is widely regarded as one of the most astute and powerful politicians in Italy. Despite his Catholic background, he has not generally favoured the radical Catholic groups, and he will be particularly watched for his responses to the problems of religious education and abortion. An early indication of the future development of abortion policy was provided by the appointment of a new Health Minister. Francesco De Lorenzo is a Liberal Deputy with a professional background as a surgeon in Naples. He replaces an assertive opponent of abortion, the DC trade-unionist Carlo Donat-Cattin.

Paul Furlong

JAMAICA 141

# JAMAICA

Numerous Christian groupings are represented amongst Jamaica's 2.5 million people, including Anglicans, Methodists, Presbyterians, numerous pentecostal and evangelical denominations, and Rastafarianism.
Pentecostal and Evangelical growth has been dramatic in the past two decades, with charismatic practice affecting Catholic and "mainstream" Protestant churches (represented by the Jamaica Council of Churches) as well. Since the mid 1970s there has been tacit alliance between the conservative Jamaica Labour Party (JLP) and its leader Edward Seaga and with the rapidly expanding conservative evangelical community (often represented by the Jamaica Association of Evangelists). A campaign by US evangelist Lowell Lundstrom was cancelled in June 1987 when the then opposition People's National Party (PNP) uncovered promotional material claiming the "gospel invasion" would help prevent communism in Jamaica. In late 1986, the PNP joined Church leaders in supporting a government decision to stop plans for casino construction. The Rastafarian movement, numbering about a hundred thousand, is currently going through a transition and its direct political influence, particularly on the PNP, has ironically declined as it has become more acceptable.
Mid-1987 witnessed Marxist/Christian debates at the University of the West Indies involving academics and Protestant theologians, at which the Anglican bishop was present. An article attacking liberation theology in the *Daily Gleaner* sparked off the debate. After a year of debate, the Jamaican Senate granted tax-exempt status to the Mormon Church in March 1988.
The Catholic Church claims about 7 per cent of the population (1984 est.) and its Archbishop, Samuel Carter, has been politically outspoken, attacking Seaga's *laissez-faire* policies in a 1987 pastoral letter and affirming labour rights in 1988. In March 1989, the Catholic hierarchy called for an end to capital punishment.
Elections held in February 1989 returned Michael Manley's social democratic PNP to power after nine years of JLP rule. Manley's earlier radicalism moderated in the interim. Church leaders had joined in a call in late 1988 for an agreement between the two major parties to avoid the widespread violence which had marked the 1980 elections.

Virgil Wiebe

# JAPAN

Those who think of Japanese religion as a couple of monoliths — Shinto and Buddhism — existing in a sea of materialist apathy have a case. But the simplicity of this view is belied by the sheer diversity of religious phenomena which is revealed by the most casual glance at the daily press. Readers of Carmen Blacker's *The Catalpa Bow* will not be surprised to learn that shamanism is alive and well and living in Okinawa. Most, if not all, of the Okinawa shamans, or *yuta* as they are called, are women, who rid houses of undesirable gods for a fee of ¥20,000 and a bag of food, and come to their vocation in their early 40s when the gods enter them (*kami sama ga hairu*).[1] At the other end of the archipelago, in Hokkaido, a French Trappist establishment dating back to the 1890s, is flourishing: the last of the French monks died in 1960, but they left behind a prosperous community, owning gardens and orchards, which is now exclusively Japanese.

An increase in cults is hardly a new phenomenon in Japanese society, but there is a considerable growth not so much in the main stream cults — Tenrikyō, Sōka Gakkai, Risshō Kōseikai, and so on — but in marginal ones which emphasize forms of magic and occultism and offer escapes from the stresses of a materialistic and highly-regulated society. Psychotherapy, not salvation, is the motivation and the levels affected are not simply the deprived: two-thirds of students in a 1987 poll said they believed in spells and psychic powers. An example of one such cult is the Sekai Mahikari Bunmei Kyōdan, founded in 1959, based in Shizuoka Prefecture but with 160 branches elsewhere and a worldwide membership of 200,000. Vast sums of money seem to be available for this cult to build itself a massive shrine in Shizuoka which makes a contrast to the straitened circumstances in which one might be led to believe some major Kyoto temples exist.[2]

A few years ago, some of these — among them very well-known temples like Kinkakuji, Ginkakuji, Nisonin — went to court to seek relief from the payment of ¥100 million, the "ancient city preservation tax" demanded by the municipality. The temples based their case on the grounds that this violated the freedom of worship guaranteed by the post-war constitution. The temples have, of course, considerable financial muscle. By exercising a threat to close, they could deprive hundreds of stall-holders of a living and drastically cut Kyoto's tourist income.

But an even more intractable conflict between religion and the state, or at least religion and the judiciary, arose in the summer of 1988, when the 15 judges of the Supreme Court handed down a verdict against a Christian woman who had protested against ceremonies carried out on behalf of her husband according to Shinto rites. Mrs Nakaya was married to an officer in the Self-Defence Forces who was killed in 1968 in a car accident while on duty. She had him buried in a Christian church in Yamaguchi, but the SDF regional authorities notified her that his soul was to be enshrined in the Gokoku (Protector of the Country) Shrine in Yamaguchi Prefecture. The ceremony went ahead despite her passionate objections that her husband's soul was already being looked after by her church. As the ceremony was privately organized by an SDF support body, not the SDF itself, the judges ruled that the enshrinement was not a state act and therefore no conflict arose between state and religion. They dismissed the widow's claim for ¥1 million damages. A leader in the *Japan Times* said that unconcern, rather than tolerance, is the commonest Japanese attitude to religion; which was acceptable, provided that it did not leave the way open to revival of State Shinto, "that pseudoreligion of an authoritarian, egoistic Japan isolated from reason and the world itself. Politics, not religion, is the name of the game. And this brand of it is too dangerous to tolerate".[3]

That Japanese are still sensitive to this particular area of the interface between religion and politics is abundantly clear from the reaction to the most significant event in the sphere of religion or politics of the last decade, the death of the Emperor Hirohito on January 7, 1989. The 62-year reign had seen Japan pass from tentative democracy in the 1920s to economic depression and militarist takeover of the civilian government in the 1930s and early 1940s, and to disastrous war and defeat; followed for the past four decades by an immense national effort at rehabilitation and the attainment of an unpredictable prosperity and economic power.

It would be a very bold historian who tried to establish cause and effect between the vicissitudes of the past six decades and the presence on the Japanese throne of the Emperor Hirohito. On the other hand, the Japanese themselves are aware that the outside world has views on the Emperor's role which are not derived from Japanese sources and do not correspond to the Japanese context at all. So that role has itself been modified in response to tacit or open outside pressure. Article IV of the Meiji Constitution defined the Emperor as "the head of the Empire", which made him an organ of the state as the head is an organ of the body. On the other hand, Article III declared "The Emperor is sacred and inviolable". There was a clear conflict of interests here, between a modified constitutional monarchy on the Prussian model, and a sacral state, a conflict symbolized by the persecution in the 1930s of the learned and courageous law professor Minobe Tatsukichi for propounding the theory that the Emperor was an organ of the state. He was hounded in the press and the Diet by militarists like General Baron Kikuchi for whom the absolutism of imperial rule was a necessary reinforcement of their own schemes of military aggrandizement. As Kikuchi put it in the House of Peers (February 1934):

> Merely to think of our Emperor as the same as the Chinese Emperor or any western sovereign is to forfeit the secret of our national polity. If we do not stamp out the thought of scholars and politicians who hold these views, the future of our nation will be threatened.[4]

These were the voices which led Japan into a war from which the Emperor, acting against his normal constitutional practice, rescued his country by transcending the impasse into which the soldiers and statesmen had led her, and ordering the acceptance of the Allied peace terms.

Much western discussion, particularly in the popular press (even in recent months) has been vitiated by the inability to cope with this sacral concept. The Emperor's so-called "divinity", i.e. his nature as "kami", a being set apart from others by reason of some vaguely numinous quality to do with descent or function, has nothing whatever in common with western notions of God as creator of the Universe and so on. There are "kami" in stones, trees, cemeteries, and distinguished artistic gifts. It is when the notion of the exclusive "kami" nature of the Japanese Emperor is linked with the overseas expansion of a unique people, militarized for the purpose, that the need for a reform of vocabulary becomes evident.[5]

Japan's war in Asia became a holy war, and in the conquered territories Shinto shrines were erected as a matter of course. The so-called liberation of Asia from western domination went *pari passu* with the enslavement of common life in terms of the most ridiculous detail, as in the regulations for office workers in Indonesia:

> One must put on one's hat correctly, not at an angle. The hat should be two inches above the two ears.
> It is not permitted to sit with one's mouth open, lest one be considered empty-headed.
> When we have no work to do we must read regulations concerning our work . . .

These Pecksniffian objugations would be bad enough in themselves; but they are always accompanied by an indication of the supposed sacral source of such authority:

> During every conversation in which the name Tennō Heika (His Imperial Majesty) occurs, one must stand at attention.[6]

The surrender of August 1945 therefore brought about not simply the liberation of the Japanese people from a repressive militarization of their religious traditions, but also freed the peoples of the Asian continent from what a recent Japanese study of war-time occupation has termed *shinsei kokka Nihon* (sacred-nation-Japan), opposition to which was not merely a political or military act but sacrilege.[7] The liberation from this misinterpretation of a burdensome past was the humanity proclamation, or *ningen sengen* of January 1, 1946, in which the Emperor renounced false conceptions of his divinity. "The ties between us and our people", the proclamation ran, "have always stood upon mutual trust and affection. They do not depend upon mere legends and myths. They are not predicated on the false conception that the Emperor is divine, and that the Japanese people are superior to other races and destined to rule the world".[8]

It is still a matter for debate whether this fateful rejection was initiated by the emperor himself in consultation with the Imperial Household Ministry, or by the offices of the Supreme Commander, Allied Powers (i.e. General MacArthur). What is certain is that the go-between between MacArthur and the Household Ministry was the English Zen and *haiku* scholar, R. H. Blyth, who had lived in internment during the war in Japan and on release had worked as a teacher of English at the Peers' School (Gakushūin) where the present Emperor was educated. The Principal of the Gakushūin at the time was Admiral Yamanashi Katsunoshin, an anglophile who had worked in Barrow-in-Furness at the beginning of the century when the Japanese Navy had ships built at the Vickers shipyards there. It is said that Yamanashi had Blyth enquire from his friends at MacArthur's headquarters what the reaction would be to a declaration of the Emperor's ordinary human nature. This was undertaken at a time, December 1945, when the Imperial Household Agency was looking for safeguards for the Imperial constitution, a time when an Imperial prince — Prince Nashimoto Morimasa — had been arrested as a war criminal, and it did not seem at all unlikely that the Emperor himself would be indicted before the International War Crimes Tribunal for the Far East.

An American Colonel Henderson, himself a translator of *haiku* and an admirer of Blyth, discussed the matter with him, and, as he remembers it, concocted a formula the Emperor could use. This was revised by Blyth and specifically stated: "His Majesty disavows entirely any deification or mythologizing of his own Person". The Education Minister, Maeda Tamon, then drafted a Japanese version of it, which was in turn rendered back into English for public consumption by the Premier, Shidehara. Yamanashi insisted that the original Henderson draft be burned. Professor Hirakawa Sukehiro, who has published an account of Yamanashi and Blyth and their connection with the *ningen sengen* has this to say about the substance of the declaration:

> Has Hirohito ever been a God–Emperor to the Japanese? I don't think he has. The English expression "God–Emperor" is itself a Christian analogy. The Shinto notion of *kami* and the Christian notion of God are different. Although there was strong Emperor-worship in war-time Japan, the Japanese did not believe that the Emperor was divine in the Christian meaning. In the Imperial Rescript of 1st January 1946, there is a famous passage: "the false conception that the Emperor is divine". Who held that false conception? War-time Japanese? Or war-time Americans? Although the present Emperor declared four decades ago that he was a human being, I am sure he will be respected as *kami* in Japan by many generations to come. A shrine will surely be built after he passes away. According to Blyth, the Emperor renounced his divinity which he did not have anyway.[9]

It was one thing to clarify a politico-theological issue which apparently didn't need clarification anyway; quite another to fend off the accusation that the Emperor was at the very least as guilty as his ministers in preparing and waging an aggressive war and permitting his forces to carry out atrocities against prisoners of war and conquered peoples; even though the Emperor made it clear, in the Rescript declaring war in December 1941, that the war was against his wishes.[10]

He did not, as far as can be ascertained, initiate planning of any operation. But he did discuss plans submitted to him, and during the Liaison Conferences between Cabinet and Supreme Command in the months running up to Pearl Harbor he certainly intervened with quite well-informed questions on the smaller details of operations, such as weather conditions on the north-east coast of Malaya or the political conditions of Thailand.[11] He was, therefore, privy to what was intended. Similarly, in the course of the war itself, although it may be true that those closest to him in the Household Ministry kept from him some of the more disagreeable facts about his armies' behaviour on the continent of Asia, some of the worst aspects undoubtedly reached him through his own brother, Prince Mikasa, who had spent some time as a staff officer in China and had been so appalled by a Chinese propaganda film about Japanese atrocities that he had brought it back with him to Tokyo and showed it to the Emperor personally.[12]

It seems clear that if General MacArthur, acting on the advice of the Joint Chiefs of Staff (whom he had in turn no doubt advised), had not resolutely ensured the removal of the Emperor's name from the list of persons to be tried by the International Military Tribunal for the Far East, the combined pressures of the other Allied nations represented on the Tribunal would have prevailed. The proceedings were presided over by the Australian judge, Sir William Webb, who remained convinced that the Emperor should have stood trial. MacArthur's reasons were pragmatic. If the Emperor appeared before the Tribunal, he was sure Japan would become ungovernable, there might even be guerrilla warfare, and the Occupation forces might reach two million and have to remain for decades. Far better use a modified imperial system.

In effect, the Emperor's guilt has been tried again and again in books, newspapers and television programmes. One Japanese professor, visiting a conference in England in September 1988 when the Emperor was gravely ill and thought to be on the brink of death, was appalled to find the man he took for the greatest Japanese of the twentieth century being greeted on his death bed by such tabloid headlines as "Hell's Waiting for This Truly Evil Emperor". One does not expect tabloid journalists to be *au fait* with the subtleties of Japanese constitutional history, but there can be little doubt they reflected the mood of a minority of readers whose views on the war had remained stationary since 1941.

Some Japanese who contributed to a massive issue, 764 pages long, of the monthly magazine *Bungei Shunjū* were aware that the omission of the Emperor from the proceedings of the IMFTE had not really provided a verdict of innocent but one of non-proven. The issue of his responsibility for Japan's behaviour in Asia between 1937 and 1945 was raised in an interesting way by a conservative emeritus professor of Tokyo University who in his time had been head of the Japan Foundation, the body whose function it is to interpret Japan to the world. Legally and substantially, Professor Hayashi Kentarō was sure, the Emperor bore no responsibility for the war. On the other hand, it was a fact that great destruction had been wrought by men acting in the Emperor's name, and one might well think that, as a human being — not morally or logically — the Emperor might well feel a sense of responsibility.[13] That was the significance of the celebrated interview with General MacArthur in November 1945, when the Emperor told MacArthur that he took upon himself fully the burden of responsibility of Japan's conduct in the war. MacArthur is said to have been much moved by this confession, made at a time when the possibility of the death penalty was not entirely excluded from the Emperor's future; but in the end it remained a mere statement, and his ministers took the actual burden upon themselves.

But the debate is not between outsiders and the Japanese. It is still an issue debated hotly between Japanese themselves, and it is likely to continue now that the fifty-year gap between the war and the present time is sure to provide fresh evidence, memoirs, letters and so forth, to form opinion in a generation of Japanese for whom the war is not experience but history.

Protests against attempts by both government and media to manipulate and glorify the Imperial role, in the wake of the nation's mourning of January 1989, sometimes took unexpected forms. The succession to the throne, under the Meiji Constitution, was limited to male heirs. This was seen by women's movements as a form of justification of the second-class citizen treatment of women, and in violation of the guarantee, under the post-war constitution, of equality between the sexes. But women's lawyers were not pleading for reform: "It does not mean that we want a woman in the position of the

Emperor. We are calling attention to one of the many irrational aspects of the Imperial system."[14]

This was not the first time the issue had been raised. A woman member of the Diet, Kubota Manae, queried in 1985 at a Diet committee whether limiting the imperial succession to the male line was contrary to the stipulations of the United Nations "Convention on the Elimination of All Forms of Discrimination Against Women" which Japan was about to sign. The then Foreign Minister, Abe Shintarō, replied that the Convention was aimed at securing basic human rights for women, and to succeed the Emperor was not a basic human right.[15]

At the moment this issue can have little more than anecdotal interest. Perhaps the most spectacular intervention on this issue of the responsibility of the Emperor for World War II, inside Japan, was from the mayor of a city of crucial importance: Nagasaki. Its mayor, Motoshima Hitoshi, made a speech on December 7, 1988, in which he declared the Emperor bore responsibility. Given the fact that the Emperor was then near death, it is not surprising that this provoked furious reaction. But Motoshima was unmoved. "Without the freedom to say anything about the Emperor", he riposted, widening the issue, "there will be no progress in Japanese democracy"; and later added that Japan would never gain the confidence of the outside world unless she reflected upon her war-time actions. Others, like the mayor of Hiroshima, refrained from committing themselves, or expressed embarrassment that the issue had been raised at all. More practically, the Liberal Democratic Party withdrew its support from Motoshima.[16]

There have also been interesting criticisms of the new Emperor's handling of his first audience. This took place on January 9, 1989, at the Imperial Palace, in the presence of 240 government leaders, only a small number of whom were elected members of the Diet. This was, it was said, to behave like a sovereign granting an audience to subjects, and ran counter to the spirit of the post-war constitution. The legal scholar Hoshino Yasusaburo, professor of constitutional law at Rissho University, claimed that the correct procedure would have been for the new emperor to appear before the whole Diet and then pledge himself to abide by the constitution. Anything else was an infringement of the constitution's declaration that sovereign power resided in the will of the people, from whom the constitution derives.

But, as Hoshino put it, this seemed really a rhetorical precaution. He expressed little fear that the new Emperor might be tempted to act *ultra vires*. Akihito, the new Emperor Heisei, grew up in war-time and had been educated as a young boy by the American Quaker, Elizabeth Gray Vining, and would be sensitive to attempts by right-wing militarists to repeat the history of the 1930s and manipulate the Imperial institution to achieve their political aims. Oddly, Hoshino is less sure of the ability of the new Crown Prince, Prince Hiro, to withstand such pressures when he in turn becomes Emperor. Hiro has been educated in the period of post-war affluence, has no experience of the horrors of war and, moreover, may have absorbed other tendencies from his time at Oxford (1983–1985):

> Looking at the fact that a British army colonel was in attendance on the Japanese prince, I cannot help but think that the prince's stay in Britain was arranged in order to make him learn the role of the royal family in a country that has been engaged in war repeatedly, most recently in the Falklands War.[17]

(It is always a relief, in Anglo-Japanese relations, to learn that paranoia is not only on one side.)

Prince Hiro should, Hoshino concluded, have gone to Sweden, where he might have learned something about the value of neutrality in war-time. Hoshino himself was called up in 1943, and his brother was killed in the war with China. His call for Japan to link war-time atrocities with the Emperor's guilt seems to have found little general echo in the Japanese young people, over half of whom, in poll interviews, seem to be indifferent to the implications of the transition from one era to another.

One political leader, Doi Takako, the chairwoman of the Japan Socialist Party, made a speech at the Japan National Press Club (January 10, 1989) very much along Hoshino's lines. The Emperor was responsible for Japan's entry into World War II, she firmly maintained, and Japan should accept criticism from other nations with humility. This is a strain the Liberal Democratic party never likes to hear, and Ms Doi was in fact countering a speech made in the same place the previous day by Abe Shintarō: the blame for Japan's entry into the war was to be laid at the door of pre-war governments, and was not the Emperor's responsibility. Abe was doing two things: replying to the Mayor of Nagasaki, and faithfully supporting the then Prime Minister Takeshita Noboru, who had declared that the late Emperor resolutely brought to an end the war that had broken out in spite of his wishes.

These declarations tend to become an endless merry-go-round. Assertions are made, little or no new evidence is produced for them, the polarisation continues. Perhaps the best example of this is the celebration of February 11, "National Founding Day", or, as it is better known to Japanese history, Kigensetsu, the anniversary of the Emperor Jimmu's accession to the throne (supposedly 660 BCE). Kigensetsu was abolished after the war but restored under its new name in 1966. Out of respect for the death of Emperor Shōwa, some groups thought it polite not to celebrate the event. Others went ahead at the Meiji Shrine Hall, which echoed to be traditional shouts of "Tenno Heika Banzai!" in deliberate opposition to what the composer Mayuzumi Toshiro, chairman of the Society for Celebrating Japan's National Founding Day, described as the increased momentum of the anti-emperor movement since the late Emperor's death. As if to confirm his fears, a symposium was held in Yamate Church in Shibuya, Tokyo, to bring together opponents of the emperor system. Yasumaru Yoshio, professor of history at Hitotsubashi University, declared that the modern emperor system was a political fiction created for political purposes. He was followed by a Shinto priest from the Tōshōgu Shrine in Nikko, Saga Hironari. The deification of the emperor was unforgivable, said Saga, because similar movements in the past had led to the deaths of three million Japanese and 20 million Asians during the war. A resolution was adopted criticizing both the Liberal Democratic Party and the government for glorifying the late Emperor, who bore the highest responsibility for wars of aggression abroad and the suppression of human rights in Japan.[18] It looks as if Shōwa is going to overshadow Heisei for a long time to come.

**Notes**

[1] *The Japan Times* (Weekly Overseas Edition), December 5, 1987, p. 4.
[2] ibid., April 18, 1987, p. 10.

[3] ibid., June 18, 1988, p. 6, p. 9; and cf. J. M. de Vera, "Church and Emperor", *The Tablet*, March 18, 1989, pp. 3–4.

[4] Minobe Tatsukichi, "Clearing up a Misinterpretation of a Constitutional Theory", in R. Tsunoda et al, *Sources of Japanese Tradition* (New York: Columbia, 1958, Vol. II, pp. 239–246).

[5] L. Allen, "The Way of the Gods", *New Blackfriars*, October 1968, pp. 27–32; "Kami Natures", *New Blackfriars*, October 1973, pp. 459–466.

[6] "Circular Letter concerning 'Spirit and Attitude' ", December 27, 1944, in H. J. Benda et al, *Japanese Military Administration in Indonesia: Selected Documents* (Yale, 1965, pp. 231–4).

[7] Suzuki Shizuo and Yokoyama Michiyoshi, *Shinsei kokka Nihon to Ajiya-senryoka no han-Nichi no genzo* (Japan the Sacral State and Asia: Origins of Anti-Japanese Movements under the Occupation), Tokyo, 1984.

[8] "The ties between Us and Our People have always stood upon mutual trust and affection. They do not depend upon mere legends and myths. They are not predicated on the false conception that the Emperor is divine, and that the Japanese people are superior to other races and fated to rule the world."

[9] Hirakawa Sukehiro, *Heiwa no Umi to Tatakai no Umi* (Sea of Peace, Sea of War), Tokyo, 1983; *Modernising Japan in Comparative Perspective* (Tokyo, 1987, pp. 106–120).

[10] "It has been truly unavoidable and far from Our wishes that Our Empire has now been brought to cross swords with America and Britain", R. Butow, *Tojo and the Coming of the War*, (Stanford, 1961, p. 410).

[11] *Sugiyama Memo*, Tokyo, 1967, Vol. I, p. 277 and pp. 387–8 *inter alia*.

[12] Mikasa no miya Takahito (Prince Mikasa), *Kodai Oriento to watakushi* (The Ancient Orient and Myself), Tokyo, 1984, pp. 18–25.

[13] Hayashi Kentaro, "Senso sekinin to wa nani ka?" (What is War Responsibility?"), *Bungei Shunju*, Special Issue, March 1989 pp. 254–265.

[14] Mayo Issobe, "Glorification of Emperor Draws Criticism from Women", *Japan Times* (Weekly Overseas Edition), December 10, 1988, p. 3.

[15] loc. cit.

[16] ibid., December 31, 1988, p. 4.

[17] ibid., January 28, 1989, p. 4.

[18] ibid., February 25, 1989, p. 4.

Louis Allen

# JORDAN

The modern state of Jordan was established by the British mandatory authorities in Palestine in 1920–1922. Originally named Transjordan, it consisted at first of the lands to the east of the Jordan river and to the west of the states of Syria, Saudi Arabia and Iraq. In 1950 the territory to the west of the river which was not part of Israel was annexed to Jordan. It remained part of Jordan until the Arab-Israeli war of 1967, when the West Bank, which included the eastern part of Jerusalem, was invaded and occupied by Israel. As a result three of the major shrines of Judaism, Christianity and Islam, the Temple Mount, the Holy Sepulchre and the Dome of the Rock, passed from Jordanian to Israeli control. The affront to Muslim sensibilities caused by the "loss" of Jerusalem continues to arouse strong passions throughout the Arab and Muslim world.

The great majority of Jordanians are Sunni Muslims; about 6 per cent of the population are Christians, mostly Greek Orthodox. As a member of the Hashemite family of Mecca, King Hussein traces his descent from the Prophet Muhammad, and his lineage is an important factor in maintaining his legitimacy. Although the regime does not insist that Jordan is an "Islamic state", such public manifestations of Islam as a large mosque building programme and numerous religious programmes on radio and television are evidence of the regime's desire to be clearly identified with the Islamic faith. Both Hussein and his grandfather Abdullah, the first ruler of the state, have been careful to cultivate good relations with the *ulama* and in Hussein's case with the less extreme wing of the Muslim Brethren. Outlawed or at least restricted in most other Arab countries, the Brethren have been permitted to function and to proselytize in Jordan, and several of its members or close associates gained seats in the parliamentary elections in 1984. For this and other reasons, in spite of its close links with the United States and other Western countries, the Jordanian regime does not seem to have been very seriously affected by the rise of popular Islamic radicalism in the late 1970s and 1980s.

Marion Farouk-Sluglett
Peter Sluglett

# KENYA

In recent years Kenya has witnessed the erosion of civil liberties, increasing human rights violations, the stifling of all opposition, and an unprecedented consolidation of power. In 1986 President Moi introduced a bill enabling him to dismiss the Attorney General and the Auditor General without, as hitherto, requiring the approval of a legal tribunal. The move was criticized by the National Christian Council of Kenya (NCCK), representing 35 Protestant Churches with a total membership of over six million people. The NCCK statement expressed "deep concern for the proposals", and the apparent ease with which the constitution could be changed. The Roman Catholic Bishops of Kenya, in a letter to President Moi dated November 13, 1986, pointed out the dangers in the drift to totalitarianism of the one-party state and the rule of the President, and regretted the subjugation of legal authority. About the same time Anglican Bishop Muge of Eldoret, supported by 28 Anglican priests, criticized the government with regard to the deterioration of human rights since 1982 and the harassment of people by security forces. He even compared Kenya to South Africa. The Rev. T. Njoya of the Presbyterian Church of East Africa (PCEA) suggested that the government hold talks with the opposition. All these interventions were met by fierce opposition from government and party officials.

Delegates to the annual conference of KANU on August 20, 1986, endorsed an open system of voting which required electors to line up publicly behind the candidate of their choice. This system was adopted for the primary elections the following year; candidates with less than 30 per cent of the vote being eliminated, and candidates getting 70 per cent or more in the primary being elected unopposed. Catholic and Anglican leaders strongly opposed this system as undemocratic, and were fiercely attacked for doing so by KANU officials. In 1986 Moi said exemption from queueing would be granted to civil servants, members of the armed forces and Church leaders, allowing them to vote by proxy in acknowledgement of the "impartial role they are supposed to play in serving the public". In the primary elections, held February 22, 1988, there was no such provision made for these people; there was violence in several places, and one candidate was even arrested; 60 candidates were declared to have obtained 70 per cent of the vote, so were declared elected to parliament unopposed, thus eliminating the secret ballot in 60 out of 188 constituencies. On the eve of the primaries, the NCCK and the Roman Catholic Bishops had called for the exercise of responsibility and justice in the elections.

In March 1988, the NCCK-sponsored magazine *Beyond* was banned by the government, the editor being accused of failing to file publication information as demanded by law. *Beyond* had been the only local paper to criticize procedures followed during the primaries and general elections of February and March, citing irregularities and questioning the fairness and the role of the administration in the process. In August the editor was jailed for nine months without the option of bail.

The KANU conference and elections in September 1988, at which Moi was elected Party President for a third term, took only a week. (The 1984 conference and elections had taken two months.) In these elections even the mildest critics were eliminated. Among the 12 major resolutions was: "We note that the NCCK no longer represents the majority of the Christian Churches in Kenya and call on the government to reconsider its stand on the NCCK." The Anglican Bishop of Mt. Kenya, the Rt. Rev. David Gitari, criticized the conference for being just a rubber stamp for resolutions drafted by a few individuals, called on the party not to destabilize institutions like the NCCK, suggested that the party elections for some districts were rigged, and called for a revival of the party's disciplinary committee where suspended members could defend themselves. Gitari earned a furious response from the Secretary General of the party, who was also the Minister for Local Government and Physical Planning, who asserted that KANU did not recognize Gitari as a Kenyan, since he was subordinate to a foreign master, the Archbishop of Canterbury, and warned that the Bishop should not be surprised if the government removed freedom of worship from him. The Secretary General lumped in "the Gitari Group" other Anglican Bishops Henry Okullu and Alexander Muge, and Dr T. Njoya (PCEA), who he claimed supported the Pretoria regime. Twelve Church leaders issued a statement supporting Bishop Gitari. In response the head of the Mombasa branch of KANU warned that KANU might be forced to defrock Church leaders who used freedom of worship to destabilize the country, and told Church leaders not to take advantage of President Moi's position as a committed Christian to create chaos in the country; KANU, he said, "would not sit idle and watch freedom of worship being misused by a few churchmen". Bishop Gitari rejected the claim that he was not a true Kenyan, and insisted that as a Kenyan citizen he was duty-bound to speak on issues of peace and justice. He appealed to politicians to stop alleging that Church leaders were serving foreign masters every time they spoke their minds. Anglican Archbishop Manasses Kuria rejected the charge that the Anglican Church of Kenya is not autonomous; and Bishop Muge denied being anti-government or anti-Kenyan and denied any link with South Africa. Bishop Philip Karanga of the Evangelistic Church in Kenya called the Secretary General's remarks "disturbing and frightening".

Thus is tension mounting between the government and mainline churchmen. At the same time, the last few years have seen the proliferation of fundamentalist Churches, mainly from the USA. This proliferation has been so marked that steps have been taken to limit the number of new denominations being registered. Some existing Churches have been banned, including the Jehovah's Witnesses in 1987. Usually no reasons are given. Most of these Churches shun any political involvement. Other Churches, too, rather than be part of any conflict with KANU, have withdrawn from the NCCK; these Churches include the Baptist Convention of Kenya, the African Inland Church, the African Gospel Church and the Full Gospel Churches. This trend is used by government and KANU officials in their attempts to discredit the NCCK. A delegation from the NCCK in February 1989 met with President Moi to try to effect better relations, but only a few weeks later the Minister of Energy denounced "misguided bishops" who attack the government. Roman Catholic and NCCK churchmen are now virtually the only opposition voices in Kenya.

Paul Gifford

# KIRIBATI

Formerly the Gilbert islands, Kiribati became an independent republic in 1979. It comprises a series of low-lying atolls spread over more than one million square miles of ocean and includes Christmas Island, the largest coral atoll in the world. The population of 68,000 people, concentrated on 33 main islands, is 93 per cent Christian. There is no real political party system although a Christian Democrat Party was set up in 1985 to oppose some actions of the parliament. The great fear for all Kiribati is that the greenhouse effect will raise the level of the waters and their land will disappear. The Catholic Church has been making representation to try and persuade Australia to give the Kiribati people free entry if the waters begin to rise.

Ron O'Grady

# KOREA

There is no country of its size and economic, political and cultural importance of which is so little known as Korea. To the historian of religion, Korea is especially significant for three reasons: (i) no other nation of East Asia was so thoroughly a Confucian society or state as Korea; (ii) Korean monastic Buddhism is more "orthodox" than elsewhere and Korean Buddhism in general is more flourishing than in other East Asian nations; and (iii) nowhere else in East Asia has Christianity developed so rapidly and extensively as in Korea. Consequently, the relation of religion and politics, particularly the impact which the religious community has on the political system, is of great interest. Conversely, because Korea is presently divided into two states espousing radically different political ideologies, the condition of religion in the two parts of the nation offers a unique East Asian laboratory to examine the effects of politics on the practice of religious faith.

The Korean people are ethnically, culturally and linguistically distinct from the Chinese. They have claimed as their ancestors races of people who inhabited southern Manchuria as well as the Korean peninsula. The autochthonous religion of the Korean people reflects this distinction from the Chinese, whatever later cultural borrowings there may have been.

The indigenous religion of Korea is a form of north-east Asian shamanism typical of Manchuria or eastern Siberia. Korean shamanism emphasizes the role of the shaman (usually a woman) who enters into an ecstatic trance to be possessed by a spirit. Through the agency of this spirit the shaman will perform ceremonies to cure disease, secure a blessing for a village, family or individual person, or escort the soul of a deceased person to the nether world. In the ancient period, the rulers of the various tribal kingdoms acted as the supreme shamans of their people by interceding on their behalf with the spirit world.

Buddhism was brought to the Korean peninsula towards the end of the fourth century and was recommended to the kings of Koguryo and Paekche (two of the ancient kingdoms) as being a superior form of spiritual protection for the state. During the early sixth century, a third kingdom, Silla, accepted Buddhism on much the same basis. During the Unified Silla period (670–926) when there was a single political authority over most of the peninsula, Buddhism was lavishly supported by the state. During the same era, the Unified Silla period, Confucian philosophy was accepted by the court. At this time, Confucianism was seen as a system of government and not a religious or philosophical system which affected the social and cultural aspects of the nation's life. The government's bureaucratic structure and the educational system were all modelled on the ideal Chinese (Confucian) pattern.

During the next historic era, the Koryŏ period (936–1392), Buddhism and Confucianism were seen to be complementary, the former dealing with the life beyond this world and the latter dealing with the ethical life of this world. More clearly than during the preceding Unified Silla period, Buddhism was seen to be the state religion.

The relation of Buddhism and Confucianism changed during and immediately after the period of Mongol rule (late thirteenth to mid-fourteenth century). Confucian scholars came to feel that one reason for the decline of the Koryŏ state had been the pernicious and corrupt influence of Buddhism at the court. Also, by the fourteenth century, Korean Confucian scholars had come to embrace the metaphysical Neo-Confucian thought of Chu Hsi (1130–1200), which, in contrast to early Confucianism, was a more all-embracing system of belief akin to a religion.

When the Chosŏn dynasty (1392–1910) was established, Neo-Confucianism was supported as the state cult and orthodox philosophy. The active suppression of Buddhism, the control of the number of clergy and the closure of all but a few temples, became state policy throughout most of the history of this dynasty except for a few brief periods.

Because of the rigid nature of Korean Neo-Confucianism, certain young scholars in the late eighteenth century became attracted to Roman Catholic Christianity through contacts with missionaries in China. It is an interesting fact that Korean Catholicism was brought to Korea and propagated for its first 50 years by Koreans and not by Western missionaries. However, because of the prohibition against the performance of the Confucian ancestor rite, and because some of the leading Catholics were members of a political group out of favour with the ruling Confucian elite, Catholicism was heavily suppressed.

One religious reaction to the development of Catholicism in Korea was the emergence of a syncretic religion, Tonghak (Eastern Learning) or Ch'ŏndo-gyo (Teaching of the Heavenly Way) during the 1860s. This religion was actually a mixture of shamanism with Confucian, Taoist and even Catholic elements and had great appeal to the poor in certain areas.

## The recent century: to 1945

With the decline of the strength of the Korean state in the nineteenth century, Korea was forced to change her status from a "Hermit Kingdom" to a state with Western-style diplomatic relations. The diplomatic ties with Japan in 1876 led to further treaties with the United States and various European powers in the 1880s. These diplomatic treaties required the government to support religious freedom. Buddhism was freed from centuries of suppression and the way was opened for the propagation of Christianity. Although there had been Protestant Christian communities established in the Korean peninsula by Koreans living in Manchuria before the advent of American missionaries in 1885, the major impetus for Christian evangelism came from North American missions representing the Methodist and Presbyterian churches. As a result of the economic and political decline of their country, and because of the spiritual vacuum left by a moribund Confucian philosophy, many young progressive Koreans turned to Christianity.

During the same period which had seen the rapid development of Protestantism, the Ch'ŏndo-gyo syncretic religion emerged as a major political and patriotic force. The local rebellions in the south-western part of the peninsula became the source for the Sino-Japanese War of 1894–95. Even in defeat, the leaders of this group were seen as anti-Japanese patriots with a considerable following.

In the 1930s, when ultra-nationalistic military groups dominated the Japanese government, the attendance at regular Shinto rituals to the divine Japanese emperor and his ancestors was seen to be the touchstone of patriotism. Large numbers of Koreans balked at this for patriotic reasons. Christians further objected to these rites on religious grounds. Although most accommodated to the situation, significant numbers of Protestants, particularly Presbyterians, refused to give in and were incarcerated and, in a few dozen instances, executed. The Shinto Shrine Question and other issues from the Japanese period have significantly influenced the subsequent development of Protestant denominationalism.

The witness of the Roman Catholic Church during the Japanese period was different from the nineteenth century. Nearly a century of persecution had given the Church a ghetto mentality and a desire to be protected from the state and to remain aloof from the affairs of contemporary society. Consequently, on the advice and suggestion of the Vatican, Catholics participated in Shinto rites. Likewise Buddhism, which was strongly supported legally and financially by the Japanese Government-General, remained quiescent during this period, with the exception of a few notable leaders.

# KOREA, REPUBLIC OF (Tae Han Min'guk, South Korea)

**Statistics** (reported to Ministry of Culture and Information, Republic of Korea, 1986): Total population, 41,658,935.

| Religion | Membership | Clergy | Places of Worship |
|----------|-----------|--------|-------------------|
| Buddhism | 15,127,710 | 21,197 | 6,443 |
| Protestantism | 9,723,576 | 43,468 | 28,447 |
| Catholicism | 2,148,607 | 6,189 | 2,414 |
| Confucianism | 10,184,723 | 17,393 | 231 |
| Ch'ŏndo-gyo | 960,867 | 4,740 | 273 |

## History from 1945 to 1986

When Korea was liberated from Japanese colonial rule in 1945, the restrictions which had been placed on all religions were lifted and the various Protestant denominations began to reform out of the United Church which had been created by the Japanese colonial authorities. Since the establishment of the Republic of Korea in 1948, prominent Protestant Christians have come to take a leading role in political and social affairs. For example, the right-wing first President of the ROK, Syngman Rhee (Yi Sŭngman, 1875–1965) and the first woman lawyer and social activist Lee Tai-young (Yi T'ae-yŏng) are both Methodists. Similar examples might be found within the Roman Catholic and other Protestant communities.

During the 1960s, following upon a decade of recovery from the Korean War (1950–3), Protestant laymen and women became notably active in various social projects to alleviate the misery of the urban workers in the newly emerging Korean industrial state. These projects often brought them into conflict with the government of General Park Chung Hee (Pak Chŏng-hŭi, 1917–79) which was striving for rapid industrialization.

With the changes in the constitution in 1972, which ensured the continuity of General Park in power, opposition to the "military" form of government grew. Throughout the 1970s and into the 1980s the leading political dissidents have been Christians. Kim Dae Jung (Kim Tae-jung, 1925–), possibly the best known Korean politician to the outside world, is a Roman Catholic while Kim Young Sam (Kim Yŏng-sam, 1927–) is a Presbyterian. The Cardinal Archbishop of Seoul, Kim Su-hwan (1922–) and members of the Korean hierarchy have given a lead to and provided considerable support for Catholic political dissidents.

It is an interesting fact that whereas many Protestant laymen have been prominent political dissidents, the clerical leaders of the Protestant denominations have been virtually silent. This contrast in the visible activity in the political sphere of the leadership of the two major branches of Christianity is, in the 1970s and '80s, dramatically different from the activities of Church leaders during the Japanese period, especially during the 1930s. At that time, it was the Protestant leadership which was more vocal and outspoken.

During the period since Liberation in 1945, the various Buddhist groups have remained virtually silent on all matters of national politics. The Ch'ŏndo-gyo syncretic religion which played such a prominent role on the national political scene from the 1890s through to the 1930s, had by the 1960s become fairly silent on political matters. Sadly, Ch'ŏndo-gyo was only prominent in the newspapers when the leadership was openly supporting some anti-dissident movement spawned by the government.

## Events of 1987–89

*1987*: This year was a year of major political turmoil in the ROK. The question of the choice of the successor to the incumbent president, Chun Doo Hwan (Chŏn Tu-hwan, 1931–) and questions over the constitutional procedures to elect the new president led to a dramatic conflict between the government and a broad spectrum of South Korean society.

At this time, Christians played a prominent part in the movement for greater democracy. A mass memorial meeting to demand a full government investigation into the death of a student who had been held in police custody — planned by various religious organizations and the New Korea Democratic Party (at that time the largest opposition party) — was held at the Roman Catholic Cathedral in Seoul on February 7. The area around the church was surrounded by 3,000 riot police. Similar gatherings in churches in other parts of the country took place at the same time.

On May 18, The Catholic Priest's Council for Justice held a mass for citizens killed by the military during an uprising in the southern city of Kwangju in 1980, and to demand further investigation of the torture death of the university student. From June 9–15, large numbers of university students participated in a sit-in and hunger strike at the Roman Catholic cathedral in Seoul, demanding democratic selection of the next president of the Republic. On June 15, following the departure of the students from the cathedral, Cardinal Kim demanded that all anti-government dissidents be released from custody. A planned march from the Anglican cathedral in Seoul to the Christian Broadcasting Building on June 11 was prevented by the police and 140 people were arrested.

Before President Chun made steps to resolve the political crisis, he spoke with prominent clerical leaders of the Roman Catholic and Protestant churches on June 25. On July 8 the government released Moon Ik-hwan (Mun Ik-hwan), leading Biblical scholar and political dissident.

*1988*: Upon his inauguration on February 27, Roh Tae Woo (No T'ae-u, 1932–) freed 1,731 political prisoners. The Korean National Council of Churches called for the release of all political prisoners. Following the election of President Roh, Korean political concerns have been less concerned with the movement for democracy and more concerned with revealing the corruption of the Chun regime and the desire for the reunification of the two halves of the Korean nation. Christians have played a prominent role in pursuing these issues.

In late April and early May, the Korean National Council of Churches hosted an International Christian Consultation on Justice and Peace in Korea attended by 200 participants from several nations. This consultation advanced such ideas as the signing of a peace treaty between North and South ʿorea. Its resolutions were strenuously objected to by the more conservative denominations which are not a part of the KNCC and also by conservative members of the constituent denominations of the KNCC.

To pursue its avowed goals of international harmony, the Seoul Olympic Organizing Committee created a Religious Advisory Council for the Seoul Olympics which embraced all of the major religious traditions in Korea.

In mid-August, Cardinal Kim spoke to the journalists' society, the Kwanhun Forum, and stated that the truth of the corruption of the Chun regime and especially of the massacre in Kwangju in 1980 must be brought to light. He also reiterated his previous statement that all political prisoners must be released.

On November 23–25, The World Council of Churches sponsored a meeting at Glion, Switzerland, at which representatives from the KNCC and the North Korean organization the Korean Christian Federation were present. The South Korean representatives were told that there were 10,000 Christians in the north, 20 ministers, and three seminaries. The Southern delegation gave a gift of money to help support their Northern brethren.

*1989*: On March 1 the liberal Protestant-oriented Academy House conference centre sponsored a "Religious Conference for National Unification" at which leading members of the Christian, Buddhist and Ch'ŏndo-gyo communities were present. In the early part of the year, taking a cue from the meetings of Protestants and Catholics with their northern counterparts, a group of South Korean Buddhists resident in Hawaii announced plans to attend an international Buddhist conference to be held in Ulan Bator, Mongolia.

From March 25 to April 3, the Rev. Dr Moon Ik-hwan accepted an invitation from the North Korean leader Kim Il Sung (Kim Il-sŏng, 1912–) in the early part of the year to come to the North to discuss the issue of reunification. During his stay, Rev. Moon met twice with Kim Il Sung, with members of the Committee for the Peaceful Reunification of the Fatherland, and with representatives of the Korean Christian Federation and the Ch'ŏndo-gyo Association. He also attended Easter services at the newly-built Protestant church in P'yŏngyang and later attended services at the newly-built Catholic church. Upon his return to Seoul on April 13, he was arrested at the airport. His arrest has spawned a political crisis which as of the time of writing (late June, 1989) has not been resolved.

# KOREA, DEMOCRATIC PEOPLE'S REPUBLIC OF (Chosŏn Minju chu'ui inmin konghwa-guk, North Korea)

**Statistics:** no definite statistics available.

## History from 1945 to 1987

Upon the surrender of the Japanese to the Allied forces on August 15, 1945, the Korean peninsula was divided into an American and a Soviet zone for purposes of taking the surrender of the Japanese forces. By 1948, these zones had become two separate states, each pursuing distinctly different political and economic policies. The Soviet installed leader, Kim Il Sung (Kim Il-sŏng, 1912–) adopted the Stalinist model of government. No independent source of political or social authority was allowed to exist. Thus, the incipient, non-Communist political organizations which had begun to develop during the twilight period of Japanese rule were either eliminated or co-opted. The centre of Korean Protestant Christianity had been P'yŏngyang, now the new communist capital. The political parties formed by the Protestants such as the Christian Social Democratic Party and the Christian Liberal Party were suppressed. Likewise, the political movements of the Ch'ŏng-u Party, the political arm of the Ch'ŏndo-gyo syncretic religion, were suppressed and the party leadership eliminated or co-opted.

Even before the formal establishment of the North Korean state, free religious associations were eliminated and state-controlled organizations were created in their place. In 1945, the Central Committee of the Buddhist Believers' Federation was created which action was followed by the creation of the Central Committee of the Korean Christian Federation, and the Central Committee of the Leaders of the Ch'ŏndo-gyo in 1946. From 1948 to 1974, nothing further was publicly known about the first two organizations. From 1949 to 1974, there was also no further news of the Ch'ŏndo-gyo Association. These groups are government creations with no free existence of their own and only serve the propaganda purposes of the government. Korean Christians in China have pointed out that north Korean "Christian" leaders whom they have met are totally ignorant of the Bible.

## Events of 1988–89

*1988*: A visitor to the new Catholic church in P'yŏngyang heard on September 30 that a Korean Catholic Association had been formed with 800 members on June 30. At the same time as the creation of the new association, the new Catholic and Protestant churches had been erected. The visitor had also been told that there was as yet no priest to celebrate the mass. He had also been informed that there was a Protestant seminary which had been open since 1971, that a hymnal and a translation of the New Testament had been published in 1983 and that the Old Testament had been published in 1984.

*1989*: On January 15, at a rite to commemorate the Enlightenment of the Buddha, a sermon was preached by the Vice-Chairman of the Buddhist Association calling for national reunification. Likewise on March 16, the Ch'ŏng-u Party, the political wing of the Ch'ŏndo-gyo Association, at the party plenary meeting approved the unification policies of the Korean Workers

Party (the communist party of North Korea). On April 7, the Korean Christian Federation sent a letter of support to the Korean National Council of Churches in the South supporting their policy for national reunification and criticizing the KNCC's critics. On May 30, a new pan-religious organization, the Council of Korean Religionists, was created for an unspecified purpose. On June 2, the south Korean priest Mun Kyu-hyon arrived in P'yŏngyang on a visit and was met by the Vice-Chairman of the Korean Catholic Association.

James H. Grayson

# KUWAIT

Kuwait is ruled by the pre-eminent sheikhs of the Sabah clan, in conjunction with prominent members of the indigenous commercial elite, who occupy many of the senior positions in the central administration. The Al Sabah are followers of the orthodox Sunni branch of Islam and adhere to the Maliki school of Islamic jurisprudence, which favours relatively strict interpretations of the Koran and the traditions of the Prophet (*Hadith*), but which also tolerates some flexibility in applying the law for the benefit of the community as a whole. The commercial oligarchy includes prominent Twelver Shias from both southern Iraq and Iran, as well as a smaller number of Sunnis following the *Shafi'i* school, who migrated to the country from southern Iran around the turn of the century. In addition, Shia tribes based in southern Iraq and the eastern province of Saudi Arabia traverse the country's northern and western borders on a regular basis, while significant numbers of poorer Twelver Shias entered the country in the years after World War II to work in the petroleum and construction sectors of the local economy. It is estimated that Shias make up a quarter of the indigenous population.

Disadvantaged Shias staged a series of demonstrations in the capital city in early 1979; police responded by deporting the country's most influential Shia notable, Hujjat ul-Islam Sayyid 'Abbas Muhri, and prohibiting the display of posters bearing the picture of the Iranian leader, Ayatollah Ruhollah Khomeini. Demonstrations recurred at the end of the year in response to the seizure of the Grand Mosque in Mecca by militants demanding an Islamic revolution in Saudi Arabia. Shortly thereafter, a group of Shia intellectuals publicly accused the government of removing Shia officers from command positions in the armed forces and police. This charge prompted a backlash against the indigenous Shia: in October 1983, militant Sunnis attacked workers building a Shia mosque in the capital and looted the site. In an attempt to defuse rising popular support for the Islamist movement, the authorities adopted severe restrictions on the sale of alcoholic beverages and placed increasingly strict limits on the public activities of women, particularly at the university, during the mid-1980s. Nevertheless, sporadic attacks on foreign diplomatic and economic installations were carried out by Islamist militants throughout the decade.

In February 1985, candidates espousing an openly religious platform suffered significant losses in elections to the National Assembly. Members of Sunni organizations were particularly hurt by the publication of a Saudi scholar's ruling concerning the evils of co-education and western music. Only one prominent Shia representative was elected to the 50-member assembly. Growing frustration within the Shia community led to a suicide attack on the ruler's motorcade at the end of May and the bombing of a cafe in Kuwait City attached to a meeting house sponsored by the ruling family for older citizens the next month. In January 1987, 11 Kuwaiti Shias belonging to the clandestine revolutionary organization, Forces of the Prophet Muhammad, were arrested and charged with planting bombs at three major oil facilities in an effort to disrupt a summit meeting of the Islamic Conference Organization in the capital. Prominent members of the local Shia elite reacted to the arrests by taking out full-page advertisements in the country's newspapers denouncing the group's actions and reaffirming their loyalty to the regime.

Fred H. Lawson

# LAOS

Laos is a land-locked country of 236,000 sq km lying between Thailand, Vietnam and China. Its population in 1985 was estimated at 3–3.5 million, 35 per cent of whom belonged to hill tribes. The economy is almost entirely agricultural, predominantly based on rice with additional revenue from timber and opium. In 1975 the Lao Patriotic Front (*Pathet Lao*) gained power after the US withdrawal from Vietnam and founded the Lao People's Democratic Republic, closely allied to Vietnam and the Soviet bloc. Relations have recently improved with the USA, China and the EC.

Laotian religion is a syncretization of elements from aboriginal peoples, Chinese culture and Theravada Buddhism from India. Buddhism provides the formal aspect of religious life but is pervaded by the cult of *phi*, popular beliefs in spirits, souls, deities and demons. Festivals and the practices of shamans, healers and mediums traditionally played a major role in Laotian society and the monasteries (*vat*) were centres of education, welfare and collective life. Although retaining popular sympathy, the role of the *vat* has diminished since 1975 as a result of more modern education and governmental promotion of a secular culture. Religion is represented at official level by the Lao Unified Buddhist Association.

Alan Hunter

# LEBANON

The mountains of the eastern Mediterranean coastline have through history
been inaccessible to successive waves of conquest. Here remnants of conquered
communities have been able to maintain their old cultures and religions; here
persecuted communities from the surrounding regions have found refuge.
Here imperial powers have had to rule with consent, if they wanted to
rule at all.

The mountain range called Lebanon provided security for peasant communities which were mainly Maronite or Druze. The former, a Christian
community, trace their origins to the fifth and sixth centuries in the coastal
mountains further north in what is today Syria. In the centuries after the
Crusades they developed increasingly strong ties with Rome and became the
first Uniate or Eastern Rite Catholic Church in the region. The Church came
to cultivate particularly strong links with the Catholic Church in France. The
Druze were a sect which had splintered off the Ismaili Shi'ite form of Islam
in the early eleventh century, a time when a dynasty of this allegiance ruled
Egypt. The sect failed in Egypt but found support in the central parts of
Mount Lebanon.

In the shelter of Lebanon — in the south where the mountains become the
Galilean hills, and on the east where the fertile Beqaa valley separates Lebanon
from the dry Anti-Lebanon range — there has survived the largest Ithna'ashari
(Twelver) Shi'ite community outside Persia. They were dependent on the land
in areas where agriculture was hard work.

The towns and villages around the mountains — along the coast, in the
north and particularly around Beirut — were the home of Sunni Muslims
and Christians belonging to the Byzantine-rite Orthodox (Greek Orthodox)
church. They tended to be traders, craftsmen, professional and religious
elites, and financiers. By the eighteenth century other Uniate churches
had appeared, especially the Greek Catholic, as well as the beginnings of
an Armenian settlement mostly of merchants in the major towns. In the
twentieth century refugees from Turkey added to the Armenian population,
both Orthodox and Uniate Catholic. There was a long-standing Jewish
community in Beirut, and further smaller Syrian Orthodox communities.
The activities of Western missionaries during the nineteenth century gave
rise to small Protestant communities of various persuasions as well as a "Latin"
Catholic Church.

The history of the Lebanese mountains reflects this communal patchwork.
Regardless of religious adherence, social structures tended to be clan-based
with groups of clans coming together in alliances under feudalistic leaderships,
whose power rested on their ability to mobilize their clients for political and
military action and to offer those same clients material protection and welfare
in an uncertain world. Religious identity was one tool in this system but only
one of many and not necessarily the strongest. However, its strength was
clearly boosted by the continuation until the present of the Ottoman system
of delegating to the religious communities responsibility for determining and
administering family law. A Lebanese citizen therefore must be a member
of a recognized religious community. At the time when the civil war broke
out in 1975, there were 27 such communities and 14 different family laws.

The tradition of local autonomy had been reluctantly accepted by the Ottoman Turkish rulers of the sixteenth to eighteenth centuries, and much of the story of Lebanon during that time was one of political and military manoeuvring among the dominant Druze princes in the mountains inland from Sidon, Beirut and Jbeil (Byblos). This was a period of practical co-operation between Maronite and Druze where the former provided the educated scribes who took care of the administration of the latters' series of small principalities. At the same time there was a general southwards migration of Maronite peasants, so that the area was quite mixed by the end of this period.

The communal wars of 1840–42 and 1859–60 were as much peasant uprisings against their feudal masters, whether Druze landowner or Maronite Church, as they were Maronite-Druze clashes. More ominously, they were the occasion for massive interference not only by the Ottoman government, still recognized by all as the legitimate power, but also by European powers, France, Britain, Austria, and Russia. The result was, on the one hand, a recognition by the Ottomans of Lebanon being a special entity within the empire (although within much narrower boundaries than the modern state) and, on the other hand, a transfer of effective power to leaders and structures identified as Maronite.

The axis of communal relationships now became Maronite-Sunni Muslim, a relationship in which sometimes Orthodox Christians were able to play a mediating role. Their concentration in the towns and the villages of the lowlands among the Sunni Muslims usefully complemented the fact that they shared a broad Christian outlook with the Maronites of the mountains.

The latter half of the nineteenth century was a period of growing prosperity for Lebanon. The production of fruit and silk in the mountains combined with the trading traditions of the coastal towns to lay the bases for the area's later position as the most important entrepot for trade between Europe and the Arab world. It also became an entrepot of ideas and culture, as Western missionaries established schools throughout, as well as colleges and two universities in Beirut, one American Protestant and one French Jesuit. Arab Christians, especially Greek Orthodox, of Lebanon and Syria became the founders of the ideas of Arab nationalism. Young educated Lebanese writers were a major influence in the revival of modern Arabic literature and the creation of an Arabic press throughout the Middle East.

During the nineteenth century, the long-standing connection between the Maronite Church and French Catholic missions began to coincide with French imperial ambitions in the area. Some sections of the Maronite community saw the potential of exploiting this in favour of achieving an autonomous Greater Lebanon dominated by the Maronites under French protection. Both French and Maronite ambitions were attained when, in 1918–20, France took control of the Syrian provinces of the defeated Ottoman empire. The French High Commissioner decreed the establishment of the State of Greater Lebanon. In 1926, the country became a constitutional republic under French mandate.

The new state incorporated not only the mountain provinces with their Maronite and Druze villages, but also the Beqaa valley, the hills of northern Galilee and the coastal plains and its towns from south of Tyre, through Sidon, Beirut, and Jbeil to north of Tripoli. Thus the whole of the religious–communal patchwork described above was being required to develop and define a common future.

The express aim of the League of Nations mandate was to proceed towards full independence, however reluctant France might be. So far as the various sectors of Lebanese society were concerned, the question was: what kind of independent Lebanon? While the Maronite leadership had little doubt, other groups were not in agreement with its ambitions. The Arab nationalist movement had in the last decade of the Ottoman empire been joined by Arab Muslims no longer able to identify with the increasingly Turkish nature of the government in Istanbul. In Lebanon, the debate over the nature of an independent entity tended to polarize between the supporters of a Christian, mainly Maronite, Lebanon with a Western, mainly French, orientation and the supporters of an Arab Lebanon committed to pan-Arabism. The more radical of the latter were for a long time unable to reconcile themselves to French creation of a Lebanon from Syria.

A number of factors combined to produce the arrangement which founded post-war independent Lebanon — personalities, the German occupation of France, rivalries between Britain and the Free French. During 1942 and 1943, political leaders from both sides agreed to a series of practical arrangements that Lebanon was to remain a fully independent state as part of the overall Arab nation. Based on the outcome of the 1932 census, the only one ever to have been held, the distribution of seats in the elected Chamber of Deputies was to be in the ratio of six Christians for every five Muslims, and within each of these blocks further quota divisions were applied for the various Christian and Muslim groups, the latter including the Druze. The quotas also applied to all government employees. It was agreed that the President and the Commander-in-Chief of the armed forces should be Maronite, the Prime Minister Sunni Muslim, and the Speaker of the Chamber Shiite. It soon became precedent that particular ministries were the preserve of particular communities; thus the Minister of Defence has tended to be Druze and the Foreign Minister Greek Orthodox, etc. Together termed the National Pact, these arrangements became the uniting force which moved Lebanon out of mandate into full independence, in time to be a founder member of the United Nations, and the final evacuation of French troops in 1946.

For many Lebanese groups the National Pact was conceived of only as a stage on the way to the achievement of a long-term national unity which would obviate the need for the confessional distribution of powers. But a number of factors existed to block progress towards that goal. As Arab nationalism grew more radical in its attitude to the Western powers during the 1950s, the debate over Lebanon's role and identity revived and culminated in civil war in 1958. Towards the end of his presidential term, Camille Chamoun had pushed Lebanese foreign policy closer to that of the United States, while large sections of the Lebanese population, particularly the urban Sunnis and Greek Orthodox, identified themselves with the Arabism of Egypt's President Abd al-Nasir. The war was ended by the landing of US marines in Beirut and the election of the armed forces commander Fuad Chehab as president.

But there still remained groups who sought reunification with Syria. There were deep cultural divides between those who had been educated in the French-speaking school sector (all schools were still private) and the English-speaking sector. Above all, there were those factors which served to perpetuate confessional distinctions in the social and political fields: the various family law jurisdictions, confessional control over educational institutions, the

164

coincidence of territorial, clan and confessional identity, and increasingly with time the quota system itself.

Between 1943 and 1974, two developments contributed to breaking the consensus on which independent Lebanon had been based. One factor was the changing nature of Lebanese society. During the 1950s and 60s, agriculture decreased in importance while the manufacturing, construction, and service industries expanded. The closing of the Suez Canal in 1967 added to the country's important position as a centre for Middle Eastern commerce by land, sea, and air. Such changes were inevitably associated with enormous population movements. By the early 1970s there were very few villages left where agriculture was more than a supplementary source of income for families who were moving to the new centres of economic activity — Tripoli, Sidon and Tyre, but above all Beirut. And it was not only the Lebanese who were migrating. Lebanon was attracting Arabs from other parts of the Middle East. Armenians and Kurds from Syria and Iraq were gathering in the suburbs of Beirut. Palestinian refugees from 1948 were joined by others, a movement accelerated by new waves fleeing the 1967 June war and the war in Jordan 1970–71. Any thought of incorporating any of these groups, overwhelmingly Muslim, into Lebanese society was out of the question, as it would upset the confessional balance, already in danger as people realized that the wealthier sectors were being overtaken by the high birth rates of the poorer parts of the country, mostly Muslim and especially Shi'ite.

Moving from village to town meant a weakening of the links to the traditional rural elites and of the dependency on the clan system. It was beginning to become possible to develop a comfortable career independently of traditional patronage. New forms of group solidarity could be discerned: trades unions, professions, international connections, shared economic interests, etc. The growing concentrations of foreigners were also to some extent outside the control of the traditional elites.

The other development which contributed to breaking the traditional pattern was the changing nature of the state itself. The first stage was the building of a national army during the 1950s. Here was an institution which was directly under the control of the state, designed to be a symbol of national unity. It failed to achieve that aim. In seeking to preserve the unity of the army by refusing to intervene in the civil war of 1958, the army command lost the confidence of the Maronite elite. When General Fuad Chehab then became president, his moves to modernize the state through the military apparatus alienated the remaining leaders. "Chehabist" policy was gradually toned down by his successor, Charles Helou, and President Sulaiman Franjieh's first priority after coming to power in 1970 was to bring the army firmly under what came to be perceived as Maronite control. The disbandment of the Chehabist centralist policy also provided renewed space for the activities of the traditional elites.

During the late 1960s and early 1970s the government sector expanded also on the civilian side. Growing health, social security, and education systems created more public employees. All were subject to the confessional quotas of the National Pact. The traditional elites seized the opportunities for exercising patronage, and corruption and nepotism became rife.

As the discrepancy grew between an outdated constitutional understanding and the economic and social state of affairs, so pressures began to be exerted to bring them into harmony again. The major political groupings which gained most from the old situation sought to consolidate their position. Former enemies came together in a Maronite entente. Under President Franjieh state control was, in popular perception, coming to be identified with purely sectional interests which, in turn, were being identified as Maronite.

The Palestine Liberation Organization and the various Palestinian groupings began to become a factor. During the 1970s, the urban concentration of groups who felt that they were being excluded from participation in the wealth of the nation, were becoming politically activated. They saw the state and particularly the army becoming the preserve of Maronite groups. They began to look to the Palestinians as a countervailing force. The Palestinian political leadership in turn welcomed this rapprochement through which it gained spokesmen within the Lebanese system. The slogans became social and political reform on the side of the National Movement and its Palestinian allies. On the side of the mainly Maronite Lebanese Front the call was for the preservation of the Lebanese state in the face of the growth of states within the state, a reference particularly to the Palestinians.

This increasingly explosive mixture was sparked off by several developments. The failure of the army to respond effectively to the increased intensity of Israeli raids, as well as its failure to be accepted as a national institution, convinced the opposition that only the Palestinians could be relied on as counterweight and protection. The failure of the army to control the Palestinians convinced the Maronite nationalists that only their own militias could do so. The views of both sides were strengthened by open warfare between the Lebanese armed forces and the Palestinians during May 1973. The scene was set for an arms race, in which the various groups increasingly looked to patrons elsewhere in the Arab world and outside to assure finance and lines of supply. The progressive breakdown of state structures and internal security began to transfer the political initiative from the politicians to the men who controlled the guns. Disagreement among the Palestinians over how to respond to the disengagement agreements and the international diplomatic moves after the 1973 Arab–Israeli war contributed to the growing anarchy.

Most ominous of all was the extraordinary inflation fuelled by oil money being pumped into Beirut's banks and property market. Prices and rents doubled between January and December 1974. People on controlled wages in the public and private sectors saw their standard of living and their aspirations for the future destroyed in a matter of months. Out of frustrated expectations concentrated in the cities on the Mediterranean coast grew the seeds of civil war. Strikes, demonstrations and roadblocks during the spring of 1975 needed joint Lebanese and Palestinian action to keep them under control or bring them to an end. This became too much for the leaders of the mainly Maronite Phalangist and National Liberal parties. It was a Phalangist massacre of a busload of Palestinians in a Beirut suburb in April 1975 which marked the outbreak of civil war.

The first phase of the war was an internal Lebanese affair. The militias of the Lebanese Front, overwhelmingly Maronite, confronted Syrian Nationalists, mainly Greek Orthodox, on the northern and eastern outskirts of Beirut and south of Tripoli. In the centre and south of Beirut they confronted other militias of the National Movement — some Sunni Nasserites, variously socialist or communist, often Christian. During early 1976, the Palestinians finally became actively involved on the side of the National Movement, but as the Lebanese Front seemed on the verge of defeat Syria engaged first in the mountains and then in the cities to redress the balance. Along the southern border, Israel began to build up a permanent presence within the country.

With no willingness on either side to move forward politically, there was a stalemate which was broken by two developments. After the Islamic revolution in Iran, Shi'ite groups were becoming more active. The main Shiite force, Amal, found itself being outflanked by more radical voices looking to Iran for leadership, a link which was at various times encouraged by Syria, once Damascus had allied with Tehran against Baghdad in the Gulf war. Israeli intervention was growing and culminated in the invasion and occupation of Beirut in the summer of 1982. These events effectively put an end to the power of the secular socialist groups and the traditional Sunni parties in Beirut. The expulsion of Palestinian armed forces also put them out of the picture. Israeli withdrawal paved the way for Shi'ite domination in West Beirut, for a time coupled with the Druze militias of the Popular Socialist Party. In East Beirut the Phalangist militias had swallowed up the smaller Maronite groups. Elsewhere in the country, Syria dominated in the Bekaa valley in co-operation with Shi'ite parties. The Druze were in control of their territory in the mountains south-east of Beirut. The northern part of the Maronite heartland was controlled by the family militia of former President Franjieh, now allied with the Syrians. In the south, the Israelis retained their "security zone" along the border.

The most recent stage in the collapse of Lebanon came when the Chamber of Deputies failed in 1988 to elect a new president. In the vacuum the outgoing president appointed the army commander Prime Minister, a clear break with the National Pact and a move which the Lebanese Forces of East Beirut and the Maronite areas accepted but which was rejected by the rest of the country and the Syrians, with the result that the country had both a Maronite and a Sunni Muslim head of government. Continuing conflict over the distribution of power within the Lebanese constitutional structure, as well as disputes over territorial control have seen the moderate Shi'ites of Amal at war with the radical Shi'ites of Hizbollah, renewed conflict between rearmed Palestinians and Syria. Since the end of the Gulf war Iraq has been free to put pressure on Syria by giving its backing to the East Beirut government, under General Aoun, in its campaign to obtain Syrian withdrawal from Lebanon.

Whatever the causes and background of the Lebanese civil war, the war has itself clearly created new factors, new chains of events, new alignments which any analysis must take into consideration. One significant result of the war has been what is often called the cantonization of the country into confessional enclaves. East Beirut, which was not exclusively Christian, has become so. Populations have been exchanged, often in horrifying circumstances which have reinforced interconfessional bitterness and laid the basis for innumerable blood feuds. The separation between Druze and Maronite in the mountains inland from Beirut has become total. Isolated Christian villages in predominantly Muslim areas and vice-versa are there no longer. One of the few areas to remain religiously plural has been so-called Muslim West Beirut, but even there the proportion of Christians is seeing a steady decline.

The place of the state has been taken by numerous political groupings and their militias. The livelihood of thousands of people has become dependent on employment by them. Traditional political groups have been transformed into paramilitary organizations functioning as governments where they are in control. The functions of the Phalangist party on the Maronite side have changed to include civil, financial, security and military administration on its territory. The same is the case with the Druze and the Shi'ite parties in their areas. It is difficult to envisage any of these freely surrendering their control to the state.

Finally, a significant effect of the war has been to throw most ordinary Lebanese back into dependence on the very kinds of structures — family, clan, patron — which were a main obstacle to the emergence of a nation state. This is ironically the case even within the framework of the large paramilitary party organizations, like the Phalangists and Amal, which have grown to a size where central control has become weak leaving room for internal factions and interest groups to manoeuvre for power and sectional interests. In this situation, religious identity continues to be an incidental but emotively very powerful factor.

J. S. Nielsen

# LESOTHO

The Kingdom of Lesotho, 1.5 million strong, which regained its independence in 1966, is completely surrounded by South Africa and dependent for half its GNP on miners' wages earned there. Nine-tenths of the Basuto people are Christian, approximately half being Roman Catholic, a quarter Lesotho Evangelical Church (deriving from the Paris Evangelical Missionary Society) and one-tenth Anglican. The pre-independence election was won, unexpectedly, by the Basuto National Party, with Catholic support, against the more radical Basuto Congress Party. Chief Leabua Jonathan held on to the Prime Ministership, with paramilitary support, despite losing the 1970 election. Latterly he became increasingly critical of South Africa and in January 1986 was deposed by a military coup. In March 1986 all political parties were banned. Legal and military power now officially resides in King Mosheshoe II, educated at Roma College, Ampleforth and Corpus Christi College, Oxford. In practice power is uneasily shared between the King, the Military Council under Major-General Lekhanya and the Council of Ministers. Although the Catholic Church distanced itself from Jonathan as a politician, it was associated with the civilian government and Catholics have been critical of the new regime's close links with South Africa. With party activity banned, political argument finds an outlet in the two main newspapers, the Catholic *Mosletsi Ou Basotho* (The Sotho Adviser) and the Protestant *Leselinyana La Lesotho* (Light of Lesotho). The main public religious event of 1988 was the papal visit in September, the high spot of which was intended to be a mass of beatification for the French missionary Father Gerard, credited with making nearly a million converts. But atrocious weather, the hijacking of a pilgrim bus by revolutionary guerrillas and its bloody suppression by Lesotho and South African forces cut attendance to a mere 25,000.

H. S. Wilson

# LIBERIA

Liberia was ruled by the True Whig Party from 1869 to 1980. Although the party made much of its Christian principles, it was really a thinly disguised mechanism for preserving power in the hands of the descendants of the freed slaves who founded the country in 1822 and for denying it to the 16 indigenous tribes. President Samuel Doe, who came to power in the coup of April 12, 1980, is the first from the local tribes to take power, but his regime has become more repressive and corrupt, and less attentive to human rights than any of the Americo-Liberian regimes before him. The mainline Churches have protested against the most glaring abuses of Doe's regime, notably Doe's manipulation of the 1985 election process, and the brutal suppression of student unrest, and the bloodbath after the unsuccessful coup in November 1985. In April 1987 a Catholic priest was expelled; though no reason was given, the expulsion was for comments critical of the regime. In April 1989 the Catholic Archbishop publicly called for the closing of the notorious top-security prisons, which drew a blank refusal from the Minister of Justice. Harassment from the regime has ensured that the Churches speak out less frequently now. There is considerable growth among the evangelical Churches that refuse to become involved in anything political. The Muslim minority, though growing, is under-represented in positions of influence because of its relative neglect of education in the past.

Paul Gifford

# LIBYA

Islam and politics have often been intertwined in Libya's modern history. In the first half of the nineteenth century an Islamic reformist movement, the Sanussiya, emerged in the Hijaz, in the Arabian peninsula, and then moved on to Cyrenaica, in Libya, where it found a welcoming environment. The Grand Sanussi, the head of the movement, set up his headquarters in Cyrenaica.

The Sanussiya was both a religious and a political movement. Its primary function was to proselytize and reform, and the Sanussiya's call spread east to Libya's neighbours in North Africa, and south to sub-Saharan Africa. The movement was structured around *zawiyas*, or lodges, which were headed by religious *sheikhs*, as well as a council made up of tribal notables. These lodges instructed their followers in matters ranging from religion to astronomy, geography, history and medicine, and in the late nineteenth century, military sciences as well. Those lodges were not merely centres of learning but military outposts as well, that could be mobilized to defend any region that was under attack. The Ottoman rulers relied on them eventually to collect taxes and to establish and maintain law and order among the tribes.

The Sanussi leaders sought to strengthen and unite the tribes of North Africa, and their role often included mediating in inter-tribal conflicts. They were so successful that they were able to recruit a very large following extending to many parts of sub-Sahara Africa. The political ties, for instance, between the Fezzan region of modern Libya and some of the territories which make up Northern Chad today, were strengthened during the nineteenth century when Sayyid bin 'Ali al-Sanussi spread his reformist movement to Chad. The Sultan of Wadai and his successors became Sanussi followers, and by the end of the nineteenth century the headquarters of the Sanussi order had moved to Gouro, in Chad.

In the twentieth century resistance to the Italian colonial power was primarily headed by Sanussi leaders. 'Umar al-Mukhtar, a hero of the independence war of the 1920s, was a Sanussi *sheikh* and a warrior. King Idris I, who became Libya's first head of state at independence in 1951, was the leader of the Sanussi Order.

It is not surprising, therefore, that Qadhdhafi's views of religion and politics bear the imprint of the Sanussi legacy. Like the Sanussiya, Qadhdhafi's Islam is primarily reformist rather than fundamentalist. According to him, Islam is the source of change and progress and is in harmony with the laws of science which govern the physical world. It is also the source of change and progress governing human society. He claimed that his "Third Theory", a form of pre-capitalist socialism, which he offered in the mid-1970s as an alternative to Capitalism and Communism, was rooted in Islam.

Like other Islamic reformers Qadhdhafi addressed the issue of legislation. To him the laws of any nation had to be based on religion and on customs. Religion provided the ethical standards upon which law was based, and therefore superseded custom. The Koran had to be the direct source of legislation. Islam, according to Qadhdhafi, is a "permanent revolution", which needs continuous new interpretation. It was the right and responsibility of all Muslims to provide this new interpretation of the Koranic verses, and was not just the exclusive privilege of the jurists and clerics. He thus downgraded the traditional role of the men of religion in Libya.

In so doing he alienated the religious establishment which became one of the most significant groups to criticize him and oppose his policies and reforms. Libyans could attend a Friday sermon at their mosque and also enjoy a political discussion of Qadhdhafi's policies. Realizing the danger of such meetings Qadhdhafi ordered in May 1975 that Friday sermons be restricted to spiritual matters, and not include such mundane subjects as politics. By the spring of 1978 those mosques that had not complied with his orders were "seized by the masses", and their *imams*, or religious leaders, removed and replaced by more compliant ones.

The attempt to curb the power of the men of religion continued throughout the 1970s and the early 1980s. The laws that were passed in 1977 on limiting private property were also imposed on religious endowments, *awqaf*, that were the main source of support for many of the clerics, *shuyukh* and *'ulama*, and created more dissatisfaction in their ranks.

One of the major critics of Qadhdhafi was the Grand Mufti of Libya, Sheikh al-Tahir al-Zawi, who had begun opposing the Libyan leader's housing laws as early as 1977. The Grand Mufti's criticisms had also been levied against the Government for taxing individual incomes despite its own extensive external revenues from oil, and against its banking transactions that included taking interest on loans. The Grand Mufti eventually resigned in January 1984 in protest against government harassment of himself and of *Dar al-Ifta'* (the office of the Mufti of Libya).

The religious establishment in Libya was traditionally associated to the prominent families of Libya, and shared the views of the Tripolitanian and Cyrenaican urban nobility on economic and political matters. Qadhdhafi's attempt at discrediting the Muslim clergy and at undermining its power, was not so much over differences on religious issues as over its opposition to his political and economic reforms.

Opposition to Qadhdhafi's regime was not limited to the religious establishment. Islamic groups generally referred to as the *Ikhwan*, or Muslim Brothers, directly challenged many of Qadhdhafi's ideas and policies. Those groups were influenced by their counterparts in Egypt and existed in Libya even before Qadhdhafi came to power. They objected to Qadhdhafi's economic reforms, especially those concerned with private property, as being against the strictures of the Koran; they accepted hierarchical structures of authority, preferring religious leadership to a secular type of authority; found Qadhdhafi's social reforms, in particular those dealing with the status of women, un-Islamic; and considered his views on the individual's right to interpret the Koran heretical.

The number of members in those organizations is not known, but they are primarily urban and petit bourgeois in contrast to those in the religious establishment. They are also popular among high-school and university students, as well as among the lower ranks of the armed forces. The *Hizb al-Tahrir al-Islami*, the Islamic Liberation Party, is perhaps the major Islamic organization in Libya. It appears to be linked to similar organizations in other parts of North Africa, in Egypt and in Jordan where the party was originally founded in the 1950s.

Qadhdhafi repressed those groups ruthlessly from the early 1970s, arresting their leaders, hanging their members, discrediting their views. Those actions only made them go underground or abroad and protest even more strongly against the policies of the Libyan regime. The persecution of the Islamic groups has continued relentlessly throughout the 1970s and the 1980s.

Amnesty International has followed closely the arrests and trials of Libyans accused of being Islamic activists. In the last five years, for instance, they reported that 18 members were arrested in September 1983 and tried by a court that sentenced them to prison terms ranging from six years to life imprisonment. In May and June 1984 two well-known religious figures, Sheikh Muhammad al-Khalifi, and Sheikh Hamidah al-Hami, were arrested, and imprisoned without trial. Al-Hami was accused of being a member of the *Ikhwan*. That same year two students accused of belonging to the Islamic

Liberation Front were hanged on the campus of the Fatih University of Tripoli. In September 1986, 26 men were arrested, accused of being members of *Jihad al-Islami*, the Islamic *Jihad* Organization, which Qadhdhafi had all but destroyed in 1973. They were alleged to be an extremist fundamentalist group, which used violence as part of its struggle. In February 1987 nine people arrested with them were hanged and their execution televized. They were accused of belonging to the Islamic *Jihad* Organization, of having carried out two assassinations, and of being involved in acts of sabotage.

By the end of 1988 the confrontation between the Islamic groups and the government had intensified. In November 1988, the state organ *al-Zahf al-Akhdar*, the Green March, published a vehement attack against Islamic groups, describing them as heretics, and threatening to destroy their organizations. A month later in December 1988, there was a crackdown on students at the university of Tripoli many of whom were purported to be members of religious organizations.

Unrest spread in January 1989 throughout Tripoli, Benghazi, Ajdabiya and al-Kufrah with Libyans protesting against deteriorating economic conditions, lack of jobs for graduating students as well as attacks on religious figures and institutions by government security forces. This followed a raid on the mosque of al-Zurayraq bil-Sabri in Benghazi by the revolutionary committees who arrested a number of worshippers suspected of being members of Islamic organizations. The teaching section of the mosque was also closed down because the *imam*, Sheikh Qussaybat, had been publicly critical of Qadhdhafi's views on religion. In Tripoli a number of mosques were raided in December 1988 and January 1989 during the time of prayer. The confrontation between worshippers and the revolutionary committees appeared to be particularly violent at the mosques of 'Ali Bin Abi Talib in Tripoli, and Al-Salmani in Benghazi. According to some reports, hundreds of arrests were made.

The government crackdown on Islamic groups was not limited to mosques but also included university campuses in Libya's two major cities. Male students wearing beards, a traditional badge of membership in Islamic organizations, and female students in conservative Islamic gear, were harassed and many were arrested by security forces or by members of the revolutionary committees in December 1988 and January 1989. In January 1989 Qadhdhafi had made a speech in the Tunisian Parliament, criticizing the practice of wearing the veil as a work of the devil.

Thus in the past year the attempt at repressing Islamic fundamentalism in Libya has intensified. Islamic opposition, on the other hand, has become more outspoken and more organized. It may become the most important opposition to the Qadhdhafi regime in the near future, and prove to be the unifying force that until now has eluded the Libyan opposition domestically and externally.

Mary-Jane Deeb

# LIECHTENSTEIN

Bordered by Austria and Switzerland, with a population of only 26,000, Liechtenstein is, under its prince, the octogenarian Franz Josef II, a survival of the Holy Roman Empire. A traditional Catholic state, women voted for the first time in the elections of 1986, but a referendum in the previous year rejected a constitutional amendment to include the principle of equality between men and women.

Stuart Mews

# LUXEMBOURG

Ninety per cent of Luxembourgers are Catholic, but this has not prevented the coexistence of liberal and socialist traditions alongside Christian democracy in many areas of life besides party politics. The historic dominance of the PCS (*Parti chrétien social*) which until 1974 secured a good third of the vote and usually provided the Prime Minister has been challenged latterly by the socialist party. But as in Belgium, compromise has prevailed and coalitions ruled. Religion is not a divisive factor here.

David Hanley

# MADAGASCAR

This former French colony became self-governing in 1958, and independent in 1960. Now about 45 per cent of inhabitants are Christian, 5 per cent Muslim and 48 per cent followers of traditional religion. Till the military took over from the arbitrary and autocratic rule of President Tsiranana in 1972, Catholics tended to remain out of politics. It was Protestants who had been more nationalistic, and the leader of the main opposition party during the 1960s was a Protestant pastor. At the end of 1972 the Catholics broke with the old order. In recent years all the Churches have expressed opposition to the regime of President Ratsiraka. In a pastoral letter of November 1987 the Catholic Bishops had deplored the economic deterioration and denounced "la minorité des nantis, affairistes et courtisans qui ignorent la masse qui s'enfonce dans la misère". At the time of the presidential elections in April

1989, the Christian Churches stated that the situation had gone from "serious to tragic" in recent years; they accused the government of "major errors in policy and management", and "failure to punish widespread embezzlement of public funds, theft and unbridled profiteering by officials". The Union of Christian Churches of Madagascar (FFKM) was instrumental in setting up the national body to supervise these elections. At these elections Ratsiraka was returned for a third seven-year term; the candidate of the moderately socialist Popular Movement for National Unity, Razanabahiny, regarded as the Catholic choice, finished third with 14% of the vote. There were numerous charges of electoral fraud. A month later the Pope paid a three-day visit; the previous week six people had been killed in violent demonstrations in Tananarive. The FFKM appealed to the opposition to suspend political meetings during the visit; the opposition leaders complied.

Paul Gifford

# MALAWI

Politics in the East African country of Malawi has been dominated for 30 years by Dr. Hastings Kamuzu Banda, who returned after 40 years' absence in 1958 to become leader of the Nyasaland African Congress. This body had been set up in 1944 to bring together some of those who had been active in native associations and independent Churches. They were largely men who had had their sights raised to the possibilities of life without white control by memories of the premature rising inspired in 1915 by the Reverend John Chilembwe, one of the Yao people converted by a British evangelist. At independence in 1964, Banda became first President, and is now President for life. Aware of Malawi's economic dependence on white-dominated countries to the south, it is not surprising that the government is one of the most conservative in Africa. From the beginning Banda took a close interest in the recruitment and training of civil servants, who form an elite managerial class.

Malawi is predominantly Christian; only about 15 per cent are Muslim, mainly from the Yao people. The first missionaries were Roman Catholics but their mission was not firmly established until the arrival of the White Fathers in 1889. Since 1950 the church has expanded rapidly and by 1987 could claim about 2.5 million, a third of the nation. Amongst the Protestants, the Church of Central Africa, Presbyterian, is largest with 90,000 members. It was formed through the merging of churches established by Scottish Presbyterians and Dutch Reformed from South Africa. There are two High-Church Anglican dioceses, which were set up in 1971.

The formation of black congregations was much encouraged by the African Methodist Episcopal Church from the USA which introduced charismatic styles of worship and speaking in tongues. The Jehovah's Witnesses have been banned by the government, which dislikes manifestations of cultural deviation.

Stuart Mews

# MALAYSIA

Malaysia is a multi-racial, multi-religious country in which ethnicity or "race" and religion form mutually reinforcing relationships. Approximately 50 per cent of the population are Malay who are almost all Muslim, with the remainder primarily Chinese (35 per cent) and Indian (11 per cent). Malaysian politics are largely defined by this ethnic–religious composition. The country has been ruled since independence by a multi-racial coalition headed by a Malay–Muslim party, the United Malay National Organization (UMNO), which has named every Prime Minister, Deputy Prime Minister and Home Minister since independence. Its major opponent on the left has been the primarily Chinese Democratic Action Party (DAP) and on the right the Parti Islam Se Malaysia (PAS), a conservative Malay-Muslim organization.

"Islam is the religion of the Federation" and in every state that has a ruler the sultan is the head of the Islamic religion. Muslim religious laws are state matters and differ from state to state. There have been demands from some Muslim politicians for the establishment of an Islamic state, although there has also been some vagueness as to its specific attributes. Malaysia upholds freedom of worship, but proselytizing Muslims is not allowed.

In the political realm religion has been a major factor in one long-term and one more recent phenomena. From the beginning of independence in 1957, UMNO and PAS and its antecedents have battled for the support of the Malay-Muslim voter. Although the UMNO leadership has found it necessary to accommodate the desires of the multi-racial coalition it heads, it has also needed to show its Malay-Muslim constituency its commitment to Islam. At the local level, UMNO politicians have been even more willing to emphasize their loyalty to Malay and Islamic expectations. PAS, on its part, has been deeply committed to the Malay-Muslim and has accused UMNO of giving in to its non Malay partners. There have been numerous cases in rural areas of party opponents accusing one another of being unbelievers and the government has sought to diminish this type of religious antagonism. In recent years PAS has suffered at the polls, winning only one parliamentary seat in the last national elections, although it received 40 per cent of the vote in the four northern heavily-Malay states. There have been efforts to find a means of establishing an electoral coalition between PAS and the DAP and PAS has toned down its more radical Islamic stance. Future prospects for PAS strengthening may be encouraged by recent divisions within UMNO, but it also must face the political and economic power of UMNO as exemplified by the arrest of party leaders from both the DAP and PAS in 1987 and several by-election defeats during 1988 and 1989.

The more recent and dominant issue has been the Islamic revival that has grown in strength over the past 15 years. This has been manifested in increased references to Islam by political leaders, change in dress and particularly the wearing of *shari'a* clothing by Malay women, rare cases of violent attacks by those demanding the immediate formation of an Islamic state, efforts to enforce the *shari'a* or increase its role, greater involvement in international Islamic organizations and causes, and the growth of religious organizations, particularly among the youth. Specific examples of the revival in recent years have been efforts to control gambling among Muslims, the establishment of an Islamic bank, anti-Zionist expressions by the Prime Minister and other UMNO politicians, and demonstrations against the visit to Singapore of the Israeli President. The revival has worried non-Muslims and is one of the factors leading to a majority of the Chinese voting against the ruling coalition in the last national elections and some brain and capital drain. Non-Muslims have also perceived themselves as endangered by recent court and legislative decisions that have strengthened the power of *shari'a* courts and allegedly targeted Christian religious activities. Among those arrested in 1987 for threatening public order were a number of Christian evangelicals. Overall, increased Islamization in recent years has created greater ethnic and religious tensions in society and politics.

Fred R. von der Mehden

# MALDIVES

The religious affiliation of the 181,000 citizens of the Republic of Maldives, which consists of 1,200 coral islands in the Indian Ocean 415 miles south-west of Sri Lanka, is almost exclusively Sunni Muslim. The first settlers on the islands came from India and Sri Lanka some 2,000 years ago. Buddhism was the primary religion until 1153 CE, when a large number of Arab merchants visited the islands, and the Maldivian king was converted to Islam. A sultanate was established, and the legal system followed Islamic law.

In 1932 a rebellion against the dictatorial powers of the Maldivian sultans led to a new constitution, and in 1953 the first attempt to establish a secular and democratic government brought about a short-lived republic. The Maldives soon reverted to a sultanate, however, until in 1957 a longer-lasting republic was established. The former Prime Minister, Ibrahim Nasir, became President. In 1978, under charges of corruption, Nasir resigned and was replaced by Abdul Gayoom.

On November 3, 1988, the Maldives received world-wide attention during a brief and quixotic coup attempt. Tamil mercenaries from Sri Lanka sailed into the harbour of the capital city, Male, and attempted to take President Gayoom hostage. Both Sri Lanka and India agreed to lend assistance to the government, and with the support of 300 Indian paratroopers, the coup was crushed.

There are no organized political parties in the Maldives, and there is no organized religious opposition to the government. The judicial system continues to be based on Islamic principles, and the President has proclaimed the Maldives to be aligned with other Muslim countries in matters of international policy.

Mark Juergensmeyer

# MALI

Mali gained independence from France in 1960. With a population of over eight and a half million, it is one of the poorest and least urbanized countries in West Africa. Ninety per cent of the population are Sunni Muslims but traditional religion survives strongly among the Dogon hill people. Perhaps one per cent of the population is Christian. The *Union Démocratique du Peuple Malien* is the sole legal party under President Moussa Traoré. Mali is heavily dependent on international aid and Traoré has been under strong pressure to cut the swollen civil service and parastatal sector. The notorious desert prison Taoudénit, officially termed "special re-education centre", where so many Malians suffered and died, established in 1969, was closed in 1988. While President of the OAU in 1988 Traoré sought to make his country and himself more prominent in international affairs. Malian marabouts have established themselves elsewhere in West Africa as presidential advisers and Traoré has his own, the Chérif of Nioro, Muhammadu Ould Chiekna.

H. S. Wilson

# MALTA

Malta has a population of 350,000, of whom 98 per cent are nominally Catholic. The Head of the Church in Malta is John Mercieca, Archbishop of Malta since 1976.

The most important event in Maltese politics in this period was the narrow victory of the Nationalist Party in the general election of 1987. This was widely regarded as signalling the onset of a period of tranquility for Church–state relations. However, Malta's fragile domestic economy and difficult international position make it unlikely that Maltese politics can remain tranquil for long, and if this is so, we can expect the linkage of religion to politics to bring back onto the agenda some of the problems now apparently shelved.

Once an anti-clerical Italian liberal grouping, the Nationalist Party now firmly identifies itself as European Christian Democrat and is supported at elections by the local clergy. These have come to regard the Nationalist Party as their natural protection against the anti-clerical and neutralist Maltese Labour Party. Bishops and senior clergy, conscious of the dangers of excessive identification with one political party in a two-party system, have usually tried to maintain communications with the Labour Party. This has recently been extremely difficult, particularly when the Labour Prime Minister Dom Mintoff declared Archbishop Mercieca *persona non grata* and asked the Vatican to remove him. This dispute (associated with Labour education and health policies) lasted from 1981 to 1984, and was resolved with Mercieca still in post.

During the 1987 election campaign the Nationalist Party supported stronger links with western Europe, and received considerable financial and technical help from the Italian Christian Democrats and the West German CDU. The pro-clerical stance of the Nationalist Party and its links with European Christian Democrat parties inevitably draw the Church into the bitter internal arguments about Malta's neutralism which have continued since the policy was adopted by Mintoff in 1979.

The Maltese Labour Party governed Malta from 1971 to 1987, for most of the time under the leadership of Dom Mintoff, who retired on grounds of ill health in December 1985. Particular targets of the Maltese Labour Party have been the extensive property interests of the Church and its domination of the education system. In 1982 Mintoff attempted to sequestrate all assets of the Church for which it could not provide clear title deeds; this was stopped by the Constitutional Court and in 1985 a joint commission was established to consider the question of ecclesiastical property. In 1983 Mintoff proposed to compel the Church's schools to accept state pupils free of charge; after violent demonstrations by both sides, this was resolved in April 1985 by a compromise which provided for the gradual introduction of free education on condition that pupils met entry standards and that the Government committed itself not to interfere in teaching.

These policies were part of a wider strategy by Mintoff aimed at making Malta less dependent ideologically and materially on the west and more open to alliances with Middle East and communist countries. Though Fenech Adami, the Nationalist Party leader, has much closer ties with the Church and seeks to promote European links, his foreign policy is necessarily constrained by the need to have close trading links with Arab countries and particularly with Libya. In so far as these involve increased Libyan cultural and economic influence in the islands, the Church is necessarily concerned even if unwilling to react too openly. The Libyans are seeking to establish mosques on the islands for visiting Libyan technicians, and in January 1989 Fenech Adami agreed with them to establish a joint radio station on Malta to be known as "The Voice of the Mediterranean".

The present Archbishop of Malta, Joseph Mercieca, is a canon lawyer trained in Rome and formerly a judge at the Sacra Rota, the Vatican's marriage tribunal. Malta is one of the few remaining western countries not to allow divorce in any form. Archbishop Mercieca is an altogether greyer and more emollient figure than his predecessor Michael Gonzi, a colourful and outspoken prelate who clashed repeatedly both with the British authorities and with the Maltese Labour Party. Arguably the most important Maltese cleric is not on the islands at all. He is Archbishop Emanuele Gerada, a Vatican diplomat who was brought back to Malta in 1966 as auxiliary bishop and heir-apparent to Gonzi. Gerada failed to survive the intense factional in-fighting which is the normal business mode of Maltese Catholicism: in 1973 he was promoted away from the island to become the Apostolic Nuncio in Guatemala and El Salvador, where he was an active supporter of the Christian Democrats and a critic of the radical Archbishop Oscar Romero. In February 1989 Gerada was appointed Apostolic Nuncio in Ireland.

Paul Furlong

# MAURITANIA

The Islamic Republic of Mauritania is on the north-west coast of Africa and links the Arabic Maghreb with Negro Africa. Colonized by the French, Mauritania gained its independence in 1960. Islam is the official religion, and almost the entire population are Sunni Muslims which is the only thing which the nomadic Berbers of the north have in common with the settled pastoral Negroes of the south. At Chinguetti the country has the seventh Holy Place in Islam.

The southern blacks who make up a third of the population have always been apprehensive of domination by the Arab north. These fears were increased when Arabic was made compulsory in secondary schools in 1966 and two years later when it joined French as an official language. At first, most Arab countries refused recognition but Morocco changed its view in 1969 and soon after, Mauritania was admitted to the Arab League. From 1975-9 the government was preoccuppied with the problems arising from its claim to that part of the Sahara, which was once a Spanish possession. This involved the vast expansion of the army, loss of life in battle, economic disruption, and the breakdown of relations with Algeria which supported those who demanded self-determination for the area. The war was very unpopular in Mauritania, particularly among the black population which had no desire to see an increase in the Arab population.

There were further black African complaints in 1986 at the growing Arab influence. The government reacted by emphasizing the Islamic rather than Arabic features of the national culture and speeded up the introduction of Islamic law.

Stuart Mews

# MAURITIUS

The politics of this small island in the Indian ocean have been complicated since independence through ethnic differences, personal rivalries and ideological disagreements. When it was a British Crown Colony, Mauritius was a one-crop economy. To cut the sugar cane, the British introduced indentured Indian labour to replace the slaves. Their descendents now form 68 per cent of the population, who are 75 per cent Hindu and 25 per cent Muslim. The Creoles make up 27 per cent and are mainly Roman Catholic. Then there are 3 per cent Chinese and 1.6 per cent Europeans, mainly French.

Throughout the 1960s the Mauritian Labour Party (MLP) led by Sir Seewasagur Ramgoolan dominated political life, but it was challenged in 1963 by Graëtan Duval, an energetic barrister who championed the Creole working class. His criticism of Hindu domination helped create a climate in which violence erupted in 1965. Five years later, more radical opposition came from the Mouvement Militant Mauricien (MMM) led by Paul Bérenger, who attacked the government's wish to avoid damaging trade by criticizing South Africa, and its acquiescence in the establishment of the U.S. naval base on the tiny atoll Diego Garcia.

In 1981 the MMM and Parti Socialiste Mauricien, (PSM) fighting together won every seat on the main island. The government they formed soon became unpopular; the Prime Minister, Aneerood Jugnauth did not inspire confidence, while Bérenger as minister of finance, imposed a tough policy, but also tried to make Creole the official language. With his party in disarray, Jugnauth in 1983 formed a new party, the Mouvement Socialiste Militante (MSM) which in alliance with the MLP and Graëtan Duval's PMSD went on to defeat his old party, led by his old colleague Bérenger. The MSM-PSD coalition was thrown into crisis in 1985 when several of its deputies were arrested in the Netherlands on a charge of drug smuggling. In the General Election of 1987, the results confirmed the communal character of Mauritian politics. the MSM polled strongly in the Hindu community, especially in the merchant caste to which Jugnauth belongs, the MCP secured the votes of high caste Hindus, the PMSD got the support of Creoles. The opposition MMM got most of its support from urban Muslims and the minority of both Creoles and Hindus. Aneerood Jugnauth is once again Prime Minister. In November 1988 a Hindu priest tried to shoot him and in March 1989 a man tried to knife him during a Hindu religious ceremony.

Stuart Mews

# MEXICO

Article 130 of the Mexican Constitution, promulgated in 1917 and still in force, states: "The law does not take cognizance of any personality in the religious bodies called Churches . . . . The ministers of religious cults shall be considered as persons who exercise a profession and shall be directly subject to the laws passed in that regard . . . . The ministers of religious cults shall never, in public meetings or in private gatherings, in the acts of their cult or in religious propaganda, criticize the fundamental laws of the country, or the authorities in particular, or the government in general; they shall have no active or passive vote nor any right to associate for political purposes." Article three of the Constitution forbade the intervention of religious bodies in the field of education. At the same time, laws passed in 1859 which nationalized all ecclesiastical property remained in force. The combined effect of this legislation was to disenfranchise the clergy and to prohibit the Catholic Church from entering the political forum, even to the point of issuing general pronouncements on questions of social justice.

To understand the historical context of Church–State relations in modern Mexico, it has to be recalled that the Liberal elite who first forged the Mexican State in the Reforma of the 1850s attacked the Catholic Church as the chief obstacle to their modernizing project. Moreover, the generals and intellectuals who came to power during the revolution of 1910–20 equally derided Catholicism as a hindrance to their radical plans. In the 1920s they succeeded in creating the structures of a one-party authoritarian regime which has dominated Mexico up to the present day. The ideology of the PRI — the Institutional Revolutionary Party — has changed from decade to decade, much depending on the circumstances at the time and the preference of the current President. Eminently socialist in the 1930s under President Lázaro Cárdenas, it became decidedly capitalist under Miguel Alemán during the late 1940s. At all times, however, it has remained authoritarian and interventionist, allowing other parties to exist and campaign, but preventing the opposition from obtaining executive office at the level of state governor. So also, it has remained resolutely hostile to any abrogation of the anti-clerical articles of the Constitution, even if it has not actively implemented the existing laws for several decades.

Relations between Church and State remain coloured by the events of the 1920s when President Calles sought to close churches and limit the number of priests, only to encounter a strong challenge from the bishops and a mass rebellion by the Catholic peasantry of western Mexico. The Cristeros, as the rebels were called, launched an extensive campaign of guerrilla warfare which revealed the inherent strength of the Church in Mexican rural society. In the end, reconciliation was effected thanks to the mediation of the American ambassador who appealed to the Vatican to force the bishops to the negotiating table. Nevertheless, it was not until the 1940s that tension eased. In effect, the Church constituted a permanent opposition to the authoritarian state that governed Mexico.

If tensions slowly eased during the post-war years, it was largely because the PRI moved to the right. During the 1930s its radical policies had alarmed the business classes and its "socialist education" had alienated parents and clergy. The effect was to promote an implicit alliance between certain business leaders and the Church hierarchy. Funds became available to revive Catholic schools and universities. The urban middle class, especially in the provinces, enrolled in numerous Catholic lay organizations and actively supported the construction of schools and churches. At much the same time, there emerged two significant Catholic forays into politics. The more ephemeral proved to be the Sinarquista movement which during the 1940s and early 1950s succeeded in mobilizing thousands of supporters in central and western Mexico. Corporatist and integralist in ideology, the Sinarquistas were both Catholic and nationalist and strongly attacked what they conceived to be the Socialist policies of the PRI, especially with respect to education and land reform. Their appeal was to the more prosperous sectors of the peasantry who feared collectivization of their land. The more lasting creation of these years was the PAN — the National Action Party — which opted for electoral opposition rather than the mass mobilization favoured by the Sinarquistas. Funded by businessmen, especially from the provincial capitals of Guadalajara and Monterrey, it enjoyed the active support of many Catholics and the implicit preference of the clergy. Its purpose was to create a political forum for non-violent opposition to the governing regime and to insist on the necessity of democratic elections. By the 1950s the Church hierarchy, led by Cardinal Luis María Martínez, had reached an unwritten accommodation with the State and no longer accorded active support to any political movement or party. Content at this point to develop its network of lay organisations and to promote its schools and colleges, the Church remained the only institution in Mexico that enjoyed freedom from government intervention, albeit subject to strict limitations as to its sphere of activity.

The Cuban revolution of 1959 and the revival of radicalism during the succeeding decades affected Mexico as much as the rest of Latin America. At first the hierarchy responded by backing a propaganda campaign against the dangers of communism. But then came the Second Vatican Council with its call for *aggiornamento*: the Church was now expected to open itself to the world and its problems rather than retreat into a confessional ghetto. In 1968 the Latin American Episcopal Conference held at Medellin insisted that Catholics should actively assist in the transformation of the continent, seeking remedies for its appalling social injustices. These pronouncements encouraged the emergence of the theology of liberation which argued that the Church should display a preferential option for the poor. It was accompanied by the formation of base communities among the peasantry and the urban poor, groups which found Biblical inspiration for their quest for social justice and human dignity.

The radical turmoil of these years found only a muted echo in Mexico since the bias of the Church hierarchy remained deeply conservative. It is significant that no theologian of any note emerged to develop the liberation thesis of their South American colleagues. It was the Jesuits who were most affected by the new trends, and they closed their college in Mexico City which had educated the social elite and turned their apostolic energies to the capital's slum districts and to the countryside. But only a handful of bishops and a small sector of the clergy embraced whole-heartedly the new emphasis on social justice. By far the most prominent was Sergio Méndez Arceo, bishop of Cuernavaca, who actively campaigned on behalf of students persecuted by the government and in favour of the workers and peasants. He travelled to Cuba and defended the

Christian preference for socialism. His outspoken interventions on social issues provoked angry response from the political bureaucracy which denounced his pronouncements as unconstitutional and irresponsible. His radical stance also alarmed the more conservative members of the hierarchy, especially as he also permitted a considerable degree of liturgical and theological diversity in his diocese.

If Méndez Arceo was viewed with disfavour by his fellow bishops, it was because during the 1970s the Church hierarchy established increasingly amicable relations with the current Presidents, Luis Echeverría and José López Portillo. The Church became an implicit supporter and beneficiary of the *status quo*. The rewards were substantial. In 1974–76 a monumental new basilica was constructed at Tepeyac in honour of Our Lady of Guadalupe, the patron of Mexico, an enterprise unimaginable in earlier years but now assisted by government funds. Catholic universities gained ground in their competition with state institutions. In 1979 permission was granted for Pope John Paul II to visit Mexico to preside over the Latin American Episcopal Conference scheduled to be held in Puebla. His triumphant tour was greeted by millions whose presence at public services held throughout the republic signified the contempt in which the Constitution was held. The ability of the Church to mobilize such masses demonstrated to the political bureaucracy its latent power. Moreover, the Pope explicitly compared the Mexican Church to its Polish counterpart, which also suffered from the intrusive vigilance of an authoritarian state.

During the 1980s the Catholic Church in Mexico has assumed an ever more important public role. In part this derived from the political bankruptcy of the PRI, which was discredited by its gross mismanagement of the oil boom and the ensuing inflationary spiral and mass impoverishment. It was this economic crisis that strengthened the role of the PAN, which emerged from the doldrums of the previous decade with renewed vigour in several states, especially in the north, acting as the chief contender for political office. But the Church hierarchy now entered the political forum by asserting in 1982 its right to pronounce in public on issues of social concern. Bishops were now heard calling for the repeal of the anti-clerical articles of the 1917 Constitution. Equally important, John Paul II's emphasis on basic human rights, nurtured no doubt by his experience of a communist government, was echoed by the Mexican hierarchy which in several instances denounced the electoral corruption and chicanery practised by the PRI. An authoritarian regime was seen as an obstacle to the exercise of political rights by the citizenry of Mexico.

The newfound political influence of the Church was most clearly illustrated in the 1987 election for state governor in the northern frontier state of Chihuahua. For the candidate of the PAN was an active Catholic, a participant in charismatic sessions, who was openly supported by peasant organizations led by a priest who was an exponent of the theology of liberation. The local archbishop intervened in the political debate to condemn electoral fraud as un-Christian and immoral. And when the official candidate was duly installed, he threatened to close all churches in the state as a protest against this denial of the basic rights of its citizens, a threat which promptly elicited a rebuke from the Vatican. Once more, the Church has emerged as the only effective opponent of the authoritarian regime which has governed Mexico since the revolution. But whereas in earlier years the lay groups it sponsored were generally integralist in philosophy, nowadays their orientation is often liberal and democratic. There is a renewal of self-confidence in the Church hierarchy and a newfound willingness to engage in public debate. At the same time, there is little desire for open confrontation with the State, and indeed a great deal of implicit support. As Pope John Paul II rightly perceived, it is a situation eerily similar to that of Poland.

D. A. Brading

# MONACO

It is hard to describe the relationship between religion and politics in this hugely-Catholic statelet, as there are no real politics (supposing politics to involve some kind of competition). All seats on the 18-man National Council went to one list in the 1988 elections (as happened in the previous two). Prince Rainier appoints his chief executive from a shortlist handed him by the French government.

David Hanley

# MONGOLIA

The People's Republic of Mongolia, with a population of only about two million, covers a huge area — some 1.5 million sq km — in Central Asia. The economy is based partly on a sedentary form of agriculture with nomadic pastoral elements, and partly on mining and industrial production. Mongolia is an independent state but heavily dependent on the Soviet Union, which is its principal trading partner. Mongolia aligned with the USSR during the Sino-Soviet split and only began to enjoy more friendly relations with China in 1986.

The Mongols have traditionally been believers in Lamaism, a hybrid of Mahayana Buddhism and shamanism evolved in Tibet. As well as acceptance of Buddhist tenets, importance was laid on practices such as contact with departed spirits and healing through trance and magic. Shamans and lamas had great influence in traditional Mongolia which was in some periods a theocracy similar to Tibet. Religion has now been largely abandoned, forgotten by the population or repressed by the pro-Soviet authorities. One Buddhist monastery still operates and traces of shamanistic practices survive in country regions. Barring unexpected changes it seems unlikely that religion will play a significant role in the country's development.

Alan Hunter

# MOROCCO

Islam in Morocco has always been associated with the state. King Hasan II and his dynasty are believed to be descendants of the Prophet Muhammad, and the King is supposed to have *baraka*, some form of spiritual power generally attributed to saints. The King's traditional legitimacy stems in part from those religious attributes. The religious establishment is very supportive of the monarch and in turn is treated well by him.

On the popular level there are the *sufi* orders, the *marabout* brotherhoods and the shrines and saints related to those groups. They are rarely if ever involved in national politics, but provide a safety valve for the grievances of the discontented among the rural and urban poor, who often form the backbone of Islamic fundamentalist movements elsewhere in the Muslim world.

The militant Islamic movement in Morocco has its roots in the Association of Islamic Youth, *Jam'iyat al-Shabiba al-Islamiya*, founded by 'Abd al-Karim Muti, a civil servant in the Ministry of Education, in 1972. It is divided into five major groups and is considered one of the most radical fundamentalist opposition movements in Morocco. These groups oppose the monarchy which they see as corrupt and subservient to the West. As the name of the organization indicates, its members come primarily from secondary schools and universities. In January 1984, they were accused of being behind major riots in Morocco and 71 Islamic militants were arrested and jailed by the authorities. In July 1987, while King Hasan was in London, four Islamic fundamentalists were accused of attempting to foment revolution.

Mary-Jane Deeb

# MOZAMBIQUE

Fifty per cent of Mozambique's inhabitants practise traditional religion, 35 per cent are Christian, 13 per cent are Muslim. Under Portuguese rule, the Catholic Church was closely allied to the State. This makes it the biggest Christian church by far, but meant that when the Marxist Frelimo took power in 1975 and nationalized all churches and hospitals, it suffered most. Since 1975 Mozambique has been engulfed in civil war by the South African backed Renamo or MNR. This has crippled the country, with 70 per cent of the country outside government control, four million starving, and by April 1988 an estimated 100,000 killed. Churches have suffered: the Anglicans have lost 50 out of 160 congregations, the Baptist Union has lost the active participation of 80,000 of 200,000 members. There are reports of US-linked fundamentalist Churches assisting Renamo (on the grounds that it is "anti-communist"). On March 23, 1988 an Australian missionary was sentenced to 10½ years in prison for collaborating with Renamo. After his trial he apologized and admitted he had been "duped".

Even before President Machel's death in October 1986, Frelimo had begun to soften its stand towards Churches. Archbishop Tutu visited in June 1987; the state provided security and he visited government ministers. He spoke in a church closed for five years and before the officials who had closed it. Between August and November 1988 the government returned church buildings seized from the Catholic Church in 1975.

The Catholic Church has refrained from open condemnation of Renamo. On May 17, 1987 the Catholic Bishops called for dialogue between Frelimo and Renamo. Government media attacked the Bishops' statement, but did not block its circulation or its reading in churches. In August 1987 a Vatican dignitary visited, seemingly to explore the possibility of the Vatican acting as an intermediary. The Catholic Church has continued to advocate dialogue: in September 1988 the Pope visited Mozambique and called for an end to war. In June 1989 there were reports of the possibility of negotiations; the same reports mentioned a role for the Catholic Church.

Paul Gifford

# NAMIBIA

Since 1920 Namibia, then known as South-West Africa, has been administered by South Africa, which has introduced its apartheid policies, and ignored continued calls to withdraw. The South West African People's Organization (SWAPO) came into existence to campaign, and since 1961, to fight for independence. To counter them, South African troops and police have behaved with savage brutality. Church reports of killings and torture have been confirmed by a succession of international church delegations.

About half of the population of just over one million are connected in some way with the United Evangelical Church, a union of two Lutheran Churches. In 1971 its African leaders condemned the politics of apartheid and called for independence. The Anglican bishop of Damaraland was deported in 1972, and later his successor.

About 66 per cent of the population are Protestant and 15 per cent Roman Catholic. There have been continuous diplomatic moves to reach a settlement, particularly since the military stalemate of 1988. In November 1989, elections supervised by the United Nations were due to take place. Whichever party claimed victory would be required to introduce a new constitution which South Africa insists must have the support of two-thirds of the representatives. The main parties in the election are SWAPO and the Democratic Turnhalle Alliance (DTA) supported by the whites, coloureds and those blacks like the Hereros who fear that a SWAPO victory would lead to domination by the Ovambo people. The elections brought thousands back from Angola, Zambia and elsewhere. The UN Commission for Refugees has asked the Council of Churches in Namibia to look after them.

Stuart Mews

# NAURU

When Nauru became an independent Republic in 1968 it was, for a time, the wealthiest nation in the world. Vast resources of phosphate had been mined from the single raised atoll of 22 sq km and the population of 8,000 people benefited from the boom in prices. The population is 82 per cent Christian, with most others Chinese Buddhist or Taoist. There are no organized political parties and the Church has its hands full trying to cope with serious social problems on the island. Drunkenness is rampant, the islanders have the world's highest incidence of diabetes and the islanders have forgotten how to grow vegetables or catch fish. When the phosphate runs out, the island may have to be abandoned.

Ron O'Grady

# NEPAL

The king of Nepal, the world's only Hindu monarch, reigns over 17 million subjects, 90 per cent of whom are Hindu; the remaining 10 per cent are Buddhist, Muslim and Christian. Nepalese Hinduism is distinctive, however, since it is heavily influenced by Hindu and Buddhist tantrism and Himalayan shamanism.

The present king is a direct descendant of Nepal's founding monarch, Prithvi Narayan Shah (eighteenth century CE). The authority of later rulers was limited, however, by a powerful hereditary lineage of Prime Ministers; in 1950 an armed revolt restored the kings to full power. In 1959, parliamentary democracy was instituted, but scarcely a year later it was declared a failure and the authority of the monarchy was re-established. In 1962 a new political system was created, based on the traditional *panchayat* system of elected councils. In 1972 the present king, Birendra, instituted further reforms, and since 1981 the country has been ruled by Prime Ministers selected by the democratically-elected national *panchayat*. Most leaders of political parties oppose the *panchayat*, but many traditional leaders, including religious leaders, support it.

In recent years King Birendra has made several symbolic gestures affirming the importance of religion in public life. In 1988 his son marked his coming of age in a colourful religious ceremony, and during the same year the king played host to the World Hindu Conference, which was attended by over 2,000 delegates from south and south-east Asia.

Mark Juergensmeyer

# THE NETHERLANDS

Dutch politics long revolved around *verzuiling* ("pillarization"). Each sub-culture or pillar had its own set of organizations — schools, unions, voluntary groups, media and a political party. Politics was a permanent accommodation, in which enlightened leaders bargained on behalf of passive followers.

The pillars (Catholic, Protestant, liberal and socialist) emerged in the nineteenth century. The Catholic south containing some 40 per cent of the population produced the beginnings of a party KVP (*Katholieke Volkspartei*) that would only really mature in 1945. In the north Protestants soon had to organize against the liberals who sought to remove state subsidies to denominational schools. They worked alongside Catholics with the joint aim of protecting their schools; by 1917 parity was won. The Protestant party split into two. The original ARP (*Anti-Revolutionnaire Partij*) catered for the more severe Calvinists of the *gereformeerde Kerk*; its opposition to the secularist humanism of 1789 was always tempered by a populist discourse on social and economic justice reflecting its lower-class support. Its offshoot the CHU (*Christelik-Historische Union*) was more conservative.

From 1917 to the mid-sixties these three formed a comfortable alliance at the centre, allying according to circumstance with either liberalism or social democracy in the shape of the PvdA (*Partij van de Arbeijt*). But declining religious identification led voters to vote on other criteria, mainly socio-economic. KVP and CHU lost on their left and right. Many held that pillarization was being replaced by polarization, especially after the merger of the Catholic and socialist unions in the late seventies. But the religious parties merged into a federation: the CDA (*Christen-Demokratisch Appel*) in 1976. Since then this united Christian Democrat party has dominated government, alongside the liberals. Some disgruntled Protestants remain outside (three Calvinist MPs were elected in 1985); radical Catholics have gone to the left. Tensions remain, such as over liberalizing abortion (Catholic reticence over this blocked a possible CDA/PvdA coalition in 1977). But the religions get on as well within one party as they did when there were three.

David Hanley

# NETHERLANDS DEPENDENCIES

## Aruba

Aruba left the Netherlands Antilles federation in 1986 and faces full independence in 1996. Following a decline in the petroleum industry, the Dutch dependency faces severe economic crisis. Approximately 80 per cent of the 67,000 population (mid-1983 est.) is Roman Catholic, with Dutch Protestants, Methodists, Evangelicals, Jehovah's Witnesses, and Adventists also present. There have been no recent reports of serious Church–State conflicts.

# Netherlands Antilles


The Netherlands Antilles (the Leeward Islands of Bonaire and Curaçao and the Windward Islands of St. Maarten, St. Eustacius, and Saba) currently faces daunting problems, with severe economic decline coupled with a demand by the strongman leader of St. Maarten for independence by 1990. To the consternation of the Hague, with long-term hopes of an independent "Antilles of Five" by 1996, Curaçao also is considering an independent path.

Approximately 80 per cent of the dependency's 250,000 people are Roman Catholic, with the majority of the Dutch Protestants found on the smaller Windward Islands. Anglicans, Methodists and Moravians have also had long presence. At a meeting of a Caribbean Council of Churches delegation held in Curaçao in late 1987, two local government officials expressed concern at the "virtual onslaught" being made by "foreign religious groups" on the island. In a condition of social upheaval, the search for moral and spiritual standards also coincides with the use of religion for ideological ends.

Virgil Wiebe


# NEW ZEALAND


The New Zealand islands are so isolated that European explorers did not discover the country until the eighteenth century. The idyllic isolation encouraged a mass migration of Europeans. The white settlers, known as "Pakeha", soon outnumbered the indigenous Polynesian tribes, the Maoris, and started a process of land confiscation which is only now being seriously challenged.

The white settlers brought Christianity to New Zealand and, after initial hesitation, Maori people accepted the new religion, especially the Anglican, Methodist or Catholic versions. Two indigenous religions, Ratana and Ringatu, based on Christianity, developed. Ratana has political importance for Maoris and has provided most of the Maori political leadership in recent years.

In 1840, when the British took possession of New Zealand, they signed a collective treaty with many of the Maori tribes. Known as the Treaty of Waitangi, it is today the focus of most political debate in the country. It is the basis of renewed Maori land claims and because it speaks of sharing sovereignty, it is being invoked in every situation from control of the fishing industry to selling the air waves for radio.

The Church has generally been supportive of Maori rights and the three major Churches have committed themselves to a policy of biculturalism. This has led to the return of Church land to Maori ownership, the growth and empowerment of the Maori bishopric in the Anglican church, the appointment of the first Maori Catholic bishop and the decision by the Methodist church to give US$1,000,000 from a trust fund to a landless Maori tribe to enable them to buy back possession of land.

In 1984, the Labour government under the Methodist lay preacher David Lange was elected to office. Nominally socialist, it soon introduced the most radical economic and social reforms in New Zealand history. These have been based on a need to reduce the national deficit and lower the inflation rate but have led to a massive rise in unemployment and social dislocation. The mainstream Churches have opposed many of the reforms, not on economic grounds, but because of their effect on the poor sections of the community.

Soon after election, the government fulfilled an election promise when it refused port entry to a nuclear-armed American ship. This isolated New Zealand from its three main allies, the United States, Great Britain and, to a lesser extent, Australia. The policy has been maintained and on June 4, 1987, the nuclear-free stand was written into law. The anti-nuclear, pacifist approach has the support of more than 70 per cent of the general population and almost total support from religious bodies. Lange resigned on health grounds in August 1989.

With increased immigration from Asia, other religious communities are growing but they are still relatively small and show little interest in political questions. The growth of conservative and charismatic Christian groups is also noticeable and although they have been politically active in questions such as homosexuality and abortion to the point where they supported candidates at the 1987 election, they have made little impression on the country as a whole.

Ron O'Grady

# NICARAGUA

The Christian churches, especially the Catholic Church, have been important political actors since the Sandinista revolution as different political forces inside and outside the country have sought ecclesiastical and religious support for their own political positions. At the same time groups within the churches have their own political, theological and ecclesial agendas.

In the Catholic Church, in parallel with other Latin American countries, there are conflicts about the role of the Church and the way it is, or should be, "inserted" into society, which, while they reflect and echo conflicts in the wider society outside the Church, are not simply a continuation of those conflicts within the confines of the Church. The Church as an institution is a meeting-place for conflicts in the wider society and specifically ecclesial concerns.

The conflict between the Catholic bishops in Nicaragua and the Sandinista government is well-known. It has its roots in Nicaragua, in the political alliances and ideological preferences of the bishops, clergy and lay people themselves and of the Sandinistas. There are external forces as well. The

Vatican has strongly supported the positions taken by Cardinal Archbishop Obando y Bravo and sought to reduce the influence of the significant number of clergy and Catholic lay people who have advocated support for the Sandinista revolution. The US government and political groups close to it, such as the Institute on Religion and Democracy, have supported Obando y Bravo while numerous agencies and Church groups in the United States and Europe, Protestant and Catholic, have provided material and political support for Church groupings sympathetic to the Sandinistas.

As the initial coalition of forces which combined to overthrow the Somoza dictatorship broke down in the year following the revolution, the Catholic bishops, and in particular Archbishop Obando y Bravo of Managua, sided with the developing opposition. At the time the opposition consisted largely of groups representing business and land-owning interests which had thrown in their lot with Sandinistas in the months leading up to the overthrow of Somoza. The official positions adopted by the Catholic bishops mirrored the development of the attitude of these sectors. On June 2, 1979 the bishops issued a pastoral letter justifying armed insurrection against the Somoza regime which they described as a "case of evident and prolonged tyranny". It has been suggested that this was an attempt to come to terms with the imminent revolution long after the possibility of a negotiated solution had been swept away. Certainly, the letter came far too late to have any influence on Christians who might otherwise have hesitated to take up arms. Those who were going to fight with or support the Sandinistas in other ways had already made up their minds. The hierarchy and the Sandinistas, however, seemed to have reached a new understanding when the bishops published a pastoral letter the following September which affirmed that the revolution was "authentically Nicaraguan".

By 1982, however, Archbishop Obando y Bravo was already being feted in the United States as an opposition leader. In September 1983, the bishops deliberately challenged the legitimacy of the government by condemning the conscription law on the grounds that the Sandinistas were drafting young men into the armed forces to serve an ideology rather than the country. This letter came after the disastrous visit of the Pope to Nicaragua had reinforced the support of the Vatican for Obando's view that the Sandinista government was a Marxist, totalitarian regime in the making. This position led inevitably to the view that the contra rebels were indeed "freedom fighters" as they had been described by President Reagan. The official position of the Sandinistas, in contrast, was that the contras were mercenaries in the service of a foreign power who did not have a legitimate role in Nicaraguan politics.

In November 1984 the Sandinistas won presidential and National Assembly elections with a two-thirds majority in a contest judged as fair by international observers. Before and after the elections there was lull in the hostility between the bishops and the government and some bishops made statements condemning the brutality of the contra attacks which were taken as a sign that the bishops were not as united as the signatures at the foot of pastoral letters indicated. In June 1985, however, Archbishop Obando was made a cardinal — at present he is the only cardinal in Central America — indicating clear Vatican support for his position of uncompromising hostility towards the Sandinistas. Obando underlined his position on his return from Rome by breaking his journey in Miami and celebrating mass for a congregation of Nicaraguan exiles including the contra leaders Adolfo Calero and Eden Pastora. "I do not object to being identified with the people who have taken up arms", Obando y Bravo was reported as saying after being photographed with the contras.

After his return Obando y Bravo made a sort of progress through Nicaragua, timing his visits where possible to coincide with the festivals of the patron saints of the towns and villages, so as to guarantee as large a turn-out as possible. Between June 15 and October 15, when the state of emergency was renewed in a stricter form, Obando y Bravo made more than 70 such visits. Each one of his visits was announced by the "15 de septiembre" FDN contra radio, broadcasting from Honduras, as if it were part of their own programme of counter-revolutionary activities. The effect of this high profile activity was to make him even more of a national figure. On October 3 he was elected President of the Bishops' Conference.

By 1986 the Sandinista leadership was beginning to refer to the "strategic defeat" of the contras. The organization of conscription, the deployment of helicopter gunships and the formation of the BLIs (Brigadas de Lucha Irregular) which sought out and pursued contra units transformed the war. Writing in mid-1986, Conor Cruise O'Brien thought that the contras were already past their peak and gauged the effects of their decline on the Nicaraguan Church:

> "To support the weaker side in a civil war, in the hope that it may be about to be rescued by a foreign invasion, is an extraordinarily high-risk policy, which prudent church-men — whatever their personal inclinations — would always wish to avoid. It rather looks as if prudent churchmen may currently be a rising force in the Nicaraguan Episcopate and that they may be beginning to rein their impetuous primate, the 'Cardinal of Central America'." (Conor Cruise O'Brien, "God and Man in Nicaragua", *The Atlantic Monthly*, August 1986, p. 54).

It is doubtful, however, whether any of the other bishops in Nicaragua was in a position to rein in Obando y Bravo with the added prestige and authority of his Cardinal's hat.

In the latter half of 1985 relations between Church and State deteriorated even further with the declaration of a new and more rigorous state of emergency in October, the closure of *Radio Catolica* and the seizing of a new church periodical, *Iglesia*, which the archdiocese had refused to submit to censorship as required by the state of emergency. The tension mounted in 1986 as the battle for contra aid heated up in the US Congress.

The appointment of a new Nuncio in April 1986, Mgr Paolo Giglio, did signal a change in Vatican policy. This was reinforced in June by cordial interviews between the Nicaraguan vice-president, Sergio Ramirez — not a "comandante" turned politician but a writer — and the Pope and Cardinal Casaroli, the Vatican Secretary of State.

At the same time, however, Obando y Bravo was undermining the Nicaraguan government in the United States and Bishop Vega of Juigalpa was campaigning openly for contra aid visiting Washington before crucial Congress votes.

On July 2, Vega criticized the judgement of the International Court upholding Nicaragua's complaint against the United States, saying that a court decision which was not based on all the facts could be only a limited judgement. On July 4, Vega was unceremoniously deposited on the frontier of Nicaragua and Honduras by Ministry of the Interior officials. At the same time the government refused re-entry into Nicaragua to Fr Bismarck Carballo, the press officer of the Archdiocese of Managua and an unconditional supporter of Obando, who was returning from a visit to France. These expulsions marked the nadir of Church-state relations.

Shortly afterwards the new Nuncio managed to restart the Church-state dialogue. This progressed slowly from September and was given a boost by the successful organization of a Eucharistic Conference in November, which brought many ecclesiastical personalities to Nicaragua, including Mother Teresa. The dialogue continued haltingly in 1987, punctuated by Obando's obstinate refusal to condemn even the worst contra atrocities, until the Guatemala Accord (Esquipulas II) was signed in early August. One of the requirements of the accord was that each Central American government should set up a National Reconciliation Commission which should include a representative of the Bishops' Conference. Obando was chosen as the representative and was unanimously elected as its President.

The Episcopal Conference published a pastoral letter on September 17, 1987 reiterating the position of earlier letters on reconciliation by warning against government manipulation and calling for a dialogue between all Nicaraguans, that is, including the contras. Two weeks later the Nicaraguan government revoked the expulsion orders on Bishop Vega and Fr Bismarck Carballo and allowed *Radio Catolica* back on the air. On September 30, the opposition paper, *La Prensa*, which was closed down in June 1986, was allowed to reopen and publish without censorship.

Although the Sandinistas could justifiably claim military victory over the contras the economic effects of the war made a settlement increasingly urgent. The Guatemala Accord had breached their rigidly held position that there could be no dialogue with the contras by specifying that governments and insurgent movements should arrange cease-fire agreements. This clearly required some shift in the Nicaraguan position. First, in November, the government agreed to indirect or mediated talks and asked Obando to act as the intermediary between themselves and the contras. Later, in January 1988, at a summit meeting of the Central American presidents convened to evaluate the peace process, Daniel Ortega announced new measures: direct talks with the contras; the lifting of the state of emergency; an expanded amnesty for all ex-National Guardsmen and contras once a cease-fire was arranged; and the abolition of the People's Anti-Somocista Tribunals, the courts used to try suspected contras.

These measures and the subsequent development of the peace process have brought about a cold and formal detente between Obando and the Nicaraguan government. The attitude of both sides is one of deep scepticism about the other's intentions. The hostility of Obando and his supporters towards the Sandinistas has been fuelled over the years by the willingness of the Sandinista leadership to use sticks as well as carrots in its dealings with the Catholic hierarchy and, in particular, by a number of "dirty tricks" mounted by the security services to discredit the Church. On August 11, 1982, for example, Fr (now Monseñor) Bismarck Carballo was paraded naked through the streets of a Managua suburb after allegedly having been chased from a house by an enraged husband who found him dallying with his wife. Whatever the facts of the case, the crudity with which it was handled by the Sandinista media and the Ministry of the Interior rebounded against the government. Two years later, in August 1984, the Sandinistas expelled 10 foreign priests who were known supporters of Obando after a march in support of a Nicaraguan priest, Fr Amado Pena, who was arrested in July after having fallen into a trap set for him by an agent provocateur. Under the state of emergency then in force the archdiocese should have asked for permission to hold the march. Naturally it did not. Of those expelled, only five had actually taken part in the protest. The others were generally regarded as effective conservative priests with a following in their parishes or schools. Most recently, in July 1988, *La Prensa* was suspended for two weeks and *Radio Catolica* was closed down again for a month for allegedly misreporting an opposition demonstration which the government claimed was part of a US plan to destabilize Nicaragua.

The other cause of the enmity is the grass-roots groups and base communities which support the Sandinista government and who have been denounced as a parallel "popular Church" by Obando and his allies. The priests and religious who advise and encourage these groups have been the victims of what they see as ecclesiastical persecution. Recent reports, however, indicate that the base community movement is at a low ebb. The base community movement, just like the traditional Church, suffers from hierarchical, "top-down" organization. Moreover the difficulties of daily life, particularly in Managua, keep people away from meetings where they are asked to deal with yet more problems. A pro-government religious said: "People are faced with going to church to gain some solace and sing a few hymns or spending hours in discussions in a base community."

Apart from the issue of the war and what they see as Obando's support for the contras, the Sandinistas and their supporters in the Church complain of ecclesiastical harassment of the base communities and the priests who work with them. In February 1989, for instance, it was reported that an Italian priest, Father Ubaldo Gervasoni, who was kidnapped and threatened by contras after denouncing the murder by a contra unit of a peasant, had been told to leave the country. Father Gervasoni publicly accused the Vatican of trying to force him to leave the country.

Although the situation of the remaining priests heading ministries in the government — Miguel D'Escoto at the Foreign Ministry and Fernando Cardenal at the Ministry of Education — has been resolved through suspension and, in Cardenal's case, expulsion from the Society of Jesus, they continue to be an irritant to the hierarchy. They provide a focus and an inspiration to Christians in Nicaragua and abroad who find in the Sandinista revolution a concrete example of how the "preferential option for the poor" can be put into practice in a poverty-stricken third world country.

In late 1988 the authority of Cardinal Obando was undermined by reports that he was paying $9,000 a month each to five consultants in Miami and Washington D.C. out of funds provided by the US Agency for International Development (USAID) to the Organization of American States ((OAS) to promote the peace process in Nicaragua. Two of these consultants, Roberto Rivas and Miguel Dominguez, were well-known aides of the cardinal. Obando, as president of the National Reconciliation Commission on Nicaragua, and OAS Secretary-General Joao Baena Soares, are authorised to draw on the funds as "witnesses" to the Sandinista–contra peace agreement. A US government auditor subsequently demanded that the employees pay back some of their salaries because USAID is not permitted to fund salaries in excess of $72,000 a year. Since the peace talks broke down in June 1988, the Nicaraguan government disputes that there is an agreement to monitor. On these grounds the government seized 17 vehicles imported by the archdiocese ostensibly for use by monitors of the peace agreement. The cardinal complained that the press revelations about the salaries, first published in the National Catholic Reporter in the United States, amounted to a "campaign of slander against the church."

New Sandinista measures have removed the last remaining formal obstacles to improvement in Church–State relations. In February 1989 they released 1,939 members of Somoza's National Guard tried and imprisoned for war crimes since 1979, leaving only 30 in prison. In March Daniel Ortega announced that the 10 foreign priests expelled from the country in 1984 would be permitted to return and that *Radio Catolica* would be permitted to broadcast news bulletins as well as religious programmes.

This account has concentrated on relations between the Catholic Church and the government. The minority Protestant Churches, accounting for about 15 per cent of the population, have had a different history, with their leaders supporting or seeking accommodation with the government while many of the faithful have been much more critical. The leadership of CEPAD (Evangelical Committee for Development Aid) in particular has supported government development programmes and has tried to nurture an understanding of social justice issues among naturally conservative evangelical pastors. The Moravian Church ministers mainly to the Miskito population of the Atlantic Coast and its attitude to the Sandinista government has followed the ups and downs of the government's relations with the Miskitos, ranging from outright hostility in 1981 to acceptance of the Sandinistas' good faith in 1988.

It is doubtful whether any practical measures can bring about a real rapprochement between the Catholic hierarchy and the Sandinista government. Over the years they have consistently interpreted each others' actions in the worst possible light. The enormous suffering caused by the contra war has widened the breach between Church and state, rather than providing opportunities for reconciliation, with each side blaming the other for being the cause, or part of the cause, of the conflict. They have separate and opposed visions of what the new, post-Somoza, Nicaragua should become. Any concessions made by the government in the meantime are seen by Obando and his supporters as tactical manoeuvres rather than evidence of a change of heart.

George Gelber

# NIGER

With a population of nearly seven million, Niger is one of the most Islamic countries in West Africa. About 97 per cent of the population is Sunni Muslim with most of the rest following traditional religion and a mere 30,000 or so Christian. The most powerful religious organizations are the Muslim brotherhoods: Tijaniyya, Senoussi and Hamalists. Adherence to Islam gives advantages in all walks of life. A bloody military coup in 1974 brought the suppression of all political parties and President Seyni Kountché to power. He gained solid support from France, the ex-colonial power, which feared that if his policy of uniting the minority tribes against the 70 per cent Hausa failed then its own influence would dwindle and that of Nigeria correspondingly rise. When Kountché died the Chief of Staff, Ali Saibu, became President by the unanimous vote of the 12-strong ruling Military Council.

H. S. Wilson

# NIGERIA

## Introduction: the vicissitudes of independence politics

There are two problems that immediately beset the study of religion and politics in Nigeria. The first is that the country has had no accurate census. In consequence, not only is the overall number of inhabitants not known but no reliable data exist for the numbers of different religious adherents. The best estimate for the number of inhabitants seems to be around 105 million. In making estimates of religious affiliation one might suggest that some 45 million are Muslim (mostly living in the northern states but forming also a third of the population in the western states); some 35 million are Christian; and some 25 million observe forms of African traditional religions.[1] The second problem is that in Nigeria it is often difficult to distinguish religion from ethnicity as a political factor. The complexity of the ethnic issue is evident from the fact that the country is made up of over 600 ethnic groups or nations — some are very small — but five at least (Hausa, Yoruba, Ibo, Bini/Ishan, and Effik/Ibibio) have populations larger than most African states. Nigerian politics, including the 1967–70 civil war, has revolved around the competition of ethnic groups.

Since independence in 1960 Nigeria has had a chequered development. It was established as a federation of three units (later four in 1964) in which the Northern Region was larger than all the others together. The governments of the first republic were toppled by a military coup in January 1966. The first military government was itself overthrown in mid-1966; the overthrow was accompanied by a pogrom against Ibo in the Northern parts of the country;

civil war then ensued between the Ibo (Biafrans) and the other peoples. The end of the civil war saw the country broken into 12 states (and later into 21). The military regime gave way to a civilian regime in 1979 but the latter was overthrown in 1983 and the country has been under military rule since then. Civilian rule is once again promised for 1992.

The civilian governments were overthrown as independence politics revealed the strains of a new and artificial country that had not had enough time to create a sense of nationhood out of a multiplicity of ethnic groups. More seriously again, constitutionalism — good law and a respect for the rules of the game, not least in refraining from pushing opponents to the wall — had not matured in the artificiality of colonial, and the insecurity of early independence, politics. Good leaders might have overcome some of the problems but the Nigerian leaders who had been formed in the politics of agitation turned out to be poor performers in the politics of governing: many proved to be incompetent in running a state with modern requirements; most were tribalist or communal in outlook and loyalties; too many were pervasively corrupt in the use of public money and in their general financial practices; and the country's intractable socio-economic problems were bound to lead elite groups to challenge out of dissatisfaction any government in power.

## Ethnicity, religion and social change

The basic political and social cleavage within Nigeria was for long between north and south — in practice between the majority far northern peoples (Hausa, Kanuri and Fulani) who formed a traditionalist and Muslim alliance and the majority southern peoples, Ibo and Yoruba (but also the Bini/Ishan and Effik/Ibibio). The southern peoples were also mostly becoming Christian and had sent their children to mission schools. The far northerners had retained the traditional social structures of the emirates relatively intact under British rule; and they had taken more slowly to modern-type education than the Southern peoples and more slowly than the middle belt peoples in the southern part of the northern region who were also becoming Christian. In consequence, they feared a federation in which the central or federal administrative structures were going to be controlled by mission-educated southerners. Though in the actual practice of politics the northern participants in power came mostly from the Hausa, Kanuri and Fulani groups, some also came from middle belt groups, most of which had allied with the far northern groups. Moreover, one of the features of all Nigerian governments since independence has been that while northerners tend to hold crucial security ministries, ministries have generally been distributed among representatives of all the main peoples.

Given this history, it might seem that religion has not appeared as a serious factor in Nigerian politics and in the Nigerian state. The dominant factor in political allegiance has tended to be allegiance to local communities (each community usually consisting of a set of towns or villages) that grouped together for political purposes along ethnic lines — Nigerians called the phenomenon "tribalism" from the old colonial term for ethnic group. The ethnic groups were also gradually evolving a sense of cultural identity alongside a capacity for political action.[2] However the link between the dominant northern coalition (Hausa, Kanuri and Fulani) and Islam led, on the one hand, northern ruling groups to use politically the

198                                                    RELIGION IN POLITICS

bonding factor of Islam, and, on the other hand, southerners to perceive
their northern opponents as Muslims. There were two other complicating
factors. First, northern Muslims, heavily influenced by Arab Islam, did not
easily accept a political regime in their country which they did not control.
Second, Muslim northerners for religious reasons as well as for reasons of
political control and the protection of their traditional social structures sought
a special place for the *sharia* or Muslim law within the Nigerian state and
affronted Christian Nigerians in the process.

While ill-will between Muslims and Christians has been a considerable
factor in recent Nigerian politics — something which I will come back to —
two earlier sets of phenomena require consideration. First, in 1966 the two
pogroms that were unleashed against Ibo in Northern, and mostly Muslim,
areas involved Muslims killing Christians. The Ibo had lived in an interstitial
way in Hausa and northern society. They had been lesser bureaucrats, small
traders and technicians who lived outside the traditional structures of the
communities and yet within rigid emirate political and social structures that
could not easily cope with social change and that were unable to contain
growing political insecurity and economic frustrations. Various politicians
and members of the northern intelligentsia turned Ibo into scapegoats for
such insecurity and frustration and had them killed in considerable numbers.[3]
In the subsequent civil war the Ibo secessionists used hatred of Islam as part
of their rallying propaganda — and they tried to depict the northern areas
as entirely Muslim, whereas they were probably 60–70 per cent Muslim.[4]

Second, in the late seventies and early eighties the same social frustrations
and uneasiness over the pace and shape of social change and inadequate
structures for coping with these problems led fundamentalist Muslim sects,
brotherhoods and extremists to rise in rebellion on different occasions in
Kano, Maiduguri, Gombe, Yola and elsewhere against the ruling authorities.
This time there were few Ibo available as scapegoats. Muslim fought against
Muslim in fratricidal strife which showed that the tensions that had led to
the Ibo pogroms were now being unleashed within socially-discordant and
class-divided northern communities. The Nigerian army was used to put
down these rebellions at a cost of hundreds, and even into thousands, of
lives.[5]

When the civilian regimes were overthrown, the military continued the
pattern of ethnic and religious balancing with ruling council members and
state governors representing a spread of groups and areas. An insensitive
break with careful politico-religious balancing came however when the present
head of state, President Babangida, a Muslim, turned Nigeria's observer status
at the Islamic Conference Organization into full membership in 1986 — with
the implication for Nigerian Christians that Nigeria was a Muslim state.[6]
The psychological impact on Christians was as sharp as the reaction was
unexpected by the government. Bitter and vocal Christian reactions left the
regime reacting indecisively and on one occasion even claiming that it had not
joined the body.[7] With the constitutional discussions that presently prepare
for a return to civilian rule the issue of *shari'a* (traditional Islamic religious)
law in the Nigerian constitution has come to the fore. Muslim members of
the Constituent Assembly want *shari'a* appeal courts at federal level; and
they also want the deletion of the "personal" restriction (which limited the
law to family and divorce law).[8] Christians want complete exclusion of *shari'a*
courts from the new constitution due to come in with a civilian regime in 1992.

Negotiations have broken down in a committee of the Constituent Assembly amidst recriminations and boycotts. In the wake of the controversy and other accusations President Babangida (on October 23, 1988) intervened to reaffirm that Nigeria would remain a secular state.[9]

These diversions and bitternesses coincided with the economic downturn of the country resulting from falling oil prices, industrial failure, economic mismanagement by the government and bureaucratic sluggishness and corruption. Before the *shari'a* controversy had reached its climax, in March 1987 riots broke out in northern areas against Christians in which communities were intimidated, persons killed and churches burnt. These Muslim riots drew on the assertiveness spreading through the Islamic world from the Iranian revolution; they were kindled by Muslim aspirations towards complete control in the areas where they were a majority; and they expressed resentment against a lack of economic growth that left groups locked in relative poverty and without much hope of breaking out of such poverty. If dissatisfaction took on a Muslim character in northern states, it is still the case that these riots differed little in underlying social character from the disturbances that broke out in 1989 in Lagos, Benin and elsewhere in the south. Again it is significant that university students — an aspiring intelligentsia arriving on the scene late and now cherishing few prospects corresponding to their education — played a central role in the disturbances in north and south.

## Rival theologies of politics and religion

Nigerian Muslims[10] not only reject Christianity as a religion but they have consistently seen Christianity as western; sure of a religion that claims to control the detail of life as well as its orientation and that is deeper than Christianity in its hold over most of its adherents they have not appreciated the Christian commitment of the southern and middle belt — educated intelligentsia; and they have also underestimated the belief shared by both the religious and the less religious members of the latter intelligentsia that not only was Islam a malign political factor in the country but that it was an unprogressive force that stood out against Nigerian modernization as well as aligning Nigeria with states that marginalized it in global and African politics. Also, southern and Christian groups have been little sensitive to how much more than the Muslim peoples they have benefited from federal resources and how much northern groups have good reason to be afraid of the southern lead in skills.

While Islam has in some measure benefited from federal sympathy and support and has in much greater measure again received considerable backing from many northern states, it has had to pay a political price for its own traditional linkages of religion and politics. A significant instance of political intervention in Muslim affairs was the manner in which a combined federal and state decision imposed a political nominee as sultan of Sokoto (traditional ruler of the largest Hausa emirate and head of Hausa Muslims as well as important to many Muslim groups) and provoked huge riots in Sokoto itself.[11] The heaviest cost of the political implications of Islam has, however, been the tendency for its sects to challenge both established religious and political orders.

Christianity has a tradition of the separation of Church and state. Moreover, the colonial state while using and helping the missionaries to construct and maintain schools and hospitals kept a certain distance from them, especially from Catholic missionaries, and took away from the churches any temptation to identify too closely with the colonial state or its successor, the independent state. After independence the Nigerian State and its regions/states took away from the Christians bodies much — though not all — of their power in education. For a period also they made it difficult — by withholding subsidies and by making it difficult to obtain visas and work permits for foreign doctors — for these bodies to run voluntary hospitals.[12] However the sheer quality of these hospitals, especially as contrasted with the better-funded but badly-run government hospitals, has offered them crucial popular support and protection. The churches have as well continued informal and community-linked development work. Finally, Christian episcopal and other appointments have avoided state intervention.

## Conclusion: politics, religion and the unity of the state

In recent Nigerian politics the defence of Islam — and conversely the defence of Christianity — has been used as a form of code for strains between far northern and southern groups.[13] Northerners have used Islam as an appropriate political ideology and organizing principle that appears to avoid the taint of ethnicity and yet enables claims to be put forward that benefit particular ethnic groups. Southern groups have taken the same approach. This religious cleavage and confrontation which mimics and further envenoms the old north-south division could in the longer run prove more serious than confrontation between straightforward ethnic alliances since this religious conflict could enter into and threaten new and cherished modernizing social identities as well as forming part of embittering and widening ethnic cleavages.

A continuing north-south split could also with time threaten the unity of the country by putting far northern groups into a position of political inferiority that they might believe they could resolve only through secession. Yet if they were to set out on a path of secession, and if southerners (and possibly most middle belters) were loath to stop them, southerners might discover that northerners provide them with a certain negative unity and that a fission principle once accepted might not easily halt with one secession.

### Notes

[1] I will say little or nothing directly in the course of this paper about these groups. They are gradually losing numbers to Islam and to Christianity. In a sense once contemporary technology through its attitudes, tools and organisation had begun to make its impact through the school system, missionary effort, and economic and technological development, traditional religion had little hope of formal survival. To put this case graphically: In Yoruba traditional religion, for example, Ogun, the god of iron, was run down by a lorry; Shonponna, the god of smallpox, was killed by vaccination; Shango, the god of the storm, was explained away by climatology; and the many spirits of the creeks were driven away by motor-boats. Yet the age-old attitudes engendered in Nigerian peoples by traditional religion, environmental conditions and social linkages endure in good measure within Muslim and Christian structures and observances.
[2] It is important to remember however that ethnic determinism grossly oversimplifies Nigerian politics and that most groups split in their approach to politics.

3 It is difficult to be sure of the numbers killed. The Biafran secessionists claimed that the number was 30,000. My own interviewing in Nigeria at that period suggested that the number was closer to 6,000–8,000, dreadful figures in themselves. Most of those killed were poor people — the well-to-do had left before the second pogrom as they saw disaster coming — who could not afford to leave their jobs and small properties.

4 In the civil war the federal infantry was composed almost entirely of Christian middle belters (Tiv, Idoma, Igalla, Southern Zaria and others), while the military technical services were mostly manned by the Yoruba.

5 There was a millennarian thrust in the fundamental insurrections. The most serious was that led by Muhammed Marwa/Maitatsine that purported to set aside western corruption among the Muslim ruling groups. In recent times states have again become afraid of religious disturbances. Gongola state banned open-air religious preaching for a second time in January 1988; and Bauchi and Kwara later in the year acted to restrict the influence of the Muslim sect, *Kungiyar yan Shia*, which draws inspiration from Iran.

6 It is fair to say that the federal government had arranged and facilitated visits by the Pope and the Archbishop of Canterbury in 1982.

7 Muslims have also been inept in assuming that the location of the new federal capital (within a small Northern emirate) gave it a quasi-Muslim identity and that they could surreptitiously forward the islamicization of the state and the capital in state-subsidised mosque-building.

8 In the 1979 constitution *shari'a* courts of appeal could be set up at the request of an individual state. Deep divisions had also manifested themselves in the pre-1979 discussions.

9 A paradoxical result of ethnico-religious confrontation may well be however, that the Nigerian state while remaining resolutely secular will not easily implement secularist or anti-religious policies; and so it is likely to avoid statist measures such as other African countries — Zaire is an obvious example — have enforced. It is ironic that in Nigeria there has been neither a Church–state problem nor a confrontation in the strict sense between politics and religion.

10 Yoruba Muslims form a considerable exception. They exhibit the religious tolerance that characterizes Yoruba society generally and in which the individual lineages contain amicably Christian and Muslim members.

11 There were three days of rioting including deaths and the storming of the local prison with the release of 2,000 prisoners.

12 At the end of the Nigerian civil war almost all the Catholic foreign missionaries — they were mostly Irish — were expelled from the former eastern states for the role they had played in siding with the secession. Throughout the federation after that time Catholic priests and sisters had difficulty in obtaining visas and residence permits. There was strong suspicion that Muslim elements in the federal government played a considerable part for both religious and political reasons in enforcing this restrictive policy.

13 From time to time argument between the religions takes on odd tones. When the government in 1983 announced a population control policy — population growth is estimated at 3.3 per cent per annum — to persuade women to reduce their average number of children to four, Muslim leaders denounced the policy as un-Islamic, while Christian leaders such as the Catholics opposed its contraceptive elements and others thought that it gave Muslim polygamists a population edge over Christian monogamists. In real truth limitation of births does not come easily to the psychology of Nigerians; and, strangely enough, comparative evidence seems to suggest that monogamy produces more children under the same conditions than polygamy.

James O'Connell

# NORWAY

The state Church in Norway, the Norwegian Church, counts 92 per cent of Norwegians as its members. Within the Norwegian Church there are strong lay movements of a pietistic and low-church character as a heritage from the revivals of the nineteenth century. It is estimated that more than 5 per cent of all Norwegians are members of at least one low-church organization. The largest free Church is the Pentecostalist movement with about 2 per cent of the population.

Norway has the oldest and the strongest religious party in Scandinavia. The Christian People's Party was founded in 1933 and got more than 12 per cent of the votes in 1977; in 1985 its percentage was 8.3. The strongholds of the party have been the southern and western constituencies, where the low-church movements have the majority of their members.

The Christian People's Party has been a member of coalition governments of centre parties on two occasions (1965–1971 and 1972–1973); its leaders held the office of Prime Minister. The party has been successful in its attempts to preserve a clear Christian profile of religious education in the schools but it has not managed to fight liberal abortion laws although it had the whole of the Christian organizations of Norway behind it on this issue. At the referendum in 1972 about Norwegian membership of the Common Market the Christian People's Party belonged to those groups which were most strongly opposing it.

The Social Democrat Party accepted the state Church already during the 1930s and nowadays regards the Norwegian Church as an institution that "fulfills legitimate welfare needs that the state has a duty to support". The Social Democrats have, however, hesitated to grant the state Church inner autonomy and the representative body the church got in 1984 still lacks the right to take decisions on many issues vital for religious life.

The Norwegian bishops and the clergy have — as a reminiscence of their acting against the German occupation power — often expressed their opinions in questions that are under political debate. The abortion laws and disarmament are only two examples.

Göran Gustafsson

# OMAN

Oman is ruled by the pre-eminent sheikhs of the Bu Sa'id clan, in alliance with senior members of the country's other leading tribal confederations and a limited number of western-educated technocrats. Since consolidating control over the government at the end of 1971, the ruler, Sultan Qabus bin Sa'id, has acted as Head of State, Prime Minister, minister of defence, minister of finance and petroleum affairs and governor of Dhofar and the national capital area. The ruling family shares with a majority of the indigenous population adherence to the heterodox Ibadi movement; this movement broke away from mainstream Islam almost immediately after the death of the Prophet, when a faction based in the Iraqi city of Basra began demanding that the leader of the community (the *imam*) be popularly elected on the basis of education and ability rather than appointed on the basis of family lineage. Struggles between successive *imams* based in the interior north and west and Sultans supported by the tribes in the south represented a basic dynamic of Omani politics until the mid-1950s, when troops loyal to Sultan Sa'id overran the heartland of the imamate and forced the *imam* to resign.

In addition to the split between the sultanate and the imamate, politics in Oman have been characterized by sharp divisions between the majority Ibadi population and minority Sunni groups in the southern province of Dhofar. Many of these groups have hereditary ties to the Hadramawt region of South Yemen, as well as to isolated communities in the Yemeni highlands. Such divisions provided a sectarian dimension to the secessionist movement in Dhofar that engaged the central government in a fierce civil war from the mid-1960s to the mid-1970s. With the suppression of the secessionists, the Omani regime began encouraging a kind of non-sectarian Islamism: a network of new government-supported mosques was constructed, Islamic law was made the basis of the legal system and the Sultan cultivated a reputation for religious devotion. These moves, along with the general prosperity that accompanied the development of the local petroleum industry in the years after 1975, for the most part precluded the emergence of an Islamist movement opposed to the regime during the 1980s.

Fred H. Lawson

# PAKISTAN

## Background

Pakistan is located in the north-western region of the Indian sub-continent and is estimated to have a population of just over 100,000,000, the majority of whom live in the countryside. The country's economy is heavily dependent on agriculture although substantial industrial bases have been developed around the cities or Karachi and Lahore.

There are four main ethnic groups: the Sindhis, the Baloch, the Punjabis and the Pathans, each with its distinctive language and culture. At independence Pakistan's administrative provinces, namely Sind, Baluchistan, Punjab and the North West Frontier Province, conformed closely to the distribution of its principal ethnic groups. In the last few years there have been growing demands, particularly in the southern province of Sind, to class Urdu-speaking Muslim migrants from India, otherwise known as *muhajirs* or migrants, as a distinct ethnic "nationality" with a claim to its own province.

Islam is the dominant religion and the majority of Pakistanis adhere to the Hanafi school of jurisprudence. There is also a substantial Shia minority and significant numbers (about 3,000,000 to 4,000,000) of Ahmadis, also known as Qadianis. The Ahmadis are followers of Mirza Ghulam Ahmad, a minor reformer who founded the sect in the Punjab in the mid-nineteenth century. Ahmadis, who regard themselves as true Muslims, believe that an inspired reformer is destined to appear in every millennium. Orthodox Muslims, however, who believe that Muhammad was the last prophet, reject the Ahmadis as heretics. Since independence, religious groups in Pakistan have campaigned strenuously for Ahmadis to be officially designated as non-Muslims. This campaign resulted in violent demonstrations in some of Pakistan's major cities in the early 1950s. In April 1984, a government decree authorized by General Zia ul-Haq declared the Ahmadis non-Muslims. The decree also made it a criminal offence, punishable by imprisonment for up to three years, for any Ahmadi to describe himself a Muslim, perform Muslim religious rites, propagate the Ahmadi faith, refer to Ahmadi places of worship as "mosques", or vote, unless registered as a non-Muslim.

Of Pakistan's small non-Muslim minorities, the most important are the Christians, the Parsis, and a handful of Hindus concentrated mostly in the southern province of Sind.

## Government and Politics

Pakistan was created in 1947 as a result of the partition of India. For many, if not all, Muslims in India it signified the right to a separate Muslim homeland. Pakistan at independence comprised two halves, East Pakistan (now Bangladesh) and West Pakistan, divided by a thousand miles of Indian territory. The emphasis upon Islamic symbols in the movement for Pakistan led many Muslims to assume that Islam would play a dominant role in the political and constitutional evolution of the new state. Their views were most forcefully expressed by the fundamentalist *Jamaat-i-Islami*, or Islamic Party, under the leadership of the late Maulana Abul Ala Maududi.

The Jamaat-i-Islami is Pakistan's most well-organized religious party. Its cadres seek to emulate the strict discipline and political loyalty characteristic of the Muslim Brotherhood in parts of the Arab world. Its founder, Maulana Maududi, although learned in some aspects of Islamic law, was not himself a formally trained religious scholar, or *alim*. Indeed, his fundamentalist and militant views have always been much closer in spirit to the thinking of activists like Sayyid Qutb of the Egyptian Brotherhood than to the more scholarly temper of the *ulama* who dominate Pakistan's religious establishment. Although the party has fared poorly in electoral contests, it enjoys considerable support among the urban lower-middle classes in the cities like Karachi and Hyderabad in Sind. The party is also known to have increased its influence among sections of the army where the secularist ethos is being steadily weakened as British-trained officers give way to younger, less literate officers, drawn from impoverished families where religion is often of overwhelming importance. The party's close links with the army were greatly strengthened in the Zia years when the Jamaat, under its new leader Mian Tufail Ahmad, took a close interest in and actively endorsed the programme of Islamization. By 1988, however, the party had begun to distance itself from the Zia regime. In common with the rest of the opposition, it called for an elected government and criticized the cosmetic nature of Islamization under Zia.

Other parties that have been active in the campaign for an Islamic State include the *Jamiat-al Ulama-i-Islam*, presently led by Maulana Fazlur Rahman, and the *Jamiat-al Ulama-i-Pakistan*, a Sunni progressive party, under Maulana Shah Ahmad Noorani. Both groups were also in the forefront of the campaign in 1952–53 to reduce Ahmadis to the status of a non-Muslim minority.

Despite the influence and popular appeal of these religious parties, Pakistan has always harboured strong secular and modernist currents which have resisted the consolidation of a strictly Islamic State. These were best represented by the westernized elite close to Muhammad Ali Jinnah who is widely credited with having wrested Pakistan from the British. Constitution-making in the early 1950s which reflected some of the existing tensions between secular and clerical forces, resulted in 1956 in a Constitution that decisively rejected a theocratic Islamic state.

In the autumn of 1958, a coup led by General Ayub Khan replaced the country's fragile civilian government by a military regime. Although the new government headed by Ayub paid lip-service to the role of Islam in public life, its policies tended to be distinctively secular in spirit. One of the government's bolder steps consisted of promulgating a new Constitution in 1962 which, in stark contrast to the document of 1956, referred to the "Republic of Pakistan" instead of the "Islamic Republic of Pakistan".

Among the government's most progressive, if controversial pieces of legislation was the Family Laws Ordinance enacted in the early 1960s. This sought, among other things, to curb polygamy, bar childhood marriage and make the process of divorce, particularly for women, more humane. Other measures introduced by Ayub's government included the constitutional equality of Muslims and non-Muslims, and the creation of an Institute of Islamic Research designed to promote modernist views.

Muslim orthodox opinion was fiercely critical of the regime's new reforms. Powerful pressure groups consisting of influential *ulama* (religious scholars) mobilized public opinion and forced the National Assembly in 1963 to adopt a constitutional amendment restoring the word "Islamic" as a preface to the "Republic of Pakistan". Orthodox Muslims were also unhappy about the nature of Islamic Studies then being conducted at the Institute of Islamic Research. By 1969, growing pressure led to the resignation of its modernist director. The organization of a common front, namely the Democratic Action Committee, against Ayub's government, served as a vehicle for religious parties like the *Jamiat-al Ulama-i-Pakistan* (JUP) and the *Jamiat-al Ulama-i-Islam* (JUI) to publicize their demands for the repeal of the Family Laws Ordinance. The participation of the most well-known of the religious parties, namely the Jamaat-i-Islami tended, on the whole, to be more muted. This was not so much because of its support for government policies, but because its more radical and fundamentalist orientation was often at odds with the more conservative thinking of the *ulama* who dominated the JUP and the JUI.

In March 1969, popular pressure forced Ayub to step aside in favour of a transitional military government headed by General Yahya Khan. Pakistan's first general election was held in December 1970. The Awami League under Sheikh Mujibur Rahman secured the largest number of votes all of which were, however, confined to East Pakistan. The Pakistan People's Party (PPP) under Zulfiqar Ali Bhutto, was returned with the largest number of seats in West Pakistan. Fundamental disagreements concerning the modalities of power, in particular the right of Sheikh Mujib to form a government, led subsequently to the secession of East Pakistan, now Bangladesh, in 1972.

In January 1972, Bhutto was formally sworn in as Prime Minister of a truncated Pakistan. High on the agenda was the question of an Islamic State. Its significance was all the more poignant as it was clear that a distinct Islamic identity which had ostensibly been the basis of Pakistan in 1947, had failed to guarantee the unity of the state. Bhutto's instinct, like that of his predecessor Ayub, was for an essentially secular constitution. Like Ayub, Bhutto had his own set of constraints; for whereas his Pakistan People's Party clearly held a majority in the provinces of Sind and Punjab, religious parties, most notably the Jamiat-al Ulema-i-Islam, dominated coalition governments in the North West Frontier Province and Baluchistan. In order for Bhutto to obtain their co-operation, these parties demanded the introduction of strict Islamic laws, including corporal punishment for theft and adultery, and a return to the veil for women. Although Bhutto's constitution of 1973 made few concessions to orthodox Muslim opinion, it is clear that he recognised the political importance of Pakistan's religious parties. This was reflected in the pains taken by the new government to describe its left-wing programme of social and economic reform as "Islamic Socialism", and its willingness to declare Islam as the state religion of Pakistan under the new constitution.

Bhutto's style of government, and in particular his intolerance of political dissent, prompted the creation of a broad-based opposition known as the Pakistan National Alliance, which included in its ranks: the *Tehriq-i-Istiqlal* led by a former Air Marshal; the Pakistan National Democratic Party; the All Jammu and Kashmir Muslim Conference; and established religious parties like the *Jamaat-i-Islami*, the *Jamiat-al Ulama-i-Islam*, the *Jamiat-al Ulama-i-Pakistan*; and the Khaksars (a group of militant Muslims whose antecedents lay in the 1940s when it gained notoriety under the leadership of Inayetullah Mashriqi).

The role assumed by religious parties in the opposition to Bhutto placed a renewed emphasis on the debate on Islamization. The conduct of Bhutto's personal life, his disregard for religious observances and his preference for alcohol, were just some of the issues which allowed the religious opposition to fuel public sentiment against his government and to press for the introduction of an Islamic State. In July 1977, Bhutto was deposed by a military coup led by the recently-appointed army Chief of Staff, General Zia ul-Haq.

## Islamization under Zia

The heart of General Zia's Islamization programme lay in the idea of "Nizam-i-Mustapha", a state where all Muslim Pakistanis would lead their lives according to the precepts of Islam. Early in 1979, Zia announced his intention to institute an Islamic system. This was followed in June 1980 by the introduction of a legal code that was deemed to be consistent with the *shari'a* (the body of Islamic law based on the Koran and Sunnah).

The new reforms provoked widespread criticism among non-Muslim minorities, women's groups and human rights organizations. Non-Muslims feared they would be reclassified as *dhimmis* (protected minorities), and claimed that this would render them subordinate in law to Muslims. Many also opposed the government's return to a system of separate electorates which restricted the right of non-Muslims to participate in a common electoral system.

Women's groups, especially the newly formed Women's Action Forum (WAF), were equally critical of the government's Islamic measures which they believed would institutionalize the inequality of women. Many denounced the attempt to introduce retrogressive legislation (later embodied in a law passed by the National Assembly in October 1984), under which the evidence of two women would be deemed equal to that of one man. Women's and lawyers groups also protested against a provision sanctioned by Islamic law which required business contracts to be signed either by two men or one man and two women. The inequality of women was seen also to be implicit in the proposal to restrict the death penalty to cases which only involved the murder of a man.

Zia's campaign for "moral regeneration" also met with criticism from human rights groups. Many expressed concern at the new measures which were regarded as both excessively punitive and inconsistent with the spirit of the Declaration of Human Rights. Human rights lawyers in Pakistan condemned as especially regressive and inhumane the government's intention to treat adultery as a criminal offence punishable by stoning, and to introduce flogging and the amputation of hands for theft.

Zia's programme of Islamization also met with resistance from Pakistan's Shia minority who were particularly critical of the government's proposals to introduce *zakat* (alms tax). In March 1979 growing concern among the Shia community resulted in the resuscitation of the *Tehrik-i-Nifaz-i-Fiqah-i-Jafria* (TNFJ) or the Movement for the Implementation of the Shia code. Under the leadership of the late Allama Arif Hussain al Hussaini, the Movement was transformed in 1987 from a religious pressure group to a political party. One of its objectives was to enable Shias to resist the application of Hanafi laws, i.e. the main Sunni code, and to opt instead for laws based on a Shia code derived from the Jafria school of jurisprudence. The party has a strong

following among the Pathans of the Parachinar region in the North West
Frontier Province and maintains strong links with political activists in Iran.
It also enjoys support in parts of Baluchistan.

In February 1983, sectarian clashes between Sunnis and Shias in the
suburbs of Karachi resulted in the death of six people. In March, a further
seven were killed in renewed sectarian violence. In October 1984, Karachi
was once again the scene of Shia–Sunni clashes following rumours that Sunnis
had set alight a Shia mosque. In July 1987, 5,000 Shias demonstrated in the
Marriabad district of Quetta in Baluchistan to demand a Shia code of practice
as part of the Islamization programme. Clashes with police resulted in the
deaths of 27 people (including 13 police). In September 1986 the traditional
Shia procession in the holy month of *Muharram* was interrupted when Sunnis
objected to the route taken in Lahore. Three people died in sectarian rioting
in Lahore, four in Leiah (320 kms to the west), and two in Dera Ismail Khan
in the North West Frontier Province.

In May 1988 Sunni–Shia clashes in northern Pakistan resulted in the
deaths of 25 people, although Shia leaders put the death-toll at around
100, including women and children. In August 1988, the leader of the TNFJ,
Allama al-Hussaini was assassinated at his home in Peshawar. Shia outrage
at the murder fuelled speculation later in August that Shia militants were
behind the plane crash which resulted in the deaths of Zia and top members
of Pakistan's military establishment.

Shias in Pakistan continue to be active under the new government of Prime
Minister Benazir Bhutto. In March 1989, Shia militants, led by the prominent
Shia politician Agha Murtaza Pooya, protested against the publication of *The
Satanic Verses* by Salman Rushdie, and staged demonstrations to coincide with
the visit of Britain's Foreign Secretary, Sir Geoffrey Howe.

The opposition to Zia's government and his programme of Islamization
gained fresh impetus with the return to Pakistan of Benazir Bhutto in April
1986. The creation of the Movement for the Restoration of Democracy
(MRD), shortly after her arrival, led to growing demands for free elections.
The government's "non-party" elections of 1985 which had resulted in a
civilian government nominally headed by Prime Minister Mohammad Khan
Junejo, were seen by the opposition to be neither free nor fair. Some parties
had refused to participate, while others were barred from doing so as
the result of an excessively dubious process of registration. Active in the
opposition to Zia at this time was the *Jamiat-al Ulama-i-Islam* under the
leadership of Maulana Fazlur Rahman.

In May 1988 General Zia, in his capacity as President, dismissed
the federal government of Prime Minister Junejo on the grounds of
"incompetence, corruption and lack of attention to the Muslim faith".
At the same time he promised to hold fresh elections within 90 days.
Opposition parties condemned Zia's move, while the Pakistan People's Party
(PPP) under Benazir Bhutto refused to take part in any poll organized by a
military dictatorship.

In the meantime, Zia announced the formation of an interim government
headed by himself whose foremost task was defined as the enforcement of
an Islamic system. In June 1988, a presidential decree formally introduced
the *shari'a* (the Islamic legal code) and simultaneously repealed all existing
secular civil laws. The new ordinance contained provisions for Islamic fiscal
laws and the creation of religious courts, or Shariat Benches, charged with the

introduction of Islamic personal law, especially in areas relating to women's rights which had so far been regulated by the Family Laws Ordinance of 1962. The ordinance also provided for two new commissions on the Islamization of the economy and education.

The ordinance was widely criticized as an assault on women's rights, a recipe for sectarian tension and a blow to modern economy. The Pakistan Women's Action Forum (WAF) condemned the "anti-female bias" of the new ordinance and described it as "a dangerously retrogressive move". Women's groups marched through Karachi and Lahore in June 1988 to protest against the new measures. Opposition to the ordinance was also voiced by the *Tehrik-i-Nifaz Fiqah Jafria* (TNFJ) whose leadership described the new code as "incomplete and ambiguous and not acceptable" to the Shias. The Jamaat-i-Islami accused President Zia of hypocrisy and cast doubt on his credentials as "a true Muslim".

## Islamization under Benazir Bhutto

In August 1988, General Zia, along with senior members of Pakistan's military establishment, were killed in an air crash on an internal flight from Bawalpur (on the Sind–Punjab border) to Islamabad, the national capital. An initial inquiry into the crash confirmed sabotage, although no one group or individual has directly been implicated.

The decision by the acting president to go ahead with the elections that had been promised by Zia in July 1988, resulted in the return to power of the Pakistan People's Party (PPP) led by Benazir Bhutto. However, while the PPP commanded a clear majority in Sind, and could depend on working a coalition in the North West Frontier Province and Baluchistan, it was unable to form a government in the Punjab. Here, a provincial government led by Mian Nawaz Sharif, represents the views of a motley coalition, the Islami Jamhoori Ittehad (IJI) or Islamic Democratic Front, which consists predominantly, although not exclusively, of groups which sought to legitimise the Zia regime in its later years. Although originally created to counter what it believes to be the "non-Islamic" ideas of the PPP and its allies, the IJI has come increasingly to reflect the crusade for greater Punjabi autonomy rather than the cause of Islamization.

The PPP's own approach to Islamization has been a cautious one. Although it is unlikely to espouse the banner of Islamization, the new government is clearly intent on not antagonizing Pakistan's religious parties. Benazir Bhutto has moved slowly to dismantle the foundations of Zia's Islamic state. Although there are some visible signs of a relaxation of traditional Islamic codes of practice as expressed in dress and the conduct of women, no move has yet been made to repeal the infamous Hudood Ordinance or redefine the law of evidence which, under Zia, required the testimony of two women to be treated as equal to that of one man.

The task of undoing Zia's Islamic system cannot be an easy one for Benazir Bhutto. As a woman in a predominantly Muslim society, she is forced to tread with care on issues which impinge directly upon greater sexual equality and freedom for women. There are also political constraints, such as the Party's dependence upon religious parties like the *Jamiat-al Ulama-i-Islam* whose members hold key posts in a government coalition in the sensitive province of Baluchistan. The support of religious parties like the JUI is also crucial if

Benazir Bhutto is to repeal the Eighth Amendment enforced by Zia, which concentrates substantial power in the hands of the President. More recently, in March 1989, Benazir's government faced a minor challenge from religious parties protesting against the publication of *The Satanic Verses*. While the present government has repeatedly condemned the publication of a book that is deemed offensive to Muslims and their faith, it is unlikely to have welcomed the revival of a debate about the Islamization, especially one launched by its fiercest political opponents.

Farzana Shaikh

# PANAMA

Neither truly Central American nor South American, Panama's strategic location and the existence of the canal make it a country of prime interest to the United States. Predominantly Catholic with a small evangelical minority, the 2.5 million people of Panama face a future of greater national control over the canal but reduction in canal revenues and US economic and military support funds and an uncertain government situation.

The current crisis, while its origins go back over a decade, began in mid-1986 with allegations originating in the US that the *de facto* leader, General Manuel Noriega, had been involved in drug-smuggling, money-laundering, and assassinations. The Catholic hierarchy, led by Archbishop Marcos McGrath, has been walking a fine line between criticism of Noriega — by objecting to violations of civil liberties and calling for free elections and the military's submission to civilian authority — and opposition to US attempts to unseat him, particularly economic sanctions imposed in 1987 leading to a drop in GDP of 20 per cent. Further charges made against Noriega by a retired colonel in mid-1987 sparked demonstrations and strikes by the middle class *Cruzada Civilista Nacional* and by slum dwellers.

In January 1988, US evangelist Jimmy Swaggart held a crusade for thousands in Panama and prayed with Noriega. In contrast, the Catholic Bishops' Conference issued letters in March and April criticizing both US pressure and governmental clamp-downs, to which President Manuel Solís responded with a sharply critical letter to the Papal Nuncio. Noriega remained in power through reliance on loyal elements within the armed forces, creation of vigilante groups and strong nationalist reaction to US sanctions.

In the run-up to the May 7, 1989 elections, the hierarchy called for a "preferential option for the poor" and joined the Papal Nuncio in calling for an end to US sanctions. The election itself was marred by widespread government fraud and intimidation with church run exit polls nonetheless giving the opposition alliance ADOC (*Alianza Democrática de Oposición Civilista*) a 3 to 1 victory over the government coalition COLINA (*Coalición de Liberación Nacional*). Amidst great national and international criticism, the elections were annulled. The presidential term was due to expire in September 1989 and attempts by the Organization of American States and the Papal Nuncio to negotiate an end to the crisis have failed. Tensions continued to mount between the US and Panama with the potential for armed confrontation not ruled out by either side.

Virgil Wiebe

# PAPUA NEW GUINEA

The largest Melanesian country in the world, Papua New Guinea, has a population of 3.1 million people living in a mountainous and inhospitable terrain. Christians make up 97 per cent of the population but there are large stretches of the land still unexplored and numerous indigenous tribes inhabit the forests. About 2.5 per cent of the population are followers of traditional religions including the Cargo Cult groups — a popular messianic movement. The country obtained its independence from Australian trusteeship in 1975 and it was the work of the Churches, particularly the Catholic Church, that promoted the independence movement.

Of the 100 members of parliament in the new government only seven are non-Christian. The new Prime Minister, Mr Namaliu, who took office in July 1988, is the only major politician in the country with an overseas university degree. Among many pressing human rights problems, the flood of refugees from the Indonesian half of Papua New Guinea, known as Irian Jaya, is the most serious. The Churches have been providing care and legal aid for the refugees, most of whom come from the Protestant Church in Indonesia. There is still argument about resettlement as against repatriation for the refugees. The church initiated talks between Indonesia and Papua New Guinea to try and resolve the dispute.

Ron O'Grady

# PARAGUAY

Paraguay is one of Latin America's poorest and more economically backward countries with an estimated population (in 1986) of 3,788,000. By contrast with most of its neighbours, over 65 per cent of its citizens live outside cities. Though its official language is Spanish, the majority of inhabitants speak Guarani, a local Indian language. In religious terms it is mainly Christian, with approximately 90 per cent being officially Roman Catholic. A small Protestant community is divided amongst such bodies as the Disciples of Christ and the Evangelical Church of Rio de la Plata.

The nation's political history has been characterized by instability, violence and a general absence of constitutional rule. Its modern political life has been overshadowed by the rule of President Alfredo Stroessner Mattauda who first came to power in May 1954 as a consequence of a military coup and who remained in office until deposed by a further coup in February 1989. The durability of his Presidency (the longest in the country's history) was due to his initial military power base; support from agrarian and business interests; and, in particular, an alliance forged at an early stage with the long-established Colorado Party. Through the party, as well as the state bureaucracy, he created a network of vested interests and a potent nation-wide instrument of political control that, in significant measure, came to be held together by corruption and participation in such technically illicit activities as smuggling. The network was underwritten by the extensive repression of opponents entailing arbitrary imprisonment, torture and other serious abuses of civil rights. Such abuses undercut the regime's five-yearly attempts to secure the legitimacy provided by general elections. In practice the Colorado Party and the state apparatus were employed to intimidate and otherwise interfere with the rights or activities of even officially-sanctioned electoral opponents. The latter were further hampered by their own divisions.

Initially the regime's opponents could not count on backing from the country's Roman Catholic Church. During the dictatorship's earlier years its leaders tended to adopt conformist positions consistent with their own theologically and politically conservative traditions. During the 1960s, however, growing portions of the local Catholic community were influenced by radical currents of opinion emerging within the wider Latin American Church. The resulting reform movement found particular expression in support for a non-violent peasant movement, the "ligas agrarias" which emerged in reaction to the country's highly unequal land-holding system. Its success in eroding Colorado support amongst peasants clearly worried the government and the extent of the Church's contribution could be gauged by official accusations that it was promoting communism. The consequent deterioration in Church-State relations was marked, in 1969, by a police invasion of Church property, the resulting excommunication of senior government officials and the withdrawal of the Archbishop of Asunción from the Council of State.

Subsequently, in 1976, the state alleged the existence of links between the "ligas agrarias" and an emergent student-led guerrilla movement. The links were used to justify massive repression which dealt the peasant movement a damaging blow. In the wake of these developments the hierarchy tended to espouse a p licy of public silence in the hope of eventually persuading the government to enter into dialogue with opposition parties. In practice, however, dialogue did not result. Economic difficulties, experienced in the pursuit of growth, led to a resurgence of opposition and four groupings, including a Christian Democratic Party, jointly sought to put pressure upon the government. The response was repression. Nevertheless, the opposition alliance (Acuerdo Nacional) maintained its unity and groups of students, peasants and trade unionists emerged to offer open challenges.

The most serious difficulties, however, arose out of mounting divisions within the Colorado Party. Popular discontent, a deteriorating economic situation and mounting uncertainty about the succession to Stroessner all tended to exacerbate factionalism within the party and to intensify competition for control over its leadership. This competition was, in the short run, resolved in favour of a harshly authoritarian clique, composed of three ministers and the President's political secretary, who were concerned to perpetuate Stroessner's model of dictatorial rule. In the longer term their attempts to check opponents, in and out of the party, provoked the coup which brought Stroessner down and brought to power General Andrés Rodriguez.

During Stroessner's final years in office the Church re-emerged as a major critic of the regime and as a focus of more widespread dissent. The regime's immobility and continuing repression led the institution to renew open attacks upon the government. It was also increasingly driven to accept the roles of ally and protector of other opposition groups. In rejecting dialogue with its adversaries the government effectively consolidated a partnership between the Church and those other party political, peasant, trade union, student and intellectual forces dedicated to substantial political change.

The underlying tensions were clearly exposed by developments surrounding or following upon the two major events of 1988: the presidential election in February and Pope John Paul II's visit in May. Thus prior to the election the National Bishops' Conference publicly objected to the nature of the electoral process and lent their support to a campaign urging voters to record blank votes. In response a pro-government newspaper said the episcopal settlement owed more to Marx that the Gospel and the government itself mounted a campaign to brand progressive clergy as Marxists.

The Pope's visit was an even more important occasion for the pursuit of ideological struggle. Both the regime and its opponents were obviously aware of the damage that could be done to the dictatorship's national and international standings as a consequence of adverse Papal comment. They were equally aware of the boost that could be given to the opposition's credibility. For example, a lay organization, "The National Lay Team", sought to draw the Pope's attention to the demands of radical groups in the Church. Consequently the state placed obstacles in the way of Catholic and other non-official agencies seeking to report the visit. There was also an unprecedented attempt to tamper with the Pope's itinerary. He was prevented from going to a rural border area characterized by high levels of social conflict and an attempt was made to cancel a meeting with opposition groups which only failed when it was made plain that the consequence of cancellation would be an abandonment of the entire visit.

As anticipated the Pope used the opportunity publicly to criticize human rights abuses and to associate himself with earlier calls of the Paraguayar bishops for agrarian reform and democracy. Equally, his appearance before dissenting political groups tended to legitimize the local Church's attempts (pioneered by Archbishop Ismael Rolon of Asunción — the president of the National Bishops' Conference) to provide protective umbrella organizations for opposition parties.

The impact of the visit seems to have subsequently manifested itself in a further heightening of Church-State tension. Immediately after the Pope's departure individuals who had seized the opportunity to voice political protests were detained. There was also a continuance of officially-inspired campaigns of harassment against Church activists. A Spanish Jesuit, Fr Juan de la Vega, was expelled from the country for promoting liberation theology (and so became one of over 20 foreign priests expelled during Stroessner's presidency). Similarly, vigilantes, organized under Colorado auspices, persisted in attacks upon local Church gatherings.

The Church responded with a refusal by the Archbishop of Asunción to say mass in Stroessner's presence. Also, in August 1988, there was a massive "procession of silence" in the capital, to show popular solidarity with the Church and, in particular, to protest against attacks upon Church leaders and Fr Vega's expulsion. It was acknowledged to be the biggest public demonstration witnessed during Stroessner's presidency and made plain the extent to which the Church had become established as a popularly recognized focus of the country's mounting political dissent. Equally, it was a pointer to the extent to which religious bodies may be constrained to fill the vacuum left by the absence or fragility of alternative sources of institutionalized opposition.

Following Stroessner's eventual overthrow, the President of the National Bishops' Conference issued a statement (February 5, 1989) expressing support for the new regime of General Andrés Rodriguez. Encouragement, clearly enough, was being offered to the promotion of significant changes. A subsequent statement by Bishop Mario Melanio Medina of the diocese of Benjamin indicated the persistence of serious reservations within at least portions of the hierarchy. In particular he criticized Rodriguez for moving so speedily toward fresh elections that there was insufficient time for full democratic debate. Certainly Rodriguez's victory suggested that the process had worked to Rodriguez's advantage and to the detriment of his divided and less well-organized opponents. He was able to capitalize upon the support of established political networks and, to that extent, confirmed the suspicions of those observers, including Churchmen, who saw the overthrow of Stroessner as the outcome of a struggle within the established governmental system rather than a major new departure.

Rodriguez's mild liberalization process may have removed some of the more immediate or serious sources of Church–State tension but his dependence on long-established military, economic and bureaucratic interests suggests a limited capacity to tackle the fundamental economic and social injustices underlying much recent conflict. The Paraguayan Church consequently seems likely to remain a significant and even radical political force.

Kenneth Medhurst

# PERU

Peru (1986 population, 20,207,100) confronts a mounting economic crisis expressed through and reinforced by inflation and external debt. Increasingly large numbers live outside its formal economy. Modern politics have been particularly overshadowed by rivalry between APRA — a once radical nationalist party — and the military. In 1968 the military established its own radical reforming regime but economic difficulties and political dissent led (1975) to a more conservative military government and then (1978) the resumption of civilian politics. In 1985 APRA obtained control of the government under the leadership of President Alan Garcia Perez. His administration initially enjoyed extensive popular support but continuing economic problems, inability to contain the "Sendero Luminoso" (a Maoist guerrilla organization), divisions in APRA and strengthened conservative opposition, spearheaded by the novelist Mario Vargas Llosa, threaten defeat in 1990 elections.

The population is officially over 90 per cent Roman Catholic. After the Medellin Bishops' Conference (1968) its hierarchy espoused progressive positions and was significantly influenced by liberation theology (which was pioneered by the Peruvian priest Gustavo Gutierrez). The bishops were affected by and supported the military regime's early radicalism. Subsequently Vatican appointments have created a conservative majority within the episcopate which is now more obviously divided. Similarly, political conservatives have attacked "Marxist influence" in the Church. Also, John Paul II during a 1988 visit privately warned the episcopate of his reservations concerning liberation theology. Nevertheless, there remains a grass-roots Church which is too strong to eradicate. It is particularly active in exploring the implications of folk religion for Catholic radicals. This points to a cleavage in Peruvian society, cutting through the Church (and other institutions) tending to divide *mestizos* and Indians from the traditional white elite.

Kenneth Medhurst

# PHILIPPINES

During this century the Philippines has followed the American concept of separation of Church and state and the new Constitution formulated under the Cory Aquino presidency again articulates that position. However, religious issues have frequently reached national importance during and after the colonial era, often with regard to education. In the 1980s three major political issues have engaged religious leaders and their lay followers: the confrontation with the regime of President Ferdinand Marcos, Church involvement in social questions, and the so-called "Moro Problem".

The primary religious actor involved in the efforts to reform or bring down the Marcos government during its last years was the Catholic Church, representing some 84 per cent of the population (approximately 3 per cent are Protestant). During the early years of the 1980s, the Church was divided in how to deal with the regime. At one end of the spectrum were those reflecting elements of Liberation Theology who called for active resistance to what they perceived to be a repressive system (some even joined the communists). At the other end were many conservative bishops who either supported the martial law system established by Marcos or argued that the Church should remain out of politics. Taking a middle ground were those exemplified by Cardinal Jaime Sin who appeared to mix accommodation with criticism of particular policies, in what the cardinal called "critical collaboration". Within the

Bishops' Conference approximately 80 per cent could be termed conservative or moderate at that time.

By 1983 a general consensus began to emerge within the Church that was increasingly critical of the Marcos government. At the Catholic Bishops' Conference of that year the bishops spoke of issues such as the arrests of priests and nuns, political torture, and government efforts to equate criticism with subversion. At the same time, the hierarchy attempted to remain "apolitical" while supporting free expression and due process.

With the death of Benigno Aquino the leadership of the church became more aggressively critical and moved more directly into the electoral process. During the abortive 1986 elections the hierarchy generally supported Cory Aquino and at the local level parish priests were a core of her strength. Both Cardinal Sin and individual priests called upon the populace to vote and for the government to hold free elections or face the moral and political consequences. When it became apparent that the results were being manipulated the bishops quickly reacted. In February 1986 a meeting of the bishops termed the elections "unprecedented in the fraudulence of their conduct" and stated that a government perpetrating such activities had no moral basis. In a major change of policy in terms of involvement in the political process, the bishops declared that: "If such a government does not itself freely correct the evil it has inflicted on the people then it is our serious moral obligation as a people to make it do so." Thus, the Catholic Church hierarchy moved from often sharp differences to a general consensus opposing the Marcos regime and its methods of retaining power.

Since the overthrow of the Marcos regime, the bishops have continued to stress democratic principles, although there are an increasing number of questions about the direction of the new government. Rather than "critical collaboration", the new phrase is "critical solidarity" with an emphasis on underscoring the positive aspects of the Aquino program. Several Churchmen have been brought in as economic and political advisors to the president, but there have also been rising criticisms of corruption and a lack of movement on peasant problems. Radical clergy, particularly those within the Christians for National Revolution, advocate "smashing the reactionary state" through social revolution and there has been continued tension within the Church and between the radicals and elements of the civil and military authorities. The military have charged that the umbrella social action organization, the National Secretariat for Social Action, has channelled money to the communists and that some priests have been dupes of the party. The military have also sought to use religion as a tool against the communists, printing pamphlets depicting the insurgents as enemies of the Church.

A second major issue or set of issues relates to the involvement of the Catholic Church in social action and social justice at the local level. Again, there have been internal divisions with more conservative bishops wishing to curtail what they consider to be more non-traditional activities. In part this view reflected fears of Marxist influences in the Church and society, but it also was grounded in the concept that the Church should concentrate on its "sacred mission". There was also the fear that the authorities might attempt to weaken the Church as an institution in retaliation for what they saw as a dangerous political challenge. A majority of the bishops reflect a conservative or moderate position in this area, but a sizeable number of parish priests have become deeply involved in social action programmes, with a small minority co-operating with the communists (the latest figure is that 21 priests that have taken up arms with the communists). A major area of contention has been the Basic Christian Communities (BCP) programme begun in the 1970s which endorsed a wide range of local community action programmes. The BCP reflected a general consensus among parish priests that a primary role for the Church was to aid the community in both religious and secular matters. These activities were attacked by the Marcos regime as subversive, leading to arrests and deportation as well as other governmental pressure. By the end of the Marcos period the hierarchy had moved to a more positive position regarding the BCP, in part as a reaction to government repression. Although social action remains an area of contention both within the church and between the BCP and local authorities, the church hierarchy has not abstained from its continuing interest in social issues. For example, the most recent Pastoral Letter condemned environmental despoliation and put the Church in the forefront of the ecological issue. The letter illustrates the mixture of theological and social thinking prevalent in the hierarchy today as it argues that the "assault on creation is sinful and contrary to the teachings of our faith". At the same time, it declares that "ruthless exploitation" derives from human greed and will lead to "an increase in political and social unrest".

There remains a conflict within the Church as to how deeply it should become involved in political issues and what methods should be employed. Only a fringe element of the priests supports armed struggle for social justice while others seek more direct political action than is acceptable to the hierarchy as a whole. For the bishops there is no question as to the limits of the tools that should be used and a recent Pastoral Letter prohibited priests from joining organizations "that espouse violence as the road to social transformation". On the other hand, the same members of the hierarchy have been equally critical of vigilante and local militia violence from the right. The bishops are also worried about the considerable increase in evangelical Protestant activity and the argument that the consciously "apolitical" stance taken by the evangelicals has aided conversions by contrasting themselves with perceptions of a more "political" Catholic Church.

Finally, there is the long-standing conflict in the southern Philippines stemming from efforts of the Muslim minority there to attain autonomy or independence. This is a long simmering conflict that extends back into the colonial period. It has regularly flared into large-scale violence (one estimate is that 50,000 died as a result of clashes in the 1970s). The problem is complicated by a variety of divisions. There is the issue as to what comprises the area under dispute. Muslims comprise approximately four million of the 14 million people in the southern Philippines. Some Muslim extremists refer to a "Bangsa Moro" state of 26 provinces, while an agreement between the Philippine government and Muslim states in 1976 referred to 13 provinces and a recent proposal of President Aquino was for 10 provinces. Secondly, the Muslims are divided internally as to tactics and organization with the largest separatist group, the Moro National Liberation Front having to contend with other groups with differing agendas. The government in Manila and the provinces has also not been united as to how to deal with the issue, with elements of the military fearing the consequences of compromise and some politicians questioning the impact of autonomy on national unity. Finally, the conflict has been internationalized, with Muslim states allegedly supplying arms to the insurgents and the Moros looking to the Muslim world to argue their case with Manila. Given the considerable number of Filipinos working in the Middle East and the dependence of the Philippines on foreign oil, this pressure is real, although the recent oil glut has limited oil as a factor and some argue that the presence of the workers gives the Philippine government some economic leverage. All of these factors complicate agreements that lead to cease-fires and political arrangements that prove temporary.

Upon attaining power Cory Aquino set out a variety of proposals including an autonomous regional government covering ten provinces, a plebiscite to assess the will of the populace — a problem for the Muslims since they are a majority in only five provinces — and a general cease-fire. These proposals remained somewhat vague as to exactly what powers were to be given the new entity. Since that period there has been a mixed reception to efforts at a solution to the problem, with some elements of the Muslim community accepting negotiations and others continuing armed resistance. The cease-fire has generally held and the MNLF has denied any intention of renewing armed hostilities. There are still up to 15,000 armed insurgents in the field, although during the past year there has been a renewed effort at agreement. However, there has been no solution to the overall problem, as both sides lack the unity or strength to make the necessary concessions for long-term peace.

Fred R. von der Mehden

# POLAND

With the outbreak of World War II and the occupation of Poland by Germany and the Soviet Union, the Catholic Church lost all of its formal privileges and the influence it enjoyed during the short-lived Second Republic (1918–39). In addition, it suffered great human and material losses, its organizational structure was wrecked and its rich religious life was undercut. On the other hand, however, sharing the fate of the people and taking an active part in the combat for liberation immensely strengthened the traditional bonds between the Church and the nation. Postwar territorial changes further improved the position of the Church since the new frontiers turned Poland into a highly homogeneous nation: more than 95 per cent of the population was now Polish, almost all of them baptized Catholics.

The communist rulers imposed on Poland towards the end of the war were aware of the influence of the Church on the Polish masses and shrewdly concealed their anti-religious attitudes. An uncertain international situation and domestic struggle with the underground and the legal opposition made such tactics a political necessity. Thus, their first public manifesto, issued in Lublin on July 22, 1944, offered assurances of religious freedom and recognition of the Church's rights.

Notwithstanding official declarations, the Marxists treated religious freedom as a narrow individual privilege and were determined to keep the Church from having any meaningful input into policy development. The unilateral abrogation of the 1925 Concordat with the Holy See (September 25, 1945) was a clear indication of their design. The fate of the Labour Party of Karol Popiel was another. This organization, a partner in the Polish government in exile, was permitted by the Yalta agreement to renew its political activities in post-war Poland. But the Communists forced the party's leadership to disband it before the March 1947 elections. The affair made it quite clear that there was no room in communist plans for a Christian political formation that could represent the interests of the Catholic majority.

While lay Catholics tried to cope with communist schemes in their own way, the episcopate initiated a multitude of activities oriented towards the healing of war wounds and toward the solution of problems created by the new socio-economic and political order. Some of their acts had considerable political significance.

In the latter category falls a communique, issued at Czestochowa during the First Plenary Conference of the Episcopate (October 4–5, 1945), in which the bishops clearly indicated their desire to promote the formation of a confessional political party to compete in the forthcoming parliamentary elections. No less meaningful was the attitude of the prelates toward the Labour Party which ranged from recognition and support when it was led by Popiel to public repudiation when control was seized by pro-Communists. An obvious attempt to influence the political process was also demonstrated by the pastoral letter of September 10, 1946 which — without mentioning any names — urged Polish Catholics to vote in approaching elections for the anti-communist opposition led by Stanisław Mikołajczyk.

The onset of the "cold war" and the servile application of the Stalinist model marked not only the end of clerical political involvement but forced the Church to focus its efforts on defence and survival. It was during this period that the episcopate entered, on April 14, 1950, into an agreement with the State which was hailed by the regime as an important step toward integrating all aspects of society under the control of the party. Yet, it did not deprive the Church of the determination and ability not only to proclaim the Faith and defend its vital interests (e.g. the famous *Non possumus* letter of Primate Wyszynski to Prime Minister Bierut of May 22, 1953) but also to champion Catholic solutions to moral issues of national importance (e.g. the pastoral letter of March 25, 1952 in defence of the unborn).

The posture of the episcopate further augmented the confidence enjoyed by the Church among the Polish masses. Many Poles — religious or not — came to the conclusion that the Church was the only institution in the country which had not been compromised or corrupted. This conviction added a new dimension to the moral status of the Church that went beyond the strictly religious sphere. In fact, a large number of Poles expected the Church to provide them with political guidance in the turmoil of the post-Stalin era.

The "Polish October" of 1956 furnished a promising opportunity and the Church, attuned to the concerns of its flock, did not hesitate to accept the call. Cardinal Wyszynski, recently released from confinement, helped to calm the explosive situation and gave a boost to Gomulka by encouraging people to vote in the January 1957 elections. Thus a precedent was established of the Church giving the communist regime support in times of national emergency.

Yet, despite the logic of this step, the episcopate was not aiming at explicit political involvement and acted in the public arena with considerable restraint. A clear demonstration of this mood was given by persistent refusals to endorse attempts to restore the pro-Church Labour Party and by constant reminders that the members of the Catholic parliamentary club "Znak" enjoyed full freedom of decision.

Undoubtedly, the bishops' attitudes were strongly influenced by a desire to escape accusations of "interfering with politics", by fears of undermining the newly reached agreement with Gomulka, and — above all — by honest, though cautious, concern for an apparent process of liberalization. But they also expressed a growing trend within the universal Church, ultimately confirmed by the constitution *Gaudium et spes*, which advocated abstention by the Church from direct interference in political affairs. Consequently, the prelates concentrated on religious activities with emphasis on the millennium of Poland's Christianity (1966).

In spite of these constraints, renewed hostility of governmental officials, and an accelerated secularization campaign, the episcopate accomplished two deeds of great political consequence. First was a message, sent in December 1965, to the West German bishops offering Christian exoneration between two hostile neighbours. The other was the determined opposition, led by Cardinal Wyszynski, to the Vatican *Ostpolitik* which attempted to establish direct links with the Warsaw regime, a step that could undermine the precarious relationship between the Church and the State in Poland.

During recent decades, the ever-increasing yearning of the Polish people for moral and social renewal as well as for an improvement in living conditions brought the Church much closer to the arena of political struggle. This did not mean that Polish bishops entered competition with the Communists for political spoils or decided on participation in underground activities. It only meant that they resolved to take a higher profile in their support of people who were in conflict with the regime. The issue which came to the forefront in the joint effort was that of human rights and civil liberties.

There is little doubt that, in spite of various misgivings and reservations, the episcopate saw the growth of the dissident movement as a hopeful development. Thus, it provided assistance to several of the opposition activities, including the so-called "flying universities" that challenged the State monopoly in education. The election of the "Polish pope" in 1978 and his trips to Poland, while greatly complicating the situation for the regime, gave a powerful momentum to the struggle for human rights. Certainly, the 1979 papal visit was instrumental in the inception of "Solidarity".

The Church offered full moral support to the trade union movement, supplied it with religious services and guidance on social problems, interceded on its behalf in dealing with the authorities, and defended its members when their rights were endangered. At the same time, however, the bishops directed their priests to abstain from engaging in organizational activities and themselves refrained from direct involvement in the internal affairs of the association.

The formation of the protest movement, crowded with the establishment of "Solidarity", was interpreted by Polish bishops as a turning point in the Church's role. Instead of continuing as a para-political opposition, the Church could now start acting from a purely evangelical position as an impartial critic of socio-political relations.

As might be expected, the triadic configuration gave rise to various fears and suppositions. Some were afraid of the fortuity of an "alliance between the crozier and the sabre". Others worried about the "Khomeinization" of the union movement. More realistic was the anxiety of the communist leaders who foresaw a possibility of direct cooperation between the Church and the opposition. Hence, several overtures were made to the episcopate in the name of national interests and unity of all Poles, accompanied by gestures of goodwill and some compromise formulas to the Church's demands.

But the episcopate, while consistently supporting the fight for pluralism and human rights, never identified itself with any of the opposition groups. At the same time, the bishops remained aloof to communist blandishment. Instead, carefully avoiding the reputation of a power broker, the Church offered itself as a mediator between the rulers and the ruled.

The prelates' behavior demonstrated several things. First, it gave evidence of their conviction that the central mission of the Church is the salvation of souls. Second, it testified to their keen awareness of the extremely explosive domestic situation and of the dangers of Soviet intervention which would inevitably result in a new blood-bath. Finally, it testified to their foresight that the existing crisis could be solved only by conciliation and co-operation of all social forces. In pastoral letters and other pronouncements (e.g. the pastoral letter of May 3, 1981), the bishops pointed out that the basic source of Polish problems lay in the moral sphere, and that the blame must be shouldered not only by the rulers but by the ruled as well. They also made it clear that the duty of overcoming the crisis rested with all Poles. Consequently, they urged both sides to engage in a constructive dialogue and offered the Church's good services to facilitate the encounter.

Unfortunately, the communist leadership failed once again to rise to the occasion. Instead of trying to channel popular discontent into a positive, mutually worked out programme of reconstruction, General Jaruzelski and his associates resorted to the use of brute force. On December 13, 1981 martial law was introduced and all previous guarantees and concessions — except those made to the Church — were rescinded. "Solidarity", deprived of its legal status, went underground.

In the face of mounting repression and dangerously escalating tensions, the Church saw as its most immediate task the prevention of bloodshed. To this end, Cardinal Jozef Glemp, who became the Primate of Poland after Wyszynski's death (May 28, 1981), urged the people to abstain from violent resistance and fratricidal strife. Simultaneously, the bishops initiated an extensive programme of spiritual and material assistance to the victims of governmental coercion and to their families. They also made it clear who was responsible for the violation of valid agreements.

The bishops were of the opinion that the military coup was not the answer to existing problems and they persisted in their conviction that a positive programme for the solution of the crisis could not be found without the participation of all significant groups, including the banned "Solidarity". In this spirit, the Church continued the difficult, often misunderstood and criticized service of mediating between two belligerent camps. But the prelates stressed that if the government were to regain the people's trust, it must sincerely revive the reform process leading to a new "social accord" that would recognize the rightful needs and aspirations of citizens. Turning to their flock, the hierarchs urged prudence, realism and a gradual approach in the struggle for obtaining desired goals. The efforts of the Polish episcopate

— not derailed even by the sadistic and provocative murder of Fr Popieluszko in 1984 — were powerfully endorsed by Pope John Paul II who in his visits to Poland insisted on "a peaceful and rational solution to the conflict".

But the authorities were unwilling to take up the Church's advice and instead started a campaign of vehement accusations against some bishops and priests. Over-confident in their own tactics, they hoped that the use of force would break down the resistance of the Polish masses while the application of some measures towards liberalization on the regime's terms would restore the nation's productive capacity. Democratization was not on their list.

The following years corroborated the bishops' view that the military *putsch* would not stop the economic morass from deepening further, would not alleviate massive resistance and would not put an end to popular aspirations. Periodic strikes, mass protests and widespread underground publications proved it beyond any doubt. Slowly, these facts started to penetrate the minds even of communist hardliners. Starting in 1987, they began to build bridges towards the unbroken, though exhausted, populace by proclaiming amnesty, liberalizing censorship and issuing passports as well as by creating a Consultative Council. Still calculating on assistance from the Church, the authorities reopened negotiations aimed at the normalization of relations between the State and the Church and upgrading of diplomatic ties between Warsaw and the Vatican. They also issued official permission to the Church Agricultural Committee, established in April 1987, to go ahead with various plans for helping private farmers. The episcopate, ever mindful of the nation's welfare, accepted the overtures as a move toward a pluralistic Poland and increased its pressures on the communist leaders in order to overcome their obstinacy in dealing with the opposition, especially with "Solidarity" and Lech Walesa.

In 1988, the Church's toil, undoubtedly augmented by the third visit of John Paul II to his homeland in the previous June, seemed to bear fruit. On January 5, the government's spokesman, Jerzy Urban, informed the public of the regime's readiness to open a dialogue with the leadership of "Solidarity". He conditioned the promise by two prerequisites: a prior renunciation by the union leaders of illegal activities and the abandonment of the "policy of negation". The declaration, however, was not followed by deeds and there were no signs that the party was ready to start a parley despite many and serious indications of growing discontent. Instead, the government continued the unproductive application of palliatives that could not solve the economic crisis and overcome the general apathy.

A wave of damaging spring strikes at major industrial enterprises, however, forced the party leaders into action. As usual in times of national emergency, they turned once again for help to the Church. The episcopate obliged and dispatched five Catholic laymen to mediate between the strikers and the administrators.

In these circumstances, the officials started anew talking publicly about an "anti-crisis pact" with the opposition as a sort of initiative to get stalled economic reforms moving forward. To win the Church's support, Jozef Czyrek and other Politburo members met with a group of bishops, and the architect of the economic reform program, Deputy Prime Minister Zdzislaw Sadowski, paid a highly-publicized visit to Cardinal Glemp.

In a parallel gesture of peace toward the intelligentsia, the authorities raised the possibility of reinstituting the PEN Club, undertook discreet explorations of allowing a Church-linked opposition, and asked leaders of the Clubs of Catholic Intelligentsia to propose candidates for the forthcoming local elections to be held in June. The response was negative and in some measure contributed to the extremely small turnout of voters, who obviously followed "Solidarity's" call for the boycott of the elections.

The bishops' reaction was expressed in a communique issued on June 18, at the close of the 228th Plenary Conference of the Episcopate held in Bialystok. The prelates ascribed the strikes to the "insufficiency of participation, especially sensed by the young generation of workers and students" and to the "progressive impoverishment of the society". "The difficulties", said the bishops, "are intensified by the lack of confidence in the efficacy of reforms since numerous declarations are not accompanied by equally energetic actions." These assertions were combined with an appeal for "courageous and farsighted transformations" which cannot be replaced by "mere improvements in the state apparatus, political or economic".[1]

Almost simultaneously, *Tygodnik Powszechny* of June 19 published a heavily-censored article by two well-known Catholic activists, Ryszard Bugaj and Andrzej Wielowieyski, entitled "In the face of diminishing chances". The authors, besides stressing the catastrophic economic and cultural situation of Poland, underlined the necessity of co-operation between the ruling elite and independent social circles. Unfortunately — they complained — at the moment not only does such a collaboration not exist, but there is even a lack of a common platform for contacts. What is more, the authorities do not seem to feel that they are desirable or expedient. And yet — they concluded — "the economic reform must be linked with the democratization of the political system".

It was not necessary to wait very long for confirmation of the above opinion. On August 15 a sit-down strike erupted in the coal mine "July Manifesto" in Jastrzebie and it shortly engulfed the other mines of Upper Silesia, involving over 75,000 miners. Their example was followed by other industrial enterprises, including the Gdansk shipyards. The strikers, in addition to economic demands, requested the re-legalization of "Solidarity". The regime, as usual, resorted to the use of recriminations and to a more rigorous curtailment of civil liberties.

The Church immediately took up the cause of the striking workers and strongly accentuated the new stage of the Polish drama. Numerous enunciations issued by the Pope and members of the Polish episcopate contained assurances of pastoral care and support. The bishops also stated that the cause of the crisis lay in the "violation of human rights and the dignity of human labour". They once again called for a dialogue which "must find ways for recognition of independent associations and trade union pluralism".[2] They also urged the end of violence and remission of punishment of the workers involved in strikes.

The seriousness of the situation forced the regime to offer new promises. It was announced that the Minister of Internal Affairs, General Czeslaw Kiszczak, was empowered to meet shortly with representatives of independent social groups in order to hold round-table discussions of current problems. According to General Kiszczak, there were no prior conditions set regarding the range of topics or participants with the exception of those who "reject legal or constitutional order". As the first step in this direction, Kiszczak met Lech Walesa in the presence of bishop Jerzy Dabrowski and Stanislaw Ciosek, a high party official designated to supervise operations of trade unions. After the meeting, Lech Walesa implored strikers to return to work and explained that he was now personally undertaking negotiations for re-legalization of "Solidarity." The strikers heeded his call, though in some places with hesitation and misgivings.

On September 15–16, Kiszczak and Walesa met again and afterwards issued a joint communique, which announced the date for the first meeting of round-table discussions (October 17), and listed approved groups of participants, which included — among others — representatives of the Church. There was, however, no new commitment on "Solidarity".

While there was not much publicity on the subject, the events demonstrated once again the role of the Church as a "catalyst of social transformations".[3] Acting as an impartial mediator and not involving itself directly in the political process, the episcopate exercised a highly constructive influence on the form and content of negotiations. Although not too happy with the aggrandizement of the Church's prestige, the authorities appreciated the bishops' help in calming a tense situation. In return, they demonstrated greater amiability in ongoing negotiations on the legal status of the Church in Poland and on diplomatic relations between Warsaw and the Vatican. The Church's stand also found recognition in Moscow which allowed Cardinal Glemp to take part in the millennial celebrations of Christianity in Russia, in May 1988, and to visit Catholic communities, largely Polish, in Belorussia. This truly historic trip took place on August 5–6.

The improvement in relations between the State and the Church, however, was not reflected in official actions towards enhancing the status of Polish society. It appeared that discussions with independent circles were the limit of the regime's reformist aspirations. As if to prove the point, the authorities initiated criminal proceedings against leaders of the August strikes, and started accusing Walesa of blocking round-table talks by including on his team several anti-communist extremists.

Suspicions were strengthened by a number of significant occurrences. First, a secret party document was leaked on September 26, which claimed that the re-legalization of "Solidarity" presented the main threat to the Communist Party and therefore would not be permitted. Two days later, an outspoken anti-"Solidarity" member of the Politburo, Mieczyslaw Rakowski, was appointed to head the new Council of Ministers. A round-table meeting, scheduled for October 17, was not convened, and on October 31, the government decided to close the cradle of "Solidarity", the Lenin Shipyard in Gdansk.

The episcopate realized the dangers of a new deadlock and forcefully acted to start the dialogue rolling again. On November 12, Archbishop Bronislaw Dabrowski, the Secretary of the Episcopate, issued a statement which openly accused the communist leadership of the stalemate in round-table initiatives. In particular, the pronouncement blamed the authorities for the propaganda campaign against social freedoms, for the failure to honour earlier promises not to punish August strikers, and for the decision to close the Gdansk shipyard that — in the Archbishop's words — was "a political act which does not support the idea of accord".

The statement claimed that ". . . big hopes were aroused by the initiative for a broad political opening attached to the idea of the round-table talks".

And it continued: "Steps towards ensuring domestic peace were supported by wide social groups and the Church."

The whole allegation formed one of the sharpest attacks on the regime since 1984, when Fr Jerzy Popieluszko was murdered by the police. In closing, the statement once again repeated the conviction of the bishops that urgently needed reforms were not possible without "the wide participation of society".[4]

The growing disquiet of the episcopate was certainly not lost on the party leaders. Yet, unable to overcome their own habits and factional dissent, they offered merely a symbolic substitute for the round-table discussions in the form of a televised debate between Alfred Miodowicz, a Politburo member and the head of the official trade union, and Lech Walesa. The plan, undoubtedly conceived as a means of discrediting Walesa and the cause for which he stood, misfired. In the polemics, held November 30, Walesa proved himself a mature statesman whose ideas on social, economic and political reforms were well-received by the audience.

The debate seemed to prompt General Jaruzelski and the moderates toward a resolution of the intra-party impasse. But the 10th Central Committee Plenum of the Party, after two days of haggling (December 20–22), adjourned without taking any decision on "Solidarity", and only after General Jaruzelski and his closest associates threw their personal authority into the scale during the dramatic second half of the Plenum (January 16–18, 1989), the Party officially — though with several conditions — endorsed the reintroduction of political pluralism and restoration of "Solidarity".

The step injected a new vigour into negotiations which, despite tensions aroused by the murder of Fr Stefan Niedzielak, started finally to move toward a constructive resolution. On January 27, Kiszczak and Walesa, accompanied by associates, met in the presence of Bishop Tadeusz Goclowski of Gdansk and Fr Alojzy Orszulik, a Deputy Secretary of the Episcopate. After 11 hours of debate, it was decided to open round-table talks on February 6.

Bringing the opponents together did not end the Church's efforts. During the whole period of the round-table talks that lasted until April 5, two Church observers (Frs Orszulik and Dembowski) attended all meetings and reported the proceedings to their superiors. When deadlocks developed and special sessions for their resolutions were held among the leaders at Magdalenka (as, for instance, on March 2 and April 3), Bishop Goclowski and Fr Orszulik were there and — as reported by both sides — played a prominent role in helping to restore goodwill and reach acceptable compromises.

There is a great deal of support for the view that the Church greeted the round-table settlement as a positive development. Already on April 11, the Primate's Social Council issued a special statement in which it called on Catholics to take part in the forthcoming elections and make a conscious choice among the candidates. Cardinal Glemp in a joint communique published after the meeting with General Jaruzelski on April 13, expressed his approval for the accord which "provides a foundation for reconciliation and national agreement". John Paul II apparently pronounced similar sentiments when meeting Walesa and his advisers at the Vatican on April 19. The 234th Plenary Conference of the Episcopate (Czestochowa, May 1–2) appraised the results "an important event on the road to societal pluralism" and called on Poles to take part in the June 4 elections though they are "only the first step towards the full subjectivity of the society".

The pre-election campaign provided a very vivid picture of support given to the "Solidarity" candidates by bishops and lower clergy. Among others, Bishop Stanislaw Szymecki of Kielce received representatives of the regional "Solidarity" Citizens Committee and Cardinal Franciszek Macharski of Cracow met with candidates from Malopolska. The involvement of the lower clergy was manifold — from offering facilities for preparatory debates of the nominating committees, collection of needed signatures, and for meetings of candidates with voters, to endorsement of "Solidarity" candidates, usually proclaimed as a personal choice of a priest. Characteristically, there were only a very few cases when bishops expressed their reservations towards candidates nominated by "Solidarity", usually on moral grounds (divorce).

The constructive outcome of the round-table bargaining led to a similar development in protracted negotiations between the Church and the state on the legal status of the Church in Poland. During the 233rd Plenary Conference (Warsaw, March 7–9, 1989), the bishops extensively discussed the text of a proposed law as prepared by the editorial team of the Joint Commission and approved it by a secret vote. A few weeks later, on April 4, Church and government officials initiated a draft law to be submitted for parliamentary approval. On May 17, the Sejm passed the statute on the relations of the State with the Catholic Church in Poland. Only two deputies voted against it and 12 abstained. Thus, over 40 years after the end of World War II, the Church regained the status of a fully legitimate social institution able to carry out its own programmes and determine its own fate. An agreement between Warsaw and the Vatican — reportedly close to conclusion — will fortify the Church's position still more.

While the round-table and the legal status were in line with the Church's interests and strengthened its already high standing with the masses, the future will present problems and will not allow the Church to follow its longing for purely pastoral work. The astounding victory of "Solidarity" in the June 4 elections will certainly intensify the latent aspirations for greater political gains. Combined with extremely difficult economic conditions, the aggressive posture of the opposition may lead to a breakdown of the existing system of government. In anticipation, the regime will again call on the Church for help. It may be expected that the bishops, afraid of the domestic and international consequences of the collapse of the political authority, will respond positively. But what, then, will be the impact of such a decision on the relationship of the Polish masses to the Church?

But this is not all. The newly gained pluralism has already brought about a multiplication of organizations with political goals. Some of them are seeking the Church's endorsement (e.g. Christian Democrats); others — dominated by the secular left, whose representatives assumed the most prominent roles at the round-table and in the election campaign — will steer away from clerical influences. What attitude should the Church take toward both groups?

And last but not least, one must remember that there exist deep sensitivities between the Catholic Church and other religious organizations. Their source lies not only in religious differences but also in dissimilar attitudes towards the regime which offered preferential treatment to smaller religious organizations. The new status of the Church is viewed by these groups with apprehension. Will the Church be able to overcome these obstacles and create a truly ecumenical spirit of the Christian brotherhood?

**References**

[1] Full text in *Lad* (Warsaw), July 3, 1988, p. 2.
[2] "Word of the Polish Diocesan Bishops from Jasna Gora", *Christian Life in Poland* (Warsaw), no. 11–12 (1988), pp. 95–6.
[3] "Zwrot?" An interview with Prof. Andrzej Stelmachowski, *Tygodnik Powszechny*, no. 37 (September 11, 1988), pp. 1–2.
[4] "Oswiadczenie Sekretariatu Episkopatu Polski", *Tygodnik Powszechny*, no. 48 (November 27, 1988), p. 1.

V. C. Chrypinski

# PORTUGAL

Though the early history of Portugal was Catholic, the developing anti-clericalism of the second half of the eighteenth century led in 1834 to the destruction of all religious orders and the confiscation of their property. The Church slowly regained ground in the second half of the nineteenth century, but again came under attack at the establishment of the republic in 1910. After Salazar came to power in 1926 the government, much under the influence of Catholic social doctrine, gradually moved to a recognition of, and support for, the Church. Though most Churchmen did not oppose the revolution of 1974, Catholicism, while promoting democracy, has remained a basically conservative force in the country, especially in the North. The Concordat of 1940 remains in force.

Michael Walsh

# Portuguese Territory

## Macao

The Portuguese established this toehold in China in 1537 to facilitate both trade and conversions to Catholicism. Despite their presence for 400 years, only 15 per cent of the 300,000 population are Roman Catholics. About 1 per cent are Protestant, mainly Baptists. Portuguese is not spoken by 97 per cent, who are mostly Chinese Buddhists, and take little interest in politics. The Portuguese accept China's sovereignty over Macao, and the Chinese tolerate the Portuguese administration.

Stuart Mews

# QATAR

Qatar is ruled by the senior sheikhs of the Thani clan, in conjunction with a few prominent members of the indigenous commercial elite and religious notables. Virtually all of these rulers adhere to the literalist Hanbali school of Sunni Islam, and more precisely to the interpretation of Islam associated with the eighteenth century puritan Muhammad Ibn al-Wahhab. Consequently, the country's religious notables exercise considerable influence over judicial and educational affairs, as well as advising the amir as to the legality of governmental decrees according to a strict reading of the Koran and the traditions of the Prophet (Hadith). A growing minority of the merchant oligarchy consists of recent Shia immigrants from southern Iran, although there is also a small number of Persian Sunnis who arrived in the country at the turn of the century. Unofficial estimates put the proportion of Shias in the indigenous population at around 16 per cent, making Qatar one of the most homogeneous of the Arab Gulf countries in ethnic/sectarian terms.

Fred H. Lawson

# ROMANIA

In 1988 there were 14 authorized religious bodies in the country, of which the Romanian Orthodox Church, with 15.5 million believers in the population of 23 million, was the largest. In addition, there existed other denominations, which did not possess legal status, including the Catholic Church, a part of which, the Uniates, was officially disbanded in 1948 and members forced into the Orthodox Church. All religious communities were tightly controlled by the State (e.g. in 1987, the Department of Cults blocked the appointment of several Baptist pastors) and all of them went through periods of harassment and persecutions. In addition, the regime was continuously engaged in militant atheist propaganda.

The regime paid special attention to relations with the Orthodox Church not only due to its size but also due to its historical commitment to Romanian nationalism and its hold on people's lives, especially in the villages. The policy used was the usual mixture of "carrot and stick" techniques with the ultimate goal of making the Church subservient to the state. The meek posture of the Orthodox hierarchy made the task easier.

But the bishops should not be entirely censured for their attitude because they only conformed to a well-established model of behavior highlighted by the biblical command of "rendering unto Caesar" and by historical experience, which taught them to avoid a martyrdom that they could hardly afford. Thus, instead of "meddling" in secular affairs, the prelates concentrated on raising the standard of Church life and maintaining religious awareness of the people. In both jobs they were quite successful. The bishops' position came in recent decades under increasing criticism by younger priests and educated laymen who were trying to liberate the Church from servility to the State and create a new, more socially-involved, concept of Orthodoxy. Not unexpectedly, the growth of religious activism was not welcomed by the authorities. Unfortunately, it was also censured by the Orthodox episcopate. The examples of Frs Gheorghe Calciu, Radu Pamfil and Alexandru Pop were cases in point. In spite of the condemnations, the opposition to both leaderships was growing. In 1987, a new group, "Romanian Democratic Action", produced a manifesto asserting the Christian roots of the dissident movement and describing the hierarchy as "the chief obstacle to the true rebirth of Christian spirituality".

The dissent manifested itself also among other religious bodies, especially among the Protestants who already in 1977 circulated documents similar to the Czechoslovak Charter 77. Since that time, the movement has been gaining strength.

V. C. Chrypinski

# RWANDA

Rwanda was a German colony until 1918, when it became a Belgian mandated territory. It became independent in 1961, and a military regime took control in 1973. Rwanda has avoided the intertribal wars of its neighbour Burundi because the majority Hutu had already gained power by 1961. The population of 4.5 million is 70 per cent Christian, 8 per cent Muslim, while 20 per cent practise traditional religions. Freedom of religion is guaranteed by the constitution (though communist propaganda and activity is banned by it). Over half the population is Catholic, and the Catholic involvement in education and social work has occasionally led to friction with the government, though in general relations are good. Between September and October 1986 300 adherents of illegal religious sects were tried on charges including incitement to rebellion, refusal to pay dues to the single ruling party, Mouvement révolutionnaire national pour le développement (MRND), and refusal to participate in communal work. The State Security Court in the capital Kigali passed sentences of up to 12 years' imprisonment, the leaders of the Jehovah's Witnesses receiving the heaviest sentences. Other religious groups involved were the People of God, the Elect, and the Central African Temperance Movement.

Paul Gifford

# ST KITTS and NEVIS

One of three dual island states in the Caribbean, the recently independent St Kitts and Nevis (1983) is home to some 46,000 people, its population remaining stable over the past 60 years due to considerable emigration. The largest denominations in the country are the Anglicans, Methodists, Pilgrim Holiness (Wesleyan) and the Catholic Church. As elsewhere in the Caribbean, the influence of fundamentalist and neo-pentecostal sects under the leadership of nationals trained primarily in the United States has been growing over the past decade, drawing membership from historical churches. During celebrations in 1988 of the fifth anniversary of the nation, one pastor was reported to have warned against party appropriation of national symbols, which should be above politics. One observer has suggested that some pastors have avoided the political arena, seeing the personalist nature of politics as "dirty".

In the elections of 1989, the People's Action Movement/Nevis Reformation Party (PAM/NRP) coalition, which has led the country since 1980 down a neo-conservative economic path, again swept to victory over the St Kitt's Labour Party. An opposition Nevisian grouping called the Concerned Citizen's Movement led by the practising Anglican Vance Amory captured one of the three seats allocated to the smaller island due in part to disenchantment by younger people with the NRP.

Virgil Wiebe

# ST LUCIA

Early French influence in St Lucia accounts for its predominantly Catholic population, but other denominations are represented. The country's population was estimated at 134,000 in 1984. Charismatic Christianity, both in terms of renewal within the Catholic Church and the arrival of USA based sects, has had success in recent years.

In late 1987, the Catholic Church was alone but successful in calling for government prevention of the partnership of a local television station with a religious broadcasting network from the USA. The director of the station accused the Church of attempting to preserve St Lucian religion for itself. Religious opposition was more widespread to government plans for casinos to attract tourist development, it being led by the Christian Council (representing 14 denominations) and the opposition St Lucia Labour Party. The ruling United Worker's Party led by Prime Minister John Compton pushed ahead with the plans in March 1988.

Virgil Wiebe

# ST VINCENT and the GRENADINES

The major religious affiliations of St Vincent's and the Grenadines' 108,000 people (1984 estimate) are Anglican, Methodist, and Roman Catholic.

Roman Catholic Bishop of Barbados and St Vincent, Anthony Dickson, presented ecclesial support for greater political and economic integration of the Eastern Caribbean on behalf of the bishops of the region in November 1987.

"Don't worry, be happy," was Prime Minister James Mitchell's message following the May 1989 landslide victory of the ruling New Democratic Party (NDP) and was directed at those concerned about the potential emergence of a one-party state. The major opposition, the St Vincent Labour Party, had promised to restore "social, economic, and moral well-being" against the NDP campaign of tight fiscal management and land reform. Of interest was the decision by NDP cabinet minister Marcus de Freitas not to run for re-election due to a "higher calling" to the religious life.

Virgil Wiebe

# SAN MARINO

One of the two remaining independent city-states in Italy (the other is Vatican City) San Marino boasts of being the oldest state in Europe, claiming to have been founded in 301CE. With a population of 28,638, there is no army but all citizens may be conscripted in an emergency. For many years, San Marino was the only state in Western Europe (and the only Catholic country in Europe) to be governed by a Communist-led coalition after free elections. Following a financial scandal, the PDCS, a right-wing Catholic and conservative party gained support and entered the government.

Stuart Mews

# SÃO TOMÉ and PRÍNCIPE

This former Portuguese territory became independent in 1975. The sole party is the Movimento de Libertação de São Tomé e Príncipe under President and Prime Minister Dr. Manuel Pinto da Costa. About 80 per cent of the population is Roman Catholic and there is a suffragan see at São Tomé under the archdiocese of Luanda in Angola. With a population of some 113,000 much of the country's politics consists of international manoeuvring to take advantage of its strategic and economic situation, with opportunities for offshore companies, without losing control of its own affairs.

H. S. Wilson

# SAUDI ARABIA

The present Saudi state has its origins in a politico-religious alliance entered into in the 1740s, when Muhammad ibn Saud, the ruler of an oasis close to the modern city of Riyadh, accepted the revivalist message of the reformer Muhammad ibn Abd al-Wahhab and made use of the latter's unitarian principles as a means of building up a power base. By the beginning of the nineteenth century the Saud family and their followers were posing a serious threat to the Ottoman state, sacking the Shii shrine of Karbala in 1801 and occupying the holy cities of Mecca and Medina in 1806.

With the aid of their viceroy in Egypt, Muhammad Ali (r. 1805–1849), the Ottomans were able to contain Saudi expansion for much of the nineteenth century, but in 1902 Abd al-Aziz ibn Abd al-Rahman al-Saud, who had taken refuge with the ruler of Kuwait a few years before, recaptured Riyadh and, over the next three decades, established the Saudi state within its present boundaries. In this he was assisted by the *Ikhwan*, an army of tribal warriors inspired by the ideals of Muhammad ibn Abd al-Wahhab. With the aid of the Ikhwan, Abd al-Aziz was able to expand from Najd into the Eastern province, and then to defeat the Hashemite rulers of the Hijaz in 1925–26. The process of territorial consolidation was completed with the addition of Asir, Najran and Jizan to the state, which became the Kingdom of Saudi Arabia in 1934.

Saudi Arabia is an Islamic state in the sense that there is no secular constitution and no secular laws apart from those concerned with the operation of commercial companies. The *shari'a* forms the basis of the legal system, but although the state is supposedly governed according to Islamic principles, it is not clear precisely what this means in practice, since (unlike, for instance, the situation in the Islamic Republic of Iran) there is no written constitution, and the day-to-day running of the country is in the hands of the King and the royal family. In addition, there is no elected assembly or official council of *ulama* and the decision-making and political processes are not open to any form of public scrutiny.

The influence of religion on politics is considerable. In the first place, Mecca and Medina, the chief shrines of the Islamic faith, are located within Saudi Arabia, and its rulers have derived much of their legitimacy, both internal and external, from their status as guardians of these two shrines. The organization of the pilgrimage to Mecca, which attracts millions of Muslims each year, is supervised by a special Saudi government department. Saudi Arabia has been the prime mover behind a series of Islamic conferences, 18 of which have been held since 1969, which seek (with varying degrees of success) to establish common "Muslim policies" on matters of general concern to the 45 participating states. The most recent meeting, held in Riyadh in March 1989, decided to condemn Salman Rushdie. the author of *Satanic Verses*, as an apostate, but refrained from endorsing Iran's call for a death sentence to be passed upon him. The conference also "hailed the heroic struggle of the Afghan people under the leadership of the alliance of Afghan *mujahadin*".

More generally, the oil price rises of the 1970s have enabled Saudi Arabia to wield increasing influence both inside and outside the Middle East and in particular to encourage and finance the spread to other countries of the conservative version of Islam favoured by its own rulers. Other Arab and Muslim states were to find that such factors as their willingness to ban alcohol or to impose Koranic punishments for criminal offences as well as a display of broad support for the USA were to be important in determining their eligibility to receive financial assistance from Saudi Arabia.

In a different way the origins of the Saudi state and the longevity of the partnership between the religious and political institutions have combined to ensure that the *ulama*, and particularly the *Al al-Shaikh*, the descendants of Muhammad ibn Abd al-Wahhab, continue to play an important if imprecisely defined role in Saudi politics. The rulers can usually block or divert reforms which they themselves may find unpalatable by raising the spectre of opposition on the part of the religious authorities, but, in addition, the rulers and the *ulama* have closed ranks in the face of the kind of populist anti-establishment Islamic reform encouraged by Muslims inspired by the "success" of the Islamic Republic of Iran.

Relations between Iran and Saudi Arabia have been strained since the Iranian Revolution, because of the new regime's attacks on Saudi Arabia's close links with the USA, its allegations of Saudi hypocrisy in matters of religion and the Kingdom's support for Iraq in the Gulf War. In the course of the pilgrimage in July 1987 there was a clash between the security forces and Iranian pilgrims which left more than 400 people dead in Mecca. Before the 1988 pilgrimage season the Saudis announced that the number of Iranian pilgrims would be limited to 50,000 and that no political demonstrations would be permitted. Iran refused to accept these conditions, and Saudi Arabia broke off diplomatic relations on April 27, 1988. The cessation of hostilities between Iran and Iraq, and signs of the beginnings of a decline in the appeal of populist Islamic radicalism, may ease this and other tensions in the region.

Marion Farouk-Sluglett
Peter Sluglett

# SENEGAL

Although there is no state religion in Senegal it is one of the most
Islamic states in West Africa with over 90 per cent of the population
Muslim and about six per cent Christian, mainly Roman Catholic. Almost
all Muslims belong to one of the three powerful Islamic brotherhoods: well
over 50 per cent are members of the Tijaniyya, about 25 per cent belong to
the Muridiyya and some 16 per cent to the Quadriyya. Prominent men in the
brotherhoods are both wealthy and politically influential. At the same time
Senegal has been held up as a showpiece of progressive pluralist democracy
in West Africa. The smooth transition when the distinguished poet Leopold
Sedar Senghor stood down from the presidency in 1981 was regarded as
exemplary. Senghor selected as his successor Abdou Diouf, a career civil
servant who had been Prime Minister since 1970. Leadership now passed
from a Christian to a Muslim, while the Socialist Party remained the party
of government.

The relationships between religion and politics were illuminated by
the February 1988 election. President Diouf was re-elected with over
73 per cent of the vote while his opponent Abdoulaye Wade of the
just left-of-centre Senegalese Democratic Party gained over 25 per cent of
the votes. Backed by the country's business and religious leadership for his
pragmatic economic policies, Diouf's victory was expected.

Yet the election was widely regarded as a disaster and proponents
of authoritarian rule like Bongo of Gabon and Mobutu of Zaire publicly
gloated. With the backing of most local religious leaders Diouf easily carried
the countryside where the majority of Senegalese live. But Wade's call for
"Sopi", ("Change"), and especially for halving the price of rice won him
urban support. There were riots in the poorer parts of the capital Dakar and
elsewhere. Troops were called out. Wade and other opposition leaders were
jailed and schools and universities were closed. The opposition denounced
the brotherhood leaders for automatically supporting the government and
demanded a separation of religion and politics. Most brotherhood leaders
are farmers, however, and had benefited from Diouf's policies, while the
opposition was willing enough to accept the support of whatever religious
leaders it could get. (The fourth most powerful, Mouride, was elected on
the PDS list.) The problem for Diouf is that Senegal's image as a democratic
society, so useful in attracting international aid, has been damaged when
that aid is essential to cope with the problem of unemployed school-leavers,
especially in the urban areas.

H. S. Wilson

# SEYCHELLES

The 92 islands of the Seychelles archipelago in the Indian ocean, were granted independence by Britain in 1976. First colonized by the French but ceded to Britain after the Napoleonic war, French and English are both spoken. Freed African slaves were brought to the Seychelles by the British navy. The present population of 60,000 is largely Creole; its religious allegiance is 80 per cent Roman Catholic, 19 per cent Anglican. In 1977 a coup backed by the OAU brought the Seychelles People's United Party under Albert René to power. Relations between the Churches and government are amicable, but the government frowns upon the continued use of French in Catholic services. Teachers in Catholic schools are appointed by the Church but paid by the state.

Stuart Mews

# SIERRA LEONE

Sierra Leone became independent in 1961, and has been a one-party republic since 1971. 50 per cent of the population of 3 million practise traditional religions, 40 per cent are Muslims and about 9 per cent Christians. However, it is the descendants of the returned slaves (Creoles) and some Mende and Temne that are Christian, and power has always been in their hands. All the heads of government, the Margai Brothers, Stevens and now Momoh, have been Christians. The United Christian Council took up several issues with President Stevens, issues like death sentences and the conduct of elections. Since President Momoh took over on 29 November 1985, Sierra Leone has experienced an economic collapse. This has led to social tensions, attempted coups (February 1986, March 1987), clashes of students and police (January–March 1987), and runaway inflation. The United Christian Council has frequently made statements over such things as rice shortages and power cuts. Iran has increased its cultural influence in recent years. Both Vice-Presidents are currently Muslims, and in 1989 an *imam* was put on the central committee of the ruling party.

Paul Gifford

# SINGAPORE

Singapore is a tiny but self-governing state of 620 sq km with a population of approximately 2.5 million, two million of whom are ethnically Chinese. The People's Action Party (PAP) has been firmly in power since 1959 and under Prime Minister Lee Kuan Yew, although criticized for an anti-democratic style of government, has created a highly successful modern economy centred on petroleum processing, electronics, banking, tourism and trade. In recent years there have been signs of economic difficulties and allegations of increasing repression of anti-government criticism.

The majority of the Chinese population are believers in Buddhism and Taoism, and also strongly influenced by Chinese popular religious beliefs. There are an estimated 400,000 Christians among the Chinese and Eurasians, while the 175,000-strong resident Indian community is mostly Hindu. A significant factor for the state's future is the large Muslim minority; Singapore lies between two much larger Islamic neighbours, Malaysia and Indonesia, with whom stable relations are vital.

During its first two decades of independence religion was not a major political issue in Singapore and even today remains a minor theme. However, in the 1980s two religiously-oriented issues have come to the fore. Initially appearing early in the decade and further emphasized since 1988, has been a government effort to foster Confucian values within the population. Arguing the need for a national ideology, spokesmen of the ruling People's Action Party have seen in Confucianism a necessary moral core to the society. These views have been criticized by Chinese academics as providing a wedge to despotism and are generally not supported by the Indian and Malay communities in the country.

Religious and political tensions have also arisen from the considerable growth in Christianity and particularly the Protestant evangelical movement in Singapore. The Christian population has risen from 10.3 per cent to 18.7 per cent in the 1980s and is particularly active among the youth. The government has watched this development closely due to fears that conversions might cause unrest in Singapore's multi-racial society and because of the alleged mixing of religion and politics by religious elements. In May 1987 the Internal Security Department claimed that a communist plot had sought to infiltrate Christian groups and many of those arrested were involved in Catholic social work. They were detained without trial and some are still in prison. Prime Minister Lee Kuan Yew stated that he would not tolerate the use of religion to cover subversive activities and that religious groups should emphasize charity and social and community work. On December 30, 1987 the offices of the Christian Conference of Asia (CCA), a regional ecumenical body, were closed by the government on the grounds that some CCA activities in the area of human rights were a threat to Singapore's security.

Alan Hunter
Fred R. von der Mehden

# SOLOMON ISLANDS

After 85 years of British rule, the Solomon Islands became independent in 1978. Under the influence of the Catholic church, the Northern Solomons sought separate independence and eventually agreed to become a semi-autonomous province of Papua New Guinea. The 300,000 Solomon Islanders are 95 per cent Christian and have one of the highest birth rates in the world. The people are well politicized and there are numerous political parties. Economic development has been slow and some indigenous religious groups have been demanding a greater say in political decisions.

Ron O'Grady

# SOMALIA
## (The Somali Democratic Republic)

The vast majority of Somalis are Sunni Muslims, and religion provides a broadly unifying element in Somali political life, especially in the context of the age-old conflict with Christian Ethiopia. Though Somalia is a "scientific socialist" state, care has been taken since the 1969 revolution to reconcile socialism with Islam, which has the constitutional status of state religion. The most significant clash between religious and secular elites occurred in 1975, when religious leaders protested at a new law giving equal inheritance rights to women, and 10 of them were publicly executed. Some tension persists, and the opposition Somali National Movement, engaged in civil war in the north of the country, emphasizes its commitment to Islam; this in turn, however, may be a tactical device designed to exploit a potential area of government weakness, disguise the SNM's own embarrassing dependence on Ethiopia, and profit from the leading role in Somali Islam of the clans from which it draws its main support. Fundamentalist Islamic sects have as yet played no prominent role in Somali politics. Though Somalis are in no sense Arabs, the country's Islamic identity is also expressed internationally through membership of the Arab League. There are 2,000 Catholics who had encountered little hostility, but the Italian Bishop of Mogadishu was shot outside the cathedral in July 1989. This seems to have sparked off a new phase of repression and conflict.

Christopher Clapham

# SOUTH AFRICA

**Population** (1984) 33 million, of which 4.8 million are classed as 'white' by the South African government, 24.1 million 'African', 0.9 million 'Asian' and 2.8 million 'Coloured'

**Land** 14% of the land is allocated to blacks and 86% to whites

**Religion** 70% Christian (including nearly 90% of whites). Important Muslim population in parts of Western Cape and Natal.

## Religion and the development of the South African political economy

South Africa has been described as a society which is "resolutely religious". While it may not be unique, it is certainly unusual in the degree to which Christianity has played and continues to play a consciously formative role in South African political life. Under the present State of Emergency (which has recently been renewed for the fourth time), the churches remain one of the few legitimate avenues for political protest. The South African Council of Churches (SACC) has consciously taken up the mantle of opposition to apartheid which the banned organizations of the Mass Democratic Movement (MDM) have been forced to lay down. What is unique, however, is the shape that South African society has assumed under the policy of apartheid. This is not to suggest that the South African reality can be explained solely in terms of the interpenetration of religion and politics, however significant the religiousness of the policy-makers was and is.

The structures of domination in South Africa are not only racial, but economic. Apartheid is an economic as well as a racial ideology. The labour relations ensure that political, social and economic power remains in the hands of the ruling group. The NP are aware that the costs of excluding the black majority from meaningful participation in the political process outweigh the benefits to the ruling group from that exclusion to the extent that the economic survival not only of South Africa but of the system is threatened. This threat has been the impetus for P. W. Botha's policy of "adapt or die" and forms the back-drop for his so-called reforms. These are aimed at giving apartheid an acceptable visage in the face of mounting world pressure for disinvestment. It is a policy of co-optation of blacks into the system (as opposed to inclusive democracy) and a changing of the language of apartheid which leaves ultimate power in Afrikaner hands. It is the non-negotiable question of who holds power upon which both the NP and the Conservative Party (CP) are agreed, despite their substantial ideological differences.

There is, however, another factor of significance that must be accounted for, namely the fact that there has been a noticeable shift by the government towards the goal of *state survivalism*, by which is meant that the survival of the state (and the maintenance of power relations) becomes the highest good which outweighs all other considerations. Within that framework, there is scope for change and adaptation; the government is actively pursuing various possible models. What will not be countenanced is a non-racial democracy in a unitary state, as this would mean a transfer of political and socio-economic power away from its present holders. The most worrying feature of state survivalism is its amoral character: fundamentally utilitarian, it is a policy which is largely impervious to moral appeal. While in the past theological justifications and criticisms of government policy carried weight, there is evidence of a growing willingness and determination on the part of the government to muzzle and crush dissent from whatever quarter. State survivalism represents the South African version of secularization.

# The South African Churches

### 1   The Dutch Reformed Churches

The term "Dutch Reformed Church" (DRC) is usually taken to refer to the largest and oldest of the families of the DRC: the Nederduitse Gereformeerde Kerk (NGK). Membership of the NGK has in the past been restricted to white persons, while the three "sister Churches", established through mission, catered for persons of other racial groups: the so-called "coloured" NG Sendingkerk ("mission church"); the (Indian) Reformed Church in Africa; and the (African) NG Kerk in Afrika. Representatives of all four Churches meet every two years in a federal council.

### i   NGK

The largest and most influential of the DRCs, the NGK has been called "the National Party at prayer" because of the number of government ministers (including P. W. Botha) who are members. Its moderator is Professor Johan Heyns. Since the adoption of the report *Church and Society* in 1986, membership has, in principle, been open to people of other races. Adoption of the report led to the founding of a break-away church, the Afrikaanse Protestante Kerk (APK) under the chairmanship of Professor Willie Lubbe.

### ii   NGS

The moderator is Dr Allan Boesak. The general synod of the NGS adopted the Belhar Confession in 1986 which rejected the theological and moral justification of apartheid. The NGS is the only one of the four NG churches to officially recognize the "Belydende Kring" ("confessing circle"), a radical movement formed in 1979 under Boesak's chairmanship and striving for structural unity between the churches concerned.

### iii   NGKA

The leadership of the NGKA, which depends on the NGK for more than 80 per cent of its finances, has, in the past, been comparatively conservative. However, the present leadership under the moderator, Rev. Sam Buti of Alexandra, is sympathetic to the *Kairos Document* and rejects the possibility of reforming apartheid in favour of the transformation of South African society.

## 2 Breakaway DRCs

### i *Nederduitsch Hervormde Kerk (NHK)*

A conservative Church, racially constituted, the NHK grew out of the Great Trek and was established in the Transvaal in 1858 as a protest against NGK opposition to the Trek. Like the NGK, this Church was suspended from the WARC in Ottowa in 1982 until it renounced all theological and moral support for apartheid. It refused to do so and has withdrawn from the WARC.

### ii *Gereformeerde Kerk (the "Doppers")*

This was founded in 1859 by a theologically conservative sub-group within the NGK. Its members include F. W. de Klerk, successor to P. W. Botha.

## 3 African Separatist Movements

Leaders have maintained a low profile in socio-political matters. They include two major groupings of Churches: the Zionist Churches and the Ethiopian Churches. While the Zionist Churches are syncretistic, blending Christianity with traditional African religions, the Ethiopian Churches are those that have broken away from established Churches to afford members self-government in religious matters. They have frequently been African nationalist in outlook.

## 4 English-Speaking Churches

These comprise the Churches of mainly European origin. Historically, for both theological and nationalistic reasons, these Churches have expressed opposition to apartheid, although this has never amounted to a serious threat to the status quo. Opposition at any level has been far more muted in the evangelical Churches (including the Pentecostal and charismatic denominations and Church groupings), although the publication of the document *Evangelical Witness in South Africa: Evangelicals Critique their own Theology and Practice* by the group known as the "Concerned Evangelicals" in 1986 is indicative of a growing awareness that the South African context demands theological engagement.

Recent years have seen the practical recognition of the fact that the majority of the English-speaking Church membership is black. Not only have black leaders been elected to key positions within the denominations; they have also significantly altered the anti-apartheid profile of the Churches which they represent, thrusting their denominations into the forefront of internal opposition to and criticism of the government, although not without considerable opposition from within the Churches.

## 5 Right Wing Christian Groups (RWCGs)

There has been a proliferation of RWCGs which are small, rapidly-growing Church-based movements and which give direct support to the state. Fundamentalist in their theology, they claim to be "apolitical" while supporting the government in its "Total Strategy" (designed to keep the present government in power by destroying meaningful opposition) while vehemently attacking Christians with different views. Some of the most militant RWCGs include The Gospel Defence League, Signposts Magazine and the Aida Parker Newsletter.

## 6 Liberation Theology (LT)

This is a form of theology associated with people such as Allan Boesak, Desmond Tutu, Albert Nolan and Frank Chikane; with theology departments such as those at the universities of Cape Town and Natal (Pietermaritzburg); and with groups such as the Institute for Contextual Theology (ICT) in Johannesburg. This theological approach has its best-known expression in the *Kairos Document* and has close associations with the Mass Democratic Movement (MDM).

Characteristic of LT is the conviction that the God revealed in Jesus Christ, according to the Bible, is the God who sides with the oppressed. In a situation of oppression, the Church cannot be neutral, but must take the side of the oppressed in the struggle for what is right and just. Social transformation is properly part of the gospel: it is the task of the Church to address not only private sins, but also public ones that have to do with social, economic and political life. *Context* is thus of crucial importance. Accordingly, an important place is afforded to social analysis. Liberationists are prepared to use Marxist analysis (as opposed to philosophy) in order to illuminate the social context.

## 7 Jewish Organisations

The South African Jewish Board of Deputies, which is the official representative body of the South African Jewish community, has an old-established policy of not entering the party political arena, considering this to be the prerogative of individual Jewish citizens. More radical are the two anti-apartheid organizations founded in 1985: Jews for Social Justice (Johannesburg) and Jews for Justice (Cape Town). A factor affecting South African Jews is the pro-Nazi sympathies of leading Afrikaner nationalists during World War II. The emergence of the neo-Nazi Afrikaner Weerstandsbeweging (AWB) is perceived as a growing militant threat to South African Jewish interests, and has led to the formation of a Jewish Defence Organization, in which members receive training in weapons and martial arts.

Rabbi Cyril Harris was appointed Chief Rabbi of South Africa by the Union of Orthodox Synagogues of South Africa in January 1988.

## 8 Muslim and Hindu Faiths

The pragmatic focus on Christianity's relationship to the politics of South Africa belies the fact that Muslims and Hindus are involved in opposition to apartheid. It is all too easy for the government to dismiss these as false religions, so that theological opposition to apartheid is not taken seriously.

A radical Muslim grouping aligned with the MDM has emerged which has been a significant factor in the development of a liberation struggle reaching beyond ideological, religious and racial differences in opposition to apartheid. *The Call of Islam*, formed in 1983, has as its ideal a free, non-racial, non-sexist, democratic and nuclear-free South Africa. Moulana Farid Esack is the movement's most prominent spokesman.

# Events: 1987–1989

## 1987

### i  Lusaka Statement

During May the WCC's Programme to Combat Racism organized a conference in Lusaka, the theme of which was "The Church and the Search for Justice and Peace in South Africa". Some 40 southern African Church and community representatives were among the 200 delegates who attended. The aim of the conference was to enable Church leaders to meet representatives of the liberation movements. The speakers included Oliver Tambo, president of the ANC, Sam Nujoma, leader of SWAPO, and Johnson Mlambo, chairman of the PAC. It was the first official meeting between the leaders of the liberation movements and the ANC and PAC leaders.

The so-called "Lusaka Document", or "Statement", issued at the conclusion of the conference, read, "While remaining committed to peaceful change we recognize that the nature of the South African regime which wages war against its own inhabitants and neighbours compels the [liberation] movements to the use of force, along with other means, to end oppression". It also concluded that "the South African regime and its colonial domination of Namibia are illegitimate", and endorsed a resolution involving civil disobedience which "regarded the rent boycott as a justified form of resistance, resolving that the SACC would not comply with any requirement in law that it deducts payment of rent arrears from employees' salaries." The Statement was adopted by the SACC on July 2 and referred to member Churches. The provincial standing committee of the CPSA met to discuss the matter at Modderpoort in November. The Statement was unanimously adopted, although it was made clear that its acceptance was far from meaning that the CPSA accepted violence. The Methodist annual conference in October referred the Statement to its Christian citizenship department and circuits for study. There had been worry among the Methodist delegation during the SACC deliberations of July that acceptance amounted to their Church justifying the use of force.

The Statement is significant for the following reasons:

a)  it recognizes that the system of apartheid is the prime cause of violence in South Africa, rather than the "Total Onslaught" being waged by the communist-inspired terror organizations of the South African government propoganda, so that there can be no facile, one-sided condemnation of the armed struggle being waged by the liberation movements.

b)  it recognizes the indispensibility of the liberation movements for any negotiated settlement in South Africa. This implies not only that they are of key military significance, but are also genuinely representative (to whatever degree) of black opinion in South Africa, a fact which is denied by the government.

c)  its acceptance by South African Churches represents a significant shift towards active opposition to apartheid on their part, and a clearly-perceived need to take sides in a struggle which precludes neutrality.

d) any meetings between South Africans and the liberation movements (particularly the ANC) are monitored and decried by the South African government.

## ii  World Conference on Religion and Peace (WCRP)

A conference on the theme of "Religion and the South African Crisis" was held in Lusaka during September, at which representatives from South Africa joined WCRP colleagues from Australia, Britain, India and the United States to meet executive members of the ANC. The South African delegation was led by Archbishop Desmond Tutu, and comprised representatives of the Christian, Hindu and Muslim faiths. Tutu emphasized that the ANC formed part of the black community in South Africa. A statement issued after the meeting maintained that interfaith co-operation was essential in South Africa to focus on religious pluralism in society, to provide a platform for continuous condemnation of apartheid, and to defuse inter-faith tensions as being politically divisive factors which the South African government sought to exploit. It was agreed that the South African government's policy of internal repression and external destabilization was blocking the possibility of a negotiated settlement. Prompt and strong measures to isolate the government were called for. A forthcoming Commonwealth summit was urged to impose comprehensive economic sanctions.

Archbishop Tutu had earlier visited Lusaka (March) for a five hour meeting with Oliver Tambo and other executive committee members of the ANC. Contrary to the way in which he is perceived by many South Africans, Tutu is first and foremost a Christian Churchman and a traditional Anglo-Catholic. His opposition to apartheid is not primarily political in motivation, but pastoral. His refusal to endorse the ANC's strategy of waging an armed struggle, while agreeing with that organization's aims to achieve a nonracial, democratic society, means that he is regarded as a sell-out by more radical blacks. His consistent call for international economic sanctions springs from his committment to the possibility of non-violent change in South Africa. He does not, however, espouse non-violence as an absolute principle. He has pointed out on many occasions that he is a member of a Church which believes that the time could come when it is justifiable for a group to overthrow an unjust system violently. He does not believe that that point has yet been reached in South Africa, nor will be, until every non-violent option has been exhausted.

## iii  Developments Within the NGK

On June 27 a mass meeting of several thousand NGK dissidents was held at the Skilpadsaal in Pretoria, at which some 80 per cent of those present voted to start a new Church called the Afrikaanse Protestante Kerk (APK). Professor Willie Lubbe was elected chairman. He told the first synod meeting in Naboomspruit in early November that membership was then about 8,000 adults and 4,000 children. More than 100 congregations were represented at the synod. The schism with the NGK arose over the adoption of *Church and Society*. When the General Synod of the NGK rejected discriminatory apartheid, Lubbe and his supporters withdrew, believing not that the decision was wrong on political grounds, but was contrary to the Bible. The APK rejected the scrapping of the Prohibition of Mixed Marriages Act (1949) and

Section 16 of the Immorality Act (1957) for the same reasons. The APK has no contact with any international ecumenical body.

## 1988

### i  SACC State Relations

1988 saw a significant polarisation in the relations between the SACC and the government. The catalyst was the government banning of 17 anti-apartheid organizations on February 24, together with restrictions against COSATU (Congress of South African Trade Unions). The government action was interpreted by the SACC as an indication that it was not prepared to allow any form of peaceful, non-violent resistance or protest against its apartheid policies.

The restricting of the organizations meant that the Church had become, in effect, the only legal extra-parliamentary avenue of political protest and opposition. The response of the SACC was to "move from passive condemnation of the system to active opposition to it". This decision led to a well-publicized march by 150 clergymen of all races and faiths to Parliament in Cape Town, in order to deliver a petition of protest to the State President. The march was dispersed with police water-cannon. Speaking of the incident, the leaders stressed that it should not be seen as disobeying the government, but rather as obeying God. Furthermore, they said, they would continue to obey God in the future.

Several factors emerged during the course of the year which shaped the position of the SACC vis-a-vis the government:

### a)  The legitimacy of the South African state

The question of the legitimacy of the state has been an acute one for the Churches since the State of Emergency in 1985. The declaration of the illegitimacy of the regime is a denial of the right of the government to govern. In this event, the only option is its removal. A convocation of South African Churches, including Anglicans and Catholics, was organized by the SACC on June 30. The two-day meeting discussed a campaign of civil disobedience based on the charge that the NP government is "illegitimate". Included in the measures was refusal to co-operate on the issue of the racial registration of births; residential segregation; taxation and military service, as well as action to persuade the international community to "withdraw their support for the apartheid system militarily, culturally, politically and economically".

### b)  Attacks on SACC personnel and property

On August 31, Khotso House, the premises of the SACC, was rendered unusable by a bomb blast. There was speculation that the bombing was the work of the Wit Wolve ("White Wolves"), a right-wing extremist group. This was dismissed by police, who suggested that the blast could have been caused by the premature explosion of explosives stored at Khotso House. This provoked angry responses by Chikane and Tutu, who condemned the implication that personnel of the SACC were involved in acts of violence. Earlier in the year, Khotso House had been raided by police.

On October 12 Khanya House, the headquarters of the Catholic Church, was destroyed by fire. Police claimed that an arms cache had been discovered on the premises. Catholic officials rejected outright the possibility that Khanya House personnel had been involved, claiming that this was a means of diverting the search for the saboteurs.

State President Botha leaked the content of a private letter from himself to Archbishop Tutu on March 16, in which he claimed that Church leaders such as Tutu and Boesak were unrepresentative of their Churches and were Marxists, receiving instructions from the ANC. The allegations were rejected in a reply to the State President on April 12, in which Tutu made a comprehensive statement of his beliefs. His letter dealt with objections to specific aspects of government policy which he backed up with biblical references. Of his relationship to Marxism, Tutu said, "I reject atheistic Marxism as I reject apartheid, which I find equally abhorrent and evil".

These incidents highlight the question of the relationship between theology and politics. Leaders such as Tutu, Boesak and Chikane refuse the government prescription that theology and politics do not mix. Chikane defended the overtly political role of the Churches in a BBC interview in July, arguing that the oppressive structures of South African society necessitate a prophetic stand by the Churches. While the government claims the allegiance and the obedience of its citizens on the grounds that it is Christian, it is vulnerable to the opposition of prominent Churchmen who enjoy a high international profile and who are willing and able to act ecumenically and corporately in opposing the state.

c) *Sanctions*

In May, a high-level delegation of South African Church leaders, representing the South African Catholic Bishops Conference (SACBC), the SACC and the Methodist Church of Southern Africa met with the British Foreign Secretary, Sir Geoffrey Howe, to call for a change in British policy towards South Africa. The demands were flatly rejected by Sir Geoffrey. These included ending flights between Britain and RSA, cutting down diplomatic links, restricting loans and intensifying pressure on trade and communication. The Church leaders rejected the belief that appeal to reason alone from the South African government, without measures that would cause real discomfort to the white community, could be effective in bringing about peaceful and lasting change in the country.

The debate over sanctions turns around the long-term intentions of the government. The Church leaders maintain that the present government strategies are not aimed at the final dismantling of apartheid in all its forms, but at giving the continued white domination of South Africa an acceptable face so as to ease international pressure on the government. "Reforms" are thus piecemeal attempts to buy time and respectability, rather than a systematic restructuring of society. The public calls by Church leaders for international sanctions, which are offences under the emergency regulations, provoked angry responses in South Africa.

d) *Elections*

On June 30, 26 church leaders from 16 churches mounted a campaign urging all Christians to boycott the forthcoming elections of October 26 to segregated municipal councils. The decision to call for a boycott, in direct violation of the emergency censorship regulations and punishable by a maximum prison term of 10 years, was taken in closed session at the annual conference of the SACC. The appeal was supported by the CPSA, Baptist, Catholic, Methodist and Presbyterian Churches, as well as the NGS and NGKA. The signatories, headed by Archbishop Tutu, said that: "By involving themselves in the elections, Christians would be participating in their oppression or the oppression of others." They maintained that no elections could be fair and free under the State of Emergency and that "the structures of the constitutional system in South Africa are based on racial and ethnic identity". Because newspapers would be prevented from publishing the appeal, they intended to disseminate it through Church newsletters and news agencies and by word of mouth in defiance of the law.

The leaders publicly repeated the calls for a boycott during the following months, earning themselves government warnings that they should not "abuse their position". The elections were being viewed as a test case for the credibility of the government's attempts to give blacks strictly controlled participation in the political process. The fact that the SACC and the SACBC between them had a potential following of 10.23 million (nearly a third of South Africa's population) meant that the threat of a widespread boycott and consequent government embarrassment was taken seriously by the authorities. The Church leaders saw the policies as aiming at co-opting blacks into the system under conditions acceptable to the whites, rather than as affording them full and free participation in the political process. In the event, the elections took place with an extremely low black voter turnout.

e) *Censorship*

Under the emergency restrictions, the Church news networks are required to register as news agencies, thus making them subject to government censorship. All publications are required to be submitted for censorship prior to distribution. The boycott call of June 30 included a refusal by the SACC to submit its magazine, *Ecunews*, to the authorities.

On September 1 police raided the Pretoria headquarters of the Catholic bishops, searching for copies of the banned pamphlet, *Standing for the Truth: understanding the municipal elections*. On the same day, police confiscated 10,000 copies of the pamphlet sent to the Durban ecumenical Church agency, Diakonia.

During September the acting Director-General of the South African Broadcasting Corporation (SABC), Mr Wynand Harmse, threatened to censor any religious broadcasts which contained material which could be regarded as "contentious and controversial". He was reacting to religious broadcasts during which prayers had been offered for detainees. Church leaders reacted angrily to the hint that the SABC would, in future, require sermons and service details to be submitted for prior approval before being broadcast.

The Orderly Internal Politics Bill, introduced in Parliament in March, was designed to gain some control over monies coming in from abroad to anti-apartheid causes. 146 humanitarian, educational and legal projects which received money from the EEC Special Programme through the channel of the Churches, the trade unions and the Kasigo Trust would be affected. One of the prime government objectives appeared to be gaining control over the finances of the SACC, 90 per cent of which come from abroad. The visit by Church leaders in May was aimed at mobilizing European support to prevent the enactment of the Bill.

These incidents are indicative of attempts by the authorities to curb the opposition of the Churches to government policies by gaining tighter control over Church resources rather than by taking direct action against the leaders.

### ii  Papal Visit

In September the Pope made a tour of Southern Africa. South Africa was to have been excluded from his itinerary; instead, he was to visit Lesotho. In the event, the papal plane had to land at Jan Smuts airport because of weather problems. The Foreign Minister, Mr Pik Botha, was on hand to welcome him. The event was regarded by the government as a propoganda victory.

### iii  Lambeth Conference

The Lambeth Conference of Anglican bishops, meeting at Lambeth Palace, England, during September, debated a draft resolution calling on governments to impose "forms of sanction" against apartheid. The motion, instigated by Archbishop Tutu, also suggested that governments take steps to ensure the military protection of the frontline states against South African military raids, and give moral and humanitarian aid to the ANC and PAC.

It called upon Anglican churches around the world to press their governments to *inter alia*:

— push for the release of Nelson Mandela and all other political prisoners and detainees;

— push for the unbanning of organizations like the ANC and PAC;

— give direct moral and humanitarian support to such organizations in the pursuit of a just order which reflects Gospel values.

The motion was seized upon by the media as signifying an endorsement of terrorism. However, its significance lies more in the fact that it is more radical than Mrs Thatcher's policy towards South Africa, so that its adoption by the Anglican communion can be expected to result in pressure on Britain from the Church to take cognizance of the significance of the MDM and the liberation movements.

### iv  Military chaplaincy

For several years there has been widespread debate concerning the appropriateness of the role of the military chaplains to the SADF, particularly over the enforced wearing of uniforms and badges of rank by the chaplains. In December a delegation from the Presbyterian Church travelled to Harare for discussions with the ANC and presented the organization with the Church's 10 principles of chaplaincy for it to consider "the whole question of establishing a ministry to the liberation organizations and to consider the possibility of ministering to both sides — the SADF as well as the ANC and PAC". Similar discussions were held with the PAC.

The convenor of the committee, the Rev Douglas Muller, told the movements that a principle of the Church supplying chaplains was that it should not be considered as support for the aims or methods of any organization. Another delegate explained that the Church regarded the military wings of the ANC and PAC as being legitimate military organisations and as such deserving of receiving military chaplains. The response of the movements was reserved: they felt that the Church should be more closely identified with "the struggle". There was also the problem of security felt by the liberation organizations as to how a minister who had served with the SADF could be expected to serve with the movements, or vice-versa. These questions were to be considered before any plans could be finalized.

The meeting is significant more for the fact that it took place at all than for what it achieved. The whole issue of military service is extremely emotive and laden with ideology. That a Church should consider it appropriate to explore the issue of chaplaincy to the liberation movements is indicative of a fundamental rejection of the government military propaganda.

## 1989

### i  Eminent Church Persons' Group (ECPG)

The Lusaka meeting of May 1987 called for the setting up of an ECPG to visit specific nations with strong economic ties with South Africa. The group was assembled by the WCC in January, with the task of mobilizing international efforts towards the imposition of comprehensive economic sanctions against South Africa.

The ECPG included the former Zimbabwean President, Rev. Canaan Banana, former General Secretary of the SACC, Rev. Beyers Naude and the current General Secretary of the SACC, Rev. Frank Chikane. The countries visited were the United Kingdom, France, West Germany, Japan, Switzerland, USA and other EEC countries. These were chosen because of their "fairly high" economic ties with South Africa. The delegation was scheduled to meet influential politicians and other people who can "help shift national policies towards the imposition and application of comprehensive, tighter and ultimately more effective economic sanctions against South Africa". While in Washington, the delegation was joined by Archbishop Tutu for their meeting with Secretary of State, James Baker. The meeting with Baker gave the delegation the greatest cause for optimism, insofar as there seemed to be a possibility for a change in policy from the Reagan administration.

### ii  Detainees' Hunger Strike

During January and February, detainees held without trial under the emergency regulations, many of whom had been detained for more than 2 years, went on a hunger strike until death demanding to be either charged or released. Church leaders, including Frank Chikane, Allan Boesak and Desmond Tutu were involved in negotiations with the Minister of Law and Order, Adrian Vlok, to prevent the death of the strikers, some of whom had been hospitalized. Boesak went on a "fast until death" in solidarity with the detainees. Meetings between Vlok and the Church leaders, as well as the detainees' lawyers, resulted in the promise of release for "hundreds" of detainees, or their being charged and tried. The strike was called off. The numbers of releases promised did not materialise, although a significant number of cases were reviewed by the Minister. The strike nevertheless brought to public notice the realities of the policy of detention without trial, which is frequently accompanied by torture, abuse and degrading prison conditions.

### iii  SA church leaders' delegation to the USA

During May four South African Church leaders — Allan Boesak, Desmond Tutu, Beyers Naude and Frank Chikane — travelled to the USA to campaign for greater economic pressure on the South African government. They went at the invitation of the American Forum on South Africa. The leaders expressed their conviction that a negotiated settlement was possible and that the Americans had the means to get the South Africans to the negotiating table. They discounted the possibility of the British Government becoming "pre-eminent broker" in such a settlement, but did not discount the possibility that Mrs Thatcher "might conceivably play a useful role in reassuring fearful white South Africans during negotiations". They remained "totally convinced" that the only way in which to get the South African government to the negotiating table was through the application of economic and dipolomatic pressure. The group reflects the growing conviction among many in South Africa that the time for peaceful means which can reasonably be expected to effect fundamental change in South Africa is beginning to run out. While the state of emergency has been effective in crushing opposition, the degree of polarization that is taking place increases the chance of an intensification of the struggle with attendant bloodshed. The only alternative is to force the government into genuine negotiations with the legitimate and authentic South African black leadership.

Lawrence Moore

# SPAIN

Though Spain was converted to Christianity early (Tarragona claims a visit by St Paul), in the eighth century it fell to Islam, which was not finally driven out until the end of the fifteenth century. The reconquest of the peninsula was closely associated with the restoration of Catholicism, and the Church has ever since been an integral part of Spanish culture. It was not until the middle of the nineteenth century that non-Catholics were officially tolerated, and until the middle of the twentieth that toleration became a reality.

Relations between Church and State, however, have rarely been smooth. There has been a strong element of anti-clericalism in Spanish society, which was at its most virulent in the years immediately preceding the outbreak of the Civil War in 1936. Franco's victory in the war was followed by a long period of "national Catholicism", in which Catholicism and Spanish nationalism were regarded as inseparable. The 1753 Concordat had given the crown the right to appoint bishops, a prerogative not finally abandoned until the death of Franco in 1975. It was the Church which took the initiative in breaking links with the Franco regime after the 1971 *Asamblea Conjunta* of priests and bishops, despite the presence in the government of a number of members of a Catholic institution, *Opus Dei*.

The restoration of a (constitutional) monarchy and a left-of-centre government was shortly followed by a move towards the right in the Church, and in recent years relations have once more been strained. The government, for instance, appointed an ambassador to the Holy See whom Church authorities regarded as wholly unsuitable, while against the Spanish government's wishes the Vatican has pressed ahead with plans to canonize "martyrs" of the Civil War. Though ecclesiastical property remains tax-exempt and Church schools receive substantial subsidies, other State support for Catholicism has gradually been withdrawn.

Michael Walsh

# SRI LANKA

The communal violence that has gripped this island nation of 16.3 million people in the last several years has ethnic, linguistic, economic and political aspects, many of which, including the opposition to Western-style secular nationalism, are expressed in religious forms. 74 per cent of the population is Sinhalese, most of whom are Theravada Buddhists; 18 per cent in the northern and eastern provinces are Tamil, and mostly Hindu; and 7 per cent are Muslims. Another 7 per cent, equally divided between Sinhalese and Tamils, are Christian.

Theravada Buddhism in Sri Lanka is distinctly Sinhalese. Buddhist dynasties have ruled Sri Lanka — or have struggled with contending Tamil kings to do so — ever since the time of Mahinda, the son of the great Indian king, Asoka. He is said to have journeyed to Sri Lanka and established the first Buddhist throne there in the third century BCE, bringing with him an offshoot of the Bodhi tree (under which the Buddha was enlightened), and the Buddha's tooth, a sacred relic that is housed in Sri Lanka's most important shrine, the Dalada Maligawa ("The Temple of the Tooth") in Kandy. From a Sinhalese perspective, the governments established by the Portuguese, Dutch and British from 1505 to 1948 were merely interruptions in the overall course of Sinhalese Buddhist history. A Buddhist monk is said to have carried the first flag for freedom in the struggle for independence from the British.

After independence the name of the country was restored from its anglicized form, Ceylon, to Sri Lanka. The symbol chosen for the national flag was the Sinhalese lion, and the suggestion that it would be more appropriate to have on the flag an ethnically-neutral symbol, such as Adam's Peak —

the mountain-top in the central part of the island that is revered equally by Hindus, Sinhalese, and Muslims — was rejected. Many Sinhalese felt that the time had come to restore Buddhism as the national religion. In 1953 a popular tract, *The Revolt in the Temple*, urged the populace to embrace a Buddhist form of nationalism. Political leaders of the country found it increasingly useful to employ the rhetoric of Buddhism to buttress their own political power. This strategy tragically misfired in the case of S.W.R.D. Bandaranaike, the Prime Minister who was killed on September 25 1959 by a Buddhist monk. He acted as part of a larger conspiracy allegedly masterminded by another monk, Mapitigama Buddharakkhita Thero, the so-called Rasputin of Sri Lankan politics, who was unhappy with the pace of Bandaranaike's efforts to make Buddhism the state religion.

The ideology of Buddhist nationalism did not sit well with minority communities, especially Hindu Tamils, the largest minority, who had lived for centuries in the northern and eastern sections of the island, and claimed it as a Tamil homeland. Tamil unrest in the north led to a severe backlash in the south, and in 1983 a storm of violence was unleashed against Tamils living in Colombo and elsewhere; hundreds — some say thousands — were killed in the riots. Soon after, the Tamil separatist movement began in earnest. Although Buddhist monks have sometimes been the target of Tamil violence — 29 monks were dragged out of a bus near the ancient Buddhist capital, Anuradhapura, and systematically gunned down — the movement's main enemy has been the government. Ironically, the favourite target of Buddhist militants has been the government as well.

The recent growth in Sinhalese Buddhist militancy is in part a response to the Tamil separatist movement, and in part a response to the government's attempt to be secular and neutral in the face of communal conflict. The Sinhalese militants are bitterly opposed to the pact made between Prime Minister J.R. Jayewardene and India's Rajiv Gandhi in May, 1987, to bring in Indian troops to quell the Tamil problem in the north and east. The pact gave greater provincial autonomy to the Tamils, and this appeared to many Sinhalese to be a sell-out to Tamil demands. Moreover, the pact did not quiet the most extreme of the Tamil separatists, the Liberation Tigers of Thamil Eelam (LTTE), who persisted in fighting on to the death, and the occupation troops of the Indian Army Peace-keeping Force did not quickly leave. Their numbers swelled to over 60,000 — more than the British had in India even at the height of the Empire. The fear spread throughout Sri Lanka that Rajiv Gandhi's gift of peace was a Trojan horse, and that even if the Indian army eventually left, the military and political ties to India would remain. The enormous popularity in India of a 1988 television presentation of the Hindu epic, the *Ramayana* — which portrays the mythic invasion of Lanka by an army of Hindu gods — did little to assuage these fears.

The antipathy to Sri Lanka's pact with the Indian military has greatly boosted support for the Janatha Vimukthi Peramuna — "the People's Liberation Front" — or simply, the JVP. The present JVP is a revival of an earlier movement of the same name that in 1971 attempted an abortive coup against Mrs. Bandaranaike, the widow of the slain Prime Minister, who succeeded him in office. Both the present and previous forms of the movement have been led by Rohana Wijewera, who once attended college in Moscow. Although supportive of the militants, Wijewera claims to have no influence over the most violent wing of JVP supporters, the Deshapremi

Janatha Viyaparaya (DJV). It is a claim that many politicians and journalists reject.

The membership of the revived version of the JVP is youthful. The most active members of the movement are young men aged 18 to 26, unemployed villagers in the southern part of the island who often use the language of Marxist revolution to express their political aspirations. Their images of an ideal society, however, often recall a glorious Buddhist past. They regard the secular, democratic government of Colombo to be an enemy of Buddhism and an obstacle to social progress.

On August 18, 1987, DJV — or JVP — supporters fired at President Jayewardene during a parliamentary meeting, and when these shots missed, hand grenades were tossed in his direction; they bounced across the table in front of him and exploded, killing a member of his cabinet and wounding 17 others. On February 16, 1988, a popular Sinhalese film star and politician, Vijaya Kumaranatunga, who was in the process of creating a new alliance among three socialist parties, was shot dead by gunmen on a motorcycle as they sped past his house in Colombo. Later in the day two bombs that had been planted inside a crowded Hindu temple near the politician's home exploded while priests were chanting their evening prayers; seven people were instantly killed and 13 more were seriously injured. Although the Reuter report of the incident said that "police could not say who was responsible," the JVP was "blamed" for the attack and the bombing.

Some observers estimate that the majority of young people in the rural areas of the southern and central provinces are sympathetic or at least non-resistant to JVP activities. Field workers in the Sarvodaya relief and development agency have reported difficulties in carrying out their activities owing to JVP interference: they have been harassed and their vehicles stolen. An indication of the JVP's strength was seen on Sri Lanka's Independence Day in 1988 when virtually no national flags were visible in the areas dominated by the JVP. Leaders of the movement had sent out the word that no one was to display them — and there was a threat of physical violence against those who did. Black flags were exhibited instead.

A number of younger Buddhist monks in rural areas have joined the JVP, and at Peradeniya University in Kandy several monks are members of the Student Action Committee, the JVP's political support group. The more established leaders of Buddhist monastic orders have admonished the young monks to resist the temptation of using violent means, but even among elder monks there is a great deal of sympathy for the JVP cause.

Many Sri Lankan politicians claimed that the Sinhalese uprising was caused by Jayewardene's refusal to tolerate democratic elections, and predicted that the situation would calm down once free elections were held. Yet some of the most savage acts of terrorism occurred after the presidential elections that brought the present leader, Ranasinghe Premadasa, into power on December 19, 1988. The JVP boycotted the elections and vowed not to relax their activities until all their demands — including the demand for a Sinhalese Buddhist state — were met. On January 10–26, 1989, eight candidates for parliamentary seats were dragged from their homes and killed by JVP supporters.

Further acts of violence occurred after the parliamentary elections on February 15, 1989. The JVP initiated a series of highly effective strikes demanding higher wages for workers and the withdrawal of Indian troops. On June 12, 1989 several people were killed when police broke up a JVP-sponsored demonstration in western Sri Lanka calling for a boycott of Indian goods and for the departure of all Indians — civilian and military — from Sri Lankan soil. On June 20, President Premadasa declared a state of emergency and arrested 3,200 suspected JVP sympathizers and other leftists; scarcely a week later he survived a bomb attack on his life at a crowded religious festival. The JVP was implicated in the attempt. In late July 1989 the Indian government agreed to a token withdrawal of Indian troops, thereby allowing Premadasa to save face. The hope was that this gesture would help to stem the tide of support for the Sinhalese militants.

Mark Juergensmeyer

# SUDAN

Religion is one of the most important dimensions of politics in the Sudan. It involves basic issues of national identity, legal structure, and organization of major political groups. It is the basis for debate and conflict because the Sudan is not a religiously homogeneous society.

The Sudan is the largest country in Africa, with an area of 2,506,000 sq km. Located in the Nile valley, it extends more than 2,000 km south from Egypt into the heart of central Africa. In this vast area there is a substantial cultural diversity among the peoples. It is generally estimated that more than 100 different languages are spoken in the Sudan by at least 50 different major ethnic groupings. However, Arabic is the language of the majority of the Sudanese and Arab language and culture have been basic to the urban and much of the rural culture in the northern two-thirds of the country for at least two centuries.

This diversity is also reflected in the religious affiliation of the Sudanese. Paralleling the importance of Arabic, most northern Sudanese are Muslims, while the majority of people in the southern third of the country are identified by the worldview traditions of their local ethnic group or are Christians. Most estimates show about 70–75 per cent of the population as formally Muslim and about 10 per cent having a Christian institutional affiliation. These estimates do not indicate the great pluralism within the broad labels.

It is specific affiliations rather than the broad identifications that have had the most importance for Sudanese politics in the modern era. This is especially true among the Muslims, where the different major Muslim groups have provided the bases for most major political organizations in modern times. Each of the major political parties in the parliamentary era of 1985–1989, for example, was based on a particular Muslim organization, and the character of the party's program reflected the historical character of the supporting group.

The major religio-political issues of 1987–1989 involve both long-term historical interactions and more recent developments. When the Sudan became independent in 1956, there were two major political groupings based on two different nationalist perspectives. The Sudan had, in the twentieth century, legally been under the dual control of Great Britain and Egypt, although in practice, the British ruled the Sudan. One nationalist sentiment advocated unity of the Sudan with Egypt while the other worked for a separate, independent Sudan.

The "unionists" were represented by a number of smaller political parties which had joined together in 1952 to form the National Unionist Party (NUP) under the leadership of Ismail al-Azhari. This party combined more secularist, modern-educated Sudanese, under al-Azhari, with the broader mass support of the Khatmiyyah, a Muslim religious brotherhood led by the Mirghani family.

The Khatmiyyah had been established in the Sudan early in the nineteenth century as a popular devotional and educational organization. The leaders from the Mirghani family developed a tradition of working with existing governments rather than taking direct roles of political leadership. In the twentieth century, Sayyid Ali al-Mirghani, who died in 1968, had continued this tradition, working first with the British and then joining the unionist nationalists but never accepting political position himself. He became the major patron of the NUP in the 1950s.

The advocates of a separate, independent Sudan formed the Ummah Party following World War II. While the Ummah Party received the support of non-unionist educated Sudanese, it closely identified with another major Muslim organization, the Ansar. This is the organization of the Mahdist movement which was begun in the 1880s when Muhammad Ahmad declared himself to be the Mahdi, or divinely-sent leader of the age. The Mahdi organized a successful Holy War against the government of the day, and he and his successor established a fundamentalist Islamic state in the Sudan which lasted until the Anglo-Egyptian conquest of the Sudan in 1898.

Although the Mahdist state had been defeated, a son of the Mahdi, Sayyid Abd al-Rahman al-Mahdi, reorganized the movement and made it into a major political force by the middle of the twentieth century. The Mahdi family and its political allies led the Ummah Party and the Ansar provided the party's mass support.

Partisan politics in the Sudan at independence in 1956 represented the competition among three groupings, the Mahdists, the Khatmiyyah, and the more secularist educated classes led by al-Azhari, who were usually allied with the Khatmiyyah. In addition to these, there were smaller groups. The southern Sudanese had not been active in the development of nationalist politics and only began to organize political parties in the 1950s. They represented a somewhat disorganized political block in the new parliament which hoped for greater recognition of the special character of the south within the Sudan. There were also some relatively smaller northern political groups at the time who were to have greater importance later, the Sudanese Communist Party (SCP) and the fundamentalist Muslim Brotherhood.

To a remarkable degree, this political configuration has provided the foundation for Sudanese politics for almost 40 years. When a revolutionary military group outlawed all political parties following a successful coup in June 1989, the parties that were outlawed were the NUP's successor, the

Ummah, various smaller southern parties, the Sudanese Communist Party, and the Muslim Brotherhood's political party, the National Islamic Front. These durable groupings have survived through a number of major changes. The first parliamentary period only survived from the pre-independence elections in 1953 until a military coup in 1958. That military regime, of General Ibrahim Abboud, was overthrown by a civilian revolution in 1964. In the second parliamentary period, the old parties again dominated the political arena and were ousted in the military coup of 1969 which brought Ja'far al-Numayri to power.

Numayri attempted, in a number of ways, to transform Sudanese politics and society. Although he ruled the Sudan for almost 16 years, he did not provide real stability. He began by attempting to implement a relatively radical socialist program but by the mid-1970s his basic policies were more pragmatic and open to private capital. In this era he succeeded in bringing an end to the major civil war which had begun with sporadic fighting in the south in 1955 and had become progressively more violent in the following 15 years. Neither northern civilian politicians nor General Abboud had been able to bring the fighting to a halt. Numayri succeeded in accomplishing this by signing an agreement with the southern opposition in 1972 which gave special recognition to southern autonomy within the Sudan.

Religion was an important part of this political system because of north-south divisions in the country tended to coincide with the boundaries between Muslim and non-Muslim majority areas. As a result, when Numayri began to adopt a more consciously Islamic political identity, the 1972 agreement came under pressure. This, combined with Numayri's increasingly authoritarian methods of rule, aroused growing opposition and resulted in the renewal of fighting in the south in the early 1980s.

The Islamization of Numayri's policies reached a high point in 1983 when he began the formal implementation of the *shari'a*, Islamic Law, in what came to be called "the September Laws". This programme involved the immediate application of Islamic rules and regulations interpreted in an authoritarian and traditional manner. Even among northern Muslims, the September Laws aroused opposition. A great grandson of the Mahdi (and leader of the outlawed but still existing Ummah Party), Sadiq al-Mahdi, was jailed for his public criticisms of Numayri's program and Mahmud Muhammad Taha, leader of a smaller modernist Muslim group, was executed in January 1985, for his opposition. Even the fundamentalist Muslim Brotherhood, which gave public support to the principle of Islamization, had significant reservations and Numayri arrested its leaders in March 1985.

Religion thus played a very significant role in the increasing opposition to Numayri in the 1980s. His policies had aroused the enmity of all of the major Islamic groups as well as the more secularist Sudanese and the southerners. In a context where he was also facing major economic problems and a growing civil war in the south, there was little public opposition to his overthrow in April 1985. At that time, a group of senior military officers took control of the government and promised a return to civilian politics within one year. The transitional military government succeeded in this with elections being held in April 1986, and a new cabinet and national assembly assumed control of the state in May.

The politics of the third period of civilian parties and parliaments were very similar to the earlier periods. The two parties winning the most seats in the new parliament were the Ummah Party, led by Sadiq al-Mahdi, and the Democratic Unionist Party, which was the direct organizational heir of the NUP and was led by Muhammad Uthman al-Mirghani, a son of Sayyid Ali. There was also a group of relatively small southern parties and a few members of the Sudanese Communist Party.

The major changes from the 1960s involved the emergence of two very important political groups, each with a special religious dimension to their programs.

The Muslim Brotherhood had been small and relatively marginal in the politics of the 1950s and '60s. While it had participated in elections and, in the 1960s, its Islamic Charter Front had gained some parliamentary seats, its appeal had been largely limited to students and younger educated professionals. However, in the elections of 1986, the Brotherhood's party, the National Islamic Front, received almost 20 per cent of the total vote in the northern provinces and its 51 seats compared well with the 64 won by the DUP and even the 99 seats won by the Ummah Party (of a total of 264 contested seats). This indicated that the Brotherhood was emerging as a more popular political force and was not confined to a small educated elite. The programme of the Brotherhood was explicitly religious: it advocated the application of Islamic Law, in a form adapted to modern conditions, in all aspects of Sudanese society.

The second major change in the political scene was the emergence of the Sudan People's Liberation Movement (SPLM). This was the organization which led the opposition in the resumed civil war in the early 1980s. It is primarily a southern movement but under the leadership of John Garang has proclaimed its goal to be the revolutionary transformation of the whole of the Sudan. The SPLM has a strong religious dimension in its programme because it opposes Muslim domination of the Sudan and strongly advocates the creation of a secular state. As a result, the SPLM refused to participate in the transitional regime or the elections of 1986 because of the continued Islamic identification of the state in Khartoum. The SPLM's ultimate condition for negotiations for an end to the civil war is the guarantee that the Sudanese state will be secular and that no form of Islamic Law will be the basis for the Sudanese legal system.

In the politics of the Sudan in the late 1980s, the Brotherhood and the SPLM provide the two extremes in the views on one of the most important political issues of the time: should the Sudanese state be Islamic or should it be secular? The Ummah Party and the DUP position has always been between the two extremes, with both parties advocating some form of recognition of Islam in the constitution and some identification of the state with Islam. However, before the September Laws, neither party had advocated the immediate implementation of the rules of the *shari'a* in its traditional form.

Numayri's Islamization program created a dilemma for the leaders of the Ummah and the DUP throughout the third era of civilian politics. Sadiq al-Mahdi was prime minister from 1986 until he was overthrown by the military take-over in June 1989. His experience reflects the basic line that this major religio-political issue followed. Sadiq had been an opponent of the September Laws and was jailed for his opposition. In the elections of 1986 he promised to rescind the September Laws and repeated this intention when he became prime minister.

One of the major issues in Sudanese politics in 1987–1989 has been to deal with Islamization. All parties agree that the September Laws are not acceptable. However, on one extreme, the Muslim Brotherhood insisted that they be maintained until a more acceptable version of Islamic Law be established in their place. At the other extreme, the SPLM refuses to stop the civil war and begin negotiations until there is agreement upon the principle of a secular state for the Sudan. Sadiq regularly attempted to bridge this gap with proposals which would change the nature of the legal context without eliminating the Islamic identity of the state.

In November 1986, al-Mahdi announced that new laws to replace the September Laws would be proposed and in June 1987 he proposed the exemption of non-Muslims from specifically Islamic legal prescriptions. Again, in April 1988 when he formed a new coalition government of national unity, his governmental charter called for replacing the September Laws by what he called the genuine *shari'a*, with special rights for non-Muslims. In October, when the National Islamic Front was included in the government coalition, the cabinet approved a more strict application of the *shari'a*, causing a cabinet crisis only resolved by withdrawing the proposal. All of these actions indicate both the importance of the issue and the inability of al-Mahdi's cabinets to resolve the problems involved in trying to replace the September Laws. The issue remained unresolved in June 1989, when the parliamentary regime was overthrown by the military government led by Umar al-Bashir.

In its early announcements in June and July 1989, the new military government attempted to avoid the issue. The new rulers simply promised that "the people" would be allowed to decide at some future date. The suggested means for making this decision was some form of national referendum. Such a solution might not be approved by the non-Muslim Sudanese.

Religion was specifically involved in the great task of achieving national unity and bringing an end to the civil war. Non-Muslim and secularist views as expressed by the SPLM were uncompromising on the need for a secular state in a unified Sudan. This was one of the major sources of disagreement between al-Mahdi and Garang, the SPLM leader. Already in October 1985, during the transitional period, Garang had set the abrogation of the *shari'a* in the Sudan as a basic precondition for SPLM participation in political dialogue. In 1986 Garang refused, in the absence of this abrogation, to allow elections in southern areas under SPLM control. Each time al-Mahdi announced a proposal to replace the September Laws the proposals were rejected as insufficient by the SPLM.

Finally, in the last months of 1988 a new approach had some success, both in the general terms of securing an end to fighting and in the specific issue of dealing with Islamic Law. In October, SPLM leaders began meetings with leaders of the DUP, which was part of the government coalition at the time but acting on its own in these meetings. These discussions were concluded by a major meeting between Muhammad Uthman al-Mirghani, the head of the DUP, and John Garang. They agreed in calling for the convening of a National Constitutional Convention following a cease-fire in the fighting. On the critical issue of Islamic Law, the agreement was to "freeze" all provisions, neither implementing them nor changing them until the National Convention.

The al-Mahdi government failed to approve this agreement and the DUP withdrew from the governing coalition. The result was a new coalition government in January 1989, made up of the Ummah Party and the National Islamic Front. This government made no progress in resolving the problems of national unity and in March senior military officials told al-Mahdi that he had to reduce fundamentalist influence in the government and make significant progress toward peace or else the military would act. In March, al-Mahdi created a new coalition which included the DUP and the Sudanese Communist Party but excluded the NIF. Although some negotiations were undertaken, little progress was made in solving the great problems facing the nation. On June 30, a group of military officers arrested most of the old political leaders and took control of the government.

The new military rulers have made the political parties illegal. However, it is not clear that they will be any more successful than the two military regimes before them in changing Sudanese society in ways that will reduce the basic political influence of the large Islamic organizations. It is clear that the new rulers will face the old problems of creating a national sense of unity that can transcend religious affiliation and trying to find a way of creating a state which will reflect the Islamic loyalties of the Muslim majority without rousing the fears of the non-Muslim Sudanese.

These issues reflect the continuing importance of religion in the politics of the Sudan, whether the political system is a civilian parliamentary one or a military regime.

John O. Voll

# SURINAME

Suriname is a former Dutch colony, bordering on Guyana, French Guiana and Brazil, which obtained independence in 1975. Its estimated (1985) population is 393,748. Political life has been characterized by instability arising out of a multi-party system and underlying ethnic divisions (involving Dutch, Indian, Chinese, Javanese and other groups). A military coup, in February 1980, precipitated a prolonged period of particular instability. The coup's leader, Désiré Bouterse, made several efforts to establish a broadly-based government but he was repeatedly hampered by left-right divisions, ethnic conflict, labour unrest, military factionalism, economic problems, and sharp external responses to the government's execution of opponents that have included the withholding of aid. A particular difficulty has been armed conflict with anti-government guerrillas (the Suriname Liberation Army — SLA) which severely damaged bauxite mining and other economic enterprises.

Many religions are represented in Suriname. Christianity, Hinduism and Islam predominate. In 1988 an ecumenical Church group, "the Committee of Christian Churches" (CCK) was accepted by a newly-elected government as mediator in efforts to end the insurgency. The military opposed peace talks but subsequently accepted the offer of mediation. This development is a measure of the political vacuum created by the failure of established political groups to agree upon a viable political system.

Kenneth Medhurst

# SWAZILAND

A land-locked country increasingly economically dependent on South Africa, Swaziland has tried to present an image of stability. Becoming independent from Britain in 1968 as a constitutional monarchy, King Sobhuza II, who began his reign in 1921, became apprehensive in 1972 when the opposition Ngwane National Liberatory Congress (NNLC) won three seats. He suspended the Constitution, dissolved Parliament and abolished political parties. In 1977 the king decided to restore traditional structures of authority by requiring popular representation to come from the *tinkhundla* or local councils. King Sobhuza died in 1981 leaving a dynastic struggle for the succession which was not resolved until 1986 when King Mswati III was crowned.

Methodism was introduced in 1825 by invitation of the king and it is now the largest denomination. Anglicans, Roman Catholics, Nazarenes and Lutherans have congregations. Independent African Churches have flourished, particularly in the inter-war period and can count on the support of about a quarter of the population. Political dissent has come mainly from the university.

Stuart Mews

# SWEDEN

The Church of Sweden is a State Church; since 1951 members have been free to withdraw, but still 93 per cent (1988) are members. Immigration has made the Catholic Church the second largest religious organization with 1.5 per cent of the population. The number of adherents of the Orthodox Churches and of Islam has also increased so that Sweden is no longer a religiously homogenous country.

Since the revivals of the nineteenth century there are a number of free Churches (the Mission Covenant Church, the Baptists, the Methodists);

today they count some 5 per cent of the population as members. The free Church people have been politically active and have traditionally cast their votes for the Liberal Party, which has a clear over-representation of parliamentary members from the free Churches. In 1964 Pentecostalists and Conservative forces within the Church of Sweden joined in forming a new party, the Christian Democratic Community Party. It has never got enough votes (2.9 per cent in 1988) for parliamentary representation but it has been more successful in local elections.

The Social Democrats dropped the claim about "the abolition of the State Church system" in 1960, and since the 1930s Christian Social Democrats have been organized in the Brotherhood Movement. By tradition the conservative Moderate Party was the party most in favour of traditional State Church religion but now the Centre Party (formerly Agrarians) has taken this position. In 1985 the most frequent attenders of worship (in all religious groups) divided their votes equally between the Social Democrats, the Liberal Party, the Moderate Party, the Centre Party and the Christian Democrats, but the Centre Party was the parliamentary party with most church attenders amongst its voters. Active Christians in parliament have formed a group with some 100 (of 350) members; they have seldom engaged in joint political actions.

The political influence of the Churches is weak: they could not stop a liberal abortion law in the 1970s. In latter years they have engaged in activities for peace, disarmament and the protection of the environment.

The present position of the State Church is the result of a political compromise in 1981. This gave the Church of Sweden a new representative body instead of the Synod, with a fixed representation for bishops/clergy and lay-people. All members of the new body, the General Assembly of the Church of Sweden, are indirectly elected through the parish councils, i.e. no seats are reserved for the bishops/clergy. The political parties contest the elections for the General Assembly and the majority of the representatives there get their seats as members of a political party.

Göran Gustafsson

# SWITZERLAND

Diversity and plurality mark out life in Switzerland. Of the total population of some 5.5 million Swiss and one million foreigners living in Switzerland, some 2.8 million are Protestant, some 3 million are Roman Catholic, 18,000 are Jewish and 480,000 profess either other religions or no religion at all. Despite a tradition of religious dissent which gave rise to different interpretations of religious practice and theory and found expression in a high number of individual Churches, communities, sects and lifestyles, a mutual understanding between Catholics and Protestants is slowly emerging because of a common shared development: while "practice" is declining, "religiosity" is increasing. The accent of church work is on pastoral work bridging the gulf between traditional norms as stipulated by the Churches and the daily life and lifestyles of the believers.

The federalist nature of the state, a democratic understanding of politics, brought about a culture of consensus but this attitude is increasingly difficult to maintain given the contradictions between political stability and rapid social changes. Green and progressive parties on the political left just as much as new conservative (anti-foreigner) parties on the right have gained votes in cantonal elections in 1987 thereby eroding the parties in the centre. In the referendum on April 5, 1987 on the asylum and legislation on foreigners the majority of voters voted decisively for the revision of the laws. A committee of left and Christian groups had forced the issue fearing a further tightening of the asylum conditions.

On April 8, 1988 in a controversial nomination Pope John Paul II created Wolfgang Haas from Liechtenstein Bishop of Chur against the wishes of the chapter of Chur Cathedral, half of which did not attend the service of consecration. Critics of the Pope see in this appointment a further example for the tendency, contrary to the 2nd Vatican Council, not only to exert more influence on local affairs, but even more so to fill vacancies with trusted traditionalists, especially as Switzerland has no Catholic archbishopric so that the dioceses are directly connected to the Holy See.

In the continuing controversy over the appointment of Wolfgang Haas the Canton Schwyz asked the Swiss government in June 1989 to intervene and take up the matter with the Holy See claiming that formal rights have been disregarded with Haas's appointment. Since an earlier protest note delivered to the nunciature drew the reply that the appointment of the bishop was the business of the Holy See alone, the Canton warned that it may be forced to take action such as suspending payments to the diocese if the new diplomatic move failed. The dean of Zurich, Fr A. Camenzind, pointed to the new bishop's unwillingness to dialogue so that his "purely legalistic way of thinking" held sway over the pastoral concerns and needs of priests and parishioners.

A long-standing unsettled affair, the movement of traditionalist Catholics led by Archbishop Lefebvre, with headquarters in Écône near Geneva, came to a head with the consecration of four bishops by Lefebvre in open confrontation with Rome in June 1988, who thereby incurred automatic excommunication by the Holy See. Lefebvre founded the International Priestly Society of St Pius X in 1970 in opposition to reforms instituted by the 2nd Vatican Council. Some 10 per cent of their members have since asked to be admitted again to the Roman Catholic Church.

The series of chemical disasters which beset Swiss multi-national companies in autumn 1986 and the business acumen of the Swiss provided the backdrop for a new platform. From May 15–21, 1988 the European Ecumenical Assembly met in Basle representing 126 Catholic, Orthodox, Anglican and Protestant churches to prepare a global meeting on "justice, peace and integrity of creation" in 1990 in Seoul, Korea to link environmental issues to broader economic ones.

Dorothea McEwan

# SYRIA

Modern Syria dates from its creation as a separate state in 1920; it became independent of French mandatory rule in 1946. Almost from the time of its creation, Syria has been one of the main centres of secular Arab nationalism, from the pan-Arabism of the 1920s to Ba'thism, the political creed of the country's rulers today. Apart from the wounds caused by the dismemberment of geographical Syria after the World War I, a further factor encouraging the rise of Arabism was the heterogeneous ethnic and religious composition of the Syrian state. Arabs form the majority of the population, but there is an important Kurdish minority, and smaller communities of Turcomans, Armenians and Circassians. Again, Sunni Muslims form 70 per cent of the population, but 12 per cent are Alawites, 14 per cent Christians, and the remainder mostly Druzes and Ismailis. During the nineteenth century, and for much of the period of the French mandate (1920–1946) many of the Christians and indeed some of the heterodox Muslim minorities, looked towards the European powers, particularly France, for protection, but there was always an important element advocating either "Syrian" or "Arab" unity on the basis of language, ethnicity and co-residence.

During the mandate the French believed that the main threat to their position in Syria came from the nationalist movement in the cities, whose leaders were mostly Sunni Muslims. They tried to contain this movement by dividing the country administratively in such a way that the compact minorities (particularly the Druzes and Alawites) were ruled separately, and generally by obstructing the formation of institutions which might promote national unity. Specifically, when Syria became independent in 1946, there was no national army, and the only body on which such a force could be built was the *Troupes Spéciales du Levant*, a kind of *gendarmerie* whose members came mainly from the rural minorities, in particular from the Druzes and Alawites. The urban Sunni elite maintained their traditional interest in agriculture and certain types of commerce and did not on the whole encourage their sons to join the armed forces, even after independence.

The history of Syria between 1946 and the Ba'th takeover in 1963 is extremely complex, reflecting great power antagonisms, struggles for regional supremacy on the part of Syria's powerful neighbours Egypt and Iraq, and the weakness of the Syrian state structure. The principal tensions within Syria itself were between the traditional landowning and mercantile classes and the rising educated middle and lower-middle classes, whose most articulate representatives were to be found in the professions and in the army. The Ba'th Party, a secular nationalist organization advocating Arab unity and state-sponsored economic development which it calls socialism, proved to be the most effective vehicle for the advancement of the "new" social classes, especially as its secularism made it particularly appealing to a significant number of army officers who were not from the traditional Sunni urban elite.

In 1963 the Ba'th came to power by means of a military coup, and the senior ranks of the Party have controlled Syria ever since, albeit with important changes in ideology and personnel. The rulers of Syria since the 1960s, and especially since Hafiz al-Assad's seizure of power in 1970, have been drawn largely from the (traditionally downtrodden) rural minorities, particularly from the Alawite community of north-western Syria. In the 1960s in particular, the Ba'th pursued fairly radical social and economic policies, which aimed to break the power of the old elite. This was combined with a genuine if somewhat premature form of secularism, in that many Ba'thists believed that it was necessary to break with what they saw as the restraints imposed by Islam in order to create a new and progressive social and economic order. That such a consensus was able to emerge was partly due to the fact that in a very broad sense and with many important exceptions, religion for the Alawites, and other heterodox Shiite sects, and to some extent for Orthodox Christians, is less a matter of profound spiritual conviction than an important means of distinguishing oneself and one's community from others, and in particular from the dominant majority.

In the climate of the late 1960s and 1970s, however, the accusation of "atheism", levelled at the Ba'th by its critics, and particularly by its Muslim fundamentalist critics, could not be dismissed lightly. In an attempt to deflect such charges, the leader of the Lebanese Twelver Shiis, Imam Musa Sadr, issued a fatwa in 1973 proclaiming that the Alawites were an authentic Shiite sect. Needless to say, many Sunni Muslims also approved of the regime's social and economic reform programmes, but others, including some of those hardest hit by its effects and those outside forces who were unhappy about the regime's closeness to the Soviet Union, joined or supported the fundamentalists. At the same time, and increasingly throughout the 1970s, although its leadership remained firmly Alawite, the regime attracted a substantial body of support from urban Sunnis, most notably members of the old Damascene commercial bourgeoisie.

Nevertheless, no amount of assertions of Islamic identity on the part of the regime could prevent a wave of serious incidents involving sectarian killings (mostly of prominent Alawites associated with the regime, but also of some of its Sunni supporters), the murder of Alawite officer cadets in Aleppo in June 1979, and attempted urban risings in Aleppo, Hama, Homs, Jisr al-Shughur and Dayr al-Zur between 1979 and 1981.

The regime's major confrontation with the fundamentalists came in February 1982, when a full-scale insurrection, organized by the Muslim Brethren, broke out in the city of Hama. The fighting lasted three weeks, and between 5,000 and 10,000 people were killed. Since 1982 there has been no overt manifestation of religion-based hostility towards the regime, which, for its part, has continued its former practice of emphasizing its Islamic credentials and generally endeavouring to avoid offending the religious sensibilities of the more conservative elements in the population.

Marion Farouk-Sluglett
Peter Sluglett

# TAIWAN

Taiwan, with a population of around 20 million, is an island of some 36,000 square kilometres lying off the south-east coast of China. After the communist victory in the Chinese Civil War, 1946–49, the defeated Chiang Kai-shek, leader of the Kuomintang party, retreated to Taiwan with approximately two million soldiers, officials and opponents of communism. He established a nationalist, anti-communist regime on the island. Chiang's essentially military government was criticised for human rights' violations but attained a high economic growth rate and successful industrialization with support particularly from the USA and Japan. Chiang Ching-kuo, Chiang Kai-shek's son, entered his second six-year term as president in 1984 and the Kuomintang still dominates politics on the island. However in 1987 martial law was lifted and there have been signs of increasing liberalism.

Taiwan has a rich and varied religious culture, partly because many senior religious figures from all sects fled to Taiwan in 1949 to escape communism. The majority of the population follows traditional Chinese popular religions, and, often at the same time, Buddhism and Taoism. There are also small numbers of Christians and Muslims. Some Protestants have been opposition activists, often on human rights issues, and two leading Protestants received 10-year jail sentences in October 1987. But generally religion has been encouraged by the regime as evidence of traditional Chinese culture in contrast to the anti-religious orientation of the communist mainland.

Alan Hunter

# TANZANIA

Tanganyika became independent in 1961 and in 1964 united with Zanzibar to become Tanzania. About 40 per cent of Tanzania's inhabitants are Christian, 30 per cent Muslim, and another 20 per cent adherents of traditional religion. Julius Nyerere was Tanganyika's first Prime Minister, a month later its first President, and then the President of the United Tanzania and chairman of the sole political party, called since 1976 Chama cha Mapinduzi (Party of the Revolution). Nyerere, a devout Catholic, and his party have pursued a policy of Tanzanian socialism or Ujamaa ("familyhood"). In 1985 Nyerere though remaining chairman of the party, stepped down as president, being succeeded by Hassan Mwinyi, a Muslim from Zanzibar. There is evidence of the rise of a more militant Islam, disturbing the peaceful coexistence between Christian and Muslim. In mid-1987 the Muslim Council of Tanzania held public "teachings" in Dar es Salaam proclaiming "There is but one God and one religion, Islam". Mwinyi has several times countered this campaign of some senior members of the Islamic community to bring a "mild jihad" to Tanzania. He stated in mid-1987: "Tanzania, CCM and its government have no religion . . . Tanzanians have religions and are free to worship". On a visit to Zanzibar in 1988 Nyerere felt he had to deny allegations that he intended to turn CCM into a Catholic movement.

In February 1987 the High Court convicted the Minister of Trade and Industry of illegal campaigning during the 1985 general elections. The charge related to his use of Catholic priests to further his candidacy. The conviction was, in November 1987, overturned by the Court of Appeal.

Paul Gifford

# THAILAND

Religion has played a relatively insignificant overt role in Thai national politics. It is true that Buddhism is one of the three foundations of the Thai state along with loyalty to the King and country. Also, during the 1960s, when there was a large active communist-led insurgency in the Kingdom, some members of the sangha (monkhood) were involved in programs emphasizing development, national unity and anti-communism. However, the *sangha* has remained relatively apolitical and tightly disciplined within a hierarchical structure under the leadership of the King. Generally, religion is outside national political debates.

Religion does play a role at the regional level in southern Thailand where it combines with ethnicity among a Malay-Muslim minority that composes about four per cent of the Thai population. Until recently neglected by authorities in Bangkok and often looking south to Malaysia, elements of this community have long sought autonomy or independence. Muslim insurgents have fought Thai authorities for decades in a simmering conflict that is now at a relatively low level. As of 1988 there were approximately 200 separatists from the Pattani United Liberation Organization and *Barisan Nasional Revolusi* serving prison sentences from 50 to more than 200 years. According to Thai military authorities there are now only about 10 per cent of the 1,800 rebels that were in the field in 1978. Thai authorities have attempted to meet Malay-Muslim demands by increasing government services and local participation in district and provincial activities. However, there are still local perceptions of being second-class citizens in a region where growing Thai immigration is looked upon with suspicion. In the late 1980s there was a limited resurgence of separatist activities, with some Thai authorities claiming external aid from Libya and Iran.

Fred R. von der Mehden

# TOGO

For most of this century, government policy has had an important influence
on the religious situation in Togo. Before the First World War, Togoland was
a German colony, and Islam was encouraged as a matter of colonial policy,
but it is mainly amongst the Kotokoli that the 11 per cent of the population
who are Muslims are to be found. The League of Nations split the country
into British and French zones. One consequence was the growth of ethnic
nationalism among the Ewe, who number half a million in Togo but live
also across the border in its neighbour, the Gold Coast. During the First
World War all the Ewe had been under British administration and a single
Presbyterian Church had been brought into being. The League split the Ewe
area into two and caused much dissatisfaction.

Togo became independent in 1960 but discontent led to army coups in
1963, and again in 1967 when Lieutenant-Colonel Etienne Eyadema became
president. He appointed a commission on national disunity which reported
in 1968 that the socio-cultural and economic differences between north and
south were unbridgeable. Eyadema's solution was to project himself as a living
symbol of unity. A personality cult was encouraged and in a referendum, he
received 99 per cent of the vote.

In 1974 Eyadema launched a new policy of "authenticity" or respect
for the country's traditional culture. It was decreed that Ewe and Kabiye
would replace French in schools. "Foreign religions" were discouraged and
foreign religious personnel found it difficult to enter the country. Traditional
religious world views which have always been held by the majority of the
population were encouraged. The Roman Catholic Church clashed with the
government over this policy.

Stuart Mews

# TONGA

The Kingdom of Tonga was established under a Constitution from King
Tupou I in 1875. After a period under British Protectorate, it became
independent in 1970. Altogether 119,000 people inhabit 36 islands, with 65
per cent on the principal island of Tongatapu. The population is 99 per cent
Christian, almost all Methodist, so the church has a unique place in the life of
the people. By Constitution, Sunday is a day of rest in which no work of any
kind can be done and everyone goes to church. The King is the centre of the
political and religious life of the islands and the Constitution makes him the
head of the Free Wesleyan Church. Until recently this has been unchallenged
but new economic pressures have placed strains on the system.

There is serious overcrowding on the islands and the King's right to
apportion land to his subjects is now a major problem. Thousands of Tongans

have migrated to New Zealand, many illegally. In the last two years a few of
the minor politicians have begun to challenge the authority of the King and
the chiefs. In 1989, a people's representative brought impeachment proceedings against the Minister of Finance for making large unauthorized payments
to members of parliament for travel and expenses. The rulers are increasingly
accused of patronage and feudalism. To try and balance the shaky economy, a
Princess of the royal family last year made an arrangement to dump hazardous
wastes from the United States in the islands. When this was challenged by
Church leadership, the project was abandoned.

Ron O'Grady

# TRINIDAD AND TOBAGO

"Here every creed and race finds an equal place" goes the national
anthem of Trinidad and Tobago, a complex and racially segmented culture
in the Caribbean, comprised of large Creole and East Indian populations
and smaller communities of Syrians, Lebanese, Chinese, Portuguese and
Jews. Roughly coincident with racial diversity comes a religious landscape
comprised of Christianity, Hinduism, Islam, and a variety of Afro-Caribbean
practices, the most notable being Shango. In 1980 it was estimated that 60 per
cent of the population were Christians (33.6 per cent Roman Catholic, 15 per
cent Anglicans) 25 per cent Hindus, and 5.9 per cent Muslims. The population of 1.2 million (1986 est.) also includes Presbyterians, Methodists, and a
dynamic evangelical and pentecostal movement. National holidays include the
Christian Christmas and Easter as well as the Hindu Diwali and the Muslim
Eid ul Fitr. All public official gatherings are opened with representatives of the
"universal faiths", although fundamentalist Christian leaders normally decline
to take part in such ceremonies (at least one fundamentalist pastor has served
on a government commission, however).

While political parties make cross cultural appeals, and thus tend to avoid
using religious sectarian rhetoric in campaigning, race based political divisions
remain of key political importance. The December 1986 elections proved a
watershed, with the multi-ethnic National Alliance for Reconstruction (NAR)
breaking the 30 year domination of the largely Black Creole-based People's
National Movement (PNM). By 1988, however, explusions from the NAR of
former leaders of an East Indian based party weakened the government. It
also faced stiff labour opoosition to International Monetary Fund structural
adjustments in early 1989.

The Anti-Apartheid movement was strengthened when South African
Anglican Archbishop Desmond Tutu visited the island in May 1987 and
was greeted by Prime Minister ANR Robinson. A major interfaith service in
March 1988, attended by government ministers, also expressed opposition to
apartheid. In June 1987 a decision taken by the Trinidad and Tobagan Anglican
diocese to ordain women broke a 4–4 deadlock in the West Indian province,

but as a ⅔ majority was necessary, it remained unclear at the time what the provincial outcome would be.

Virgil Wiebe

# TUNISIA

The Islamist movement in present-day Tunisia, *al-Ittijah al-Islami* (the Islamic Tendency Movement), has its roots in the Quranic Preservation Society founded in 1970. The Tunisian Government permitted its development to counterbalance a growing leftist movement on the campuses of the University of Tunis. It is only in the late 1970s that a loose coalition of Islamists many of whom had links to the Quranic Preservation Society, emerged as an important element in Tunisian politics, voicing the economic, social and political grievances of many Tunisians.

This coalition, which became known as the Islamic Tendency Movement (MTI) set up organized committees primarily in urban centres of Tunisia and began openly criticizing the government and calling for economic and political reforms based on a return to the true principles of Islam.

Realizing that the MTI was developing into a major opposition force, the Tunisian government began to crack down on its members as early as 1979. By 1981 MTI members were being arrested in significant numbers and accused of various political crimes. In September 1981, 61 members identified as leaders of the MTI began serving jail sentences ranging from two to 10 years; their publications were suspended and the movement was forbidden to teach in the mosques on Friday afternoons.

The MTI tried unsuccessfully to gain acceptance as a political party within the constitutional framework of Tunisia throughout the 1980s. On the other hand, more extremist fringe groups such as the Islamic Jihad, who refused to play the political game and openly espoused the use of violence, began to gain support and attention in Tunisia in the second half of the 1980s.

In August 1987 Islamic Jihad claimed responsibility for the bombing of four tourist hotels. This affected tourism in Tunisia which is one of the sources of revenues for the state. The police cracked down on Islamic Jihad members. Earlier that year 90 MTI members were arrested and accused of being in collusion with the Iranian government and plotting to overthrow the government. In August 1987 when they came to trial large anti-government demonstrations took place in protest and the judge presiding over their trial was sprayed with hydrochloric acid.

In September 1987, the State Security Court sentenced seven of the 90 MTI members to death, Rachid Ghanouchi one of the principal leaders of the MTI to life imprisonment, 67 members from two years to life in jail, while 14 were acquitted. In October 1987 the first death sentences were carried out and two MTI members Mehrez Boudegga, and Boulbaba Dekhil were hanged. In October two MTI leaders Ali Laaridh and Fadel Beldi were captured by the security forces, after having been sentenced to death and to hard labour respectively, *in absentia*, in September.

On the eve of the November 1987 ouster of Bourguiba it was reported that the Tunisian President was planning on re-opening the trials and extending the death penalty to other members of the MTI. The fear that such an action would lead to more violence and bloodshed was apparently behind the timing of the overthrow of the ailing head of state.

The government's policy since then has been one of compromise rather than one of confrontation with the Islamists. In December 1987, the new Tunisian leader Ben Ali granted amnesty to 2,487 prisoners including 608 MTI members. He also commuted the death sentence of Ali Laaridh to hard labour, and dropped charges against another 60 MTI members. In May 1988 he pardoned Rachid Ghannouchi and set him free and in July a number of MTI members who were imprisoned for crimes "against public rights" were released from jail. In September 1988 he allowed the Secretary-General of the MTI Abd al-Fattah Mourou to return to Tunisia after two years in exile.

In the Spring of 1989 the Tunisians went to the polls to elect their president as well as their deputies for parliament. The Islamists were once again not allowed to run as Islamists and so ran as independents under the banner of the Renaissance Party which is not recognized as a legal political institution yet. They were well organized and able to mobilize significant support. There were reportedly 1,200 Islamist observers in Tunis alone ensuring that the elections took place fairly. Although the Constitutional Rally, the government party, won all the seats, the Islamists won 15 per cent of the national votes, and reportedly 30 per cent in some urban centers.

Mary-Jane Deeb

# TURKEY

The Republic of Turkey has been a secular state since the abolition of the Caliphate in March 1924. The majority of Turks are Sunni Muslims, although religious sects like the Alawis subscribe to a branch of Shiism. Turkey has a small minority of non-Muslims of which the most important are Jews and Christians of various denominations.

Despite its secular constitution, Turkey continues to be dominated by the debate on the role of Islam in public life. Interest in religion has been sustained not only by the popular appeal of "folk" Islam, especially Sufism, but also by the emergence in the 1960s and '70s of religious parties, most notably the National Salvation Party (NSP) which advocates the restoration of Islamic law and practice and closer ties with the Muslim world. The importance of religion is also reflected in the persistent sectarian tensions between the Sunni majority and the minority of Alawi Shias. Some Turks fear that the resurgence of Shia revivalism in neighbouring Iran could exacerbate these tensions.

Like most other Muslim countries, Turkey has recently witnessed the rise of religious fundamentalism. The 1980s have been characterized by an increase in "anti-secular activities". Whilst the government has acted firmly to control the politics of Muslim fundamentalists, some concessions have had to be made. The most significant of these was a decree (subsequently overturned by the Turkish Supreme Court) permitting Turkish women to wear the traditional head-dress. Present curbs on the activity of fundamentalist groups which tend to emphasize Turkey's Islamic identity, are likely to remain in force especially at a time when Turkey is keen to become a full member of the European Community.

Farzana Shaikh

# TUVALU

One of the world's smallest independent nations, Tuvalu, has 8,000 citizens many of whom live and work overseas on other islands. The few islands of the group (Tuvalu means "eight islands together") control half-a-million square miles of ocean and the sale of fishing rights is a useful source of income. The country is 96% Christian, almost all Protestant. Until 1964 there was a law preventing Catholics from working in the islands. Even though the law has been changed, local prejudice prevents the building of Catholic churches on several islands there and are still only 100 Catholics in Tuvalu.

Ron O'Grady

# UGANDA

Uganda is nearly 80 per cent Christian (50 per cent of the total population is Catholic, 25 per cent Anglican), and only 6 per cent Muslim. There have been tensions between Catholics and Anglicans since the civil war in the 1880s, and these continued after independence in 1962 with Obote's Uganda People's Congress being predominantly Anglican, and the Democratic Party predominantly Catholic. Under Amin (1971–79), the Muslim minority became influential for a short time, and the Anglican church in particular suffered terribly — the Anglican Archbishop Janani Luwum was murdered in 1977. Religious rivalry has been complicated by rivalry between the Bantu South and the non-Bantu North. In Museveni's drive to pacify the country after Obote's second overthrow (1985), a lengthy resistance was offered in late 1987 by the Holy Spirit Movement of Alice Lakwena, a 27-year-old Acholi woman, whose followers included members of Obote's regime. These used stones and witchcraft against Museveni's armour. In 1987 Museveni closed several missions in the north, and expelled 10 Catholic priests to stop them aiding rebels and to remove witnesses to the methods used to crush the resistance. By the beginning of 1989 church people were reporting numerous human rights abuses. In June 1988 the Anglican Archbishop was accused of being involved in a 1986 abortive coup to overthrow Museveni. In February 1989 Cardinal Nsubuga called on Museveni to restore the four provinces which existed before Obote changed the constitution in 1986. In the 1989 elections, two Catholic priests were elected to the Uganda parliament; Cardinal Nsubuga and the Catholic Bishops insisted they must resign in accordance with Canon Law.

Paul Gifford

# UNION OF SOVIET SOCIALIST REPUBLICS

## Christianity

The year 1988 was marked as the millennium of Christianity in Russian lands. In the course of it, on April 29, a well-publicized meeting took place between the most powerful man in the officially atheist state, the general secretary of the CPSU, Mikhail Gorbachev, and the Holy Synod of the Russian Orthodox Church. There were informal and no doubt significant discussions, of which no substantial account has yet been given. But even the formal declarations made on behalf of either body went beyond the customary proprieties of the day. Although it was still too early in the development of *glasnost* for euphemisms to be discounted altogether, Gorbachev was already willing to make unprecedented admissions in respect of his Party's anti-religious past. Admittedly, his "not everything was easy and straight forward in Church-state relations" might well have read "everything was done to diminish, despitefully use and demolish the Church". But it was at least a partial truth. Even more striking was the response of Pimen, Patriarch of Moscow and all Russia: "not all problems of church life are as yet resolved". For Church leaders had hitherto been expected to refrain from any plaints against the State. Such were generally restricted to the Church intelligentsia, or at least to that minority of churchmen who had been prepared to take the risk and pay the price. In previous years the price was often heavy.

As if to reassure the members of the Church that such a price would no longer be exacted in the future, nor in as arbitrary a fashion as before, new legislation on "freedom of conscience" was envisaged. In Gorbachev's phrase, it would reflect "even the interests of religious organizations".

Not the least of its provisions might involve the granting of full juridical status to the Church, something that has been withheld since the earliest days (Lenin's decree on the separation of Church and State, January 23, 1918) and throughout the Soviet period. Be that as it may, the anniversary of the April 1988 meeting was to pass without the publication, let along the promulgation of new laws.

The delay did not express any lessening of dissatisfaction with the old, existing legislation. In its essential parts this dates back to April 8, 1929. At the very least it was anachronistic. It was also undisguisedly repressive. The function of religious life was narrowly defined as "performance of the cult". The latter was reluctantly permitted, so long as the registration of the relevant persons and places had been granted. But even this was difficult to achieve as the result of arbitrary action by administrators and party personnel.

Yet nothing else was allowed. The 1929 regulations (clause 8) list most prohibited activities in detail. They rule out social, educational and charitable activity. Within a month, (May 22, 1929) the previously accorded right of citizens to religious or anti-religious propaganda was withdrawn. "Freedom of religious worship and anti-religious propaganda" was guaranteed instead. Anti-religious propaganda, already intensively practised, was thus released from any limitations. It was deemed to justify the most brazen action in the support of brazen words. The 1930s saw the acceleration of church closures, the dissolution of all monastic communities, the end of all theological schools and — symbolic of it all — the burning of icons on bonfires. Above all, it was a time of terror and of persecution. There was decimation of clergy and laity alike, and in all denominations.

Here was an arbitrary and improper application of vulgar Marxist principles: religion ought not to exist on the basis of the newly-developed infrastructures; its disappearance, inevitable though it was, could well be accelerated. Millions died in the process.

The respite gained by the Church in the years of the Second World War, and particularly after an unwritten, or at least unpublished concordat with Stalin (September 4, 1943), was largely the result of the latter's just if belated appreciation of the Church's potential as a patriotic and cohesive power in times of demoralization and disruption. The year 1943 was to see the state-approved revival of the Moscow patriarchate; also the establishment of two parallel state councils, one for the supervision of that patriarchate, the second for other denominations and faiths. These were later to be amalgamated (1965) as the Council for the Affairs of Religions, responsible to the Council of Ministers of the USSR. Its successive chairmen, V. A. Kuroedov (1965–84; previously — 1959–65 — chairman of the Council for Russian Orthodox Affairs), K. M. Kharchev (1984–9) and (from 1989) Iu. N. Khristoradnov, were to preside over a powerful body, whose role will need to be re-examined in the light of all the changes (more anticipated than achieved) associated with the present *perestroika*. Certainly, K. M. Kharchev was uncertain of the Council's future role, and said as much when visiting Great Britain (November 1988). Meanwhile, the abolition of its Hungarian counterpart (July 1, 1989) may have helped to prompt fresh thought.

When N. S. Khrushchev launched a concerted attack on religion in the years 1958–64, it was the Council in its previous form, working through its local plenipotentiaries, which acted as a decisive agent for it. The religious revival of the post-war years was cast under a shadow. Something like two-thirds of the (largely re-opened) Orthodox churches were arbitrarily closed.

The 10 theological schools which had been re-opened at the end of the year were reduced to five. Even more drastic was the reduction in monastic houses. These had already declined from over 100 (virtually all re-opened under Nazi occupation) to 69. Only 16 were to survive into the 1970s. The accompanying anti-religious campaign helped to poison social relations for decades to come. The Churches were required to be passive and silent or mendacious in their response to the campaign. Their leaders lost prestige among the faithful, as was intended by the state.

Nevertheless, by way of a response, an embryonic group of dissidents came into being. Its very independence provoked persecution and the eventual arrest of most of its comparatively few spokesmen. Yet even in the darkest years their voice remained unstilled.

Much of Khrushchev's campaign was conducted by "administrative means" (*administrirovanie*). Secret instructions were issued and adherence to them was required by word of mouth. Some of these went far beyond the provisions of the published laws. When some of these instructions (concerning baptism procedures) were withdrawn — also by oral *fiat* — early in 1988, the beneficiaries of such unwonted relaxation in the life of Christian bodies confronted it initially with some bemusement, even disbelief.

But formal regulations also played their part. In order to maintain a semblance of church autonomy in the management of spiritual and pastoral concerns, the State required the bishops themselves to formulate and promulgate amended statutes for their Church. To this end, a bishop's council was convoked in July 1961. Here was agreed the virtual disruption of parish life. Exclusively lay leadership was to prevail: no longer could the parish priest participate in meetings of the parish council, let alone preside at them (as previously had been the norm). As a result, the parish council was too often taken over by Communist Party nominees. The dissolution of the given parish could be furthered with all the greater ease. The Brezhnev years were to see no change in respect of this disastrous innovation, and the Russian Orthodox Church Council of 1971 was required to confirm it. Nor was there any serious reassessment of Church–State relations : in this respect, as in others, "stagnation" prevailed. Thus the plight of the Orthodox and other Churches was not alleviated, though their decline in status became less abrupt than in the Khrushchev years.

Since each administration, in its turn, peripheralized religion and, in its wake, morality, the social fabric of the state at large suffered a certain deprivation. Only in retrospect was this to be (albeit guardedly) acknowledged by Gorbachev's administration, who paused in genuine dismay before the amorality, disorientation and lack of motivation of the Soviet working population.

It was K. M. Kharchev who suggested to members of the church intelligentsia towards the end of 1988 that the Orthodox Church itself may have been affected by these ills. Hence "spirituality needs to be rekindled in the Church, and then rekindled — through the Church — in society at large". His "through the Church" acknowledges a vital role for what was previously dismissed as nothing other than a parasitic institution.

Such thoughts were far from being uttered at the beginning of the decade, when church plans for the millennium of Russian Christianity were first advanced (December 23, 1980). The propriety of holding any celebration of this kind was doubted in some party circles: at the very least such an occasion should be matched and neutralized, at least internally, by a corresponding presentation of the atheist case. As for the presentation proper, it was expected to be a ceremonial affair: it would serve to demonstrate to the outside world that Western discourse about the subjugation and suppression of religion in the Soviet world was altogether ill-conceived. In fact, these were the days of Brezhnev (1964–82), Andropov (1982–4) and Chernenko

(1984–5). There was no talk or expectation of religion gaining ground as the result of these millennium celebrations, however much they might impress or move observers. The declaration of a policy of *perestroika* was eventually to modify all that.

For the whole context of Church life was changing. No longer (or at least, not only) was it to be peripheralized and scorned. Christian activities or attitudes which had previously merited conviction as detrimental to the Soviet state — article 70 of the penal code ("anti-Soviet propaganda and agitation") and 190/1 ("anti-Soviet slander") had frequently been used to bring religious activists to court and to the camps — were now to be reviewed, and sentences suspended in an ever-increasing number of cases.

Thus religious "offenders" formed a good proportion of those 120 prisoners who were released on February 2, 1987. There were more to come. The release of Fr Gleb Iakunin, a notable campaigner for believers' rights, and the first to utter a public protest against their abuse in the immediate aftermath of Khrushchev (November 21, 1965), was symbolic of the new trend. It was followed by the release of Alexander Ogorodnikov (founder of the Moscow Christian Seminar in 1974) and, after a considerable delay (October 21, 1988) of deacon Vladimir Rusak (the author of an unvarnished history of the Russian Orthodox Church since the October revolution).

On a much wider level, the perceived changes in atmosphere allowed for easier church-going. In particular the State's withdrawal of its own bureaucratic requirements for (and thus impediments to) baptism involved an immediate increase in the number of those baptised. In Leningrad the increase was said to be threefold. Not that the overall figures for the preceding period were negligible: according to the Chancellor the Moscow patriarchate, indeed, no less than 30 million had taken place over the years 1971–88 alone. In the early 1930s, with massive closure of churches and open persecution of believers, such figures could hardly have been envisaged. Even so, the infant Mikhail Gorbachev was among these baptised at the time, as he revealed during his visit to France (July 5, 1989).

The bishops of the Russian Orthodox Church who assembled for a pre-conciliar consultation in Moscow in March 1988 were faced with unexpected and unprecedented possibilities. There was promise in the air. In awareness of it, one of their number, Archbishop Kirill of Smolensk, had prepared new statutes for the formal ordering of church life, the first since 1945. After due scrutiny, it was to be presented to that summer's plenary Council.

From the outset it was that Council (*Sobor*) which had been intended to provide the ceremonial centre of the millennium celebrations. Further discussion and (unanimous) acceptance of the statutes were to transform it into a landmark in the history of the modern Church. Almost equally important was the way in which this and other weighty matters were discussed. Gone was the domination of leaders' pre-digested keynote speeches.

The statutes overthrew the negative decisions of 1961 and 1971. This was no mere tinkering with administrative detail. Rather, it was calculated to release new and creative forces at the grass-roots level of church life. At the same time collegiality (*sobornost*') was safeguarded. Indeed, it was actively promoted by provision for regular assemblies at the level of the parish (twice a year), diocese (annually) and national Church (at least once per quinquennium). Such assemblies had hitherto been noteworthy for their rarity or simply non-existence. Nor were they freely elected.

With new confidence in the immediate future, the question of Church education was widely discussed. The inadequacies of the present theological schools' syllabus was noted by some. Nevertheless, the need for more schools was self-evident. In addition, the question of less specialized education for laity and Church personnel was addressed. For this, new institutions were required (and within the following year established — at Kishinev, Minsk, Smolensk and Stavropol). Even more important was the need for catechetical centres throughout the land, possibly attached to centres like cathedrals. But were there books for centres such as these? There was blunt criticism of the patriarchate's publishing house, which had failed to make the necessary provisions in this as well as other fields. Less vocal and less frequent were appeals to recognize (if not to canonize) the martyrs of the Soviet period. Only one lay delegate spoke briefly on this point: otherwise, support came from abroad (Metropolitan Anthony of Sourozh, Metropolitan Theodosius of Washington and All America, and the Archbishop of Canterbury, Dr Robert Runcie). Nevertheless, the Holy Synod was at least to establish a commission for the posthumous rehabilitation of "unjustly suppressed" believers before the year was out, and this was to hold its inaugural meeting in June 1989.

The uneven and inadequate provision of churches and monasteries hardly needed to be laboured. All the more heartening for the Council to learn of the restoration to the Church of one of its most venerated holy places, the Kievan Caves Monastery, appeals for which (one of them by a forthright prelate, Archbishop Feodosii of Astrakhan) had previously, so it had seemed, fallen on deaf ears (1987). However, the state itself had begun to set a pattern for such restitutions. As early as 1983 the semi-derelict Danilov Monastery in Moscow had been given back to the Church. This was followed in 1987 by the return of the monastery at Optino, the Tolga Convent at Iarolavl, and soon, at a surprising rate, by several others. Even more important was an upsurge in the registration of new parishes and (not to be confused with the latter) the re-opening of churches in the years 1987–9.

Not all re-openings could go forward unimpeded. Old habits die hard. Local authorities were not infrequently unwilling to yield to the appeals of Church people, and several ugly episodes ensued.

The church at Ivanovo attracted particular attention. The refusal of the local authorities to accept the ruling of Kharchev's Council and permit the opening of a second Orthodox church in this sizeable industrial town led to a hunger strike in the town square by four women on March 21, 1989. The strike gained support far beyond Ivanovo and far beyond Church circles. Andrei Sakharov was one of those who interceded on behalf of the strikers and their case, appealing to a member of the Politburo (V. Medvedev) on April 4. The seriousness of the hunger strikers' condition led to apparent concessions by the local authorities, and the strike was discontinued on April 6. Even so, the church was not made over to the petitioners. A narrow majority in the regional executive (*obispolkom*) against any such action further delayed the resolution of the conflict, which dragged on well into the summer. The case reminded Soviet society that die-hard administrators could still prevail in cases where the law, not to mention propriety or public opinion, required the contrary to be the case.

But the church at Ivanovo was not alone. Statistics about the comparatively massive increase in the number of functioning churches have to be read against this background. Even when Kharchev stated that in the first 10 months of 1988 as many as 650 churches and "other religious institutions" of various faiths had been re-opened, he added that no less than 50 churches were granted permission after opposition had been overruled by his (all-union) Council.

Nevertheless, the Chancellor of the Moscow patriarchate, Metropolitan Vladimir of Rostov, who had reported the existence of 6,893 registered parishes to the church Council of June 1988, was able to speak of 1,700 new parishes coming into existence over the year since the April 1988 meeting with Gorbachev.

That meeting had involved the promise of new legislation. In the event, even the publication of official legal drafts was to be delayed for well over a year. Speaking in London on July 24, 1989 Kharchev still envisaged only "autumn" publication at the earliest. Meanwhile a single kite was flown in print, an individual (and carefully reasoned) proposal by a legal expert, Iu. Rozenbaum. This appeared in the journal *Sovetskoe gosudarstvo i pravo* of February 1989. At least three other drafts were privately circulated. One was prepared by the official committee established under Kharchev's auspices, and on which religious bodies were given representation; another recorded amendments proposed by Church specialists; and a third, which emanated from the critical Church intelligentsia, with distinct proposals of its own.

In direct contradiction to Lenin's decree on the Separation of Church and State (January 23, 1918), all these drafts propose that religious organizations should be recognized as persons-at-law. In various degrees, all foresee a widening of their input into social life, not least by engaging in "dialogue with society", including perhaps the use of mass media. This would involve a reversal of the Stalinist decision to withhold the right of religious propaganda (May 22, 1929). As to atheist propaganda and its prominent expression in the schools, Church proposals would have it reduced in status:"the State finances neither religious nor atheist education"; schools would allow either, and on a voluntary basis.

Meanwhile, local initiatives have anticipated changes in the law, and Sunday schools have ceased to be the rare (prohibited) exception. In Kharchev's words (December 1988), "nowadays it is life itself which is rendering the law null and void".

In the event, Kharchev's newly-developed permissiveness may have proved excessive, and he was not to implement the more liberal legislation which he had earlier promoted. In June 1989 he was abruptly transferred back into the diplomatic corps from which he had earlier been seconded, and his place was taken by a former chairman of the Council of the Union within the Supreme Soviet, Iu. N. Khristoradnov.

The new legislation would affect all religious bodies, Christian and non-Christian alike. The Russian Orthodox Church is the most prominent among them. Indeed, fears are not infrequently expressed that it could once more be moulded into what it once was, the "established" Church of the realm. Even in Stalin's day it was required to function as such. When the western regions of the Ukraine were incorporated into the USSR at the end of the World War II, several million Eastern-rite Catholics (Uniates) found themselves confronted with an increasingly antagonistic situation. Their ultimate allegiance to Rome could find no favour with a blinkered Stalin, the less so since it had earlier played its part in furthering the separatist Ukrainian cause. After a brief period of apparent toleration (1944–6), secret orders were issued for the dissolution of the Uniate Church. As in pre-Revolutionary times, it was the Russian Orthodox Church which was required to be the agent for this, and the rigorously controlled Church Council of Lvov (March 8–10, 1946) marked the moment of the Uniates' forced assimilation into the Moscow patriarchate. The clergy who refused (including each and every bishop) disappeared into the well-populated camps and prisons of the day.

Destruction of the local Eastern-rite Church in Transcarpathian Ukraine followed (without the pretence of any council) in 1948. But demolition of the structures by no means guaranteed the disappearance of commitment. An underground ministry persisted; in recent years it has become increasingly more public. By the beginning of 1988, the bishops of the suppressed Church (its preferred designation — formerly "Greek Catholic" — is now Ukrainian Catholic) allowed their names and location to be announced. A campaign has been mounted for the legalization of their body, despite the reluctance of the Ukrainian state administration to tolerate any such thing. But the social and ecclesial disruption which it would undoubtedly occasion has also led the Russian Orthodox hierarchy to resist moves in this direction. Few have expressed themselves more negatively on this question than Metropolitan Filaret of Kiev, both at a press conference on the eve of the millennium celebrations (June 4, 1988) and in various statements since, not least in the one which appeared in *Radianska Ukraina* for May 9, 1989. Nevertheless, members of the formidable Vatican delegation to those same celebrations, headed by Augustino Cardinal Casaroli, was at least able to meet two bishops and three priests of the Ukrainian Catholic Church on June 10, 1988. No doubt this meeting helped to fuel the discussion which Casaroli held with Gorbachev three days later. Since the Cardinal has stated that he brought a message from Pope John Paul II about the desirability of opening a seminary for Ukrainian Catholics (there were formerly two), the related question of the Church's legalization can hardly have been ignored.

Meanwhile, no larger body of Christians remains in the shadows. A year later (June 18, 1989), an international day of prayer was set aside; hundreds of thousands of Ukrainian Catholics in the USSR openly took part in services that day, regardless of harassment. Nor did their representatives neglect to picket the Moscow sessions of the World Council of Churches Central Committee (July 21, 1989). But Kharchev, speaking in London three days later, foresaw no easy or immediate resolution of their problems.

The Western-rite Catholics of the USSR occupy a somewhat different place in Soviet life. They are most prominent in western regions, and in Lithuania above all, where they form the majority of the population. For fear of national resurgence (Lithuania had been an independent state until June 1940), the Catholic Church was kept strictly in check by the Soviet authorities. Those who sought to transgress the narrow bounds laid down were speedily restrained. A bishop like Julionas Steponavičius (a cardinal since 1988) was exiled to the provinces and remained, peripheralized and wasted, in Zagore from 1961 to 1988. There were others like him, as the *Chronicle of the Catholic Church in Lithuania* steadfastly bore witness from 1972 to the present. In recent years two priests who had promoted the (Lithuanian) Catholic Committee for the Defence of Believers' Rights, Alfonsas Svarinskas and Sigitas Tamkevečius, were imprisoned, (1983–8). Their release in the course of 1988 was a prelude to remarkable changes in Church–State relations which accompanied the advent of *perestroika*. These changes were to be signalled and furthered by the return of two cathedrals to the Church: that of Kleipeda in 1988 (it had been built in 1954–61, but seized by the state immediately after its completion) and, on February 5, 1989, that of Vilnius itself (used as an art gallery since its seizure in 1949).

The Baltic republics provide a home for Lutherans, whose presence in other parts of the Soviet Union was radically curtailed by Stalin in the 1930s. Both Latvia and Estonia have sizeable Lutheran populations, even though it is no longer possible to speak of a majority in either case. Here too the pressures of the past are gradually receding in response to *perestroika*. Of particular interest are dramatic changes in the Latvian Synod of the Lutheran Church, which may be symptomatic of the reinvigoration of the Church at large. Previously, the ruling Consistory had firmly criticized the work and attitudes of a widely-supported movement of reform, "Rebirth and Renewal". Indeed, several of its clerical members, like the rector of the Latvian theological seminary, Robert Akmentins, had been suspended from office. But by the spring of 1989, and contrary to expectations, the situation had changed radically. At its sessions of April 11–12, the General Synod of the Church (consisting of 95 clergy) proceeded to overturn the existing administration and relieve the Lutheran archbishop of Latvia himself of his post. The displaced leader, Eriks Mesters, had been appointed as recently as 1986. The new archbishop Karlis Galitis — a member of the Latvian National Independence Movement — now heads a consistory which is composed entirely of "Rebirth and Renewal" personnel.

It would appear that any schism among Latvian Lutherans has been avoided. By contrast, the Evangelical Christian-Baptist communities of the USSR have had to live with schism for the last 28 years. One of the principal reasons for the division in their ranks were differing attitudes to the instructions issued by Khrushchev (instructions which were to be formally rescinded only in April 1989). A significant minority in the Evangelical Christian-Baptist Union (formed in 1944) had regarded them as unacceptable in any shape or form and thus decided to remain unregistered, hence beyond the pale of the law. Many such protesters were to suffer imprisonment for their stance in the subsequent decades. In a year which marked the lessening of pressures on a variety of Christian bodies, unregistered communities of this kind were still to suffer intimidation. Services at such towns as Gorky, Kulebaki, Murom, Naryshkino, Odessa and Salsk were disrupted by militia and fines were imposed. An unregistered church at Rostov-on-Don was demolished on April 4, 1989. In February that year another was mysteriously burned down at Kharkov, and this despite the fact that it had earlier been tacitly tolerated by an official of the local Council for Religions. In recent years even the "separatist" members of the Church (in 1968 they had formed their own Council of Churches of Evangelical Christian-Baptists) chose to apply for registration and, furthermore, received it.

But the "parent" body (with which some "separatists" have sought reconciliation) was better placed to pursue its life, at least in circumstantial terms. For them also, the Khrushchev and the Brezhnev years had been bleak. But by the year of the millennium, they were emerging into full view of the public. Open-air services and mass-baptisms were not uncommon. Together with the Orthodox, the Union embarked on voluntary work in hospitals and mental institutions (prohibited until this time). In retrospect, the president of the Church's Council, Vasili Logvienko, felt able to designate 1988 as "the year of charity".

In the aftermath of that year (February 28, 1989), the Church at last received (after a decade of negotiations) permission to open a seminary for the full-time education of its ministers and preachers. Comparable permission had meanwhile been received by the smaller Church of Seventh Day Adventists (January 27, 1987).

Another educational institution which was founded in these years is the Theological Academy of the Georgian Orthodox Church in Tblisi (October 1, 1988). Earlier there had been a single seminary at Mtskheta (founded in 1963). This ancient Church had not escaped the rigours of earlier years. But since the election its present catholicos-patriarch, Ilia II (December 22, 1977), it had unobtrusively proceeded with its own internal *perestroika*, of which the new foundation was the latest fruit.

As well-defined in its cultural and geographical distinctness is the Armenian Apostolic Church. But despite his Church's potential as a validator of national concerns, the present patriarch-catholicos Vazgen I (elected as long ago as 1955) has preferred to keep a low profile during such crises as that occasioned by Nagorno–Karabakh (1988). Even so, it was he who eventually pronounced (both on Armenian television and in a telegram addressed to Gorbachev) that the Armenian cause was "natural, legal and constitutional". At the same time he appealed for calm. The Armenian earthquake later that year involved the Church in an important pastoral, even charitable role.

Indeed, it provoked — as also did Chernobyl — donations from a wide range of Churches and church people. Here, too, real life had superseded the Instructions of the Khrushchev period regardless of whether they were yet revoked.

Their replacement by a code of laws which will be coherent, tolerant and viable is eagerly awaited: one that will take "even the interests of the Church organizations" into account, and thus distinguish it from all that went before.

Sergei Hackel

# Soviet Jewry

Ever since the 1917 revolution, the Jews of the Soviet Union have led a chequered existence. Following the establishment of an independent Poland in 1919, and the Baltic states, the number under Soviet rule totalled about three million. Under the tsarist regime, they had been compelled to live in the "Pale of Settlement", consisting mainly of the western provinces of the Tsarist empire. This was one of the manifold forms of anti-Jewish discrimination which also limited the entry of Jews to the professions, universities, government positions and, particularly after 1881, took the form of violent physical assaults on Jews (pogroms). In fact, tsarist Russia was regarded as the classic country of modern antisemitism. All the legislation which gave effect to this policy was abolished after 1917 and the propagation of antisemitism was made a criminal offence. On the other hand, all Jewish political parties were suppressed; the practice of Judaism was driven underground and Zionism and the study of Hebrew were regarded as reactionary forces. The immediate sequel to the victory of the Bolsheviks was an outburst of pogroms in the Ukraine in 1919–1920 where the Jews were trapped between the Red Army and various forms of Ukrainian nationalism and White-interventionist forces. About a quarter of a million Jews are estimated to have been killed in the fighting. These various factors help to account for the urbanization of Russian Jewry, for towns were considered more secure. At the time of writing there are just under two million Jews in Russia of whom 300,000 live in Moscow and about 130,000 each in Leningrad and Kiev. Other major centres are Odessa (120,000), Kharkov (80,000), Kishinev (60,000), Minsk (47,000).

The same background also helps to account for the element of antisemitism that has at times characterized the Soviets' Jewish policy, especially during the later years of Stalin's rule. In 1952, 24 Jewish writers, artists and poets were executed on charges of being "agents of American imperialism". This aspect of Russian policy was also partly determined by the emergence of Israel in 1948. Soviet Russia had been prominent in its support for Zionism at the United Nations but internally the suppression of any Zionist manifestation was as ruthless as ever.

At the time of writing Russian Jewry falls into three categories: Asian Jews living in Central Asia and the Caucasus region; Western Jews in the territories annexed by the Soviet Union in World War II (the Baltic region, Bessarabia and eastern Poland); "core" or "heartland" Jews who had lived in European Russia since 1917 and had become Russified, secularized and integrated, if not assimilated. In addition, about 14,000 Jews live in the officially sponsored Jewish autonomous region of Biro–Bidzhan. Overwhelmingly the Jews are urbanized, well educated and disproportionately represented in professional and scientific occupations. But there is considerable evidence that antisemitism survived Stalin's death e.g. in the reaction to Yevtushenko's poem "Babi Yar" (1961).

A decisive turn in the modern history of Soviet Jewry came in the late 1960s and early 1970s. This coincided with the Israeli victory in the 1967 Six-Day War and the inception of detente which led to a relaxation of internal political controls in the Soviet Union. Although the Soviet Union broke off diplomatic relations with Israel at the time of the war, this did not prevent increasing permission being given to would-be Jewish emigrants to Israel. These were justified on the grounds of re-uniting divided families.

The first Jews to leave were those from the periphery, Asian and Western. They went in the main to Israel. From the mid-1970s onwards increasing numbers of "core-Jews" joined the exodus, not out of religious or cultural motives but in order to escape discrimination and to seek improved prospects in the West. They were less attracted to Israel because of political instability in the Middle East, the liability to military service and the country's limited opportunities. Since then the number of emigrants has fluctuated widely — e.g. 15,000 (1971), 51,000 (1979), 914 (1986), 8,000 (1987), 19,000 (1988) and in the current year (to May) nearly 13,000 Jews have been allowed to leave.

The major determinant in these fluctuating figures is foreign rather than domestic politics — especially the Soviet-American relationship. The warmer the relationship, the higher the volume of emigration. Recently, the growing diplomatic rapprochement between Israel and the Eastern bloc has also become influential. Hungary and Poland have opened interest sections in Israel and allowed Israel to do likewise in their countries. The Soviet mission to Israel, investigating church property, and an Israeli delegation in Moscow, are other operative factors. Estimates of those Jews waiting for exit permits varies from about 30,000 to 400,000. Their fate continues to depend on the foreign relations of the USSR and, increasingly so, on the state of Western public opinion.

Soviet Jewry has welcomed the period of *glasnost* and *perestroika*. Not only have they facilitated emigration but they have also permitted various forms of Jewish culture to find expression. One of the most important of these is the Solomon Mikhaels centre in the heart of Moscow's theatreland (named after one of the Jewish actors killed in 1952). This includes a theatre, exhibition hall, library and cinema. The centre also provides courses on the teaching of Hebrew. Similar centres are planned for Riga, Minsk, Kiev and Leningrad. At the USSR Academy of Sciences courses are to be introduced in Jewish religious studies. In Moscow a Jewish newspaper has appeared for the first time — "News about Soviet Jewish culture". To the same liberalization belongs the return to a Moscow synagogue of one of its former buildings and the opening of Moscow's first motza factory, just before the Passover festival. Much of this activity is co-ordinated under the auspices of the Jewish Cultural Association of Moscow, which does not yet however, enjoy official recognition. There is apprehension in certain Jewish circles lest recognition lead to manipulation and control by the authorities. By contrast the officially sponsored anti-Zionist committee remains in existence and has expressed hostility to the independent Jewish cultural movement.

*Glasnost* has not been an unmixed blessing to Soviet Jewry. It has allowed the emergence of the anti-semitic Pamyat ("Memory") movement which has harked back to the anti-semitism of the past. The celebration of the millennium of Christianity in Russia in 1988 was accompanied by leaflets threatening "death to Jews" but no untoward incident occurred until 1989. A synagogue in the Siberian city of Krasnoyarsk was vandalized and during the March election campaign in Moscow an election meeting called by Vitaly Korotych, the liberal-minded editor of the magazine *Ogonyok*, was broken up by Pamyat supporters. In Leningrad about 7 per cent of the city voted for candidates from Pamyat. The organization draws most of its support from low-ranking bureaucrats and workers. The Moscow Writers' Union also includes amongst its members several writers whose Russian nationalism verges on anti-semitism.

Lionel Kochan

# Muslims of the USSR

The USSR has one of the largest Muslim populations in the world, ranking in size after such countries as Bangladesh, Pakistan, Indonesia and India. In 1979 it numbered some 45.5 million; data from the most recent census are not yet available, but today it probably exceeds 55 million. However, the Soviet Muslims are by no means a homogenous group. They are of different ethnic origins, speak a great variety of languages and have very different historical and cultural backgrounds. Geographically, too, they are spread over a wide area. Approximately 60 per cent live in Central Asia, 20 per cent in Transcaucasia and the northern Caucasus, and 20 per cent in the Volga region and Siberia.

They constitute the titular people, though not always the majority in six Union republics: in Azerbaidzhan (Azerbaidzhanis 78.1 per cent), Kazakhstan (Kazakhs 36 per cent), Kirghizia (Kirghiz 47.9 per cent), Tadzhikistan (Tadzhiks 58.8 per cent), Turkmenia (Turkmen 68.4 per cent) and Uzbekistan (Uzbeks 68.7 per cent); they also have 10 eponymous Autonomous republics: the Tatar, Bashkir, Chuvash, Daghestan, Checheno–Ingush, Kabardino–Balkar, Nakhichevan, Karakalpak, Northern Ossetian and Abkhazian ASSRs (though some of the Abkhazians, and many of the Ossetians, are not Muslims, but traditionally Christian).

Some 85 per cent of the Soviet Muslims are of Turkic origin; they include the Uzbeks (12.5 million), who represent the third largest ethnic group in the USSR (after the Russians and the Ukrainians), the Tatars (6.3 million), the Kazakhs (6.5 million) and the Azerbaidzhanis (5.4 million). Just over half the remainder are of Iranian origin (including 2.9 million Tadzhiks), the others being Caucasian (Chechen, Ingush, Kabardians, Avars and others, all numbering under 100,000), and small groups such as the Dungans (Chinese Muslims — 52,000).

International frontiers frequently do not coincide with ethnic boundaries and this is the case with several of the Muslim peoples of the USSR. There are Kazakhs, for example, in the USSR, as well as in the adjoining regions of China (some one million) and Afghanistan; Turkmen in Iran (some one million), and in Afghanistan and Iraq (some 500,000 in each); Azerbaidzhanis in Iran (some five million). Uighurs, Kurds and many other groups are similarly divided. In most cases the international boundaries have not undergone significant modification this century, but ease of passage across them has varied greatly. Civil war, famine and political change have given new impetus to an age-old tradition of migration from one region to another. There were sizeable movements of Kirghiz, Kazakhs and Turkmen out of the USSR in the 1920s–1930s, and of Uighurs into the USSR in the 1950s. Formal cross border contacts were severely restricted for many years, but during the last decade there has been a marked relaxation; family visits, as well as cultural and academic exchanges are now being actively developed; trade links, too, are being strengthened. It is impossible to judge the extent to which clandestine cross border links exist, but there does appear to be some traffic of this nature, particularly from Iran into the USSR. Radio broadcasts are another form of contact; they are beamed in both directions across the frontiers. In some parts of Soviet Turkmenia these are in fact the only broadcasts that can be heard (which goes some way to accounting for their popularity); the content is sometimes overtly political or religious, but programmes of music and poetry are also popular.

The great majority of Soviet Muslims are Sunni of the Hanafi school. However, about 70 per cent of the Azerbaidzhanis (some 3.8 million) are Shia of the Jafari school; the remainder are Sunni. In the northern Caucasus the Muslims are Sunni, but they follow the Shafi'i school. There are small groups of Ismailis in the mountains of Tadzhikistan (the Pamiri peoples), who acknowledge the Aga Khan as their spiritual leader. There are also a few other groups, not normally considered to be Muslim, although there are some Muslim elements in their worship; these include the Yazidis (adherents among the Kurdish population) and the Bahais (Ashkhabad used to be the largest Bahai centre outside Iran, but there are very few Bahais now left in the USSR).

Islam in the USSR has had a chequered career. After a brief, initial period of relative tolerance it came to be looked on as inimical to the state. Every aspect of Muslim life came under attack: the *shari'a* (Koranic) courts and *madrassah* (religious schools) were phased out by 1927; *waqf* lands (charitable endowments) were confiscated and many mosques were closed, some destroyed, some turned over to secular use. The actions which are incumbent on every Muslim — that is to say, the daily prayers, the keeping of the fast of Ramadan, the giving of alms, the performance of the pilgrimage to Mecca — were either prohibited (in the case of the pilgrimage) or else so severely discouraged that it became dangerous to attempt to observe them. The link with the old, all-embracing religious way of life was weakened yet further by the persecution of the *ulama* (the religious scholars and leaders), as a result of which many were executed, while others fled abroad or went into hiding. The final blow was the change of scripts, first from the Arabic to the Latin (1930), then from the Latin to the Cyrillic (1940). This effectively severed the children of the Soviet state from their roots.

The outbreak of World War II brought about a small, but very significant improvement in the formal status of Islam in the USSR. Two Muslim Spiritual Directorates were created, the first in Ufa (Bashkir ASSR) in 1942, the second in Tashkent (Uzbek SSR) in 1946; two others were added a few years later, one in Baku (Azerbaidzhan SSR), the other in Makhachkala (Daghestan ASSR). Run by Muslims, under the leadership of a Mufti (or, in the case of the Baku Directorate, a Sheikh ul-Islam), each of these Directorates is responsible for a geographic region: that of Ufa for the whole of European Russia, of Tashkent for Central Asia (including Kazakhstan), of Baku for Transcaucasia (Sunni and Shia populations) of Makhachkala for the northern Caucasus. Their powers are very limited, their chief function being to maintain the formal fabric of Soviet Islam: they register and find employment for the small number of new Muslim graduates each year, and oversee the upkeep of the small number of mosques open for worship. They also play host to foreign delegations of Muslims and take part in Muslim conferences abroad. They are in theory all equal and independent bodies; however, the Mufti of Central Asia, who has by far the largest constituency, is regarded as the *de facto* leader of all the Soviet Muslims. The Directorates are self-governing and self-financing, but they come under the Council for Religious Affairs of the Council of Ministers of the USSR. In the past they were often regarded as no more than extensions of the Soviet state apparatus. While this was certainly true, the fact that they did have formal recognition and were allowed to develop an administrative structure of their own undoubtedly helped to prepare them to take advantage of the new opportunities provided by the era of *glasnost* and *perestroika* in the 1980s.

A number of other concessions were gained for the Muslim community in the post-war years. One was the re-opening of two *madrassah*, one in Bukhara (1956), the other in Tashkent (1971). The former provides a seven-year preparatory course; the latter provides a four-year course at a more advanced level. The best graduates from Tashkent are sent abroad to Muslim universities in the Middle East to complete their training (for example, to Egypt, Libya or Morocco). This also gives them the opportunity to perfect their Arabic and to make personal contacts with Muslim scholars from many different countries. This is an important aspect of their preparation, since most of them are subsequently employed in the Directorates, where great emphasis is laid on international relations. The less successful graduates are appointed to mosques in various parts of the USSR. The number of functioning mosques has been slowly but steadily increasing; by the early 1980s there were some 450 registered mosques open for worship. A trickle of religious publications began to appear, including six editions of the Koran, a collection of the Hadith of al-Bukhari, and a quarterly journal, *Muslims of the Soviet East*; this, however, is intended mainly for foreign consumption. The pilgrimage to Mecca was also reinstated, though only for a small number (15–20 per year) of carefully selected believers.

Although so much of the formal structure of Islam in the USSR has been destroyed, or reduced to a mere skeleton framework, private belief has certainly survived. For the most part it is a matter of sentiment rather than a reasoned conviction, of popular practices tinged with superstition rather than a clear understanding of Koranic law. This is not surprising, since there is very little religious literature available, and virtually nothing to illustrate and explain the basic practices of Islam. The official imams attached to the mosques have little time and even less inclination to assume a teaching role. Although the Soviet Constitution guarantees its citizens freedom of conscience, the infringements of this right have been so great in the past that there is undoubtedly a legacy of fear and confusion to be overcome before such matters can be discussed openly. On the other hand, the cultural influence of Islam is probably more pervasive, and stronger, than that of most other religions. It has proved to be impossible to draw a dividing line between the national and the religious, hence Islam remains an integral element in the major life-cycle rituals (circumcision, marriage, death), in popular festivals and in dietary laws. Partly because of the uncertainty surrounding the status of religion, partly because of a genuine shortage of trained, officially registered religious leaders, a number of "popular" practitioners of greater or lesser sincerity and learning officiate at important family events; from time to time they are caught and severely castigated in the Soviet press. There is rarely any political intent to be discerned in their activities, but they certainly do contribute to a general maintenance of an Islamic identity. To that extent "parallel" Islam, as it is sometimes called, is important. Whether it has any significance beyond this, as a source of serious political opposition to the Soviet state, is not clear, but on the evidence available to date it seems unlikely.

New developments are, however, taking place in the Islamic establishment. All the leaders of the Directorates today are relatively young men, with no personal experience of the periods of worst oppression. They came of age in a time of greater freedom, and are now caught up in the demands for greater democratization. The 36-year old head of the Tashkent Directorate, Mamayusupov Muhammadsaddyk, typifies this new approach. Formerly Rector of the al-Bukhari *madrassah*, he was elected to his present post in March 1989, replacing the disgraced former incumbent Mufti Babakhanov. The ostensible cause for the downfall of the latter was his immoral behaviour, but the underlying reason was surely that he represented the old spirit of accommodation and patronage, with its attendant implications of corruption; of complacency and an acceptance of the *status quo*. He was certainly not the man to spearhead new demands, to be a champion of the long-awaited new law on religious practices that promises a "more just" relationship between

Church and State. Although Central Asia is by no means in the vanguard of reform, Mufti Muhammadsaddyk has, by contrast, already requested, and received important concessions. Fifteen new mosques were opened in the first two months of his taking office (10 in Uzbekistan, five in Tadzhikistan); permission has been received for the building of new hostels for the *madrassahs* in Bukhara and Tashkent and there are plans to greatly increase the intake of students; a new edition of the Koran is promised. Something that has not yet been achieved, but is nevertheless being discussed with some optimism is the pilgrimage: permission for many more believers to undertake this fundamental duty has been requested. The question of the teaching of the Arabic script in schools has also been raised, with all its implications for re-establishing a link with the past, and in particular, with the region's Islamic heritage.

The recent developments augur well. However, this by no means signals the end of Moscow's uncertainty about its Muslim population. Crude, insensitive attacks still appear in the press, indicative of a startling lack of familiarity with the situation, an impatience with this alien culture and an all-too-ready tendency to make Islam the scapegoat for the whole gamut of contemporary economic and social ills. On the other hand, however, there is a very real, and seemingly contradictory, tendency to give Islam more support and more freedom. The primary intention here is surely less to strengthen Islam within the Soviet Union (though that is the inevitable consequence of this line of policy),than to build up a strong, authentic and yet reliable (that is to say, controllable) counterbalance to fundamentalist tendencies elsewhere in the Muslim world. The return of the greatly revered Othman Koran to the religious authorities may be seen as an attempt to underline the legitimacy of the Central Asian interpretation of Islam. The appointment of a bright, well-trained young scholar, who is able to project himself as a fighter for Islam, as head of all the Soviet Muslims, is an appropriate corollary to this.

**Notes**
[1] All statistical data taken from the 1979 Soviet census.

Shirin Akiner

# UNITED ARAB EMIRATES

The United Arab Emirates is governed by an alliance of the ruling families of the seven smaller Arab Gulf states lying along the former Trucial Coast, in conjunction with prominent members of the indigenous commercial elite, who occupy many of the senior positions in the bureaucracies of both the federal administration and the individual emirates. The ruling families share adherence to the Maliki school of interpretation of Sunni Islam, which favours relatively strict interpretations of the Koran and the traditions of the Prophet (Hadith), but which also tolerates some flexibility in applying the law for the benefit of the community as a whole. The merchant oligarchy is divided into a number of distinct sectarian groups: in Dubai, the most prominent families consist of Sunni immigrants from southern Iran, although there is also a significant community of Twelver Shiis; in Sharjah, Shiis from South Asia predominate; Abu Dhabi's much smaller rich merchant elite is made up primarily of Sunnis with roots in the tribes of eastern Arabia, although there is a growing cluster of Twelver Shiis within the country as well. For the federation as a whole, Shiis are estimated to account for almost 20 per cent of the indigenous population.

Fred H. Lawson

# UNITED KINGDOM

The United Kingdom of Great Britain (England, Scotland, Wales) and Northern Ireland is a constitutional monarchy which exhibits several different types of arrangement between the State and the Churches. The Church of England is a national Church "by law established". Its head is the sovereign who is crowned by the Archbishop of Canterbury, it is represented in Parliament by bishops in the House of Lords, its bishops are nominated by the Prime Minister. The Church of Scotland is also an established church but Presbyterian in its organization and free from government interference. There are no established Churches in Wales or Northern Ireland. Under the Synodical Government measure of 1969, Parliament conceded some authority to the General Synod of the Church of England but retained its right to decide on fundamental changes in worship and doctrine. In 1977 James Callaghan, then Labour Prime Minister, agreed to a new procedure for appointing Anglican bishops. A Crown Appointments Commission selected by the Church and presided over by an archbishop would present two names to the Prime Minister.

Religion was once an important factor in British politics, but outside Northern Ireland it has not been deemed significant by political scientists. In a *Times* survey of 1971, only 2% thought that the Church of England was "very influential" in public life. There are some indications, however, that in the 1970s, issue politics began to replace class politics, and this may have made the opinions of Church spokesmen more significant when contributing to national debates.

## England

The election of a Conservative government under Margaret Thatcher in 1979 introduced a new element of strain in the relations of Church and State. The new prime minister declared that her government was to be one of conviction not consensus and set out to restore the authority of the State. It combined certain elements in the programme of liberal political economy with some traditional Tory values and a new populism. For churchmen who had long preached a gospel of reconciliation and social concern, these new emphases were profoundly disturbing. "The goal posts have changed", reflected Bishop Mark Santer of Birmingham in 1989, "the things I said could be associated with old style *noblesse oblige* Conservatism and they're suddenly felt to be outrageous".

Throughout Mrs Thatcher's first and second terms of office (1979–87), there were frequent clashes between the government and the churches. Two Anglican reports *The Church and the Bomb* (1982) and *Faith in the City* (1985) put forward alternatives which were not welcomed by a prime minister who had declared, "There is no alternative". The Archbishop of Canterbury and Dean of St Paul's displeased the government by insisting that the predominant note in the service to mark the end of the Falklands campaign should be thanksgiving not triumph. In 1984, the appointment of David Jenkins as Bishop of Durham brought a new name to the demonology of Thatcherism. His exposition of a moderate liberalism in theology and call for a compromise solution to the miners' strike was expressed in tones which aroused that resentment of intellectual elitism which also found expression in the semi-paranoid loathing of many Tories for the BBC and University of Oxford.

In 1987 Mrs Thatcher won her third consecutive election victory. A significant feature of the results was the representation of ethnic minorities; four blacks had been elected. However Jewish representation was reduced to 23. Significantly 16 of them were elected as Conservatives to 7 Labour, which was a drastic change from the 1950s and '60s when most Jewish MPs were Labour. However if Jewish representation was reduced in the Commons it was powerfully reinforced in the Lords by the ennoblement of the Chief Rabbi, Dr Immanuel Jakobovits. He had long been admired by Mrs Thatcher. Alone amongst religious leaders he had criticized *Faith in the City*, attacked trade unions, rejected government intervention and scorned the demands of Blacks.

If one religious leader was praised and promoted by the Prime Minister in 1987, another was passed over. Bishop Jim Thompson of Stepney had strongly supported *Faith in the City* but although first on the list sent to Downing Street, was turned down by Mrs Thatcher for the vacant bishopric of Birmingham. Several Midlands Conservative MPs had lobbied against him. Said one of them, "Birmingham has had enough left-wingers".

Mutterings persisted not just about the widening gap between the episcopal elite and the government but also, it was claimed, between the bishops and the rest of the Church. These misgivings found expression in an unsigned preface to *Crockfords Clerical Directory* which appeared in December 1987. The author was later revealed, after he was driven to commit suicide, to be Dr Gareth Bennett, an Oxford historian of the seventeenth century. Surveying the current condition of the Church of England Bennett mocked the Archbishop of Canterbury Dr. Robert Runcie for indecision and lack of firm principles, and alleged that he and the Archbishop of York had foisted on the Church an unrepresentative liberal elite. In the subsequent General Synod debate, Canon George Austin, a High Churchman, claimed that the preface truly represented the anger and indignation of thousands. This attempt to portray the bishops as isolated both from "sensible opinion" and the rest of the Church played into the hands of those Conservatives who resented episcopal criticisms of their policies. In an attempt to heal the breach between the government and the Church, a private meeting was called by Mrs Thatcher in November 1987 when she told eight senior bishops that she wanted a new emphasis on personal morality. Two months later, the Home Secretary Douglas Hurd, himself an Anglican of traditional tastes, gave the same message to members of the Synod.

The government's olive branch was, however, snapped off by one of its own members. John Gummer, a High Church clergyman's son was himself an elected member of the Synod. In that role, Gummer along with the arch-traditionalist and Tory backbencher, John Stokes, had stoutly maintained the government's case whenever it was attacked. At the February 1988 session, Gummer lined up with the Evangelicals in condemning what he called "the condom culture". His intervention in the House of Laity debate was on an amendment requesting the bishops to issue a clear statement of policy on sexual morality, including homosexuality and lesbianism. Several factors lay behind the debate. A working party on homosexual clergy had been appointed in 1986. A year later, a debate on homosexual behaviour had been promoted within the General Synod by Evangelicals, a rising force in the Church. An amendment calling on the bishops to exercise "appropriate discipline" was passed by the House of Laity but failed in the other two houses. Undeterred, the Anglican Evangelical Assembly in January 1988 returned to the topic and clearly intended to make a determined stand. A Gallup opinion poll among the clergy showed that nearly three-quarters agreed that the "Church can never approve homosexual acts" and only 19 per cent disagreed. However, the same poll also revealed that 28 per cent of the High Church group disagreed with the proposition. Clearly, in the struggle for predominance in the Church of England, the homosexual issue was one in which the Evangelicals could take the lead. They could count on the support of some traditional High Churchmen who hoped that a swing back to tradition and away from a liberal stance on sexuality would carry over into resistance to the ordination of women to the priesthood. In the debate on Feb. 8, 1988 Gummer beat the Thatcher drum in attacking the bishops for failing to give "the unambiguous moral lead which the nation demands". On both that occasion and in a radio interview on the *Jimmy Young Show*, broadcast on the same day as Douglas Hurd's call for co-operation, Gummer attacked the Archbishop of York, drawing a tart rebuke from his colleague at Canterbury. One consequence of the debate was to draw the attention of the pro-government popular press to the existence of a small gay element within the ministry of the Church and to provide several sensationalist reports which had the effect of bringing the Church of England into disrepute.

Hopes that the Thatcher meeting and Hurd's address might open a new chapter in Anglican-government relations had received a setback from Gummer's maladroit attack on the Archbishop of York. They were further damaged from the Church's side on Easter Sunday when Bishop Jenkins of Durham enraged Conservatives by describing the government's economic policy as "wicked". On this occasion Jenkins had to receive not just the predictable rebukes of John Stokes but also public criticism from a fellow bishop, Bill Westwood of Peterborough.

In March 1988 Archbishop Runcie turned to the Free Churches and in a candid speech referred to the "curious expectations" of politicians that the legal status of the established Church had to be paid for by uncritical support of the government. There was a political consensus shared in all Churches, he said, in supporting the common Christian philosophical principles of the welfare state. The Archbishop's words brought a ready response from Free Churchmen and in June the Methodists Conference voted overwhelmingly to "declare its sense of outrage" at the way government policies were increasing the wealth of the rich at the expense of the poor. The conference designated one of its most radical ministers, John Vincent from Sheffield's Urban Theology Unit as its next president. The Urban Theology Unit had been attended as part of her training by Ms Barbara Harris, a black divorcee, who to the consternation of traditionalists was elected as first woman bishop in the Anglican communion by the Episcopal Church of the United States in the autumn of 1988.

The question of how a communion of Churches can live together when it develops divergent practices on the ministry of women was in everyone's minds at the Lambeth Conference in the summer of 1988. It was also part of the hidden agenda when proposals passed by the General Synod in February 1987 to lift the ban on the ordination of those divorced or married to divorced persons were sent to Parliament. All Synod measures have to secure the approval of Parliament's ecclesiastical committee made up of 15 MPs and 15 peers. This committee has come to be dominated by rigorists such as John Gummer and the Anglo-Catholic Labour spokesman Frank Field. It voted that it was "not expedient" to approve the Synod measure, with the consequence that a statutory special conference had to be held in February 1989 between the ecclesiastical committee and the Synod's legislative committee headed by the two archbishops. As a result the Clergy (Ordination) measure was put to and approved by the House of Lord's, but defeated in the Commons in July by 51 votes to 45 after a debate that began at 2 a.m. and ended 90 minutes later. To Bishop Colin Buchanan the defeat was a humiliation and pointed logically to disestablishment.

Bishop Buchanan had earlier in the year felt bound as a matter of honour to resign as suffragan bishop of Aston when a tour of the diocese of Birmingham which he organized for the Archbishop of Capetown, Desmond Tutu, had been poorly attended and a financial disaster. It had been thought that such a courageous fighter against racism would appeal in an area with large numbers of people belonging to ethnic minorities. This miscalculation was perhaps only too typical of the well-intentioned blunders which have followed when Churchmen have assessed what they intuit to be the needs of ethnic minorities. The number of that minority has been estimated at 2.6 million which is about 5% of the total population. The 1981 census shows that about half a million are of Afro-Caribbean origin and are highly concentrated in the South-East, while the 1.2 million which are of Asian origin have strong communities in Yorkshire, Lancashire and the West Midlands. The *Faith in the City* report revealed a disturbing state of affairs, and its findings were echoed in reports, all published in 1986 by the three main denominations, *Anglicans and Racism, Members one of another* (Methodist), *With You in Spirit* (Roman Catholic). These publications have led one observer to suggest that "the Churches have moved from echoing the political elite to challenging it".[1] The coldness of many mainline denominations in the period of peak immigration had pushed many black Christians into black-led Pentecostal churches which have discouraged political involvement. However in 1976 the Afro-Westindian United Council of Churches (AWUCOC) was formed to address "social and educational issues". Its 1984 handbook contains an article by Robinson Milwood on "How is Theology political?" which suggested that "the Pentecostal Churches are now beginning to break out into the world of political consciousness". For many Afro-Caribbeans politics was not so much thought out as danced out. An event with quasi-political overtones which provides an opportunity for self-expression and defiance of authority is the annual Notting Hill Carnival which since 1976 has often been the scene of violent clashes between the police and black youths. Despite the election in 1989 of a more professional black leadership (notably Claire Holder, a barrister born in Trinidad who chairs both the Methodist Church's committee on race relations and the carnival committee), it once again in 1989 ended in arrests and allegations against the police. The substantial presence of blacks in some inner London Methodist churches was underlined by suggestions that if Labour did not select a black candidate for the Parliamentary by-election at Vauxhall in 1989, a black candidate would be nominated by a group substantially consisting of Methodists.

The religion of the largest ethnic minority in Britain is Islam. In 1987 the Home Office, concerned at the vast sums of money being channelled from Arab countries into Muslim causes in Britain, decided that its Research Department should investigate. The Government was concerned that internal Muslim politics in Britain might become a microcosm of the conflicts of the wider Islamic world. At a time when British Muslims are searching for a common identity, they are subject to internal pressures from competing sects and rival leaders, and to external pressures, both ideological and financial. Most Muslims in Britain are Sunnis; the majority belong to the Barelwi sect, with no ready source of funds. This has led some to fall back on money supplied by Libya and Iraq. The minority sect is Deobandi which is a quietist movement and can call on the financial resources of the fabulously rich government of Saudi Arabia.

The Muslim community as a whole has not yet accepted any one body as its agreed mouthpiece. The Union of Muslim Organizations (UMO) set up in 1970 by Dr Syed Pasha, an Indian, claims to be an over-arching representative body, and was at first financed by Saudi Arabia but later by Iraq. Another body which claims a representative role is the UK Council of Imams and Mosques set up mainly with Libyan money by Dr Zaki Badawi, once director of the London Central Mosque at Regent's Park. Until recently there has been no single issue which could unite Muslims. In 1985 proposals to ban the *halal* slaughter of animals led to protests about the denial of religious freedom, but on that issue, Muslim protests only joined those of the well-connected Jewish lobby. The other subject of passionate concern is the provision of Muslim schools on the same lines as those of the Church of England and Roman Catholic church. This however, involves negotiations with local education authorities, which have been reluctant to give their agreement.

In 1988 the publication of a novel, *The Satanic Verses*, written by the Indian-born but Cambridge-educated Salman Rushdie aroused a storm of anger and outrage which grew to international proportions. First to be aroused seems to have been the Islamic Society for the Promotion of Religious Tolerance which quickly pinned the label of blasphemy to the book. But it was Faiyazuddin Ahmad of the Islamic Foundation in Leicester who photocopied the offending pages and in October despatched them to all the main Islamic organizations in Britain. Next the photocopies were delivered to the 45 embassies in Britain of the member states (including

Iran) of the Organization of the Islamic Conference (OIC), whose headquarters is in Saudi Arabia.

On Oct. 9, Dr Zaki Badawi, chairman of the Imams and Mosques Council, not only confirmed the distress caused by the book, but skilfully linked the Muslim reaction to that of Christians who were calling for a ban on the film, *The Last Temptation of Christ*. On Oct. 15 an emergency meeting was called by UMO, which resolved that the novel ought to be banned. The secretary of UMO, Dr Syed Pasha wrote to the Prime Minister calling for both Rushdie and his publisher, Penguin, to be prosecuted under the Public Order and Race Relations Acts. Mrs Thatcher replied that there were no grounds to justify government action. Pasha persevered in letters to the Home Office and Lord Chancellor, Lord Mackay of Clashfern, a man used to dealing with sensitive consciences (he had been disciplined and effectively forced out of the tiny Free Presbyterian Church of Scotland in the summer of 1989 for attending a Roman Catholic requiem Mass). On Dec. 2, 8,000 Muslims took part in what has been described as "the largest ethnic minority demonstration ever staged in Britain".[2] Yet these restrained and responsible protests, not only failed to produce results, but were played down by the mass media.

In a desperate bid to draw media attention and stir politicians into action, an increasingly frustrated Muslim community added a dramatic touch by publicly burning a copy of the book in Bradford on Jan. 14, 1989. The leaders of Britain's Muslims have taken great care to keep their protests within the law. They used their influence at the ICO meeting in Riyadh in March to tone down an Iranian demand that the Ayatollah Khomeini's death sentence of Feb. 19 should be supported. In an attempt to keep their protest within the channels of parliamentary democracy, Sher Azam, president of the Bradford Council of Mosques, challenged members of parliament: "We don't have a single Muslim M.P. In the past large numbers of Muslims have traditionally voted Labour. We feel our cause is just. If they will not help we will switch our vote". But Labour M.P. for Bradford South, Bob Cryer, described the Muslim campaign as "foolish and intemperate". In the County Council elections in May, one of the seats which Labour unexpectedly lost in Blackburn was to a Muslim standing as a Conservative. Blackburn's Labour M.P. Jack Straw, the party's education spokesman, has come out in favour of Muslim schools.

Bradford's Sher Azam has seen the Rushdie protest as providing a focus for deeper discontents. In Bradford, 78 per cent of young Asians and blacks are still without a job one year after leaving school, compared with 60 per cent of white youths. Young Muslims have higher expectations than their elders, and a correspondingly deeper sense of injustice. Sher Azam admits that an increasing number of young Muslims are losing faith in the moderate policies of their leadership. In June violence broke out after Muslim demonstrations in London and Bradford. Bookshops in various parts of the country have been damaged by firebomb attacks.

Muslim hopes are now pinned on a change in the law of blasphemy, which applies only to Christianity. However in July 1989, John Patten, Minister of State at the Home Office, informed Muslim leaders that the government is not willing to extend the law because it might lead to a spate of litigation which could exacerbate instead of ease relations between faiths. The Archbishop of Canterbury is supporting the conclusions of a committee, chaired by the Bishop of London, which in March 1988, before the Rushdie affair erupted, suggested a new offence of "insulting or outraging the religious feelings" of any group in the community.

In July 1989 the Archbishop of Canterbury at the opening of the General Synod, attacked in York Minster, fundamentalisms of all faiths, describing them as leading to "ecclesiastical apartheid". He had in mind, he said, Islamic fundamentalism in the Middle East, Christian fundamentalism in Ulster, and Jewish fundamentalism in Israel. Commenting, Mr. Mohammed Yasuf Quamar, secretary of the Muslim Liaison Committee at Birmingham Central Mosque, agreed that all faiths should live in peace. He stressed that British Muslims had been law-abiding in their attempts to get the law changed. "There has been no call for the death sentence here . . . We condemn the attacks on the bookshops, and the events in Ulster and Israel are something we should all want to avoid."

Notes

[1] Mark Johnson, "The Spirit still moves in the inner city: the Churches and race", *Ethnic and Racial Studies* 11 (1988) p. 371.
[2] Tariq Modood, "Religious Anger and Minority Rights", *Political Quarterly* (1989) p. 282.

Stuart Mews

# Scotland

There is an interesting critical and creative tension in the present relationship between Church and State in Scotland. And yet here of all places there should be little controversy about the principle of the Church's involvement in the political arena. Since the Reformation the Scottish theological tradition has seen the spheres of Church and State as distinct and yet profoundly related under the over-arching Lordship of Christ, and the Church (particularly the Church of Scotland as "national" Church) still occupies a significant place in the public eye and has brought this independence of approach to bear in addressing social and political issues in recent years.

Since the Conservative Government came to power in 1979 voting patterns and opinion polls have shown that Scotland has become increasingly alienated from Westminster and Whitehall: of the 72 Scottish Members of Parliament only 10 are Conservative; Government policies in fields such as education and health are seen as insensitive to Scottish traditions and needs; social and economic indicators show that Scotland, like the north of England and Wales, is falling farther behind the prosperous South-East; and established centres of power in the Scottish community, such as local authorities and universities, are being undermined. In this situation, the Churches, particularly the Church of Scotland and the Roman Catholic Church, have been active in expressing concern and in calling for adjustments of Government policy. This has inevitably provoked a debate about the appropriateness of the Church's engagement with political issues.

Two important events occurred in 1988 which carried the discussion forward.

First, in May the Prime Minister, Mrs Margaret Thatcher attended the Church of Scotland's General Assembly and delivered a speech which sought both to state her own Christian beliefs and to provide a Christian justification for her Government's policies. Her approach, implicitly accepting the connection between religion and politics, did not prevent subsequent criticism of Church opposition to the new system of local government finance (the community charge or "poll tax") on social justice grounds or to new proposals in the field of education. Church spokesmen have been particularly critical of the values underlying the Government's social policies and the apparent acceptance of a widening gap between rich and poor. A speech at Kirkcaldy in February 1989 by the Church of Scotland's Moderator, the Right Rev. Professor James Whyte, in which he suggested that there was undue emphasis on the individual at the expense of the community, attracted considerable attention and carried the debate forward. Meanwhile the Centre for Theology and Public Issues, established at New College, Edinburgh in 1984 has provided valuable resource material and arranged occasional events that have served as a focus for the Churches' continuing part in the political process.

The second event in 1988 was the publication of *A Claim of Right*, a document produced by an independent group, including two churchmen, proposing the establishment of a broadly based Scottish constitutional convention to reach agreement on plans for a democratically elected Scottish Assembly for the government of Scotland within the United Kingdom framework. These proposals, along with certain excitement generated by Parliamentary by-elections and elections for the European Parliament, have enlivened the Scottish political scene and attracted widespread interest throughout the Scottish community. The Convention was set up with the support of most of the political parties (but not the Conservatives or Scottish Nationalists) with a view to producing proposals for an Assembly by March 1990. The close involvement of Church representatives in the discussions, with four members of the Convention itself and the Chairman and another member of the Executive Committee, has been encouraged by other participants and formally endorsed by the Churches themselves, reflecting their interest in the greater good and future well-being of Scotland. It has been recognized that the Churches will have an important part to play in promoting the widest possible public participation as consultations proceed.

The field of education is a further area in which religious and political interests have arisen, not only in the opposition of the Churches to new policy proposals, but also in relation to denominational schools where, with falling rolls and the possibility of school closures, difficult decisions have to be taken and differences of opinion have arisen between Church interests, particularly in the Roman Catholic Church, and secular ones.

Finally, it is interesting to note that 1988 was the 350th anniversary of the signing of the National Covenant, one of the highpoints of Scottish history, where the Church took a lead in resisting moves to introduce English measures into Scottish life and worship: despite the significance of this event, from both the religious and political standpoints, the occasion was celebrated in a fairly low-key fashion. Only a year or so later it has become clear that religious and political feeling has reached a higher level; it remains to be seen what surprises and further developments lie in store.

Norman J. Shanks

# Northern Ireland

There has been much debate about whether the communal conflict in Northern Ireland is a religious conflict or a struggle between conflicting cultures: Gaelic, English, Anglo-Irish and Ulster Protestant. Northern Ireland was created in 1921 through the partition of the overwhelmingly Catholic island. Of the one and a half million people in the province of Ulter, over a quarter, 28 per cent, are Roman Catholic. Of the remaining 72 per cent, the majority are fiercely determined Protestants divided into Presbyterians (22.9 per cent), Church of Ireland (19 per cent), Methodist (4 per cent) and other small sects (7.6 per cent).

For the first 50 years of its existence, the province was controlled by the Unionist party whose choice for Prime Minister was a member of the Anglo-Irish gentry. The attempt of Captain Terence O'Neill to improve relations with Eire and the protests of the Civil Rights Movement at the anti-Catholic discrimination in employment and housing, sparked off a popular Protestant backlash which swept Protestant zealots like the Reverend Ian Paisley of the Free Presbyterian Church and the Reverend Martin Smyth, a Presbyterian minister and Grand Master of the Orange Order, into positions of prominence. There are now two Unionist parties, the Official Unionists and Paisley's Democratic Unionists, each trying to outdo the other as "super-loyalists" though they will usually come to agreements to avoid the risk of splitting the anti-Catholic vote.

The Social Democratic and Labour Party (SDLP) is the largest anti-partition party but its lack of success has led to some increase of support for Sinn Fein, the political wing of the Irish Republican Army (IRA). This was apparent in the Assembly elections of 1985. However in the 1987 General Election, the SDLP recovered some ground, particularly in the Catholic areas along the border, though Sinn Fein could not be dislodged from the Catholic working class enclave in West Belfast.

Since 1972 Northern Ireland has been under the direct rule of Whitehall. While ministers and clergy help to maintain a culture which produces men and women who are prepared to fight and die for their beliefs, they are plainly not in control. A new spirit of populist solidarity has arisen in working class areas with its own leaders who dislike the paternalism of the clergy. Appeals from Church leaders for an end to the violence by both sides have fallen on deaf ears. In November 1987 the Catholic bishops issued their strongest denunciation of the IRA following the bomb blast at Enniskillen when 11 Protestants were killed at a Remembrance Day service. Concerned that the revulsion among Catholics against terror tactics was fading and being replaced by renewed anger against the British for such incidents as the shooting of IRA members in Gibraltar, the Catholic bishops in March 1988 produced a new statement which condemned both the British army and the IRA. In 1989 the Bishop of Down and Connor, Dr Cahal Daly, urged Catholics to join the Royal Ulster Constabulary, whose members are 90 per cent Protestant. Dr Daly also said it was necessary for houses to be searched in north and west Belfast and that the IRA was chiefly responsible for any damage which might result. In July 1989 the Archbishop of Armagh, Dr Robin Eames told the Church of England General Synod that the withdrawal of British troops would be disastrous, Eames also criticized some Catholic attitudes to inter-Church marriages where some parish priests were unco-operative. This may account for the findings of two demographers, Paul Compton and John Coward that nearly four times as many mixed marriages in Northern Ireland take place in register offices.

Stuart Mews

# UK Dependent Territories

## Anguilla

Anguilla, a tiny self-governing colony of the United Kingdom, broke away from St Kitts and Nevis in 1967. Its population was estimated at 7,019 in 1984. The Anglican and Methodist churches predominate. Political life is notably personalist, with at least four political parties active. Chief Minister Emile Gumb's Anguilla National Alliance was retained in power with 73 per cent of the vote in the February 1989 elections.

Virgil Wiebe

## Bermuda

Bermuda's population of 70,000 is predominantly Anglican reflecting long British influence, though an established Evangelical community is also present. Considerable class- and race-based cleavages exist between blacks and whites and while still a British Crown Colony, Bermuda maintains internal self-rule. In the February 1989 election, the multi-racial, moderate, and predominantly white led United Bermuda Party (UBP) was returned to power with a reduced majority. The main opposition Progressive Labour Party (PLP) (characterized as mainly black, pro-independence and left-wing) has since the late seventies relied on the black Churches, adopted much of the rhetorical style of evangelical revivalism, and doubled its number of seats in the House of Assembly. The May 1989 call by UBP Premier John Swan for a referendum on the retention or abolition of the death penalty may well have repercussions for Church–State relations.

Virgil Wiebe

## Falkland Islands

The Falkland Islands (known to Argentinians as "Las Islas Malvinas") became a British Crown Colony in 1833 following the expulsion of settlers from the recently created Argentinian Republic. Their (1986) population is 1,919 (plus a British military garrison of approximately 2,000). Britain has continued to assert its claims to sovereignty on the basis of the length of British occupation and the right to self-determination of British settlers. Argentina's claims based on history, proximity and British neglect are backed by all sections of Argentinian opinion. In 1982 General Galtieri's military government launched an invasion in an effort to resolve the problem by force. Britain's victory precipitated the military regime's overthrow and helped to secure the re-election of Mrs Thatcher's government.

The Anglican Church is the largest of several Christian denominations on the islands. They help to underwrite the islanders' British identity. The 1982 war also made the Falklands an important issue for British and Argentinian churchmen. On both sides Church leaders, sometimes reluctantly, supported their respective national causes. Ensuing contacts between British and Argentinian churchmen have been one of the few lines of communication between the two countries from 1982–1988.

Kenneth Medhurst

## Gibraltar

A self-governing British colony at the entrance to the Mediterranean, Gibraltar was captured in 1704 and been used ever since as a military base. The population of 27,000 is 77 per cent Roman Catholic, 9 per cent Muslim, 8 per cent Anglican and 1.5 per cent Jewish. While the Jewish community has halved since 1900, Islam which was only brought to the colony in the 1960s by Moroccan Arab workers has grown rapidly through immigration. The main political issue is Spain's claim to sovereignty which is more likely to be treated seriously by Britain now that Spain has returned to democracy and joined the EEC. There is no established Church but each denomination gets a small annual government grant.

Stuart Mews

## Hong Kong

Hong Kong is a British colony of 1,070 sq. km. with a population of about six million, mostly ethnic Chinese. The colony is governed by a Governor, representing the Crown, who is supported by an Executive Council and a Legislative Council. In 1997 the colony will revert by agreement to China, and a mini-constitution is being negotiated which will become the future political framework for the ex-colony. In the early 1980s the prospect of

Chinese government caused anxiety for many and a slump in property values and business. After a period of recovery, confidence in the colony was severely damaged by the suppression of the 1989 student movement in China. Large numbers of Hong Kong residents, professionals in particular, may emigrate in the next few years.

Hong Kong has a lively religious life, with most Chinese families believing in Buddhism, Taoism and Confucianism as well as traditional Chinese folk religions — often all these elements are to be found in the same temple. There are important Buddhist and Taoist monasteries and seminaries. Christianity has had an important role in Hong Kong, particularly through educational work, and there are an estimated half million Chinese Christians, whose interests are promoted by the Hong Kong Christian Council among other organizations. Some Christian groups have recently been demanding safeguards for freedom of speech and belief under the future Chinese government. Many Christians were actively involved in support for the 1989 Beijing student movement and in the protests at its suppression.

Alan Hunter

## Montserrat

Montserrat, a British Dependent Territory, had an estimated population of 13,000 in 1985. A number of religious denominations are represented, most notably Anglicans and Methodists.

Ongoing conflict has occurred since 1984 between the Montserrat Christian Council and the ruling People's Liberation Movement (PLM) led by Chief Minister John Osborne. A decision in 1986 to deport an Anglican priest for alleged interference in political matters led to widespread strikes. The priest later left voluntarily. Also in 1986 the Christian Council strongly opposed a planned casino in a tourist development. The casino issue figured in the August 1987 elections, won narrowly by the PLM which took four of the seven seats. Two seats went to the newly formed National Development Party and one went to the Progressive Democratic Party. The Rev. Cecil Weekes, long-time critic of the government and head of the Montserrat Methodist Church, left the country in 1988 for a new post in Guyana.

Virgil Wiebe

## St Helena

The Crown Colony of St Helena in the Atlantic ocean has a population of only 5,310 who are mostly Anglican and worship in the 12 Anglican churches. There are also small numbers of Roman Catholics, Baptists, Salvation Army and Seventh Day Adventists.

Stuart Mews

## Turks and Caicos Islands

This multi-island British Dependent Territory of less than 10,000 people returned to internal self-rule following elections in March 1988. The former opposition People's Democratic Movement swept 11 of 13 seats on the legislative council. This followed two years of direct British rule due to a drugs and bribery scandal beginning in 1985 involving the then Chief Minister of the ruling Progressive National Party. Several Christian denominations are represented on the islands, notably Anglicanism. No major Church–State conflicts have been reported in recent years.

Virgil Wiebe

# UNITED STATES OF AMERICA

Religion continues to makes its mark on American society and politics. Indeed, events in the past three years cap an extraordinary decade of religious-political developments, including the rise and fall of television evangelists, the Church-based presidential campaigns of Jesse Jackson and Pat Robertson, and a deepening schism over abortion.

Rooted in a unique historical legacy, these episodes reflect the peculiar pluralism and vibrancy of religion in the United States. To a great degree, the nation was forged by religious dissenters from Europe, who learned that elimination of state-established Churches and a guarantee of religious freedom were the price of civil comity in a pluralistic society. Ironically, Churches thrived when cut loose from the paternalistic hand of government, and evangelical activism has become a regular phenomenon of society. Hence, even in a supposedly secular age Americans are a decidedly Church-rooted and believing people. Some 40 per cent of all Americans attend church in a given week, and 70 per cent consider themselves church or synagogue members. Moreover, an astonishing 95 per cent express a belief in God, and 70 per cent affirm the divinity of Jesus Christ.

American religion is also dynamic. Thus recent political developments arise out of key trends in religious life. Notably, the precipitous decline that began in the 1960s in the mainline Protestant denominations had levelled off by 1987, but affiliation with the Methodist, Presbyterian, and Episcopalian churches was still down one third from 1967.[1] Theologically conservative evangelical churches, on the other hand, saw dramatic growth in the same period, reflecting a major restructuring of religious alignments. The Southern Baptist Convention (SBC), for example, is now by far the largest Protestant denomination, and the fastest growing Churches include Assemblies of God, Nazarenes, Seventh Day Adventists, and Mormons.

Pollsters and scholars are just beginning to get a handle on the politically-salient religious cleavages in American society. The Protestant-Catholic divide that once defined society has been replaced by a growing split between orthodox pietists and theological liberals, a schism that crosses denominational boundaries.[2] Evangelical Christians, united theologically by a shared born-again experience and adherence to a "high" view of scripture, now comprise approximately one third of the adult population, or some 60 million Americans. This pietist group includes some Catholics and many blacks, whose cultural conservatism often blends with liberalism on other matters. More consistently conservative are the white Protestant evangelicals (about 20 per cent of the population), who appear to act on their beliefs with growing militancy.

The split between theological liberals and evangelicals highlights the potentially pivotal role of the Roman Catholic Church. "Mainline" Protestant denominations now claim only a quarter of the population, barely on par with their feisty, and growing, evangelical competitors. Thus Catholics, who comprise 28 per cent of the population, hold the balance of power in a keen cultural and political struggle. It is not surprising that both mainline Protestants and conservative evangelicals pay close attention to the American bishops and trends in lay Catholic opinion. Once "aliens" in a Protestant land, Catholics now feel comfortable and prominent in American society. The bishops grow politically assertive, and the Catholic voting block, once heavily Democratic, is up for grabs. Moreover, the public witness of the Church gives hope to both sides of the cultural divide. The bishops' pastoral letters on nuclear arms and the economy give ammunition to social gospel liberals, while pro-life witness and support for public accommodation of faith buoy the cultural conservatives. Indeed, so strategically placed is the Church, that one Lutheran scholar claimed it was "the Catholic Moment" in American history.[3]

Rounding out the pluralist picture are Jews, firmly established in American political circles, blacks, whose evangelical heritage contains a prophetic political witness, and Muslims, who are just now emerging as a visible force. Comprising only 2–3 per cent of the US population, Jews exercise impressive influence through robust organizations, eminent leadership, and focussed political agendas. Politically liberal and historically aligned with the New Deal Coalition, Jews must contend with increasing criticism of Israel in liberal circles. Blacks, the most loyal of the Democratic constituencies, comprise 12 per cent of the population and are concentrated in Baptist and Methodist denominations that continue to be the centre of political activity. Finally, the previously minuscule Muslim population is growing, both from immigration and conversions of inner city blacks. Though still small, it is beginning to exercise clout in such strategic cities as Detroit.

Clearly, the pluralism of American religion shapes and constrains Church political influence. Perennially divided theologically and socially, religious Americans do nonetheless exercise political influence, sometimes through coalitions, sometimes through fervency of commitment, but nearly always within the boundaries of the system's rules and norms.

## Religion in the presidential campaign

American political parties, unlike their counterparts in Europe, choose their national candidates through a relatively open process of electoral appeals to average citizens. Thus the presidential campaign becomes a marathon of fund-raising, organizing, and publicity — all aimed at mobilizing voters to participate in the state primaries and caucuses. This approach puts a premium on strategic political resources — money, forums, media exposure, volunteers — which evaporate quickly and spell the end of most conventional candidates.

However, the system also creates an opportunity for outsiders to penetrate the party by mobilizing their own followers to gain, if not nomination, then clout in some form.

One consequence of this porousness has been to open the parties to religiously-based mobilization, both on the right and the left. Thus the Rev. Jesse Jackson sustained his presidential campaigns in 1984 and 1988 with support from a network of black evangelical churches, winning such tangible concessions as rules changes and slots for supporters on the Democratic National Committee, and seeing his convention manager, Ron Brown, selected chairman. Similarly, the New Religious Right moved into a Republican Party formerly dominated by affluent, non-pietist elites, altering the party agenda and creating tension with the blue blood establishment, a process that accelerated with the infusion of the Robertson forces.

Remarkably, then, each party in 1988 faced the candidacy of a minister[4] with no prior elective service, but with access to a tightly-knit community of churches for political mobilization. Jesse Jackson's organizational base, of course, was the tested and formidable network of congregations led by some 40,000 black ministers. For Pat Robertson, it was the more unpredictable cluster of conservative Pentecostal churches that comprise only a portion of the evangelical world. Different though they are, however, black evangelical congregations and conservative Pentecostal churches share one thing in common: they are profoundly central to the life of their members.

The role of congregation as political precinct emerged most forcefully with the Jackson campaign for president, a fact not surprising in light of black history. It is an ironic legacy of slavery and Jim Crow that black Churches emerged from the Civil War as the one institution "owned and operated" by the blacks themselves. Indeed, for a century prior to the civil rights movement, the black congregation was the social centre, the refuge, the place where messages of comfort for the afflicted and judgement of oppressors could be heard. If America was the new Israel for the Puritans, it was Pharaoh's Egypt for many American blacks; thus biblical themes of liberation and the promised land possessed special poignancy and power. The centrality of the black minister flowed in part from his economic independence from the white power structure, but also owed to his dynamic oratorical powers, a legacy of the evangelical heritage of the black experience. With the civil rights revolution the black Church emerged the most highly politicized sector of religious America. Black ministers now routinely endorse candidates from the pulpit, mobilize voter registration drives, raise money for candidates, and solicit volunteers for campaigns. Thus in launching his first presidential bid Jesse Jackson quipped that while Mondale might have Big Labor, "We have Big Church."

In 1988 Jackson criss-crossed the nation, preaching of poverty and oppression from pulpits and igniting crowds with his command of religious imagery. On Easter Sunday he evoked resurrection themes in addresses before Denver congregations, at one point comparing Reagan to Pilate. The Jackson campaign, meanwhile, expanded on the Church-based organization developed four years earlier. When organizers moved into a state, even one with a small black population, they began with the Churches. This is not to minimize racial solidarity as a leaven for the Jackson campaign, but followers had to be mobilized, campaign workers recruited, and supporters solicited for donations of time and money — tasks co-ordinated largely through the network of black congregations. Indeed, fund-raising techniques typically involved the hard sell in congregations, with the passing of collection plates and a variation of the altar call, often to provide Jackson's plane fare to his next stop.

The political clout of the black community was shown on March 8, or Super Tuesday, when 21 states, most of them from the south, held primaries and caucuses. The Rev. Jackson's victories in Georgia, Virginia, Louisiana, Alabama, and Mississippi, plus a strong showing elsewhere, gave him a plurality of the total votes cast and catapulted him into a tight delegate race with Michael Dukakis and Albert Gore. Had Gore been able to remain in the race, thus splitting the white vote with Dukakis, Jackson might have emerged as the kingmaker at the convention. The field narrowed too quickly, however, owing to the bandwagon effect, and Jackson had to settle for extracting concessions from Dukakis in return for keeping his people from disrupting the convention.

It was in Michigan, the high-water mark of the Jackson campaign, where the strategic role of churches revealed itself most forcefully. The Michigan caucuses, held on March 27, placed a premium on strong local organization because the 600 district boundaries had recently been redrawn and the process was confusing. Jackson's surprising landslide victory there was aided by his Church-based organization. The Jackson campaign used the local parish as a meeting site for supporters on election night. After coffee and instructions the group would caravan or bus to the caucus, led by the local minister.

It was also in Michigan where Jackson's embrace of the Palestinian cause won tangible support in the growing Arab-American community in Detroit and elsewhere. An estimated 250,000 Americans of Arab descent reside in metropolitan Detroit, and Jackson was their clear choice. Jackson was free to develop this relationship because he had written off gaining more than a token Jewish vote, a fact that clearly hurt him in the New York primary, where Mayor Koch publicly attacked Jackson's support for an independent Palestinian homeland and said Jews would be "crazy" to vote for him. The solidifying alliance between blacks and Arab-Americans was evident at the Democratic National Convention. For the first time in American politics Arab-Americans were given a forum to air their concerns. Dr. James Zagby, close adviser to Jackson, orchestrated the debate over a proposed Palestinian plank at the convention, an unprecedented effort that disturbed Jewish leaders. While Zagby and Jackson ultimately agreed not to bring the issue to a vote on the convention floor, the development spotlighted the heightening tensions between blacks and Jews.

Jesse Jackson's two political campaigns for president altered the political landscape in a number of significant ways, not the least of which was to make himself the spokesman for the aspirations of American blacks. By 1988 Jackson's commanding leadership in the black community gave him an overwhelming 92 per cent of the black vote, which coupled with a respectable 12.5 per cent of the white vote, earned 1,200 delegates to the Democratic convention (or about 30 per cent of the total). His eloquent campaign against drug abuse helped to crystallize a tougher approach for Democrats once perceived as permissive, thus helping to forge a national consensus on the issue. Moreover, his campaigns also galvanized the black electorate. Black registration and voting soared dramatically in the 1980s, altering the political dynamics in congressional and state races. Ironically,

Jackson's greatest impact may have come two years before his second run for the presidency, when the Democrats regained control of the Senate in 1986, thanks to a robust black vote in half a dozen closely contested races. Indeed, in four southern states, Alabama, Georgia, Louisiana and North Carolina, the increased black vote was clearly the margin of victory for Democrats, whose white vote averaged only 40 per cent.

Jackson remains a forceful and unpredictable player on the national scene. In 1989 the talk of Washington DC was of a possible run by Jackson for mayor of the city. Plagued by drug-related violence and a tainted mayor, the city's 70 per cent black population would likely be receptive to a bid by Jackson. Should this happen, many Democrats would breathe a sigh of relief that presidential politics in 1992 might take place without the mercurial Reverend. Time will tell.

On the Republican side much has been written about the quixotic presidential campaign of Pat Robertson, a "faith-healing" charismatic minister with no prior elective experience. As host of the 700 Club Pat Robertson cultivated a religious constituency for years. His unique appeal was to the distinctive group of evangelicals who emphasize gifts of the holy spirit, speaking in tongues, and faith healing, all characteristics that separate the faithful from the broader culture and enhance social bonds. Like Jackson, Robertson's experience mirrors that of many of his followers in significant respects. His religious conversion not only changed the direction of his life, but also brought him into the culturally distinct world of Pentecostal faith. Robertson confesses to have lived, as did St. Augustine, a life of "wine, women, and song" before his born-again experience, and thus he can argue persuasively about the need for, and the power of, the religious revival he calls for. Moreover, his years as a minister have enabled him to hone his message — a withering critique of the chaos of a modern culture cut adrift from its moral and religious moorings.

Robertson's campaign staff capitalized on this aroused constituency in their attempt to penetrate the Republican Party. The early organizational effort to secure names on endorsing petitions was almost entirely church-based. In addition, the highly successful fundraising effort was conducted through lists that included many ministers, evangelical associations, and, of course, contributors to the 700 Club. Finally, through churches and networks of religious individuals Robertson built a formidable political organization.

The Robertson bid was viewed as profoundly threatening to a number of "regular" Republicans. The State GOP Chair in Michigan, for example, said the Robertson contingent looked like "the bar scene out of Star Wars", and in South Carolina a party leader termed them "Nazis". Robertson's early success in the Michigan caucuses sent the stale party into a year long chaotic struggle, complete with court challenges, rump conventions, and shoving matches. Similar protracted struggles occurred in South Carolina and Georgia, where "country club" Republicans found themselves challenged by moralist neophytes and, in many cases, former Democrats. Thus, a decade after the rise of the Religious Right and Reagan's adroit appeals to both "enterprisers" and "moralists"[5] in the Republican coalition, strains are still being felt between populist outsiders and well-established insiders.

On one level the Robertson campaign was highly successful. He raised $29 million in contributions and federal matching funds, second only to George Bush, and received slightly over a million votes in GOP primaries and caucuses, or 9 per cent of the total. His campaign scored outright victories in Hawaii, Alaska, Nevada, and Washington, and made respectable showings in Iowa, Michigan, Minnesota, and Oklahoma, primarily by enlisting new participants into Republican politics. Moreover, even in primary states where Robertson was defeated by Bush, his supporters packed party caususes to elect delegates, draft platform statements, and control party machinery. The battle that ensued over the control of these state parties is, perhaps, the most important legacy of the Robertson campaign.

On the other hand, the campaign fell far short of either the fears of opponents or expectations of supporters. Indeed, Robertson's million votes pale in comparison with the total evangelical vote,[6] and are dwarfed even by the petitions of 3 million supporters he purportedly secured prior to announcing his candidacy. Moreover, Robertson failed to broaden his base beyond the large charismatic Churches, and remains a highly divisive figure among Republicans.

Robertson lieutenants were well aware of the "negatives" attached to a television minister, and sophisticated marketing strategies were employed to overcome them. In Iowa, for example, full page ads featured Robertson and John Kennedy side by side, with the message that prejudice against Robertson's religion was comparable to Protestant hostility to Kennedy's Catholicism. Robertson, moreover, emphasized his role as a businessman and broadcaster. A sequence of events, however, undercut efforts to make Robertson more socially acceptable to average voters. First came the Bakker scandals, then Oral Roberts' unconventional fund-raising pleas. Then, in what must be some of the worst timing in recent campaign history, prominent evangelist Jimmy Swaggart fell from grace just two weeks before Super Tuesday, raising anew public doubts about the seamy world of televangelism. Robertson compounded the problem by his assertion that the Bush organization might have been behind the Swaggart downfall to hurt his candidacy. This statement, of course, occurred at just the time when campaign strategy called for distance from the world of TV evangelists.

In spite of Robertson's mis-steps, the campaign itself can be viewed as part of a process of assimilation of conservative evangelicals into the Republican coalition. He brought new people into active participation in the party, especially charismatic evangelicals from so-called "super churches" (independent congregations with thousands of members) that constituted his base. These individuals are indeed a distinctive group of Republicans, with passionate concerns about the collapse of moral codes and the disintegration of the family. However, their infiltration of the party machinery in a number of states has created turmoil at times. In Arizona, for example, Robertson backers joined forces with hard core supporters of former governor Evan Mecham to write a state platform declaring the United States "a Christian nation" and asserting that the US Constitution created "a republic based upon the absolute laws of the Bible, not a democracy". The embarrassing national publicity that ensued — including the remark by Barry Goldwater that the party had been taken over by a "bunch of kooks" — delighted Democrats who see the turmoil as enhancing their chances of keeping the governorship in 1990.

One could hardly find a more dramatic contrast than the way Dukakis and Bush dealt with the insurgent challenges of the two charismatic ministers. Dukakis conceded the black vote to Jackson in the primaries and then could not develop a coherent strategy for dealing with the Jackson forces in the general election. Moreover, Dukakis failed to seize early the populist economic themes of Jackson's message that might have energized Democratic voters.[7]

The Bush campaign, on the other hand, anticipated the Robertson effort, monitored its growth, designed strategies to blunt its impact, and co-opted its potential supporters. For example, a quiet but thorough effort began in 1985 to arrange meetings for Bush with key evangelical leaders, appearances on Christian television programmes, and feature stories in evangelical publications. A promotional biography of George Bush's life and faith, written by a Bush lieutenant, appeared in Christian bookstores. Between 1985 and 1988 Bush was photographed with almost 1,000 evangelical leaders. During the campaign, the Bush staff identified organizers in 200 "super churches" in the south to neutralize Robertson's base.[8] After the convention the Bush organization, under the leadership of James Baker III, hired all the former Robertson campaign consultants, thus ensuring loyalty.

The Bush people concluded that they could court the evangelical vote in ways that did not undercut their support among other key voting blocks. Moreover, the Bush staff discovered through experiments with focus groups[9] that themes articulated by Robertson[10] in the primaries — the pledge of allegiance, the ACLU's attack on religion — were devastating when aimed at Dukakis. In the general election Bush got around 80 per cent of an evangelical vote[11] that included many culturally conservative Democrats. Thus Bush not only blunted Robertson by courting the born-again vote in the primaries, but benefited tremendously from his cultivation of that constituency in the general election.

A breakdown of the national vote in 1988 also reveals other key cleavages in the American electorate. In addition to his commanding support among white fundamentalists, Bush also got 66 per cent of the overall white Protestant vote, and split the Catholic vote almost evenly with Dukakis. Democrats thus regained some of the Catholic presidential vote they lost in 1984, but these figures mask a significant erosion of white Catholic support, once a bulwark of the New Deal Coalition. Hispanic and black Catholics, a growing portion of the Church, continue to vote heavily Democratic, while white Catholics have moved solidly into the Republican presidential camp. The majority of Jews voted for Dukakis, but Bush got a respectable 35 per cent. Black support for the Democrats was down slightly, but still a commanding 86 per cent.[12] Perhaps most ominous for the Democrats, a new trend appeared in voting in the 1980s. Among white voters — Catholic, mainline Protestant, and evangelical — survey researchers discovered that the higher the church attendance the more likely the voter will be Republican.[13] This trend, not present prior to the Reagan era, suggests that a secular-religious cleavage characteristic of some parties in Europe may be developing in the US. One factor in this complex picture, no doubt, is the growing schism over the scope and limits of reproductive freedom.

## Politics at the cultural divide: Abortion

Abortion, the most divisive issue in American society since the Vietnam War, flared up in 1987 with the emergence of a militant new organization devoted to disruption of the "abortion industry". Operation Rescue, founded by Randall Terry, blossomed from a local protest in Binghamton, New York, to a national movement of Christian fundamentalists willing to be arrested blocking the doors of abortion clinics. Borrowing tactics and rhetoric from the 1960s, Terry's movement gained national prominence when more than 1,200 protesters were arrested in Atlanta before and during the 1988 Democratic National Convention in July.[14]

Randall Terry is an unlikely movement leader. A high school drop out and former used car salesman, the 29-year old born-again Christian and his wife began a daily vigil at a Women's Centre in Binghamton in 1984. The term Operation Rescue was coined to depict the effort to stop women from entering abortion centres or convince them to change their minds. Terry's local following grew and their tactics became more aggressive; they once stormed a clinic and chained themselves to equipment. By 1987 Operation Rescue had expanded beyond New York, and by 1988 it galvanized a nationwide following. In addition to the Atlanta arrests in the summer, Operation Rescue staged a National Day of Rescue on the last Saturday of October, in which 2,631 protesters were arrested in 42 cities located in 19 states and Canada. Another 2,019 risked arrest by sitting or lying in front of clinics, and an estimated 5,000 others supported with hymns and pickets.[15] Arrests continued into 1989, and totalled over 17,000 by March.[16]

The militancy of this group, and the possibility that the Supreme Court might overturn its 1973 Roe v. Wade decision legalizing abortion, spurred pro-choice forces to heightened activity in 1989. On April 9 the National Organization for Women sponsored a "March for Women's Equality, Women's Lives" in Washington DC. The largest demonstration of its kind, the march drew a crowd estimated at 300,000. It was cosponsored by liberal church groups and their umbrella organization, the Religious Coalition for Abortion Rights. At the rally pro-choice banners and signs were interspersed with depictions of clothes-hangers and other images of life prior to legalized abortion. The battle of the airwaves also heated up, as the National Abortion Rights Action League spent $2.5 million on dramatic national ads. Perhaps it was not too much of an exaggeration for one national newsmagazine to term abortion, "America's new civil war".[17]

The politics of abortion also tested the limits of overt activism by the Roman Catholic Church. Steadfast in its official opposition to abortion, the Church in 1988 appeared to back away from its flirtation with partisan activities in the previous quadrennial election. The immediate question was the tax-exempt status of the Church, important in itself, but also symbolic of the lines demarcating acceptable political witness by Church organs.

The issue had been brewing for at least a decade. In 1979 the National Abortion Rights Action League began presenting the Internal Revenue Service with pro-life documents distributed by Catholic groups. Lawyers for the organization argued that this political activity violated the Church's tax-exempt status, one of the most firmly rooted Church-State practices in the US. Then in 1981 a New York group, Abortion Rights Mobilization (ARM), filed suit to revoke the tax-exempt status of the National Conference of Catholic Bishops and its staff arm, the US Catholic Conference. Lawyers for ARM argued that the Church had violated the anti-electioneering provision of the tax code, citing as an example a Church document that called for creation of pro-life groups to "work for qualified candidates who will vote for a constitutional amendment".[18] During legal manoeuvring the Catholic

Conference refused to turn over documents subpoenaed by ARM, and found itself held in contempt by a New York Judge. Remarkably, the judge assessed fines of $50,000 for each day of non-compliance. The contempt order was stayed pending the appeal by the Church. Early in 1988 the US Supreme Court heard the appeal, but instead of adjudicating the matter, remanded the case back to the Circuit Court of Appeals on the basis of complex jurisdictional issues. This removed the immediate threat to the Church, but the episode was sobering and could return.

The Church's activities during the 1988 election campaign, consequently, were framed in a highly charged atmosphere. In 1984 Cardinal John O'Connor, then Archbishop of New York, flirted with election politics with his statement that he could not see how a Catholic could vote for anyone not opposed to abortion, a thinly-veiled attack on Democratic Vice-Presidential candidate Geraldine Ferraro. More directly, he criticized Ms Ferraro for "giving the world to understand that Catholic teaching is divided" on abortion. Acting in so public a way, the Archbishop ignited a storm of controversy, including highly scripted responses by such prominent Catholic Democrats as Ted Kennedy and Mario Cuomo. To head off similar controversy, the US Catholic Conference, in July 1988, issued guidelines for bishops and priests on election activities. The document clearly stipulated that bishops and other Church leaders who label a candidate "pro-abortion" or otherwise praise or condemn office seekers, jeopardize the tax-exempt status of the Catholic Church. Church leaders could speak to issues, but not personalities. The document stated that bishops or priests, as private individuals, could participate in political functions, but noted that they must avoid any official Church sanction for their activities. While arguing that the document was merely an update, the general counsel for the Catholic Conference admitted that the IRS had tightened its regulations. In the spirit of these guidelines, Cardinal O'Connor announced in mid-July that while he could not personally vote for a candidate supporting abortion, he would avoid explicitly recommending that other Catholics should so vote.

Ironically, barely a month after the Conference issued its guidelines, Archbishop John F. Whealon of Hartford, Connecticut, declared that he was "unable in conscience to remain a registered Democrat", because the party is "officially in favour of executing unborn babies whose only crime is that they temporarily occupy their mother's womb." The general counsel for the Catholic Conference said that the Archbishop's announcement "seems to be within his constitutional right and not a violation of the tax laws". However, Rev. Richard McBrien, liberal chairman of the Theology Department at the University of Notre Dame, demanded that such public denunciations of the Democratic Party be repudiated by other bishops.[19] The controversy within the Church continues.

Abortion, of course, became an issue in the 1988 presidential campaign, as Bush and Dukakis took clearly opposing positions in nationally televised debates. The issue apparently polarized those voters most committed (either way), pushing fervent pro-choice voters toward Dukakis and fervent pro-lifers toward Bush. The clear beneficiary from this exchange, however, was George Bush. Nearly one third of voters surveyed on election day cited abortion as the issue most important to them, and of those the majority (55 per cent) voted for Bush.[20] Republican strategists, indeed, see this issue as one that can realign evangelical and Catholic Democrats toward the GOP.

Political forces are clearly pushing party organizations toward the extremes on the issue. The 1988 National Democratic Party Platform states that "the fundamental right of reproductive choice should be guaranteed regardless of ability to pay," while the Republican language calls for a human life amendment and argues "that the unborn child has a fundamental individual right to life which cannot be infringed". Christian fundamentalists and pro-life groups now dominate the Republican platform on the issue no less than feminists and Planned Parenthood frame the Democratic response. Intriguingly, Republican and Democratic voters as a group are indistinguishable on the issue, with a majority favouring neither an absolute ban nor absolute choice. However, most voters of both parties favour restricting abortion to a very few circumstances, providing the edge for the moment to the pro-life activists.[21]

Inner-party dynamics also nudge national candidates toward the activists in their respective parties. Thus George Bush moved toward a more pro-life position throughout the 1980s, and Congressman Dick Gephardt backed away from his pro-life position as his presidential aspirations blossomed. No one personifies the inner-party dynamic better, however, than Jesse Jackson. As a minister Jackson had frequently denounced abortion in the 1970s and early '80s, and he even wrote a passionate pro-life article in the National Right to Life newsletter.[22] As a presidential candidate in 1984, however, he shifted abruptly to embrace the pro-choice position, an imperative for a candidate seeking to unite the progressive wing of the party. By 1988 he was actively courting feminist groups within the Democratic Party, in part by championing public funding for abortions.

It is against this complex and tumultuous backdrop that the United States Supreme Court decided to review its historic decision in Roe v. Wade. On April 26, 1989, the court heard oral arguments in Webster v. Reproductive Health Services, which tests the constitutionality of a Missouri law limiting access to abortions. No case has generated such interest. A record number of *amicus curiae* (friend of the court) briefs have been filed, including extensive medical and scientific documentation, personal "stories" of women who had abortions, and legal argumentation by members of Congress. The Bush administration, through its Solicitor General, called upon the court to overturn Roe. Remarkably, an estimated 200,000 letters reached the court by April 26.[23]

What sparked this intensity, in part, is the changing composition of the court. Roe v. Wade was decided in 1973 by a 7–2 vote, but its support has eroded over the years with the addition of new justices. The court last affirmed the Roe decision in 1986 by a thin 5–4 margin, in Thornburgh v. American College of Obstetricians and Gynaecologists. Since then, two new Reagan appointees, Antonin Scalia and Anthony Kennedy, have joined the court.

The complexity of the issues, and the uncertainty about how some justices will vote, makes predicting the outcome difficult. The court could simply overturn the Missouri law, upholding the *status quo*. It could conceivably uphold the Missouri law even while affirming major features of Roe v. Wade. This is because decisions subsequent to Roe actually gave greater latitude for women to abort than the original trimester formula. Or the court could overturn Roe v. Wade outright and return the entire issue to the states, igniting 50 state battles. Whatever the outcome, it is likely that states will be given more room to regulate some abortions, thus intensifying the political fallout in Governor's races and state legislative campaigns in 1990.

Given the delicate political balance in the court, much of the speculation about what it will do has centred on Justice Sandra Day O'Connor, the only female justice, whose past statements contain considerable nuance. On the one hand she has intimated that a woman might have some absolute privacy rights with respect to reproduction; on the other hand she has stated that Roe v. Wade is "on a collision course with itself". In a staging that Hollywood could not improve for dramatic suspense, a woman may indeed decide the issue.

## The holy wars and their aftermath

From 1987 to 1989 the world of television evangelists was rocked by one scandal after another, unmasking a vulnerability behind the veneer of power often associated with this uniquely American form of religious proselytizing. The political fallout weakened Pat Robertson's presidential campaign, diverted attention off fundamentalist leaders, and undermined fund-raising by lobbying groups dependent on member loyalty. A blend of Greek Tragedy and soap opera, the scandals occurred at the height of the video ministry's greatest influence and widest viewership, a growing billion dollar industry. Scripture says that pride goes before the fall, a maxim tellingly accurate in this tale of money, seduction, arrogance, and celebrities.

It all began in early spring 1987, when the PTL empire founded by Jim and Tammy Bakker began to unravel. PTL, which stands for Praise the Lord and People that Love, raised nearly $130 million in 1986, making it one of the three largest of the TV ministries, along with those headed by Jimmy Swaggart and Pat Robertson. The ministry included, of all things, Heritage USA, a 2,500 acre theme park and resort in South Carolina, complete with luxury hotel, swimming pools, condominiums, shops, and a water slide. In March, shortly after Mrs Bakker disclosed that she was being treated for drug addiction, reports of a sexual tryst between Jim Bakker and a church secretary surfaced. Among those exposing the story was Mr. Swaggart, who had previously denounced "sissified preachers" and "pretty little boys with their hair done and their nails done, who called themselves preachers," a thinly-veiled reference to the saccharine "happiness" gospel preached by Bakker. As news organizations probed into the story, they discovered that thousands in hush money had been paid to Jessica Hahn of Long Island, New York, who confirmed the liaison in 1980 and alleged that Bakker forced himself on her. Bakker resigned from his ministry following the disclosure, claiming he was "wickedly manipulated by treacherous former friends", and alleging that Swaggart was attempting a hostile takeover of the PTL ministries. Bakker was later stripped of his ordination by the Assemblies of God church, which shockingly accused Bakker of numerous sexual sins, including bisexual activity. Then came revelations of gross financial mismanagement in PTL and the Bakkers' lavish lifestyle, which included a $600,000 mansion in Palm Springs, California, other homes or apartments in South Carolina, Florida, and Tennessee, and an assortment of expensive cars (Rolls Royce, Mercedes-Benz), boats, clothing, jewelry, gold plumbing fixtures, and an air-conditioned dog-house. Amazingly, while the Bakkers had been paid $4.6 million during a period of 39 months, the ministry could not account for $92 million in contributions. This brought investigations by the US Justice Department and the Internal Revenue Service.

This embarrassing publicity was not welcome, of course, for other prominent religious figures, who heaped criticism on the Bakkers. Swaggart called the affair a "cancer that needed to be excised from the body of Christ", while the Rev. Jerry Falwell said that greed and self-centredness had brought the Bakkers down. In spite of this the Bakkers attempted to re-capture PTL from Falwell and the board of trustees. The holy war was on.

Sordid happenings of this sort would have been sufficient to hamper fund-raising and political forays by televangelists, but there was also Oral Roberts' claim in January 1987, that God would "take me home" if the ministry did not raise $8 million by the end of March. Roberts got his money, but his controversial, and to some extent "extortionist", fundraising techniques undermined his ability to sustain his over-extended ministry, including a financially ailing Oral Roberts University in Tulsa, Oklahoma.

If the Bakkers' downfall was fitting of their bathos, and Roberts' chastisement apropos of overweening ambition, the fall of Jimmy Swaggart reads like a Gothic tragedy of poverty, triumph, temptation, and disgrace. In a way, he is the most formidable of the television ministers to emerge in 1980s, certainly the most dramatic. His adroit use of satellite technology is evocatively modern, yet his message rings with the cadence of the old-time circuit-riding Pentecostal preachers of the depression era. Swaggart refers to himself, indeed, as "an old-fashioned, Holy Ghost-filled, shouting, weeping, soul-winning, gospel-preaching preacher", a disarmingly accurate depiction. He roars, sweats, paces, sings, and shakes his Bible in programmes edited and translated into 13 languages for airing in 142 countries. Louisiana-born to a poor itinerant labourer and Pentecostal minister, Swaggart worked his way up from the back-woods to head an electronic ministry based in Baton Rouge with a $140 million budget and arguably the largest following of all the televangelists.

Swaggart had twice accused fellow ministers, first the Rev. Marvin Gorman, then Jim Bakker, of sexual improprieties, but on February 21, 1988, he stunned his 8,000 member congregation by confessing to sins of his own. In a tearful address he said he had sinned against God, his family, fellow ministers, and his faithful followers, and he announced that he was stepping down from his ministry for an indeterminate period. It was later revealed that Swaggart had confessed to hiring prostitutes for pornographic poses, a fact revealed by the Rev. Gorman acting on a tip. The Assemblies of God again was confronted with an errant minister, but Swaggart's fortright confession and apparent repentance led the body to recommend a one-year suspension from the ministry and enrollment in a rehabilitation program to deal with his obsession. Swaggart argued, however, that the punishment would jeopardize a ministry dependent on his persona, and he vowed to return within three months. Because of his unwillingness to submit to discipline, Swaggart was defrocked as an Assemblies of God Minister. Still, amidst declining revenues and staff layoffs, he continues to preach, down but not out.

The scandals and internecine strife left the electronic Church seriously weakened politically. Contributions diminished and the public grew increasingly sceptical. The preoccupation with damage control also left the televangelists with less time and capital for political battle. Falwell relinquished active leadership in the Moral Majority, Robertson returned to the 700 Club, and fundamentalist lobbies struggled to keep going.

## Jews and Israel

Historically unified and politically formidable, American Jews found themselves divided over Israel's handling of Palestinian uprising in the occupied West Bank and Gaza Strip. The *intifada* movement also strained relations between American Jews and Israelis, especially as events were broadcast nightly on the evening news. When Israeli Defence Minister Yitzhak Rabin announced in January 1988, a policy of "might, power, and beatings" to quell the uprising, some Jews criticized Israel publicly. Indeed, the report that Israeli troops had entered Arab homes and indiscriminately broken the hands of Arab youths sent a chill through the American Jewish community. The venerable Hyman Bookbinder, Washington representative of the American Jewish Committee, said that the policy had caused "great dismay" among even Israel's best supporters, and he assured his followers that this dismay was being communicated to Israeli authorities.[24] Albert Vorspan, senior Vice-President of the Union of American Hebrew Congregations, expressed his shock in the *New York Times Magazine*: "Is this possible? Deliberately breaking bones? Israel? Come on."[25] The Conference of Presidents of major American Jewish Organizations held an "emergency" meeting to discuss the situation, and some liberal Jews responded by contributing to The New Israel Fund, an organization that promotes tolerance and improved Arab-Jewish relations in the Israel. Israel's continued military occupation thus produced an enormous soul-searching in the Jewish community, replete with an outpouring of articles, letters to the editor, and conferences. Even when American Jews kept their criticism within the family, they expressed their anguish directly with the Shamir government. On the other hand, some American Jews, such as *Commentary* editor Norman Podhoretz, voiced alarm that such criticism might lead to dangerous concessions to Israel's enemies.

Late in 1988, another remarkable turn of events occurred. A small delegation of Jews, led by attorney Rita Hauser, took the bold and controversial step of meeting in Stockholm, Sweden, with Yasser Arafat, head of the Palestinian Liberation Organization (PLO), and extracting from him an apparent recognition of the state of Israel. Although ambiguous, Arafat's shift played into the hands of the Reagan Administration, which was seeking a means of opening dialogue with the Palestinians.

The growing tension between American Jews and Israel appears to have weakened Israel's political position in the US. While still assured of its continued foreign and military aid, some $3 billion per year, Israel cannot depend on reflexive support from American Jews. In December 1988, when the Reagan administration responded to the Stockholm window of opportunity by opening talks with the PLO, Israeli leaders were stunned. In response, they sent Benjamin Netanyahu, a decorated soldier and veteran diplomat, to convince Jewish leaders and wealthy supporters in the United States to protest the Reagan policy. Remarkably, no major organization agreed to lobby in Washington against the initiative. So troubling was this, that Israel's leaders held an extraordinary conference in Jerusalem (in the spring of 1989) with some 1,500 Jewish representatives from the United States and Europe, who expressed their continued support for Israel, even while some continued to express doubts about particular policies.[26]

These strains come at a time when even the legendary pressure group, The American Israel Public Affairs Committee (AIPAC), is facing increasing competition from a growing Arab lobby, which includes foreign governments and the small but increasingly assertive Arab-American Anti-Discrimination Committee. Meanwhile, AIPAC's leader, the redoubtable Thomas Dine, found himself under unusual criticism for the organization's supposed tilt toward the GOP in the 1988 election, and its surreptitious efforts against Jesse Jackson.[27]

Even more painful for some American Jews than Israel's occupation of the West Bank and Gaza, was the serious consideration by Yitzhak Shamir to accede to religious parties in Israel and change the Law of Return defining who is a Jew. Currently any Jew can emigrate to Israel and receive instant citizenship. At issue in 1988 was whether those Jews converted by Reform and Conservative Rabbis would be considered Jews by Israeli authorities. Under current Israeli law they are, but ultra-orthodox groups demanded that the law be changed to allow only conversions under guidance of Orthodox Rabbis. The issue was moot until November 1, 1988, when orthodox parties, spurred by an aggressive Hasidic group in New York, emerged from Israeli parliamentary elections holding the balance of power in the 120 member *knesset*.

At the centre of the dispute is an American Jew, Rabbi Menachem Mendel Schneerson of Brooklyn, New York, the 87-year old charismatic leader of the ultra-orthodox Lubavitcher sect of Hasidim. The Lubavitcher Rebbe (Yiddish for Rabbi) traces his roots seven generations back to the legendary eighteenth-century European mystic and founder of Hasidim, Baal Shem Tov. While his following in the United States is only around 100,000, Rabbi Schneerson has something of a cult following around the world, including orthodox believers in Israel, who constructed an exact replica of his Brooklyn Victorian house in Kfar Habad, just off the highway from Tel Aviv to Jerusalem. Strict adherence to Jewish law and reassertion of "Yiddishkeit", or Jewishness, is the *raison d'être* of the exuberant Lubavitchers, whose missionary activities embrace modern techniques and technology. Not content with passive isolation from the secular world, the Rebbe broke ground in September 1988 on a new $23 million headquarters in Brooklyn.

Rabbi Schneerson sees a dangerous trend toward secularization and assimilation of Reform and Conservative Jews, and has taken his fight to Israel, demanding that "easy" conversions be abolished. Although he has never set foot in Israel, Schneerson intervened forcefully in the Israeli elections, orchestrating fund-raising and sending video-taped instructions to his followers to vote for Agudat Israel, one of four orthodox religious parties.[28] This effort doubled Agudat's vote, which won five seats in the 120-member parliament. Altogether, the religious parties emerged with control of 18 seats and a sense of destiny owing to the delicate balance between Israel's two major parties. Likud and its allies won only 47 seats in the 120 member parliament, while Labour controlled just 49. Neither party wanted a repeat of the previously strained coalition, so the religious parties held the balance of power in the formation of a new government. In return for their support, the ultra-orthodox leaders pressed for such religiously-based concessions as restrictions against public activities on the Sabbath, equal funding for their schools, and elimination of abortions and autopsies. Most fatefully, they demanded a change in the Law of Return which would only recognize conversions by Orthodox Rabbis. Yitzhak Shamir, desperate to avoid another coalition government with Labour and unaware of the explosive symbolic power of the issue, pledged categorically to amend the Law of Return in exchange for religious parties' support.

This caused a firestorm in the United States, where fewer than 10 per cent of the six million Jews identify themselves as Orthodox. Intensely loyal to Israel, many American Jews were stunned and disturbed by Shamir's move. For several weeks, indeed, it was intensely discussed in synagogues and Jewish community centres around the country.[29] Technically, the move would only bar from automatic citizenship those *converted* by non-orthodox Rabbis (or born to mothers so converted), but at the symbolic level it struck at the heart of Jewish identity and was profoundly threatening to many.

Reaction was swift and forceful. Twenty-seven Jewish organizations claiming to represent 90 per cent of American Jews issued a call for Israel to "heed the overwhelming voice of diaspora Jewry" and renounce the amendment of the Law of Return. Reform Rabbi Alexander M. Schindler, President of the Union of American Hebrew Congregations, termed Shamir's actions "dangerous and divisive", and added that: "Israeli politicians have persistently misread the temper of the American Jewish community."[30] Seymour Reich, President of B'nai B'rith, sent a letter to Shamir pleading that he reconsider and warning that the proposed change "would inflict a terrible wound on diaspora Jewry and in the end would prove to be harmful to Israel's interests". Abraham Foxman, President of the Anti-Defamation League, simply termed the proposal "catastrophic". Remarkably, even non-Hasidic Orthodox leaders asked Shamir to back down. The Rabbinical Council of America, an alliance of 90 per cent of the Orthodox rabbis with major congregations, sent a telegram to the Prime Minister asking that the issue be dropped from the political agenda. The Alliance Rabbis said that while they continue to support the primacy of Orthodox conversions, they felt that issue should be decided by religious authorities and not the Israeli parliament.[31] After three weeks of this wrangling, Labour leader Shimon Peres announced that he was willing to engage in another coalition with Likud to stave off a rift with US Jews. This move, plus the shock of US initiatives toward the PLO, spurred Likud to patch together a coalition with Labour, ending its erstwhile alliance with the religious parties. The American link to Israel thus came full circle.

## Church and state

Thorny Church-state disputes continue to bedevil the courts and Congress. A perennial controversy, with a new wrinkle, involves public religious displays. Litigation often pits municipal or state governments against Jewish groups and the American Civil Liberties Union seeking to ban such exhibits, but in 1988 the Supreme Court accepted several cases involving both nativity scenes and Menorah displays on public grounds. Inspired by none other than Rabbi Schneerson of Brooklyn, Hasidic Jews have pressed local governments to exhibit Hanukkah Menorahs along with Christmas displays, a move that put them at odds with other Jewish groups. A US circuit court of appeals ruled that because the Menorah and the nativity scene were religious displays, they had no place on public grounds. The US Supreme Court will decide what limits exist, if any, on official recognition of religious holidays. The dispute illustrated an emerging division within the Jewish community over Church-state practice, and produced an unusual alliance of ultra-orthodox Jews and fundamentalist Christians, who object to the ACLU's perceived hostility to public recognition of the nation's religious heritage.

Another issue concerns the impact of secular laws on religious institutions. In Washington DC, Jesuit-run Georgetown University found itself under suit for violation of the city's anti-discrimination statute that bans discrimination on the basis of sexual preference, along with race, creed, gender, and colour. The Gay Rights Coalition of Georgetown University Law Centre and the Gay People of Georgetown University sued the university and won the right to use facilities and compete for funding with other student organizations. The University decided not to appeal against the ruling, arguing that such provisions did not imply any endorsement of homosexuality on the part of the Church. Prominent conservatives, feeling that the university had caved in, thought the action set a bad precedent. Senator William Armstrong, a conservative Republican of Colorado, reacted by attaching to the DC appropriation bill a provision that would block all federal funds to the district unless it exempts religious schools from the anti-discrimination statute. The provision passed the Senate and the House, but the District will likely appeal the measure in court. Ironically, Georgetown officials declined to endorse the congressional provision.

In other action the Supreme Court settled the issue of clergy malpractice that had simmered for several years. In Nally v. Grace Community Church, the parents of Kenneth Nally had sued pastors and counsellors of the California Church because their son committed suicide after receiving spiritual counselling by clerical officials. The case was viewed as a test of the extent of liability that ministers faced in their role as counsellors. The Supreme Court held unanimously for the Church and against the parents, indicating that pastors are generally protected from such action.

Two highly-publicized cases involving the emotionally charged issue of the public school curriculum were addressed by higher courts in 1987 and 1988. Christian fundamentalist parents in Tennessee and Alabama brought suits in 1986 against public school districts, arguing that the books their kids were required to read promoted secular humanism. In Tennessee parents objected to secondary readers (published by Holt, Rinehart, & Winston), claiming that they claimed promoted magic, new age ideas, situation ethics, and a blurring of sex roles. Among the stories cited were Cinderella, Macbeth, The Wizard of Oz, and the Diary of Anne Frank. In what was termed a replay of the celebrated Scopes Monkey trial, each side weighed in with national authorities. Though the parents originally won their case before a federal judge, the decision was overturned by an appeals court, and in 1988 the Supreme Court let the appeals decision stand.

If the Tennessee case was narrowly focussed on parents' rights to keep objectionable material from their children, in Alabama the suit involved far-reaching implications. Judge Brevard Hand facilitated a suit by some 600 parents and teachers, who argued that textbooks used in Alabama schools promoted the "religion" of secular humanism and thus were unconstitutional. This was a more cunning tactic, because it turned the strict separation doctrine against the schools. Judge Hand's decision in favour of the parents, however, was overturned on appeals in 1987, so the plaintiffs lost their battle. But in another way they won the wider war of public attention. National experts found themselves unexpectedly supporting many of the contentions of the plaintiffs. Witness after witness testified to the systematic exclusion of the religious impact on society and history. Historian Timothy Smith of Johns Hopkins University expressed profound shock at the lack of religious references in the state's 11th grade history text. New York University psychologist Paul Vitz reported the "total absence of any reference to American religious life of any kind, Protestant, Catholic, or Jewish," noting that in a story by Isaac Bashevis Singer the phrase "Thank God" was changed to "Thank goodness". But it was Robert Coles, prolific writer and child psychologist from Harvard, who caused the biggest splash. Originally brought in by the defendants, Coles, after reading the textbooks, concluded that they were "crap," "psychological trash," that they did indeed promote a "religion" of the self and a militantly secular world view, and that he would not want his kids reading them. An illustration of the material found offensive was a 10th grade home economics text that offered Jesus and Gandhi as examples of the "irrational conscientious" character type whose "repressed hostility makes them cold and unfeeling". The plaintiffs quickly adopted Coles' deposition.

The fallout of the Alabama case was that scholars and reporters in the elite press began paying closer attention to the concerns of Christian parents. Even the fundamentalists' *bête noire*, People for the American Way, concluded in its own study of the textbooks that they were woefully deficient in depicting the religious heritage of the nation. Indeed, by 1989 efforts were underway in California, the largest book market, and among publishers, to address the deficiency.

The teaching of evolution, a controversy that keeps coming back, was also dealt with by the Court. In 1987 the US Supreme Court addressed a 1982 Louisiana statute that required the teaching of both evolution and creation in the public schools. In Edwards v. Aguillard, the Court struck down the statute, arguing that because it had an exclusively religious purpose, it violated the Establishment Clause of the First Amendment. This will likely not settle the issue, as states keep searching for means of accommodating the complaints of creationists.

The courts will continue to sort through the Church-State thicket, dealing with perennial issues and new ones, such as how to treat religious concerns in divorces of inter-faith couples, a case now in process.

Church-State issues also emerged on the Congressional agenda, as religious lobbies confronted secular initiatives they perceived as threatening. The Civil Rights Restoration Act, championed by liberals, finally passed Congress in 1988 over the objections of evangelical groups. The Act was proposed in 1984 in response to a Supreme Court ruling that narrowed civil rights laws barring discrimination in institutions (notably colleges) that receive federal funding. It had stalled initially because of objections of the US Catholic Conference, which argued that language in the bill might force Catholic colleges and hospitals to offer abortion services. Proponents finally agreed to accommodate Catholic concerns and an amended bill passed. Evangelical and fundamentalist groups, however, were not happy with even the amended version, which they viewed as intrusive — possibly forcing them to accommodate gay rights. The fundamentalist community, though weakened by holy war scandals, did mount a blitz against the bill. Indeed, when James Dobson, child psychologist and host of the popular radio program, "Focus on the Family", asked his listeners to voice their opposition, the flood of calls overloaded the Capitol switchboards. The law passed anyway, demonstrating that constituent pressure alone is not sufficient in a city that thrives on insider networks.

Day Care is also looming as a thorny Church-state issue. The Act for Better Child Care (or ABC Bill) stalled in 1988 when congressional proponents could not accommodate religiously-oriented objections from the right and the left. Since a third of all centres in the United States are run by churches or are housed in church buildings, federal grants could be construed as support for religious institutions. Thus such liberal groups as the ACLU and the American Jewish Committee object to the bill on the grounds that it supports religion. Conservative groups, on the other hand, oppose the bill because they feel it subjects religious institutions to intrusive regulation by the federal government. Congressional sponsors found themselves buffeted. When they tried to accommodate concerns of liberal groups by placing restrictions on the sectarian nature of the centres (such as requiring removal of religious symbols), they lost support of the Catholic Conference. When they eliminated the restrictions, they lost support of the National Education Association. The bill is back in 1989, but its ultimate fate is still in doubt. Should it pass the Congress in some form, it will surely be tested in the courts.

Tensions also surfaced in the executive branch, in this case over the explosive issue of AIDS and its prevention. Surgeon General C. Everett Koop, concerned that ignorance spreads the disease, took the unusual step of mailing an explicit brochure on AIDS to every household in America. This produced a tiff with Education Secretary Edward Bennett, who articulated what many religious conservatives felt, that promotion of condom usage would give a false sense of security to sexually promiscuous persons. The episode highlighted the complex social issues surrounding the containment of the disease, with religious traditionalists arguing that promotion of chastity and married fidelity are the answers, while Koop, once the darling of the religious right for his opposition to abortion, asserts that other methods may be necessary.

The Presbyterian Church avoided a major Church-state clash in 1988 by modifying its statement on Christian responsibilities in the nuclear age. An earlier paper, distributed in 1986, termed the US nuclear arsenal "idolatrous" and "demonic," and proposed that the Church support massive civil disobedience, including tax resistance. But on June 15, 1988, the General Assembly of the Presbyterian Church (USA), adopted a document that placed a greater emphasis on obedience to civilian authorities as the "normal" standard, even while it questioned the morality of nuclear deterrence as a "permanent means to national security". The inner politics of the nuclear debate highlighted a split between liberal (or radical) Church officials and more moderate lay members, a common pattern in the mainline Churches.

## Conclusion

As this remarkable decade draws to a close, religion remains an important social and political force in American society, though clearly not a unified one. Church political witness is now firmly institutionalized in the growing religious lobby in Washington. Liberal Church groups continue to press their case for "peace and justice", fresh on the heels of their successful effort against Reagan's aid to the Nicaraguan contras. To contend with them are conservative fundamentalists, who struggle with what they see as cultural chaos in American society. Catholics and Jews find themselves allied on one side or another as circumstances demand. And new groups will join the pluralist universe, as illustrated by the American Bahais, who opened a lobby in Washington to gain US support for their fight against persecution in Iran and elsewhere.

A trend to watch is the changing composition of the clergy. The Episcopal Church, of course, ordained its first woman Bishop, Rev. Barbara Harris, straining its relationship with the Anglican Church in England. But this celebrated case belies a broader social trend: the dramatic movement of women into the ministry. The National Council of Churches released a study in 1989 documenting the doubling of ordained women in the decade. Intriguingly, while a mainline Lutheran body had the greatest percentage increase, it was the Assemblies of God that emerged with the greatest absolute number of women ministers. Thus both sides of the cultural divide share this emerging pattern, whose political implications are by no means clear.

On the eve of the 1990s, religion has clearly not withered away in America, and its political witness is more varied than in any time in recent history. If the past three years are any indication, we can expect a full religious docket for political authorities in the years ahead.

### Notes

[1] "Emerging Trends", Vol. 9, No. 2 (February 1987), Princeton Religion Research Center.
[2] Robert Wuthnow, *The Restructuring of American Religion* (Princeton: University of Princeton Press, 1988).
[3] Richard John Neuhaus, *The Catholic Moment: The Paradox of the Church in the Postmodern World* (San Francisco: Harper and Row, 1987).
[4] Pat Robertson actually resigned his commission as a Baptist minister shortly before running for president.
[5] The massive psychographic survey of the electorate conducted by Gallup for the Times Mirror organization revealed the cultural gulf between the two most loyal voting constituencies in the Republican Party. On some social issues, indeed, "Enterprisers" were closer to some of the socially liberal Democratic groups, while the "Moralists" lean right with culturally conservative Democratic voters.
[6] According to *The New York Times* exit polls Robertson got only 45 per cent of the born-again evangelical vote on Super Tuesday, compared to Bush's 30 per cent (March 10, 1988:10).
[7] Garry Wills, "The Power Populist," *Time Magazine*, November 21, 1988.
[8] Doug Wead, "The Vice President and Evangelicals in the General Election", Campaign Document, April 1988.
[9] Top Bush strategists assembled focus groups of average Democrats supporting Dukakis and found that such issues as the Pledge of Allegiance and the ACLU

were extremely damaging (Paul Taylor and David Broder, "Early Volley of Bush's Exceeds Expectations", *Washington Post,* October 28, 1988).

10   Radio spots for Pat Robertson in Iowa featured the Pledge of Allegiance and an attack on the ACLU's protection of pornography and hostility to public religion.

11   *The New York Times* exit polls gave him 80 per cent on the basis of a very restrictive definition, other surveys give him fully 70 per cent of an even larger pool of evangelical voters.

12   *The New York Times*, November 10, 1988.

13   Thomas B. Edsall, "The GOP Will Have to Work to Get Back the Big Mo". *The Washington Post Weekly Edition*, January 23–29, 1989.

14   Howard Kurtz, "Operation Rescue: Aggressively Antiabortion", *The Washington Post Weekly Edition*, March 13–19, 1989, pp. 13–14.

15   Michelle Hiskey, "Thousands Join 'Rescue Movement' Around Nation", *Christianity Today*, December 1988.

16   Kurtz, Ibid.

17   *U.S. News and World Report*, October 3, 1988, Cover Story.

18   David Burnham, "After the Catholic Church's Tax Status", *The New York Times*, July 29, 1988.

19   Peter Steinfels, "Hartford Archbishop Assails Democrats on Abortion", *The New York Times*, August 26, 1988.

20   ABC-TV's Exit Poll, as reported in *USA Today*, Wednesday, November 9, 1988.

21   "New York Times/CBS News Poll", *The New York Times*, December 1, 1987.

22   The Rev. Jesse L. Jackson, "How We Respect Life is Over-Riding Moral Issue", *National Right to Life News*, January 1977.

23   *Congressional Quarterly,* April 29, 1989, pp. 973–975.

24   David Shipler, "U.S. Jews Are Torn by Arab Beatings", *The New York Times*, January 26, 1988.

25   Tamar Jacoby, "A Family Quarrel", *Newsweek*, April 3, 1989.

26   *Newsweek*, April 3, 1989.

27   *Congressional Quarterly*, February 18, 1989, pp. 297–300.

28   Daniel Williams, "Tremors in Israeli Political Life Emanate from, of All Places, Brooklyn", *Los Angeles Times*, November 26, 1988.

29   John Kifner, "American Jews protest Israeli Threat to Identity", *The New York Times*, November 21, 1988.

30   Marvine Howe, "U.S. Jews Criticize Plan to Redefine Who is a Jew", *The New York Times*, November 13, 1988.

31   Ari Goldman, "U.S. Orthodox Rabbis Break With Israeli Religious Parties", *The New York Times*, November 23, 1988.

Allen D. Hertzke

# US DEPENDENT TERRITORIES

In 1947, the United States received trusteeship from Japan of the Melanesian islands in the Caroline, Mariana and Marshall group. Although there are 2,141 atolls in the three groups, only 96 are inhabited by an estimated 135,000 people The strategic military value of the islands to the United States is enormous and in recent years many of the islands have become household names around the world: Bikini where early American atomic weapon tests took place; Enawetak made uninhabitable and radioactive from testing; Guam, the huge military base administered separately from the other territories; Kwaijalein and Rongelap, highly radioactive and Palau, the small island state which declared itself nuclear-free at independence and ever since has been resisting intense pressure from America to change its Constitution. The islanders are predominantly Christian, 98 per cent, and they have been increasingly vocal at the abuse of human rights by the American government. The islanders claim they have little say in running their own affairs and are controlled by American military policies.

Ron O'Grady

### Puerto Rico

Puerto Rico is an island in the Caribbean which was ceded by Spain to the USA in 1917. Although self-governing, there are those who would prefer to be one of the states of the USA; a radical minority backed by Cuba would prefer independence. The three million population is 87 per cent Roman Catholic. There are 67,000 Pentecostalists, 15,000 Baptists and 14,000 United Methodists. Among Catholics the charismatic movement has been strong. The Constitution of 1952 requires the separation of Church and State. Catholic bishops have traditionally kept out of politics, but Catholic youth movements have nurtured priests who favour socialism and national independence.

Stuart Mews

# URUGUAY

Uruguay is South America's smallest but most urbanized society. Of its 2,982,600 inhabitants approximately 1,300,000 live in the capital, Montevideo. Its relatively large middle class have also helped to make it the area's most secularized society. Though 60 per cent are baptized, fewer than 4 per cent call themselves practising Catholics. There is also a poor ratio of priests to people and unusually high divorce and abortion rates. At the official level, Church and State are rigidly separated.

Until the 1960s it was known for its welfare state and stable democracy — principally based on the competition of a liberal, anti-clerical *Colorado* party and its conservative *Blanco* opponents. Economic crisis, labour unrest and urban terrorism finally led, in 1973, to the establishment of a repressive military regime. That experience helped to move the Church from the preaching of a privatized religion to a more socially conscious position. Middle-class activists, already influenced by the Second Vatican Council and the Latin American Bishops' meeting at Medellín, created grass-roots communities which offered shelter to many seeking to evade arrest. Similarly, opposition networks, offering resistance to the regime, were built up around Church premises. Since return to democratic rule in 1984 many who had used Church structures to organize opposition turned elsewhere but with their previous anti-clericalism much reduced. Moreover, the national episcopal conference emerged, after 1984, as a sharp critic of divisive and unjust economic policies.

Though still possessing relatively little political influence, as the welcome given to the Pope in May 1988 suggests, the Church now commands some previously absent if still low-key and diffuse popular esteem.

Kenneth Medhurst

# VANUATU

With 94 per cent of the population Christian, the politics of the Republic of Vanuatu are dominated by religious leaders. Father Walter Lini, a New Zealand-trained Anglican priest, became Prime Minister at independence in 1980 and formed a cabinet of whom more than half were former clergymen. His Vauna'aku Pati is based on the organizational system of the Protestant Church. Vanuatu pursues an independent foreign policy which has angered many of the Western powers. They have declared their country non-aligned, announced a nuclear-free policy, recognized Cuba and maintained friendly relations with Russia. Rioting and divisions in the capital, Vila, in 1989 have been the result of old tribal differences.

Ron O'Grady

# VATICAN CITY

An independent city-state ruled by the Pope, Vatican City with a population of 830 is an enclave of the city of Rome. It is the last remnant of the Pope's once considerable temporal power in Italy. The Vatican maintains its own diplomatic service and appoints nuncios to many foreign states, which maintain ambassadors or representatives at the Holy See. In the two World Wars, both sides attached importance to the influence of the Roman Catholic Church and found it expedient to maintain good diplomatic relations. Security was increased after the attempts on the Pope's life in 1981 and 1982.

Stuart Mews

# VENEZUELA

Since the overthrow of military dictatorship, in 1958, Venezuela has experienced uninterrupted constitutional government. Stability has been underwritten by petroleum-based wealth and a significant degree of consensus within the political elite and particularly between the two parties that have alternated in power: the social democratic *Acción Democrática* and the Christian democratic *COPEI*. Declining oil revenues and resulting stabilization measures increased tensions that found expression in the riots of early 1989 but they do not appear to constitute a major threat to the system.

The bulk of the country's 17,791,412 inhabitants are Roman Catholic. Its Church, lacking obvious incentives to radically re-assess its stances, has continued to espouse relatively conservative positions. *Acción Democrática* assaults upon Catholic educational interests was one factor underlying the failure of an earlier democratic experiment (1945–48) and the post-1958 elite has consequently avoided confrontations with the Church.

Recent economic difficulties have elicited some socially critical responses. The hierarchy has attacked corruption and supported electoral reform proposals designed to diminish the influence of entrenched political leaders. Most episcopal statements, however, reflect the persistence of conventional pastoral preoccupations. The marital infidelity of President Lusinchi (1983–88) was a particular cause for concern. A radical change in the Church's political role therefore seems unlikely.

                                                                Kenneth Medhurst

# VIETNAM

As in all Communist countries, especially during the early decades after the revolution, religious activity in Vietnam has experienced various constraints since the rise to power of the Viet Minh in North Vietnam (in 1954) and the reunification of the whole country under Communist rule (in 1975–6).

Traditionally, Vietnamese religion was strongly influenced by China. The northern half of the country was ruled as a Chinese province until the tenth century CE, and the independent kingdom of Dai-Viet became increasingly Confucian in character between then and the nineteenth century. Its Buddhism, too, took the Mahayana form based on Chinese versions of the scriptures. Central Vietnam, under the rule of "Indianized" Cham states down to the late fifteenth century, was initially influenced by Sanskritic forms of Mahayana Buddhism — which found expression in ancient temples still to be seen along the coast; and which may have indirectly influenced the modern Buddhist fanaticism of that area. Southernmost Vietnam, including the Mekong delta, was conquered by the Vietnamese from Cambodia in the seventeenth and eighteenth centuries. Its character as a frontier region made it especially receptive to the syncretic sects brought in by early Chinese and

Vietnamese settlers. The religious tradition of pre-colonial Vietnam was thus very diverse. By the nineteenth century (following unification of the country under a single ruler in 1802) we find a Confucian court with its scholar elite, a diversity of Buddhist and Daoist sects, and a popular religion which incorporated elements of Buddhism and Daoism into the veneration of ancestors and the worship of local spirits.

Christianity also fitted into this pattern, as another kind of sect. The missionaries who arrived in Vietnam from the early seventeenth century — Jesuits, Dominicans, Franciscans, and later the French *Société des Missions Etrangéres* — had considerable success despite frequent persecutions. During the period of French colonial rule (roughly 1860–1945) Catholicism became even more important, with the result that by the mid-20th century Vietnam was estimated to have around two million Catholics, perhaps more.

Confucianism, together with knowledge of classical Chinese language, declined in the twentieth century. Other developments in the colonial period, however, constituted an important revival of "traditional" religion. In the South (once known as "French Cochinchina") two apocalyptic and highly syncretic religions emerged: the *Buu-Son Ky-Huong*, originating in the mid-nineteenth century and responsible for an anti-French movement between 1912 and 1916, subsequently gave birth to the *Hoa-Hao* religion (calling itself a form of Buddhism); while the *Cao-Dai* cult (a form of hierarchical spiritism, strongly influenced by Daoism) generated a number of distinct but related sects during the 1920s and 1930s. Also in the 1930s, in the urban areas, a revival of Mahayana Buddhism occurred in which the dominant elements were popular Amidism and (especially in Central Vietnam) the politically conscious Buddhism associated with the "Lotus of the Good Law". Both this Buddhist revival and the activities of the *Hoa-Hao* and *Cao-Dai* sects received encouragement from the Japanese — whose military occupation of Vietnam began in 1941, although they did not abolish the French administration until March 1945. Christianity had less appeal for the Japanese; but it was sufficiently deep-rooted by now, with its own Vietnamese bishops after 1933, to survive the apparent collapse of French political authority.

During the "August Revolution" of 1945–6, and the war against the French which followed, the Viet Minh presented itself as a genuinely nationalist movement capable of embracing all religions and political groups. Nevertheless, the advent of Communist power following the Geneva Partition (1954) led many Catholics — perhaps 800,000 — as well as a substantial number of Buddhists to flee from North to South Vietnam. The area south of the 17th parallel became the Republic of Vietnam, under the presidency of the Catholic Ngo Dinh Diem. It embraced around two million Catholics; several hundred thousand *Cao-Dai* and *Hoa-Hao* followers; and a number of Buddhist organizations, which attracted a growing membership during the late 1950s and early 1960s. (Statistical precision is impossible where claims made by religious leaders cannot be verified.) Diem alienated the southern sects at an early stage, leaving certain localities to be dominated by *Cao-Dai* and *Hoa-Hao* leaders who enjoyed no influence at the centre. But serious tensions began to arise between Buddhists and Catholics, which came to a head in 1963. An incident at Hue in May of that year, involving refusal of permission to fly Buddhist flags, led to a full-scale Buddhist revolt which spread to Saigon and other towns (but not to the Mekong Delta) during the next few months. The Buddhists themselves were rudely suppressed on August 21, when Diem's special forces occupied their pagodas and made many arrests; but the crisis which ensued led the Americans to withdraw support from Ngo Dinh Diem and to permit his overthrow in a military coup on November 1, 1963.

The Buddhists, who now formed a "Unified Buddhist Church" and an "Institute for Propagation of the Dharma" (*Vien Hao-Dao*) in Saigon, played an increasingly militant role in the political crises of 1964–65. The main result of the chaos, however, was the emergence of a military directorate in June 1965 — coinciding with the deployment of large numbers of United States forces to assist in the war against the Communists. Buddhists in Hue and Danang, opposed to the American build-up and virtually advocating compromise with Hanoi, started an open revolt in Central Vietnam during the early spring of 1966; they also brought large crowds onto the streets of Saigon. But the military moved to suppress the revolt by the end of June, leaving the Buddhists with little power to oppose the war. The latter continued to manage their own affairs, as did the *Cao-Dai* and *Hoa-Hao* groups, during the presidency of another Catholic (Nguyen Van Thieu) from 1967 to 1975. One group of Buddhists, associated with the An-Quang temple in Saigon, remained militantly opposed to the government and even assisted the Communists during the "Tet Offensive" of 1968. But the treatment of that group after 1975 suggests that it was by no means a mere Communist front organization, as some alleged.

Meanwhile in North Vietnam the Communist regime took steps to impose firm limits on religious freedom, including the suppression of the one significant Catholic revolt which occurred (in Quynh-Luu district, Nghe An province) in autumn 1956. (There remained about one million Catholics in the North.) The Fatherland Front, created in September 1955, was designed to mobilize the masses in support of the regime. Besides mass organizations of workers, peasants, women and youth, and some non-Communist political parties, it included acceptable leaders from the principal religious communities: the Catholics and Buddhists. (The *Hoa-Hao* and *Cao-Dai* sects were also represented in what was claimed to be a national organization, but they were numerically weak in the North). This pattern was reproduced in the National Front for the Liberation of South Vietnam, created as an ostensibly non-Communist organization in December 1960. Some elements in the southern sects probably did offer support; but for the most part the *Hoa-Hao*, *Cao-Dai* and Buddhist leaders — and most Catholics — remained vigorously anti-Communist. Following reunification in 1975–6, therefore, gaining firm control over southern religious movements presented serious problems for the new regime. It was anxious to isolate any groups which engaged in political revolt and to deal harshly with them, without alienating the "mainstream" organizations and their leadership.

Thus a group of Catholics was arrested in February 1976, following a gunfight at a church in Saigon; they were put on trial and two were sentenced to death (including a priest) in September. But a conciliatory attitude towards the Archbishop of Saigon (Nguyen Van Binh) succeeded in winning him over and in late September that year he was received in Hanoi by Prime Minister Pham Van Dong. In October 1977, Archbishop Binh and Cardinal Trinh Van Can (of Hanoi) were permitted to attend a synod of bishops in Rome. Likewise the reunification of the Fronts, at a conference in Ho Chi Minh City (Saigon) in February 1977, was made the occasion for isolating unsympathetic Buddhist elements: a group of An-Quang monks were arrested for "counter-revolutionary" activity and later put on trial, while other groups were assiduously cultivated.

In April 1980 the regime took further steps towards establishing its own leadership over both Catholic and Buddhist communities. A Congress of Vietnamese Catholics in Hanoi, attended by the three archbishops (from Hanoi, Hue and Ho Chi Minh City) and other senior clergy issued an appeal to Catholics throughout the country to adapt to present realities and to join in constructing the country. In the same month another Hanoi meeting set up the committee for the unification of Buddhist organizations. It brought together seven southern and two northern organizations, and was headed by Thich Tri Thu of the *Vien Hoa Dao*. This led to the convening of a national conference on Buddhist reunification in November 1981; but passive resistance continued in some quarters. The prominence of Archbishop Binh and Thich Tri Thu was reflected in their attendance, in May 1982, at a Moscow conference of world religious leaders opposed to the dangers of nuclear war; and in August that year Tri Thu went to Mongolia for the eighth Asian Buddhist Congress for Peace.

The years 1983–4 were less harmonious from the point of view of relations between the State and religious organizations, partly perhaps because of a revival of "resistance" groups inside Vietnam as well as the growing seriousness of the situation in Cambodia. In July 1983 five Jesuit priests were given prison sentences for "counter-revolutionary" activities in association with a former officer of the RVN armed forces. It had earlier been reported that even Cardinal Trinh Van Can had been placed under house arrest, and that over 100 priests (out of the total of perhaps 2,500 in Vietnam) were being sent to "re-education camps". In November 1983 the authorities created a new "Solidarity Committee of Patriotic Vietnamese Catholics", but there was continuing opposition to its programme. The following June, the Archbishop of Hue was said to have been placed under house arrest for criticizing it. Nor was the new assault on religious leaders confined to Catholics. A number of An Quang monks and nuns were arrested in spring 1984; and when Thich Tri Thu suddenly died soon afterwards, there were rumours that he too had been arrested and had died in detention. A report in August 1983 said that two Caodaists had been sentenced to death for their part in a Chinese-inspired plot in Ho Chi Minh city.

The situation became calmer during 1985–6. The religious organizations had to accept what had happened thus far, but they may also have benefitted from the beginnings of a new "openness" in government policy stemming from the influence of Gorbachev's new Soviet line. There was, nevertheless, another case of Catholic involvement in opposition activities in 1987: in August the "Solidarity Committee" was obliged to dissociate itself from a dissident group in Ho Chi Minh City led by Fr. Tran Dinh Thu, whose leaders received prison sentences in October. The following year it became clear that the authorities in Hanoi were also still very sensitive to the activity of Catholic exiles. They expressed disapproval of an emigré-sponsored ceremony at the Vatican in June 1988 when 117 martyrs (96 Vietnamese and 21 Europeans) who died in Vietnam in the eighteenth and nineteenth centuries were formally canonized. But there was no indication that this affected the trend towards kinder treatment of Catholics and other religious groups inside Vietnam

R. B. Smith

# WESTERN SAHARA

Bounded by Morocco, Mauritania and the Atlantic ocean, this strip of desert contains about 75,000 people, and scarcely qualifies as a nation-state. Spain ended its colonial presence in 1976, and Morocco and Mauritania divided the country between them. This was not, however, acceptable to the Polisario Front, a movement for an independent Sahara, backed by Algeria. The guerrilla war which ensued caused Mauritania to withdraw in 1979. Almost the entire population is Sunni Muslim. Most of them lived as desert nomads until the development of the phosphate mines at Bu Cra'a which now employs a quarter of the population.

Stuart Mews

# WESTERN SAMOA

The mountainous Pacific islands of Western Samoa have a population of 158,000. Before independence in 1962, they were administered from New Zealand. A member of the Commonwealth, Western Samoa has a Constitution which, like Britain, combines heredity with democracy. One of the Paramount chiefs is head of state for life, but the Prime Minister is answerable to an elected Legislative Assembly. Christianity is the predominant religion, having been brought to the islands by Congregational missionaries of the London Missionary Society. Roman Catholics claim 24 per cent of the population.

Stuart Mews

# NORTH YEMEN

Following the overthrow of the absolutist regime of the Zaydi Imam of San'a by a cabal of army officers in 1962, the Yemen Arab Republic (North Yemen) has been led by an alliance of senior military commanders and progressive civilian politicians. The successive republican governments, including that of President 'Ali 'Abdullah Salih which was re-elected to a five-year term in office by plebiscite in 1988, have generally represented the country's majority Sunni Muslim community; this community, based along the coast and in the southern highlands, adheres to the Shafi'i school of Islamic jurisprudence, in which the principle of consensus is a crucial criterion for establishing the validity of legal judgements. The Zaydis of the interior mountains represent an ancient branch of Shii Islam and make up some 40 per cent of the indigenous population. Zaydi politicians dominated the national assembly throughout the 1970s and worked consistently to derail efforts by the government to effect a merger with the People's Democratic Republic of Yemen (South Yemen), with which many members of the Shafi'i elite have close social and economic ties. During the mid-1980s, an Islamic Front closely related to the Egyptian Muslim Brethren attracted a considerable following among university students and Sunni intellectuals, perhaps including a number of government ministers.

Fred H. Lawson

# SOUTH YEMEN

Since becoming independent in 1967, the People's Democratic Republic of Yemen (South Yemen) has been governed by members of an overtly Marxist-Leninist party organization, now called the Yemeni Socialist Party. This party went to considerable lengths during its first 15 years in power to suppress the expression of religious beliefs and sectarianism in the country's social and political affairs. But with the ouster of the more doctrinaire wing of the party in April 1980, the new president, 'Ali Nasir Muhammad, began to allow greater latitude for public piety both for the elite and among the general population. 'Ali Nasir himself attended Friday prayers on ceremonial occasions during the early 1980s, and by mid-decade a wide range of family and morals matters had been relegated to the authority of resurrected Islamic legal proceedings in the outlying towns. In January 1986 a brief but devastating civil war engulfed the country, resulting in the forced exile of 'Ali Nasir and his replacement by a cabal of party militants associated with the earlier regime. The new leadership devoted most of its attention over the subsequent three years to repairing the extensive damage to the local economy and infrastructure caused by the fighting and consolidating its control over the party apparatus. These efforts left little concern and few resources available for a wholesale reimposition of state control over religious affairs, but there has been no more encouragement of public expressions of devotion to Islam nor official sanction for the Islamic courts under the new regime.

Fred H. Lawson

# YUGOSLAVIA

The making of the communist religious policy in Yugoslavia was significantly complicated by the great ethnic, cultural, and confessional diversity of
the people. The situation was made even more difficult by two other factors.
First, was the circumstance that none of the major denominations could claim
the allegiance of the majority of the population: Orthodoxy was professed by
about 40 per cent of Yugoslav citizens (Serbian about 7 million and Macedonian
about 2 million), Catholicism by a little over 32 per cent (about 5 million Croats
and about 2 million Slovenes), and Islam by about 18 per cent (Muslimani in
Bosnia-Herzegovina and Albanians in the autonomous province of Kosovo).
Second, was the very close relationship between religion and ethnicity as
manifested by the Catholic Croats and Orthodox Serbs. Unfortunately, the
past tainted relations among the major religious groups with nationalistic
animosities.

The communist rulers of Yugoslavia were well aware of the circumstances
and attempted to utilize them in achieving their own political and social objectives at home and abroad. On the whole, they were rather successful in keeping religious organizations under control. At the same time, however, their
failure to satisfy the material and spiritual needs of the citizenry as well as the
monopolistic mode of exercising political power by the communist party drew
the churches increasingly into socio-political activities. Not surprisingly,
it led recently to deteriorations in state-church relations.

In the early post-war period, Tito found it necessary to co-operate with all
religious groups, except those which openly fought against the communists.
Thus, in 1945 he initiated talks about future collaboration with the Catholic Archbishop of Zagreb, Alojzije Stepinac. He conditioned, however, his
offer on a number of unacceptable proposals such as the establishment of a
schismatic Croatian Catholic Church. Meeting a refusal, he decreed at first a
clandestine execution of the hierarch (not carried out due to the protest of the
Croatian party chief, Vladimir Makaric) and later on imprisoning him under
the fabricated accusations of war crimes.

The persecution of Stepinac was followed by other trials and repressions
against the clergy, both Catholic and Orthodox. At the same time, the regime
attempted to weaken both Churches by creating splinter groups which were
crowned with some success among Catholic priests in Slovenia and among
Orthodox ecclesiastics in Macedonia and Montenegro.

After the split with the Cominform in 1948, however, the menace
from the Kremlin forced Tito to seek the Churches' help in dealing
with domestic and international problems. As an important step in this
direction, Archbishop Stepinac was discharged from jail in December 1951
and exiled to his birthplace, the village of Krasic, where he remained until
his death in 1960. But improved relations with the Vatican were short lived
since Tito broke diplomatic ties after the Pope, Pius XII, elevated Stepinac
to Cardinal in November 1952.

In order to avoid undesirable effects of the rupture, Tito tried to come
to a reconciliation with the remaining bishops. But his endeavours produced
tangible results only in Slovenia, while in Croatia strained relations lasted until
the demise of Cardinal Stepinac.

Since that time, the relations followed a somewhat uneven track of "peaceful coexistence" that was marked by the conclusion in 1966 of a special agreement with the Vatican, followed by the re-establishment of diplomatic relations in 1970, and a visit by Tito with Pope Paul VI in 1971. The startling burst of Croatian nationalism in 1960, while attracting many younger priests, did not substantially affect the basis of *modus vivendi*. The "Croatian spring," however, strongly underlined the Church's role as champion of Croatian national interests.

In the 1980s, the Croatian episcopate also started to exhibit more nationalistic sentiments. The lead was assumed by Cardinal Franjo Kuharic who called for the rehabilitation of the late Cardinal Stepinac. As might be expected, the re-opening of the case did not contribute to the improvement of relations. The Church's resolve to maintain close contacts with the Croats abroad who on every occasion (e.g. John Paul II's visit to Austria in 1983) demonstrated the overt nationalist spirit did not do it either. The National Eucharistic Congress added another aspect to evolving tensions which erupted in anti-government demonstrations in Split, on Christmas Eve in 1984. The regime claimed that it was incited by local priests who sympathized with the *Ustashe* and promoted Croatian separatism.

The economic crisis as well as the influence of liberalization taking place in other East European states caused a significant growth of a dissident movement, which was joined by a number of Catholic priests and lay activists. At the same time, the Catholic Church was becoming more assertive and more vocal in matters of human rights. In 1980, 43 Catholic intellectuals, including Archbishop Joze Pogacnik of Ljubljana submitted a request demanding the release of all political prisoners. In 1982, the theological institute in Zagreb hosted an international conference on human rights despite the government's opposition. In 1987, Slovenian bishops issued a declaration calling for democratization of the system and for respect of the rights of believers. Recently, a Christian-Democratic movement began operating in Slovenia, and its chairman, Franc Miklavcic, appealed to the authorities for the revision of criminal proceedings falsely instigated against Slovene priests and monks.

The authorities responded with repression and by 1983 about 10 priests were in prison for various offences, including Fr. Jozo Zovko of Medjugorje in whose parish an apparition of the Virgin Mary occurred. In 1986, Fr. Filip Lukenda was jailed for "clerico-nationalism".

The Serbian Orthodox Church was always committed to Serbian nationalism and viewed itself as the primary guardian of the national ethos, culture and interests. The claim was recognized by a great majority of the Serbs and this fact gave the Church a unique leadership role in the nation. This position was greatly enhanced by the sufferings the Church endured together with the people in World War II.

The communist leadership, always keen on making use of all available means to enhance its own position, was eager to establish good relations with the Church and channel its traditions and symbols for political purposes. The Church, led by Patriarch Gavrylo, a former inmate of German concentration camps who was allowed to return to the country only in 1946, responded favourably, although governmental decisions on a number of issues: marriage, birth, church property, religious education, etc. were causing deep anxieties among clergy and believers. But the striving for social peace and Yugoslav unity prevailed.

At the same time, however, the Church demanded acknowledgement of its rights, and asked for material assistance for its activities, especially for the recuperation from war losses. It also firmly opposed governmental interference with Church affairs and decried the formation of splinter groups among the clergy.

In addition, the Church claimed jurisdiction over all Orthodox believers in Yugoslavia. The assertion became a source of conflict with the regime, which for political reasons promoted the autonomy of Macedonian and Montenegrin Churches as a check on Serbian hegemonic aspirations. In the case of the Macedonian Church, the government also considered the creation, in 1967, of the Autocephalous Macedonian Church as an important move in the territorial dispute with Bulgaria and Greece. But the Serbian Orthodox Church refused to recognize the new religious organization and treated it as a schism. A similar attitude was adopted by the Serbian Church toward the Montenegrin attempts to follow the Macedonian example. The government, however, disregarded the objections and castigated Serbian opposition as a manifestation of reactionary "clerico-nationalism". It also resorted to jailing the more vocal priests and even bishops. For instance, Bishop Vasilije of Zica was sentenced in 1972 to 30 days imprisonment for allegedly making nationalist comments in a church sermon.

Despite the official animosity, the Serbian Orthodox Church became in the 1980s engaged in ethnic politics more than ever before. The immediate cause for involvement was the rise of Albanian nationalism in the autonomous province of Kosovo. The destruction of the Serbian national shrine, the Pec Monastery, desecration of graves, and the forced flight of Serbs and Montenegrins from the area pushed the Church to call for, and later to defend, tough "anti-irredent" measures. A Serbian church paper, *Vesnik*, proclaimed that "the Serbian Church is an inalienable element of national identity, conscience and honour of the Serbian people," while another periodical warned that if "Kosovo ceases to be ours . . . we cease to be what we are."

There were also other signs of the Church's activism. In 1982, the Bishops' Assembly expressed its dissatisfaction over the Macedonian schism, unjustified persecution of members of a religious renewal group *Bohomolci*, the fate of Serbs in Kosovo, and difficulties with conducting catechism classes and building of churches. In 1985, Patriarch German overcame long governmental resistance and won permission to construct in Belgrade a church commemorating St. Sava, the national hero and most celebrated Serbian martyr. In 1985, the Church refused to deal with the Chairman of the Federal Commission for Relations with Religious Communities who criticized Church bishops for their constant referrals to the past. It must be stated, however, that Church leaders, on the whole, demonstrated considerable restraint in politically sensitive matters.

Although the regime did not consider the Orthodox clergy disloyal, and the relations between the State and the Church were generally satisfactory, the authorities were inordinately concerned over the Church's involvement in ethnic affairs. As a result, they often over-reacted as was the case when two priests were imprisoned for singing nationalistic songs at a christening.

Muslims in Yugoslavia include Albanians, Macedonians, Montenegrins, Serbs and Turks. But, unlike Orthodoxy in Serbia and Catholicism in Croatia, Islam is not identified with a particular ethnic group and was not a standard-bearer for any local nationalism. In fact, until the early 1970s,

Muslims displayed little national consciousness and did not demonstrate any political aspirations.

There were several reasons for the situation. First, Yugoslav Muslims were spread all over the country, with the majority living in Bosnia-Herzegovina, where they amounted to almost 40% of the population, and in the Kosovo province (1.7 million). Second, the largest group, about 2 million (i.e. about 50 per cent of all believers), were of Slavic origin who converted to Islam during the Turkish occupation of the Balkans (Muslimani). Third, the communist rulers decided only in about 1968 to give Muslims the status of a nation. Before that, they were listed as "Serbian" or "Macedonian Muslims," and, since 1961, as "Muslims in an ethnic sense".

The decision to upgrade the Muslim rank was caused primarily by Belgrade's desire to hinder either Serbs or Croats from controlling the federation. A separate Bosnian republic and a Muslim nation were to preserve the balance between the two major ethnic groups and reinforce the newly created and very unstable federal system. Another important cause were foreign policy considerations, namely Tito's design to get partners for his scheme of a "non-aligned bloc" and assure himself a supply of Arab oil.

Perhaps to the communists' surprise, these factors led to self-assertion and politization of the Muslims, first in Bosnia-Herzegovina and later in Croatia. In each of them Islam became the foundation of a rapidly developing conscience of Muslim nationality. A similar process also took place among the Albanians in the Kosovo province.

The rise of Islamic fundamentalism and the success of Ayatollah Khomeini in Iran gave a significant impetus to the growth of Islamic and Albanian nationalism in Yugoslavia. Although practically all Yugoslav Muslims were Sunnites, they were attracted by the Shi'ite dynamism and pan-Islamic movement.

The turn of events caused a serious dilemma for the regime. On the one hand, it did not want to abandon the policy of using the Muslims as a check on Serbian and Croatian ambitions and a helpful factor in commercial relations with Iraq, Iran and Libya. Hence, the continuing affirmation of Muslim ethnicity, easy building permits — in late 1987 a magnificent mosque was opened in Zagreb — substantial educational activities, and non-interference with confessional affairs. On the other hand, the authorities were afraid of the uncontrolled expansion of Muslim nationalism that might pose a threat to the national integrity. Hence, severe measures against overtly political actions of the *ulema* and other Muslim activists. In 1983, 13 of them received harsh sentences for attempts to "destroy the brotherhood, unity and equality" of the peoples of Bosnia-Herzegovina and of the federation, and in 1987, in Sarajevo, three Muslims were imprisoned for "propagating Muslim nationalism, demanding the setting up of a purely Islamic state, and inciting *Jihad*".

State-Church relations in Yugoslavia presented an example of the well-known paradigm that the communist religious policy was a mixture of pragmatic and ideological considerations. The proof of the first was provided by a relatively impartial treatment of all religious groups, the utilization of Islam as well as disciplinary actions against excesses of "clerico-nationalism," including those of Bosnian *ulama* preaching "positive political activity". The ideological motivation was shown in the persistent view that religion was a false ideology and a deterrent in the building of socialism. The attitude was demonstrated by the prosecution of anti-atheist propaganda (e.g. punishing of Fr. Peter Solic of Split in 1987) and of attempts to raise the level of religious indoctrination of the people (e.g. of *Bohomolci* in Bosnia, in 1981).

V. C. Chrypinski

# ZAIRE

In colonial days the Belgians made Catholicism almost the state religion. Some estimate that almost 50 per cent of Zaire's 30 million inhabitants may be Catholic today. In the upheavals following independence in 1960, especially in the popular rebellion in the north-east (1964–65), scores of missionaries were maltreated or killed. In 1965 General Mobutu and his *Mouvement Populaire de la Révolution* came to power; the regime is notoriously corrupt and despotic and has presided over increasing economic collapse and disregard for human rights. In the early 1970s Mobutu's campaign for *authenticité*, which included the abolition of all Christian names, led to a head-on conflict with the Catholic Church and the expulsion of Cardinal Malula, the Archbishop of Kinshasa; only after considerable negotiation on the part of the Vatican was he able to return 5 months later. Mobutu has employed a policy of carrot and stick towards the Church. The Church for its part has avoided direct confrontation, concentrating on ecclesiastical matters like the Africanization of the liturgy and the introduction of lay ministers, but by the time of Cardinal Malula's death in June 1989 relations between the Church and the regime were seriously strained. The evangelical churches, and the large independent Kimbangist church, do not interfere in politics, and the Jehovah's Witnesses were banned in 1987 over their refusal to salute the flag.

Paul Gifford

# ZAMBIA

Zambia's population is 70 per cent Christian, less than 1 per cent Muslim, with about 20 per cent adhering to traditional religion. The country became independent in 1964, and has been a one-party republic since 1972. Kenneth Kaunda has been chief executive since independence; he is a committed Christian, and his policy of "humanism" includes religious liberty for all. There have been religious clashes: the Lumpa (Visible Salvation) Church founded in 1954 by Alice Lenshina was banned in 1965 after clashes with government troops cost 700 lives. Alice Lenshina was still in detention when she died in 1978. The

Jehovah's Witnesses, enormously influential in Zambia (over a million people, 25 per cent of the population, are said to have been involved with the church at some time in their lives), were briefly persecuted in 1969 because of their refusal to vote; their foreign missionaries were expelled then, but Zambian Witnesses practise their religion unhindered today.

Recent friction has stemmed largely from Zambia's economic collapse. The ruling party reacted negatively to the creation of a Catholic Justice and Peace Commission in 1987, at a time of harsh economic restructuring. In February 1988 the government expressed concern over the mushrooming of splinter churches in the country. In 1988 the Ministry of Health recalled a booklet on Aids (which is rampant in Zambia), and replaced offending passages with language more acceptable to Christians. In April 1988 Kaunda lamented corruption in the United Church of Zambia (his own church and the country's biggest Protestant church); in August 1988 churches were included in a government decree demanding 6-monthly reports on foreign exchange received. The same year the Catholic Bishops, the Christian Council of Zambia and the Evangelical Fellowship of Zambia produced a 45-page booklet "Christian Liberation, Justice and Development — the Churches' concern for Human Development" in which they referred to the growing number of parastatal executives and government officials involved in corruption with no punitive measures being taken against them, reforms causing unprecedented and disproportionate hardships to the poor; they attributed the situation to bad planning, mismanagement of available resources and the piling up of external debt.

Paul Gifford

# ZIMBABWE

In the elections marking the transition from Southern Rhodesia to Zimbabwe, Robert Mugabe's ZANU(PF) won an absolute majority, beating Joshua Nkomo's ZAPU, and virtually eliminating the UANC of Abel Muzorewa, the Methodist Bishop who had for a few months been Prime Minister of the short-lived state of Zimbabwe–Rhodesia. The Marxist Mugabe adopted a policy of reconciliation, and frequently called on the Christian Churches to play a major role in the new order. He appointed the Methodist Minister, Rev. Canaan Banana, the country's first President (1980–87). Between 1982 and 1986 there was considerable friction between the government and the Catholic Church in particular over the Government's handling of dissident activity in Matabeleland. Church leaders, however, played a key if unobtrusive role in bringing about in December 1987 the unity agreement between Mugabe's predominantly Shona ZANU(PF) and Nkomo's almost exclusively Ndebele ZAPU. After this, and Mugabe's April 1988 offer of amnesty to all dissidents, the security problem was virtually resolved. In general, the mainline Churches enjoyed good relations with the government, though government spokesmen have expressed concern over the recent increase in fundamentalist Christian sects, most of which are opposed to socialism. On the occasion of the Pope's visit in September 1988, Mugabe publicly disagreed with the Pope when the latter stated that violence could never be justified as a means of social change.

Paul Gifford